CAMBRIDGE LIBRARY COLLECTION

Books of enduring scholarly value

Classics

From the Renaissance to the nineteenth century, Latin and Greek were compulsory subjects in almost all European universities, and most early modern scholars published their research and conducted international correspondence in Latin. Latin had continued in use in Western Europe long after the fall of the Roman empire as the lingua franca of the educated classes and of law, diplomacy, religion and university teaching. The flight of Greek scholars to the West after the fall of Constantinople in 1453 gave impetus to the study of ancient Greek literature and the Greek New Testament. Eventually, just as nineteenth-century reforms of university curricula were beginning to erode this ascendancy, developments in textual criticism and linguistic analysis, and new ways of studying ancient societies, especially archaeology, led to renewed enthusiasm for the Classics. This collection offers works of criticism, interpretation and synthesis by the outstanding scholars of the nineteenth century.

The Golden Bough: The First Edition

This work by Sir James Frazer (1854–1941) is widely considered to be one of the most important early texts in the fields of psychology and anthropology. At the same time, by applying modern methods of comparative ethnography to the classical world, and revealing the superstition and irrationality beneath the surface of classical culture, and also by examining Christianity using the same techniques, it was extremely controversial. Frazer was greatly influenced by E.B. Tylor's *Primitive Culture* (also reissued in this series), and by the work of the biblical scholar William Robertson Smith, to whom the first edition is dedicated. That edition, reissued here, was published in two volumes in 1890; the third edition, greatly enlarged to twelve volumes, and published between 1911 and 1915, is also available in this series. Volume 1 considers the motif of the ritual murder of the priest/king in classical mythology.

D0861472

Cambridge University Press has long been a pioneer in the reissuing of out-of-print titles from its own backlist, producing digital reprints of books that are still sought after by scholars and students but could not be reprinted economically using traditional technology. The Cambridge Library Collection extends this activity to a wider range of books which are still of importance to researchers and professionals, either for the source material they contain, or as landmarks in the history of their academic discipline.

Drawing from the world-renowned collections in the Cambridge University Library and other partner libraries, and guided by the advice of experts in each subject area, Cambridge University Press is using state-of-the-art scanning machines in its own Printing House to capture the content of each book selected for inclusion. The files are processed to give a consistently clear, crisp image, and the books finished to the high quality standard for which the Press is recognised around the world. The latest print-on-demand technology ensures that the books will remain available indefinitely, and that orders for single or multiple copies can quickly be supplied.

The Cambridge Library Collection brings back to life books of enduring scholarly value (including out-of-copyright works originally issued by other publishers) across a wide range of disciplines in the humanities and social sciences and in science and technology.

The Golden Bough

The First Edition

A Study in Comparative Religion

VOLUME 1

J.G. FRAZER

CAMBRIDGE
UNIVERSITY PRESS

CAMBRIDGE UNIVERSITY PRESS

Cambridge, New York, Melbourne, Madrid, Cape Town,
Singapore, São Paolo, Delhi, Mexico City

Published in the United States of America by Cambridge University Press, New York

www.cambridge.org
Information on this title: www.cambridge.org/9781108047524

© in this compilation Cambridge University Press 2012

This edition first published 1890
This digitally printed version 2012

ISBN 978-1-108-04752-4 Paperback

This book reproduces the text of the original edition. The content and language reflect
the beliefs, practices and terminology of their time, and have not been updated.

Cambridge University Press wishes to make clear that the book, unless originally published
by Cambridge, is not being republished by, in association or collaboration with, or
with the endorsement or approval of, the original publisher or its successors in title.

THE GOLDEN BOUGH

THE
GOLDEN BOUGH

A STUDY
IN COMPARATIVE RELIGION

BY

J. G. FRAZER, M.A.

FELLOW OF TRINITY COLLEGE, CAMBRIDGE

IN TWO VOLUMES

VOL. I

London

MACMILLAN AND CO.

AND NEW YORK

1890

All rights reserved

TO

MY FRIEND

WILLIAM ROBERTSON SMITH

IN

GRATITUDE AND ADMIRATION

PREFACE

FOR some time I have been preparing a general work on primitive superstition and religion. Among the problems which had attracted my attention was the hitherto unexplained rule of the Arician priesthood; and last spring it happened that in the course of my reading I came across some facts which, combined with others I had noted before, suggested an explanation of the rule in question. As the explanation, if correct, promised to throw light on some obscure features of primitive religion, I resolved to develop it fully, and, detaching it from my general work, to issue it as a separate study. This book is the result.

Now that the theory, which necessarily presented itself to me at first in outline, has been worked out in detail, I cannot but feel that in some places I may have pushed it too far. If this should prove to have been the case, I will readily acknowledge and retract my error as soon as it is brought home to me. Meantime my essay may serve its purpose as a first attempt to solve a difficult problem, and to bring a variety of scattered facts into some sort of order and system.

A justification is perhaps needed of the length at which I have dwelt upon the popular festivals observed

by European peasants in spring, at midsummer, and at
harvest.   It can hardly be too often repeated, since it
is not yet generally recognised, that in spite of their
fragmentary character the popular superstitions and
customs of the peasantry are by far the fullest and
most trustworthy evidence we possess as to the primitive religion of the Aryans.   Indeed the primitive
Aryan, in all that regards his mental fibre and texture,
is not extinct.   He is amongst us to this day.   The
great intellectual and moral forces which have revolu-
tionised the educated world have scarcely affected
the peasant.   In his inmost beliefs he is what his
forefathers were in the days when forest trees still
grew and squirrels played on the ground where Rome
and London now stand.

Hence every inquiry into the primitive religion of
the Aryans should either start from the superstitious
beliefs and observances of the peasantry, or should at
least be constantly checked and controlled by reference
to them.   Compared with the evidence afforded by
living tradition, the testimony of ancient books on the
subject of early religion is worth very little.   For
literature accelerates the advance of thought at a
rate which leaves the slow progress of opinion by
word of mouth at an immeasurable distance behind.
Two or three generations of literature may do more
to change thought than two or three thousand years
of traditional life.   But the mass of the people who
do not read books remain unaffected by the mental
revolution wrought by literature ; and so it has come
about that in Europe at the present day the superstitious beliefs and practices which have been handed

down by word of mouth are generally of a far more archaic type than the religion depicted in the most ancient literature of the Aryan race.

It is on these grounds that, in discussing the meaning and origin of an ancient Italian priesthood, I have devoted so much attention to the popular customs and superstitions of modern Europe. In this part of my subject I have made great use of the works of the late W. Mannhardt, without which, indeed, my book could scarcely have been written. Fully recognising the truth of the principles which I have imperfectly stated, Mannhardt set himself systematically to collect, compare, and explain the living superstitions of the peasantry. Of this wide field the special department which he marked out for himself was the religion of the woodman and the farmer, in other words, the superstitious beliefs and rites connected with trees and cultivated plants. By oral inquiry, and by printed questions scattered broadcast over Europe, as well as by ransacking the literature of folk-lore, he collected a mass of evidence, part of which he published in a series of admirable works. But his health, always feeble, broke down before he could complete the comprehensive and really vast scheme which he had planned, and at his too early death much of his precious materials remained unpublished. His manuscripts are now deposited in the University Library at Berlin, and in the interest of the study to which he devoted his life it is greatly to be desired that they should be examined, and that such portions of them as he has not utilised in his books should be given to the world.

Of his published works the most important are, first, two tracts, *Roggenwolf und Roggenhund*, Danzig 1865 (second edition, Danzig, 1866), and *Die Korndämonen*, Berlin, 1868. These little works were put forward by him tentatively, in the hope of exciting interest in his inquiries and thereby securing the help of others in pursuing them. But, except from a few learned societies, they met with very little attention. Undeterred by the cold reception accorded to his efforts he worked steadily on, and in 1875 published his chief work, *Der Baumkultus der Germanen und ihrer Nachbarstämme*. This was followed in 1877 by *Antike Wald- und Feldkulte*. His *Mythologische Forschungen*, a posthumous work, appeared in 1884.[1]

Much as I owe to Mannhardt, I owe still more to my friend Professor W. Robertson Smith. My interest in the early history of society was first excited by the works of Dr. E. B. Tylor, which opened up a mental vista undreamed of by me before. But it is a long step from a lively interest in a subject to a systematic study of it; and that I took this step is due to the influence of my friend W. Robertson Smith. The debt which I owe to the vast stores of his knowledge, the abundance and fertility of his ideas, and his unwearied kindness, can scarcely be overestimated. Those who know his writings may form some, though a very inadequate, conception of the extent to which I have been influenced by him. The views of sacrifice set forth in his article " Sacrifice " in the *Encyclopaedia*

---

[1] For the sake of brevity I have sometimes, in the notes, referred to Mannhardt's works respectively as *Roggenwolf* (the references are to the pages of the first edition), *Korndämonen, B. K., A. W. F.,* and *M. F.*

Britannica, and further developed in his recent work, *The Religion of the Semites*, mark a new departure in the historical study of religion, and ample traces of them will be found in this book. Indeed the central idea of my essay—the conception of the slain god—is derived directly, I believe, from my friend. But it is due to him to add that he is in no way responsible for the general explanation which I have offered of the custom of slaying the god. He has read the greater part of the proofs in circumstances which enhanced the kindness, and has made many valuable suggestions which I have usually adopted ; but except where he is cited by name, or where the views expressed coincide with those of his published works, he is not to be regarded as necessarily assenting to any of the theories propounded in this book.

The works of Professor G. A. Wilken of Leyden have been of great service in directing me to the best original authorities on the Dutch East Indies, a very important field to the ethnologist. To the courtesy of the Rev. Walter Gregor, M.A., of Pitsligo, I am indebted for some interesting communications which will be found acknowledged in their proper places. Mr. Francis Darwin has kindly allowed me to consult him on some botanical questions. The manuscript authorities to which I occasionally refer are answers to a list of ethnological questions which I am circulating. Most of them will, I hope, be published in the *Journal of the Anthropological Institute*.

The drawing of the Golden Bough which adorns the cover is from the pencil of my friend Professor J. H. Middleton. The constant interest and sympathy which he has shown in the progress of the book have been a great help and encouragement to me in writing it.

The Index has been compiled by Mr. A. Rogers, of the University Library, Cambridge.

J. G. FRAZER.

TRINITY COLLEGE, CAMBRIDGE,
   8th March 1890.

CONTENTS

CHAPTER I

THE KING OF THE WOOD, pp. 1-108

CHAPTER II

THE PERILS OF THE SOUL, pp. 109-212

CHAPTER III

KILLING THE GOD, pp. 213-409

CHAPTER I

THE KING OF THE WOOD

" The still glassy lake that sleeps
Beneath Aricia's trees—
Those trees in whose dim shadow
The ghastly priest doth reign,
The priest who slew the slayer,
And shall himself be slain."

MACAULAY.

§ 1.—*The Arician Grove*

WHO does not know Turner's picture of the Golden
Bough ? The scene, suffused with the golden glow
of imagination in which the divine mind of Turner
steeped and transfigured even the fairest natural
landscape, is a dream-like vision of the little woodland lake of Nemi, " Diana's Mirror," as it was called
by the ancients. No one who has seen that calm
water, lapped in a green hollow of the Alban hills,
can ever forget it. The two characteristic Italian
villages which slumber on its banks, and the equally
Italian palazzo whose terraced gardens descend steeply
to the lake, hardly break the stillness and even the
solitariness of the scene. Dian herself might still
linger by this lonely shore, still haunt these wood-
lands wild.

B

In antiquity this sylvan landscape was the scene
of a strange and recurring tragedy. On the northern
shore of the lake, right under the precipitous cliffs on
which the modern village of Nemi is perched, stood
the sacred grove and sanctuary of Diana Nemorensis,
or Diana of the Wood.[1] The lake and the grove
were sometimes known as the lake and grove of
Aricia.[2] But the town of Aricia (the modern La
Riccia) was situated about three miles off, at the foot
of the Alban Mount, and separated by a steep descent
from the lake, which lies in a small crater-like hollow
on the mountain side. In this sacred grove there
grew a certain tree round which at any time of the
day and probably far into the night a strange figure
might be seen to prowl. In his hand he carried a
drawn sword, and he kept peering warily about him
as if every instant he expected to be set upon by an
enemy.[3] He was a priest and a murderer; and the
man for whom he looked was sooner or later to
murder him and hold the priesthood in his stead.
Such was the rule of the sanctuary. A candidate for
the priesthood could only succeed to office by slaying
the priest, and having slain him he held office till he
was himself slain by a stronger or a craftier.

This strange rule has no parallel in classical
antiquity, and cannot be explained from it. To find
an explanation we must go farther afield. No one will
probably deny that such a custom savours of a barbar-

---

[1] The site was excavated in 1885
by Sir John Savile Lumley, English
ambassador at Rome. For a general
description of the site and excavations,
see the *Athenaeum*, 10th October 1885.
For details of the finds see *Bulletino
dell' Instituto di Corrispondenza Archeo-
logica*, 1885, pp. 149 *sqq.*, 225 *sqq.*

[2] Ovid, *Fasti*, vi. 756 ; Cato quoted
by Priscian, see Peter's *Historic. Roman.
Fragmenta*, p. 52 (lat. ed.) ; Statius,
Sylv. iii. 1, 56.

[3] ξιφήρης οὖν ἐστιν ἀεί, περισκοπῶν τὰς
ἐπιθέσεις, ἕτοιμος ἀμύνεσθαι, is Strabo's
description (v. 3, 12), who may have
seen him "pacing there alone."

ous age and, surviving into imperial times, stands out in striking isolation from the polished Italian society of the day, like a primeval rock rising from a smooth-shaven lawn.   It is the very rudeness and barbarity of the custom which allow us a hope of explaining it. For recent researches into the early history of man have revealed the essential similarity with which, under many superficial differences, the human mind has elaborated its first crude philosophy of life.   Accord-ingly if we can show that a barbarous custom, like that of the priesthood of Nemi, has existed elsewhere ; if we can detect the motives which led to its institution ; if we can prove that these motives have operated widely, perhaps universally, in human society, producing in varied circumstances a variety of institutions specifically different but generically alike ; if we can show, lastly, that these very motives, with some of their derivative institutions, were actually at work in classical antiquity ; then we may fairly infer that at a remoter age the same motives gave birth to the priesthood of Nemi.   Such an inference, in default of direct evidence as to how the priesthood did actually arise, can never amount to demonstration.   But it will be more or less probable according to the degree of completeness with which it fulfils the conditions indicated above.   The object of this book is, by meeting these conditions, to offer a fairly probable explanation of the priesthood of Nemi.

I begin by setting forth the few facts and legends which have come down to us on the subject.   According to one story the worship of Diana at Nemi was insti-tuted by Orestes, who, after killing Thoas, King of the Tauric Chersonese (the Crimea), fled with his sister to Italy, bringing with him the image of the Tauric Diana. The bloody ritual which legend ascribed to that goddess is familiar to classical readers; it is said that every stranger who landed on the shore was sacrificed on her altar. But transported to Italy, the rite assumed a milder form. Within the sanctuary at Nemi grew a certain tree of which no branch might be broken. Only a runaway slave was allowed to break off, if he could, one of its boughs. Success in the attempt entitled him to fight the priest in single combat, and if he slew him he reigned in his stead with the title of King of the Wood (*Rex Nemorensis*). Tradition averred that the fateful branch was that Golden Bough which, at the Sibyl's bidding, Aeneas plucked before he essayed the perilous journey to the world of the dead. The flight of the slave represented, it was said, the flight of Orestes; his combat with the priest was a reminiscence of the human sacrifices once offered to the Tauric Diana. This rule of succession by the sword was observed down to imperial times; for amongst his other freaks Caligula, thinking that the priest of Nemi had held office too long, hired a more stalwart ruffian to slay him.[1]

Of the worship of Diana at Nemi two leading features can still be made out. First, from the votive-offerings found in modern times on the site, it appears that she was especially worshipped by women desirous of children or of an easy delivery.[2] Second, fire seems

---

[1] Virgil, *Aen.* vi. 136 *sqq.*; Servius, *ad l.*; Strabo, v. 3, 12; Pausanias, ii. 27; Solinus, ii. 11; Suetonius, *Caligula*, 35. For the title "King of the Wood," see Suetonius, *l.c.*; and compare Statius, *Sylv.* iii. 1, 55 *sq.*—

" *Jamque dies aderat, profugis cum regibus aptum*
Fumat Aricinum Triviae nemus;"
Ovid, *Fasti*, iii. 271, "*Regna tenent fortesque manu, pedibusque fugaces;*" *id. Ars am.* i. 259 *sq.*—

" *Ecce suburbanae templum nemorale Dianae,*
Partaque per gladios regna nocente manu."

[2] *Bulletino dell' Instituto*, 1885, p. 153 *sq.*; *Athenaeum*, 10th October 1885; Preller, *Römische Mythologie*,[3] i. 317. Of these votive offerings some represent women with children in their arms; one represents a delivery, etc.

to have played a foremost part in her ritual. For
during her annual festival, celebrated at the hottest time
of the year, her grove was lit up by a multitude of
torches, whose ruddy glare was reflected by the waters
of the lake ; and throughout the length and breadth of
Italy the day was kept with holy rites at every domestic
hearth.[1] Moreover, women whose prayers had been
heard by the goddess brought lighted torches to the
grove in fulfilment of their vows.[2] Lastly, the title of
Vesta borne by the Arician Diana[3] points almost
certainly to the maintenance of a perpetual holy fire in
her sanctuary.

At her annual festival all young people went through
a purificatory ceremony in her honour ; dogs were
crowned ; and the feast consisted of a young kid, wine,
and cakes, served up piping hot on platters of leaves.[4]

But Diana did not reign alone in her grove at
Nemi. Two lesser divinities shared her forest sanctuary. One was Egeria, the nymph of the clear water
which, bubbling from the basaltic rocks, used to fall in
graceful cascades into the lake at the place called Le
Mole.[5] According to one story the grove was first
consecrated to Diana by a Manius Egerius, who was
the ancestor of a long and distinguished line. Hence
the proverb " There are many Manii at Ariciae."
Others explained the proverb very differently. They
said it meant that there were a great many ugly and

---

[1] Statius, *Sylv.* iii. 1, 52 *sqq.* From
Martial, xii. 67, it has been inferred
that the Arician festival fell on the 13th
of August. The inference, however,
does not seem conclusive. Statius's
expression is :—

" *Tempus erat, caeli cum ardentissimus*
    axis
Incumbit terris, ictusque Hyperione
    multo
Acer anhelantes incendit Sirius agros."

[2] Ovid, *Fasti*, iii. 269 ; Propertius,
iii. 24 (30), 9 *sq.* ed. Paley.
[3] *Inscript. Lat.* ed. Orelli, No. 1455.
[4] Statius, *l.c.* ; Gratius Faliscus, *v.*
483 *sqq.*
[5] *Athenaeum*, 10th October 1885.
The water was diverted a few years
ago to supply Albano. For Egeria,
compare Strabo, v. 3, 12 ; Ovid,
Fasti, iii. 273 *sqq.* ; *id. Met.* xv. 487
sqq.

deformed people, and they referred to the word *Mania* which meant a bogey or bugbear to frighten children.[1] The other of these minor deities was Virbius. Legend had it that Virbius was the youthful Greek hero Hippolytus, who had been killed by his horses on the sea-shore of the Saronic Gulf. Him, to please Diana, the leech Aesculapius brought to life again by his simples. But Jupiter, indignant that a mortal man should return from the gates of death, thrust down the meddling leech himself to Hades; and Diana, for the love she bore Hippolytus, carried him away to Italy and hid him from the angry god in the dells of Nemi, where he reigned a forest king under the name of Virbius. Horses were excluded from the grove and sanctuary, because horses had killed Hippolytus.[2] Some thought that Virbius was the sun. It was unlawful to touch his image.[3] His worship was cared for by a special priest, the Flamen Virbialis.[4]

Such then are the facts and theories bequeathed to us by antiquity on the subject of the priesthood of Nemi. From materials so slight and scanty it is impossible to extract a solution of the problem. It remains to try whether the survey of a wider field may not yield us the clue we seek. The questions to be answered are two : first, why had the priest to slay his predecessor? and second, why, before he slew him, had he to pluck the Golden Bough? The rest of this book will be an attempt to answer these questions.

---

[1] Festus, p. 145, ed. Müller ; Schol. on Persius, vi. 56 *ap.* Jahn on Macrobius, i. 7, 35.

[2] Virgil, *Aen.* vii. 761 *sqq.* ; Servius, *ad l.* ; Ovid, *Fasti*, iii. 265 *sq.* ;

id. Met. xv. 497 *sqq.* ; Pausanias, ii. 27.

[3] Servius on Virgil, *Aen.* vii. 776.

[4] *Inscript. Lat.* ed. Orelli, Nos. 2212, 4022. The inscription No. 1457 (Orelli) is said to be spurious.

§ 2.—*Primitive man and the supernatural*

The first point on which we fasten is the priest's title. Why was he called the King of the Wood? why was his office spoken of as a Kingdom?[1] The union of a royal title with priestly duties was common in ancient Italy and Greece. At Rome and in other Italian cities there was a priest called the Sacrificial King or King of the Sacred Rites (*Rex Sacrificulus* or *Rex Sacrorum*), and his wife bore the title of Queen of the Sacred Rites.[2] In republican Athens the second magistrate of the state was called the King, and his wife the Queen; the functions of both were religious.[3] Many other Greek democracies had titular kings, whose duties, so far as they are known, seem to have been priestly.[4] At Rome the tradition was that the Sacrificial King had been appointed after the expulsion of the kings in order to offer the sacrifices which had been previously offered by the kings.[5] In Greece a similar view appears to have prevailed as to the origin of the priestly kings.[6] In itself the view is not improbable, and it is borne out by the example of Sparta, the only purely Greek state which retained the kingly form of government in historical times. For in Sparta all state sacrifices were offered by the kings as descendants of the god.[7] This combination of priestly functions with royal authority is familiar to every one. Asia Minor, for example, was the seat of various great religious capitals peopled

---

[1] See above, p. 4, note 1.
[2] Marquardt, *Römische Staatsver-waltung*, iii.[2] 321 *sqq.*
[3] G. Gilbert, *Handbuch der griechi-schen Staatsalterthümer*, i. 241 *sq.*
[4] Gilbert, *op. cit.* ii. 323 *sq.*

[5] Livy, ii. 2, 1; Dionysius Halic. iv. 74, 4.
[6] Demosthenes, *contra Neaer.* § 74, p. 1370. Plutarch, *Quaest. Rom.* 63.
[7] Xenophon, *Repub. Lac.* c. 15, cp. *id.* 13; Aristotle, *Pol.* iii. 14, 3.

by thousands of "sacred slaves," and ruled by pontiffs
who wielded at once temporal and spiritual authority,
like the popes of mediaeval Rome.   Such priest-ridden
cities were Zela and Pessinus.[1]   Teutonic kings, again,
in the old heathen days seem to have stood in the
position, and exercised the powers of high priests.[2]
The Emperors of China offer public sacrifices, the
details of which are regulated by the ritual books.[3]   It
is needless, however, to multiply examples of what is
the rule rather than the exception in the early history
of the kingship.

But when we have said that the ancient kings were
commonly priests also, we are far from having exhausted the religious aspect of their office.   In those
days the divinity that hedges a king was no empty
form of speech but the expression of a sober belief.
Kings were revered, in many cases not merely as
priests, that is, as intercessors between man and god,
but as themselves gods, able to bestow upon their
subjects and worshippers those blessings which are
commonly supposed to be beyond the reach of man,
and are sought, if at all, only by prayer and sacrifice
offered to superhuman and invisible beings.   Thus
kings are often expected to give rain and sunshine in
due season, to make the crops grow, and so on.
Strange as this expectation appears to us, it is quite
of a piece with early modes of thought.   A savage
hardly conceives the distinction commonly drawn by
more advanced peoples between the natural and the
supernatural.   To him the world is mostly worked
by supernatural agents, that is, by personal beings

---

[1] Strabo, xii. 3, 37. 5, 3 ; cp. xi. 4,
7. xii. 2, 3. 2, 6. 3, 31 *sq.* 3, 34. 8,
9. 8, 14.   But see *Encyc. Brit.*, art.
" Priest," xix. 729.

[2] Grimm, *Deutsche Rechtsalterthümer*, p. 243.
[3] See the *Lî-Kî* (Legge's translation),
passim.

acting on impulses and motives like his own, liable like him to be moved by appeals to their pity, their fears, and their hopes. In a world so conceived he sees no limit to his power of influencing the course of nature to his own advantage. Prayers, promises, or threats may secure him fine weather and an abundant crop from the gods; and if a god should happen, as he sometimes believes, to become incarnate in his own person, then he need appeal to no higher power; he, the savage, possesses in himself all the supernatural powers necessary to further his own well-being and that of his fellow men.

This is one way in which the idea of a man-god is reached. But there is another. Side by side with the view of the world as pervaded by spiritual forces, primitive man has another conception in which we may detect a germ of the modern notion of natural law or the view of nature as a series of events occurring in an invariable order without the intervention of personal agency. The germ of which I speak is involved in that sympathetic magic, as it may be called, which plays a large part in most systems of superstition. One of the principles of sympathetic magic is that any effect may be produced by imitating it. To take a few instances. If it is wished to kill a person an image of him is made and then destroyed; and it is believed that through a certain physical sympathy between the person and his image, the man feels the injuries done to the image as if they were done to his own body, and that when it is destroyed he must simultaneously perish. Again, in Morocco a fowl or a pigeon may sometimes be seen with a little red bundle tied to its foot. The bundle contains a charm, and it is believed that as the charm is kept in constant motion by the bird a corresponding restlessness is kept up in the mind of him or her against whom the charm is directed.[1] In Nias when a wild pig has fallen into the pit prepared for it, it is taken out and its back is rubbed with nine fallen leaves, in the belief that this will make nine more wild pigs fall into the pit just as the nine leaves fell from the tree.[2] When a Cambodian hunter has set his nets and taken nothing, he strips himself naked, goes some way off, then strolls up to the net as if he did not see it, lets himself be caught in it and cries, "Hillo! what's this? I'm afraid I'm caught." After that the net is sure to catch game.[3] In Thüringen the man who sows flax carries the seed in a long bag which reaches from his shoulders to his knees, and he walks with long strides, so that the bag sways to and fro on his back. It is believed that this will cause the flax crop to wave in the wind.[4] In the interior of Sumatra the rice is sown by women who, in sowing, let their hair hang loose down their back, in order that the rice may grow luxuriantly and have long stalks.[5] Again, magic sympathy is supposed to exist between a man and any severed portion of his person, as his hair or nails; so that whoever gets possession of hair or nails may work his will, at any distance, upon the person from whom they were cut. This superstition is world-wide. Further, the sympathy in question exists between friends and relations, especially at critical times. Hence, for example, the elaborate code of rules which

[1] A. Leared, *Morocco and the Moors,* p. 272.

[2] J. W. Thomas, "De jacht op het eiland Nias," in *Tijdschrift voor Indische Taal-Land-en Volkenkunde,* xxvi. 277.

[3] E. Aymonier, "Notes sur les coutumes et croyances superstitieuses des Cambodgiens," in *Cochinchine Française, Excursions et Reconnaissances,* No. 16, p. 157.

[4] Witzschel, *Sagen, Sitten und Gebräuche aus Thüringen,* p. 218, No. 36.

[5] Van Hasselt, *Volksbeschrijving van Midden-Sumatra,* p. 323.

regulates the conduct of persons left at home while a party of their friends is out fishing or hunting or on the war-path. It is thought that if the persons left at home broke these rules their absent friends would suffer an injury, corresponding in its nature to the breach of the rule. Thus when a Dyak is out head-hunting, his wife or, if he is unmarried, his sister, must wear a sword day and night in order that he may always be thinking of his weapons; and she may not sleep during the day nor go to bed before two in the morning, lest her husband or brother should thereby be surprised in his sleep by an enemy.[1] In Laos when an elephant hunter is setting out for the chase he warns his wife not to cut her hair or oil her body in his absence; for if she cut her hair the elephant would burst the toils, if she oiled herself it would slip through them.[2]

In all these cases (and similar instances might be multiplied indefinitely) an action is performed or avoided, because its performance is believed to entail good or bad consequences of a sort resembling the act itself. Sometimes the magic sympathy takes effect not so much through an act as through a supposed resemblance of qualities. Thus some Bechuanas wear a ferret as a charm because, being very tenacious of life, it will make them difficult to kill.[3] Others wear a certain insect, mutilated but living, for a similar purpose.[4] Other Bechuana warriors wear the hair of an ox among their own hair and the skin of a frog on their mantle, because a frog is slippery and the ox from

---

[1] J. C. E. Tromp, "De Rambai en Se-broeangDajaks,"*TijdschriftvoorIndische Taal-Land-en Volkenkunde*, xxv. 118.

[2] E. Aymonier, *Notes sur le Laos*, p. 25 *sq.*

[3] J. Campbell, *Travels in South Africa* (second journey), ii. 206; Barnabas Shaw, *Memorials of South Africa*, p. 66.

[4] Casalis, *The Basutos*, p. 271 *sq.*

which the hair has been taken has no horns and is therefore hard to catch ; so the warrior who is provided with these charms believes that he will be as hard to hold as the ox and the frog.[1]

Thus we see that in sympathetic magic one event is supposed to be followed necessarily and invariably by another, without the intervention of any spiritual or personal agency. This is, in fact, the modern conception of physical causation ; the conception, indeed, is misapplied, but it is there none the less. Here, then, we have another mode in which primitive man seeks to bend nature to his wishes. There is, perhaps, hardly a savage who does not fancy himself possessed of this power of influencing the course of nature by sympathetic magic ; a man-god, on this view, is only an individual who is believed to enjoy this common power in an unusually high degree. Thus, whereas a man-god of the former or inspired type derives his divinity from a deity who has taken up his abode in a tabernacle of flesh, a man-god of the latter type draws his supernatural power from a certain physical sympathy with nature. He is not merely the receptacle of a divine spirit. His whole being, body and soul, is so delicately attuned to the harmony of the world that a touch of his hand or a turn of his head may send a thrill vibrating through the universal framework of things ; and conversely his divine organism is acutely sensitive to such slight changes of environment as would leave ordinary mortals wholly unaffected. But the line between these two types of man-god, however sharply we may draw it in theory, is seldom to be traced with precision in practice, and in what follows I shall not insist on it.

To readers long familiarised with the conception of

---

[1] Casalis, *The Basutos*, p. 272.

natural law, the belief of primitive man that he can rule the elements must be so foreign that it may be well to illustrate it by examples. When we have seen that in early society men who make no pretence at all of being gods do nevertheless commonly believe themselves to be invested with supernatural powers, we shall have the less difficulty in comprehending the extraordinary range of powers ascribed to individuals who are actually regarded as divine.

Of all natural phenomena there are perhaps none which civilised man feels himself more powerless to influence than the rain, the sun, and the wind. Yet all these are commonly supposed by savages to be in some degree under their control.

To begin with rain-making. In a village near Dorpat in Russia, when rain was much wanted, three men used to climb up the fir-trees of an old sacred grove. One of them drummed with a hammer on a kettle or small cask to imitate thunder; the second knocked two fire-brands together and made the sparks fly, to imitate lightning; and the third, who was called "the rain-maker," had a bunch of twigs with which he sprinkled water from a vessel on all sides.[1] This is an example of sympathetic magic; the desired event is supposed to be produced by imitating it. Rain is often thus made by imitation. In Halmahera (Gilolo), a large island to the west of New Guinea, a wizard makes rain by dipping a branch of a particular kind of tree in water and sprinkling the ground with it.[2] In Ceram it is enough to dedicate the bark of a certain tree to the spirits and lay it in water.[3] In New Britain

[1] W. Mannhardt, *Antike Wald-und Feldkulte*, p. 342, *note*.
[2] C. F. H. Campen "De Gods-dienstbegrippen der Halmaherasche Al-

foeren," in *Tijdschrift voor Indische Taal-Land-en Volkenkunde*, xxvii. 447.
[3] Riedel, *De sluik-en kroesharige rassen tusschen Selebes en Papua*, p. 114.

the rain-maker wraps some leaves of a red and green
striped creeper in a banana-leaf, moistens the bundle
with water and buries it in the ground ; then he imi-
tates with his mouth the plashing of rain.[1] Amongst
the Omaha Indians of North America, when the corn
is withering for want of rain, the members of the sacred
Buffalo Society fill a large vessel with water and dance
four times round it. One of them drinks some of the
water and spirts it into the air, making a fine spray in
imitation of a mist or drizzling rain. Then he upsets
the vessel, spilling the water on the ground ; whereupon the dancers fall down and drink up the water,
getting mud all over their faces. Lastly they spirt the
water into the air, making a fine mist. This saves the
corn.[2] Amongst the Australian Wotjobaluk the rain-
maker dipped a bunch of his own hair in water, sucked
out the water and squirted it westward, or he twirled
the ball round his head making a spray like rain.[3]
Squirting water from the mouth is also a West African
way of making rain.[4] Another mode is to dip a
particular stone in water or sprinkle water on it. In a
Samoan village a certain stone was carefully housed as
the representative of the rain-making god ; and in time
of drought his priests carried the stone in procession,
and dipped it in a stream.[5] In the Ta-ta-thi tribe of
New South Wales the rain-maker breaks off a piece
of quartz crystal and spits it towards the sky ; the rest
of the crystal he wraps in emu feathers, soaks both
crystal and feathers in water, and carefully hides them.[6]

[1] R. Parkinson, *Im Bismarck Archi-pel*, p. 143.
[2] J. Owen Dorsey, " Omaha Socio-logy," in *Third Annual Report of the Bureau of Ethnology* (Washington), p. 347. Cp. Charlevoix, *Voyage dans l'Amérique septentrionale*, ii. 187.
[3] *Journal of the Anthropological In-stitute*, xvi. 35. Cp. Dawson, *Australian Aborigines*, p. 98.
[4] Labat, *Relation historique de l'Ethi-opie occidentale*, ii. 180.
[5] Turner, *Samoa*, p. 145.
[6] *Journ. Anthrop. Inst.* xiv. 362.

In the Keramin tribe of New South Wales the wizard retires to the bed of a creek, drops water on a round flat stone, then covers up and conceals it.[1] The Fountain of Baranton, of romantic fame, in the forest of Brécilien, used to be resorted to by peasants when they needed rain; they caught some of the water in a tankard and threw it on a slab near the spring.[2] When some of the Apache Indians wish for rain, they take water from a certain spring and throw it on a particular point high up on a rock; the clouds then soon gather and rain begins to fall.[3] There is a lonely tarn on Snowdon called Dulyn or the Black Lake, lying "in a dismal dingle surrounded by high and dangerous rocks." A row of stepping stones runs out into the lake; and if any one steps on the stones and throws water so as to wet the farthest stone, which is called the Red Altar, "it is but a chance that you do not get rain before night, even when it is hot weather."[4] In these cases it is probable that, as in Samoa, the stone is regarded as in some sort divine. This appears from the custom sometimes observed of dipping the cross in the Fountain of Baranton, to procure rain; for this is plainly a substitute for the older way of throwing the water on the stone.[5] In Mingrelia, to get rain they dip a holy image in water daily till it rains.[6] In Navarre the image of St. Peter was taken to a river, where some prayed to him for rain, but others called out to duck him in the water.[7] Here the dipping in

---

[1] *Journ. Anthrop. Inst. l.c.* Cp. Curr, *The Australian Race*, ii. 377.

[2] Rhys, *Celtic Heathendom*, p. 184; Grimm, *Deutsche Mythologie*[4] i. 494. Cp. San-Marte, *Die Arthur Sage*, pp. 105 *sq.*, 153 *sqq.*

[3] *The American Antiquarian*, viii. 339.

[4] Rhys, *Celtic Heathendom*, p. 185 *sq.*

[5] *Ib.* p. 187. So at the fountain of Sainte Anne, near Gevezé, in Brittany. Sébillot, *Traditions et Superstitions de la Haute Bretagne*, i. 72.

[6] Lamberti, "Relation de la Colchide ou Mingrélie," *Voyages au Nord*, vii. 174 (Amsterdam, 1725).

[7] Le Brun, *Histoire critique des pratiques superstitieuses* (Amsterdam, 1733), i. 245 *sq.*

the water is used as a threat; but originally it was probably a sympathetic charm, as in the following instance. In New Caledonia the rain-makers blackened themselves all over, dug up a dead body, took the bones to a cave, jointed them, and hung the skeleton over some taro leaves. Water was poured over the skeleton to run down on the leaves. "They supposed that the soul of the departed took up the water, made rain of it, and showered it down again."[1] The same motive comes clearly out in a mode of making rain which is practised by various peoples of South Eastern Europe. In time of drought the Servians strip a girl, clothe her from head to foot in grass, herbs, and flowers, even her face being hidden with them. Thus disguised she is called the Dodola, and goes through the village with a troop of girls. They stop before every house; the Dodola dances, while the other girls form a ring round her singing one of the Dodola songs, and the housewife pours a pail of water over her.

One of the songs they sing runs thus—

> " We go through the village;
> The clouds go in the sky;
> We go faster,
> Faster go the clouds;
> They have overtaken us,
> And wetted the corn and the vine."

A similar custom is observed by the Greeks, Bulgarians, and Roumanians.[2] In such customs the leaf-dressed girl represents the spirit of vegetation, and drenching her with water is an imitation of rain. In Russia, in the Government of Kursk, when rain is much wanted, the women seize a passing stranger and

---

[1] Turner, *Samoa*, p. 345 *sq.*

[2] Mannhardt, *Baumkultus*, p. 329 *sqq.*; Grimm, *D. M.*[4] i. 493 *sq.*; W. Schmidt, *Das Jahr und seine Tage in* *Meinung und Brauch der Romänen Siebenbürgens*, p. 17; E. Gerard, *The Land beyond the Forest*, ii. 13.

throw him into the river, or souse him from head to foot.[1] Later on we shall see that a passing stranger is often, as here, taken for a god or spirit. Amongst the Minahassa of North Celebes the priest bathes as a rain-charm.[2] In the Caucasian Province of Georgia, when a drought has lasted long, marriageable girls are yoked in couples with an ox-yoke on their shoulders, a priest holds the reins, and thus harnessed they wade through rivers, puddles, and marshes, praying, screaming, weeping, and laughing.[3] In a district of Transylvania, when the ground is parched with drought, some girls strip themselves naked, and, led by an older woman, who is also naked, they steal a harrow and carry it across the field to a brook, where they set it afloat. Next they sit on the harrow and keep a tiny flame burning on each corner of it for an hour. Then they leave the harrow in the water and go home.[4] A similar rain-charm is resorted to in India ; naked women drag a plough across the field by night.[5] It is not said that they plunge the plough into a stream or sprinkle it with water. But the charm would hardly be complete without it.

Sometimes the charm works through an animal. To procure rain the Peruvians used to set a black sheep in a field, poured *chica* over it, and gave it nothing to eat till rain fell.[6] In a district of Sumatra all the women of the village, scantily clad, go to the river, wade into it, and splash each other with the water. A black cat is thrown into the water and made to swim about for a while, then allowed to escape to the

[1] Mannhardt, *B. K.* p. 331.

[2] J. G. F. Riedel, "De Minahasa in 1825," *Tijdschrift v. Indische Taal-Land-en Volkenkunde*, xviii. 524.

[3] J. Reinegg, *Beschreibung des Kaukasus*, ii. 114.

[4] Mannhardt, *B. K.* p. 553 ; Gerard, *The Land beyond the Forest*, ii. 40.

[5] *Panjab Notes and Queries*, iii. Nos. 173, 513.

[6] Acosta, *History of the Indies*, bk. v. ch. 28.

bank, pursued by the splashing of the women.[1] In these cases the colour of the animal is part of the charm ; being black it will darken the sky with rain-clouds. So the Bechuanas burn the stomach of an ox at evening, because they say, " the black smoke will gather the clouds, and cause the rain to come."[2] The Timorese sacrifice a black pig for rain, a white or red one for sunshine.[3] The Garos offer a black goat on the top of a very high mountain in time of drought.[4]

Sometimes people try to coerce the rain-god into giving rain. In China a huge dragon made of paper or wood, representing the rain-god, is carried about in procession ; but if no rain follows, it is cursed and torn in pieces.[5] In the like circumstances the Feloupes of Senegambia throw down their fetishes and drag them about the fields, cursing them till rain falls.[6] Some Indians of the Orinoco worshipped toads and kept them in vessels in order to obtain from them rain or sunshine as might be required ; when their prayers were not answered they beat the toads.[7] Killing a frog is a European rain-charm.[8] When the spirits withhold rain or sunshine, the Comanches whip a slave ; if the gods prove obstinate, the victim is almost flayed alive.[9] Here the human being may represent the god, like the leaf-clad Dodola. When the rice-crop is endangered by long drought, the governor of

[1] A. L. van Hasselt, *Volksbeschrijving van Midden-Sumatra*, p. 320 sq.

[2] *South African Folk-lore Journal*, i. 34.

[3] J. S. G. Gramberg, " Eene maand in de blnnenlanden van Timor," in *Verhandelingen van het Bataviansch Genootschap van Kunsten en Wetenschappen*, xxxvi. 209.

[4] Dalton, *Ethnology of Bengal*, p. 88.

[5] Huc, *L'empire chinois*, i. 241.

[6] Bérenger-Féraud, *Les peuplades de la Sénégambie*, p. 291.

[7] *Colombia, being a geographical* etc. *account of that country*, i. 642 sq.; A. Bastian, *Die Culturländer des alten Amerika*, ii. 216.

[8] A. Kuhn, *Sagen, Gebräuche und Mährchen aus Westfalen*, ii. p. 80 ; Gerard, *The Land beyond the Forest*, ii. 13.

[9] Bancroft, *Native Races of the Pacific States*, i. 520.

Battambang, a province of Siam, goes in great state to a certain pagoda and prays to Buddha for rain. Then accompanied by his suite and followed by an enormous crowd he adjourns to a plain behind the pagoda. Here a dummy figure has been made up, dressed in bright colours, and placed in the middle of the plain. A wild music begins to play; maddened by the din of drums and cymbals and crackers, and goaded on by their drivers, the elephants charge down on the dummy and trample it to pieces. After this, Buddha will soon give rain.[1]

Another way of constraining the rain-god is to disturb him in his haunts. This seems the reason why rain is supposed to be the consequence of troubling a sacred spring. The Dards believe that if a cowskin or anything impure is placed in certain springs, storms will follow.[2] Gervasius mentions a spring into which if a stone or a stick were thrown, rain would at once issue from it and drench the thrower.[3] There was a fountain in Munster such that if it were touched or even looked at by a human being, it would at once flood the whole province with rain.[4] Sometimes an appeal is made to the pity of the gods. When their corn is being burnt up by the sun, the Zulus look out for a "heaven-bird," kill it, and throw it into a pool. Then the heaven melts with tenderness for the death of the bird; "it wails for it by raining, wailing a funeral wail."[5] In times of drought the Guanches of Teneriffe led their sheep to sacred ground, and there

---

[1] Brien, "Aperçu sur la province de Battambang," in *Cochinchine française, Excursions et Reconnaissances*, No. 25, p. 6 *sq.*

[2] Biddulph, *Tribes of the Hindoo Koosh*, p. 95.

[3] Gervasius von Tilburg, ed. Liebrecht, p. 41 *sq.*

[4] Giraldus Cambrensis, *Topography of Ireland*, ch. 7. Cp. Mannhardt, *A. W. F.* p. 341 *note.*

[5] Callaway, *Religious System of the Amazulu*, p. 407 *sq.*

they separated the lambs from their dams, that their
plaintive bleating might touch the heart of the god.[1]
A peculiar mode of making rain was adopted by the
heathen Arabs. They tied two sorts of bushes to the
tails and hind-legs of their cattle, and setting fire to
the bushes drove the cattle to the top of a mountain,
praying for rain.[2] This may be, as Wellhausen suggests,[3] an imitation of lightning on the horizon. But
it may also be a way of threatening the sky ; as some
West African rain-makers put a pot of inflammable
materials on the fire and blow up the flames, threatening that if heaven does not soon give rain they will
send up a flame which will set the sky on fire.[4] The
Dieyerie of South Australia have a way of their own
of making rain. A hole is dug about twelve feet long
and eight or ten broad, and over this hole a hut of
logs and branches is made. Two men, supposed to
have received a special inspiration from Mooramoora
(the Good Spirit), are bled by an old and influential
man with a sharp flint inside the arm ; the blood is
made to flow on the other men of the tribe who sit
huddled together. At the same time the two bleeding
men throw handfuls of down, some of which adheres
to the blood, while the rest floats in the air. The
blood is thought to represent the rain, and the down
the clouds. During the ceremony two large stones
are placed in the middle of the hut ; they stand for
gathering clouds and presage rain. Then the men
who were bled carry away the stones for about fifteen
miles and place them as high as they can in the tallest
tree. Meanwhile, the other men gather gypsum, pound

---

[1] Reclus, *Nouvelle Géographie Uni-*
verselle, xii. 100.

[2] Rasmussen, *Additamenta ad histo-*
riam Arabum ante Islamismum, p. 67 *sq.*

[3] *Reste arabischen Heidentumes*, p.
157.

[4] Labat, *Relation historique de*
l'Ethiopie occidentale, ii. 180.

it fine, and throw it into a water-hole. This the Mooramoora is supposed to see, and at once he causes the
clouds to appear in the sky. Lastly, the men surround
the hut, butt at it with their heads, force their way in,
and reappear on the other side, repeating this till the
hut is wrecked. In doing this they are forbidden to
use their hands or arms; but when the heavy logs
alone remain, they are allowed to pull them out with
their hands. "The piercing of the hut with their
heads symbolises the piercing of the clouds; the fall
of the hut, the fall of rain."[1] Another Australian
mode of rain-making is to burn human hair.[2]

Like other peoples the Greeks and Romans sought
to procure rain by magic, when prayers and processions[3]
had proved ineffectual. For example, in Arcadia,
when the corn and trees were parched with drought,
the priest of Zeus dipped an oak branch into a certain
spring on Mount Lycaeus. Thus troubled, the water
sent up a misty cloud, from which rain soon fell upon
the land.[4] A similar mode of making rain is still
practised, as we have seen, in Halmahera near New
Guinea. The people of Crannon in Thessaly had a
bronze chariot which they kept in a temple. When
they desired a shower they shook the chariot and the
shower fell.[5] Probably the rattling of the chariot was
meant to imitate thunder; we have already seen that
in Russia mock thunder and lightning form part of
a rain-charm. The mythical Salmoneus of Thessaly
made mock thunder by dragging bronze kettles behind
his chariot or by driving over a bronze bridge, while

---

[1] S. Gason, "The Dieyerie tribe," in
Native Tribes of S. Australia, p. 276 *sqq.*

[2] W. Stanbridge, "On the Aborigines
of Victoria," in *Trans. Ethnol. Soc. of
London*, i. 300.

[3] Marcus Antoninus, v. 7 ; Petronius,

44 ; Tertullian, *Apolog.* 40 ; cp. *id.* 22
and 23.

[4] Pausanias, viii. 38, 4.

[5] Antigonus, *Histor. Mirab.* 15
(*Script. mirab. Graeci*, ed. Westermann, p. 65).

he hurled blazing torches in imitation of lightning. It was his impious wish to mimic the thundering car of Zeus as it rolled across the vault of heaven.[1] Near a temple of Mars, outside the walls of Rome, there was kept a certain stone known as the *lapis manalis*. In time of drought the stone was dragged into Rome and this was supposed to bring down rain immediately.[2] There were Etruscan wizards who made rain or discovered springs of water, it is not certain which. They were thought to bring the rain or the water out of their bellies.[3] The legendary Telchines in Rhodes are described as magicians who could change their shape and bring clouds, rain, and snow.[4]

Again, primitive man fancies he can make the sun to shine, and can hasten or stay its going down. At an eclipse the Ojebways used to think that the sun was being extinguished. So they shot fire-tipped arrows in the air, hoping thus to rekindle his expiring light.[5] Conversely during an eclipse of the moon some Indian tribes of the Orinoco used to bury lighted brands in the ground; because, said they, if the moon were to be extinguished, all fire on earth would be extinguished with her, except such as was hidden from her sight.[6] In New Caledonia when a wizard desires to make sunshine, he takes some plants and corals to the burial-ground, and makes them into a bundle, adding two locks of hair cut from a living child (his own child if

---

[1] Apollodorus, *Bibl.* i. 9, 7; Virgil, *Aen.* vi. 585 *sqq.;* Servius on Virgil, *l.c.*

[2] Festus, *svv. aquaelicium* and *manalem lapidem,* pp. 2, 128, ed. Müller; Nonius Marcellus, *sv trullum,* p. 637, ed. Quicherat; Servius on Virgil, *Aen.* iii. 175; Fulgentius, *Expos. serm. antiq., sv. manales lapides, Mythogr. Lat.* ed. Staveren, p. 769 *sq.*

[3] Nonius Marcellus, *sv. aquilex,* p.

69, ed. Quicherat. In favour of taking *aquilex* as rain-maker is the use of *aquaelicium* in the sense of rain-making. Cp. K. O. Müller, *Die Etrusker,* ed. W. Deecke, ii. 318 *sq.*

[4] Diodorus, v. 55.

[5] Peter Jones, *History of the Ojebway Indians,* p. 84.

[6] Gumilla, *Histoire de l'Orénoque,* iii. 243 *sq.*

possible), also two teeth or an entire jawbone from the skeleton of an ancestor. He then climbs a high mountain whose top catches the first rays of the morning sun. Here he deposits three sorts of plants on a flat stone, places a branch of dry coral beside them, and hangs the bundle of charms over the stone. Next morning he returns to this rude altar, and at the moment when the sun rises from the sea he kindles a fire on the altar. As the smoke rises, he rubs the stone with the dry coral, invokes his ancestors and says : "Sun! I do this that you may be burning hot, and eat up all the clouds in the sky." The same ceremony is repeated at sunset.[1] When the sun rises behind clouds—a rare event in the bright sky of Southern Africa—the Sun clan of the Bechuanas say that he is grieving their heart. All work stands still, and all the food of the previous day is given to matrons or old women. They may eat it and may share it with the children they are nursing, but no one else may taste it. The people go down to the river and wash themselves all over. Each man throws into the river a stone taken from his domestic hearth, and replaces it with one picked up in the bed of the river. On their return to the village the chief kindles a fire in his hut, and all his subjects come and get a light from it. A general dance follows.[2] In these cases it seems that the lighting of the flame on earth is supposed to rekindle the solar fire. Such a belief comes naturally to people who, like the Sun clan of the Bechuanas,

[1] Glaumont, "Usages, mœurs et coutumes des Néo-Calédoniens," in *Revue d Ethnographie*, vi. 116.

[2] Arbousset et Daumas, *Voyage d'exploration au Nord-est de la Colonie du Cap de Bonne-Espérance*, p. 350 *sq.*

For the kinship with the sacred object (tchem) from which the clan takes its name, see *ib.* pp. 350, 422, 424. Other people have claimed kindred with the sun, as the Natchez of North America (*Voyages au Nord*, v. 24) and the Incas of Peru.

deem themselves the veritable kinsmen of the sun. The Melanesians make sunshine by means of a mock sun. A round stone is wound about with red braid and stuck with owl's feathers to represent rays; it is then hung on a high tree. Or the stone is laid on the ground with white rods radiating from it to imitate sunbeams.[1] Sometimes the mode of making sunshine is the converse of that of making rain. Thus we have seen that a white or red pig is sacrificed for sunshine, as a black one is sacrificed for rain.[2] Some of the New Caledonians drench a skeleton to make rain, but burn it to make sunshine.[3]

In a pass of the Peruvian Andes stand two ruined towers on opposite hills. Iron hooks are clamped into their walls for the purpose of stretching a net from one tower to the other. The net is intended to catch the sun.[4]

On the top of a small hill in Fiji grew a patch of reeds, and travellers who feared to be belated used to tie the tops of a handful of reeds together to detain the sun from going down.[5] The intention perhaps was to entangle the sun in the reeds, just as the Peruvians try to catch him in the net. Stories of men who have caught the sun in a noose are widely spread.[6] Jerome of Prague, travelling among the heathen Lithuanians early in the fifteenth century, found a tribe who worshipped the sun and venerated a large iron hammer. The priests told him that once the sun had been invisible for several months, because a powerful

[1] Codrington, in *Journ. Anthrop. Instit.* x. 278.
[2] Above, p. 18.
[3] Turner, *Samoa*, p. 346. See above, p. 16.
[4] Bastian, *Die Völker des östlichen Asien*, iv. 174. The name of the place is Andahuayllas.
[5] Th. Williams, *Fiji and the Fijians*, i. 250.
[6] Schoolcraft, *The American Indians*, p. 97 *sqq.*; Gill, *Myths and Songs of the South Pacific*, p. 61 *sq.*; Turner, *Samoa*, p. 200 *sq.*

king had shut it up in a strong tower; but the signs
of the zodiac had broken open the tower with this very
hammer and released the sun. Therefore they adored
the hammer.[1] When an Australian blackfellow wishes
to stay the sun from going down till he gets home, he
places a sod in the fork of a tree, exactly facing the
setting sun.[2] For the same purpose an Indian of
Yucatan, journeying westward, places a stone in a tree
or pulls out some of his eyelashes and blows them
towards the sun.[3] South African natives, in travelling,
will put a stone in a branch of a tree or place some
grass on the path with a stone over it, believing that
this will cause their friends to keep the meal waiting
till their arrival.[4] In these, as in previous examples,
the purpose apparently is to retard the sun. But why
should the act of putting a stone or a sod in a tree be
supposed to effect this? A partial explanation is
suggested by another Australian custom. In their
journeys the natives are accustomed to place stones in
trees at different heights from the ground in order to
indicate the height of the sun in the sky at the moment
when they passed the particular tree. Those who
follow are thus made aware of the time of day when
their friends in advance passed the spot.[5] Possibly
the natives, thus accustomed to mark the sun's progress,
may have slipped into the confusion of imagining that
to mark the sun's progress was to arrest it at the point
marked. On the other hand, to make it go down
faster, the Australians throw sand into the air and
blow with their mouths towards the sun.[6]

[1] Aeneas Sylvius, *Opera* (Bâle, 1571), p. 418 [wrongly numbered 420].

[2] Brough Smyth, *Aborigines of Victoria*, ii. 334 ; Curr, *The Australian Race*, i. 50.

[3] Fancourt, *History of Yucatan*, p. 118.

[4] *South African Folk-lore Journal*, i. 34.

[5] E. J. Eyre, *Journals of Expeditions of Discovery into Central Australia*, ii. 365.

[6] Curr, *The Australian Race*, iii. 145.

Once more, the savage thinks he can make the wind to blow or to be still. When the day is hot and a Yakut has a long way to go, he takes a stone which he has chanced to find in an animal or fish, winds a horse-hair several times round it, and ties it to a stick. He then waves the stick about, uttering a spell. Soon a cool breeze begins to blow.[1] The Wind clan of the Omahas flap their blankets to start a breeze which will drive away the mosquitoes.[2] When a Haida Indian wishes to obtain a fair wind, he fasts, shoots a raven, singes it in the fire, and then going to the edge of the sea sweeps it over the surface of the water four times in the direction in which he wishes the wind to blow. He then throws the raven behind him, but afterwards picks it up and sets it in a sitting posture at the foot of a spruce-tree, facing towards the required wind. Propping its beak open with a stick, he requests a fair wind for a certain number of days; then going away he lies covered up in his mantle till another Indian asks him for how many days he has desired the wind, which question he answers.[3] When a sorcerer in New Britain wishes to make a wind blow in a certain direction, he throws burnt lime in the air, chanting a song all the time. Then he waves sprigs of ginger and other plants about, throws them up and catches them. Next he makes a small fire with these sprigs on the spot where the lime has fallen thickest, and walks round the fire chanting. Lastly, he takes the ashes and throws them on the water.[4] On the altar of Fladda's chapel, in the island of Fladdahuan (one of

---

[1] Gmelin, *Reise durch Sibirien*, ii. 510.

[2] *Third Annual Report of the Bureau of Ethnology* (Washington), p. 241.

[3] G. M. Dawson, "On the Haida Indians of the Queen Charlotte Islands," *Geological Survey of Canada, Report of progress for* 1878-1879, p. 124 B.

[4] W. Powell, *Wanderings in a Wild Country*, p. 169.

the Hebrides), lay a round bluish stone which was always moist. Windbound fishermen walked sunwise round the chapel and then poured water on the stone, whereupon a favourable breeze was sure to spring up.[1] In Finnland wizards used to sell wind to storm-staid mariners. The wind was enclosed in three knots; if they undid the first knot, a moderate wind sprang up; if the second, it blew half a gale; if the third, a hurricane.[2] The same thing is said to have been done by wizards and witches in Lappland, in the island of Lewis, and in the Isle of Man.[3] A Norwegian witch has boasted of sinking a ship by opening a bag in which she had shut up a wind.[4] Ulysses received the winds in a leather bag from Aeolus, King of the Winds.[5] So Perdoytus, the Lithuanian wind-god, keeps the winds enclosed in a leather bag; when they escape from it he pursues them, beats them, and shuts them up again.[6] The Motumotu in New Guinea think that storms are sent by an Oiabu sorcerer; for each wind he has a bamboo which he opens at pleasure.[7] But here we have passed from custom (with which alone we are at present concerned) into mythology. Shetland seamen still buy winds from old women who claim to rule the storms. There are now in Lerwick old women who live by selling wind.[8] When the Hottentots wish to make the wind drop, they take one of their fattest skins and hang it on the end of a pole,

---

[1] Miss C. F. Gordon Cumming, *In the Hebrides*, p. 166 *sq.*; Martin, "Description of the Western Islands of Scotland," in Pinkerton's *Voyages and Travels*, iii. 627.

[2] Olaus Magnus, *Gentium Septentr. Hist.* iii. 15.

[3] Scheffer, *Lapponia*, p. 144; Gordon Cumming, *In the Hebrides*, p. 254 *sq.*; Train, *Account of the Isle of Man*, ii. 166.

[4] C. Leemius, *De Lapponibus Finmarchiae etc. commentatio*, p. 454.

[5] *Odyssey*, x. 19 *sqq.*

[6] E. Veckenstedt, *Die Mythen, Sagen, und Legenden der Zamaiten* (*Litauer*), i. 153.

[7] J. Chalmers, *Pioneering in New Guinea*, p. 177.

[8] Rogers, *Social Life in Scotland*, iii. 220; Sir W. Scott, *Pirate*, note to ch. vii.; Shaks. *Macbeth*, Act i. Sc. 3, l. 11.

believing that by blowing the skin down the wind will lose all its force and must itself fall.[1] In some parts of Austria, during a heavy storm, it is customary to open the window and throw out a handful of meal, chaff, or feathers, saying to the wind, " There, that's for you, stop!"[2] Once when north-westerly winds had kept the ice long on the coast, and food was getting scarce, the Eskimos of Alaska performed a ceremony to make a calm. A fire was kindled on the shore and the men gathered round it and chanted. An old man then stepped up to the fire and in a coaxing voice invited the demon of the wind to come under the fire and warm himself. When he was supposed to have arrived, a vessel of water, to which each man present had contributed, was thrown on the fire by an old man, and immediately a flight of arrows sped towards the spot where the fire had been. They thought that the demon would not stay where he had been so badly treated. To complete the effect, guns were discharged in various directions, and the captain of a European vessel was asked to fire on the wind with cannon.[3] When the wind blows down their huts, the Payaguas in South America snatch up fire-brands and run against the wind menacing it with the blazing brands, while others beat the air with their fists to frighten the storm.[4] When the Guaycurus are threatened by a severe storm the men go out armed, and the women and children scream their loudest to intimidate the demon.[5] During a tempest the inhabitants of a Batta village in Sumatra have been seen to

[1] Dapper, *Description do l'Afrique* (Amsterdam, 1686), p. 389.

[2] A. Peter, *Volksthümliches aus Oesterreichisch Schlesien*, ii. 259.

[3] *Arctic Papers for the Expedition*

of 1875 (R. Geogr. Soc.), p. 274.

[4] Azara, *Voyages dans l'Amérique Méridionale*, ii. 137.

[5] Charlevoix, *Histoire du Paraguay*, i. 74.

rush from their houses armed with sword and lance. The Raja placed himself at their head, and with shouts and yells they hewed and hacked at the invisible foe. An old woman was observed to be especially active in defending her house, slashing the air right and left with a long sabre.[1]

In the light of these examples a story told by Herodotus, which his modern critics have treated as a fable, is perfectly credible. He says, without however vouching for the truth of the tale, that once in the land of the Psylli, the modern Tripoli, the wind blowing from the Sahara had dried up all the water-tanks. So the people took counsel and marched in a body to make war on the south wind. But when they entered the desert, the simoom swept down on them and buried them to a man.[2] The story may well have been told by one who watched them disappearing, in battle array, with drums and cymbals beating, into the red cloud of whirling sand. It is still said of the Bedouins of Eastern Africa that " no whirlwind ever sweeps across the path without being pursued by a dozen savages with drawn creeses, who stab into the centre of the dusty column in order to drive away the evil spirit that is believed to be riding on the blast."[3] So in Australia the huge columns of red sand that move rapidly across a desert tract are thought by the blackfellows to be spirits passing along. Once an athletic young black ran after one of these moving columns to kill it with boomerangs. He was away two or three hours and came back very weary, saying he had killed Koochee (the demon), but that Koochee

---

[1] W. A. Henry, "Bijdrage tot de Kennis der Bataklanden," in *Tijd-schrift voor Indische Taal-Land-en Volkenkunde*, xvii. 23 *sq.*

[2] Herodotus, iv. 173 ; Aulus Gellius, xvi. 11.

[3] Harris, *Highlands of Ethiopia*, i. 352.

had growled at him and he must die.[1] Even where these dust columns are not attacked they are still regarded with awe. In some parts of India they are supposed to be *bhuts* going to bathe in the Ganges.[2] Californian Indians think that they are happy souls ascending to the heavenly land.[3]

When a gust lifts the hay in the meadow, the Breton peasant throws a knife or a fork at it to prevent the devil from carrying off the hay.[4] German peasants throw a knife or a hat at a whirlwind because there is a witch or a wizard in it.[5]

§ 3.—*Incarnate gods*

These examples, drawn from the beliefs and practices of rude peoples all over the world, may suffice to prove that the savage, whether European or otherwise, fails to recognise those limitations to his power over nature which seem so obvious to us. In a society where every man is supposed to be endowed more or less with powers which we should call supernatural, it is plain that the distinction between gods and men is somewhat blurred, or rather has scarcely emerged. The conception of gods as supernatural beings entirely distinct from and superior to man, and wielding powers to which he possesses nothing comparable in degree and hardly even in kind, has been slowly evolved in the course of history. At first the supernatural agents are not regarded as greatly, if

[1] Brough Smyth, *Aborigines of Victoria*, i. 457 *sq.* ; cp. *id.* ii. 270 ; *Journ. Anthrop. Inst.* xiii. p. 194 *note.*

[2] Denzil C. J. Ibbetson, *Settlement Report of the Panipat Tahsil and Karnal Parganah of the Karnal District*, p. 154.

[3] Stephen Powers, *Tribes of California*, p. 328.

[4] Sébillot, *Coutumes populaires de la Haute-Bretagne*, p. 302 *sq.*

[5] Mannhardt, *A.W.F.* p. 85.

at all, superior to man ; for they may be frightened
and coerced by him into doing his will. At this stage
of thought the world is viewed as a great democracy ;
all beings in it, whether natural or supernatural, are
supposed to stand on a footing of tolerable equality.
But with the growth of his knowledge man learns to
realise more clearly the vastness of nature and his
own littleness and feebleness in presence of it. The
recognition of his own helplessness does not, however,
carry with it a corresponding belief in the impotence
of those supernatural beings with which his imagination
peoples the universe.   On the contrary it enhances his
conception of their power.   For the idea of the world
as a system of impersonal forces acting in accordance
with fixed and invariable laws has not yet fully dawned
or darkened upon him.   The germ of the idea he
certainly has, and he acts upon it, not only in magic
art, but in much of the business of daily life.   But the
idea remains undeveloped, and so far as he attempts
consciously to explain the world he lives in, he pictures
it as the manifestation of conscious will and personal
agency.   If then he feels himself to be so frail and
slight, how vast and powerful must he deem the beings
who control the gigantic machinery of nature ! Thus
as his old sense of equality with the gods slowly
vanishes, he resigns at the same time the hope of
directing the course of nature by his own unaided
resources, that is, by magic, and looks more and more
to the gods as the sole repositories of those supernatural
powers which he once claimed to share with them.
With the first advance of knowledge, therefore, prayer
and sacrifice assume the leading place in religious
ritual ; and magic, which once ranked with them as a
legitimate equal, is gradually relegated to the back-

ground and sinks to the level of a black art. It is now regarded as an encroachment, at once vain and impious, on the domain of the gods, and as such encounters the steady opposition of the priests, whose reputation and influence gain or lose with those of their gods. Hence, when at a late period the distinction between religion and superstition has emerged, we find that sacrifice and prayer are the resource of the pious and enlightened portion of the community, while magic is the refuge of the superstitious and ignorant. But when, still later, the conception of the elemental forces as personal agents is giving way to the recognition of natural law; then magic, based as it implicitly is on the idea of a necessary and invariable sequence of cause and effect, independent of personal will, reappears from the obscurity and discredit into which it had fallen, and by investigating the causal sequences in nature, directly prepares the way for science. Alchemy leads up to chemistry.

The notion of a man-god or of a human being endowed with divine or supernatural powers, belongs essentially to that earlier period of religious history in which gods and men are still viewed as beings of much the same order, and before they are divided by the impassable gulf which, to later thought, opens out between them. Strange, therefore, as may seem to us the idea of a god incarnate in human form, it has nothing very startling for early man, who sees in a man-god or a god-man only a higher degree of the same supernatural powers which he arrogates in perfect good faith to himself. Such incarnate gods are common in rude society. The incarnation may be temporary or permanent. In the former case, the incarnation—commonly known as inspiration or possession—reveals itself in supernatural knowledge rather than in supernatural power. In other words, its usual manifestations are divination and prophesy rather than miracles. On the other hand, when the incarnation is not merely temporary, when the divine spirit has permanently taken up its abode in a human body, the god-man is usually expected to vindicate his character by working miracles. Only we have to remember that by men at this stage of thought miracles are not considered as breaches of natural law. Not conceiving the existence of natural law, primitive man cannot conceive a breach of it. A miracle is to him merely an unusually striking manifestation of a common power.

The belief in temporary incarnation or inspiration is world-wide. Certain persons are supposed to be possessed from time to time by a spirit or deity ; while the possession lasts, their own personality lies in abeyance, the presence of the spirit is revealed by convulsive shiverings and shakings of the man's whole body, by wild gestures and excited looks, all of which are referred, not to the man himself, but to the spirit which has entered into him ; and in this abnormal state all his utterances are accepted as the voice of the god or spirit dwelling in him and speaking through him. In Mangaia the priests in whom the gods took up their abode from time to time were called "god-boxes" or, for shortness, "gods." Before giving oracles as gods, they drank an intoxicating liquor, and in the frenzy thus produced their wild words were received as the voice of the god.[1] But examples of such temporary inspiration are so common in every part of the world

---

[1] Gill, *Myths and Songs of the South Pacific*, p. 35.

and are now so familiar through books on ethnology,
that it is needless to cite illustrations of the general
principle.[1] It may be well, however, to refer to two
particular modes of producing temporary inspiration,
because they are perhaps less known than some others,
and because we shall have occasion to refer to them
later on.   One of these modes of producing inspiration
is by sucking the fresh blood of a sacrificed victim.   In
the temple of Apollo Diradiotes at Argos, a lamb was
sacrificed by night once a month ; a woman, who had
to observe a rule of chastity, tasted the blood of the
lamb, and thus being inspired by the god she
prophesied or divined.[2]   At Aegira in Achaea the
priestess of Earth drank the fresh blood of a bull
before she descended into the cave to prophesy.[3]   In
Southern India a devil-dancer "drinks the blood of
the sacrifice, putting the throat of the decapitated goat
to his mouth.   Then, as if he had acquired new life,
he begins to brandish his staff of bells, and to dance
with a quick but wild unsteady step.   Suddenly the
afflatus descends.   There is no mistaking that glare,
or those frantic leaps.   He snorts, he stares, he
gyrates.   The demon has now taken bodily possession
of him ; and, though he retains the power of utterance
and of motion, both are under the demon's control,
and his separate consciousness is in abeyance. . . .
The devil-dancer is now worshipped as a present
deity, and every bystander consults him respecting his
disease, his wants, the welfare of his absent relatives,
the offerings to be made for the accomplishment of his

---

[1] See for examples E. B. Tylor, *Primitive Culture*,[2] ii. 131 *sqq.*

[2] Pausanias, ii. 24, 1. κάτοχος ἐκ τοῦ θεοῦ γίνεται is the expression.

[3] Pliny, *Nat. Hist.* xxviii. 147.

Pausanias (vii. 25, 13) mentions the draught of bull's blood as an ordeal to test the chastity of the priestess. Doubtless it was thought to serve both purposes.

wishes, and, in short, respecting everything for which
superhuman knowledge is supposed to be available."[1]
At a festival of the Minahassa in northern Celebes,
after a pig has been killed, the priest rushes furiously
at it, thrusts his head into the carcass and drinks of
the blood. Then he is dragged away from it by force
and set on a chair, whereupon he begins to prophesy
how the rice crop will turn out that year. A second
time he runs at the carcass and drinks of the blood; a
second time he is forced into the chair and continues
his predictions. It is thought there is a spirit in him
which possesses the power of prophecy.[2] At Rhetra,
a great religious capital of the Western Slavs, the
priest tasted the blood of the sacrificed oxen and sheep
in order the better to prophesy.[3] The true test of a
Dainyal or diviner among some of the Hindoo Koosh
tribes is to suck the blood from the neck of a decapitated goat.[4] The other mode of producing temporary
inspiration, to which I shall here refer, is by means of a
branch or leaves of a sacred tree. Thus in the Hindoo
Koosh a fire is kindled with twigs of the sacred cedar;
and the Dainyal or sibyl, with a cloth over her head,
inhales the thick pungent smoke till she is seized with
convulsions and falls senseless to the ground. Soon
she rises and raises a shrill chant, which is caught up

---

[1] Caldwell, "On demonolatry in
Southern India," *Journal of the
Anthropological Society of Bombay*, i.
101 *sq.*
[2] J. G. F. Riedel, "De Minahasa
in 1825," *Tijdschrift v. Indische Taal-
Land-en Volkenkunde*, xviii. 517 *sq.*
Cp. N. Graafland, *De Minahassa*, i.
122; Dumont D'Urville, *Voyage autour
du Monde et à la recherche de La Perouse*,
v. 443.
[3] F. J. Mone, *Geschichte des Heidenthums im nördlichen Europa*, i. 188.

[4] Biddulph, *Tribes of the Hindoo
Koosh*, p. 96. For other instances of
priests or representatives of the deity
drinking the warm blood of the victim,
cp. *Tijdschrift v. Nederlandsch Indië*,
1849, p. 395; Oldfield, *Sketches from
Nipal*, ii. 296 *sq.*; *Asiatic Researches*,
iv. 40, 41, 50, 52 (8vo. ed.); Paul
Soleillet, *L'Afrique Occidentale*, p. 123
sq. To snuff up the savour of the
sacrifice was similarly supposed to produce inspiration. Tertullian, *Apologet.*
23.

and loudly repeated by her audience.[1] So Apollo's prophetess ate the sacred laurel before she prophesied.[2] It is worth observing that many peoples expect the victim as well as the priest or prophet to give signs of inspiration by convulsive movements of the body ; and if the animal remains obstinately steady, they esteem it unfit for sacrifice. Thus when the Yakuts sacrifice to an evil spirit, the beast must bellow and roll about, which is considered a token that the evil spirit has entered into it.[3] Apollo's prophetess could give no oracles unless the victim to be sacrificed trembled in every limb when the wine was poured on its head. But for ordinary Greek sacrifices it was enough that the victim should shake its head ; to make it do so, water was poured on it.[4] Many other peoples (Tonquinese, Hindoos, Chuwash, etc.) have adopted the same test of a suitable victim ; they pour water or wine on its head ; if the animal shakes its head it is accepted for sacrifice ; if it does not, it is rejected.[5]

The person temporarily inspired is believed to acquire, not merely divine knowledge, but also, at least occasionally, divine power. In Cambodia, when an epidemic breaks out, the inhabitants of several villages unite and go with a band of music at their head to look for the man whom the local god is

---

[1] Biddulph, *Tribes of the Hindoo Koosh*, p. 97.

[2] Lucian, *Bis accus.*, 1 ; Tzetzes, *Schol. ad Lycophr.*, 6.

[3] Vambery, *Das Türkenvolk*, p. 158.

[4] Plutarch, *De defect. oracul.* 46, 49.

[5] D. Chwolsohn, *Die Ssabier und der Ssabismus*, ii. 37 ; *Lettres édifiantes et curieuses*, xvi. 230 *sq.*; *Panjab Notes and Queries*, iii. No. 721 ; *Journal of the Anthropological Society of Bombay*, i. 103 ; S. Mateer, *The Land of Charity*, 216 ; *id.*, *Native Life in Travancore*, p. 94 ; A. C. Lyall,

Asiatic Studies, p. 14 ; Biddulph, *Tribes of the Hindoo Koosh*, p. 131 ; Pallas, *Reisen in verschiedenen Provinzen des russischen Reiches*, i. 91 ; Vambery, *Das Türkenvolk*, p. 485 ; Erman, *Archiv für wissenschaftliche Kunde von Russland*, i. 377.   When the Rao of Kachh sacrifices a buffalo, water is sprinkled between its horns ; if it shakes its head, it is unsuitable ; if it nods its head, it is sacrificed. *Panjab Notes and Queries*, i. No. 911.   This is probably a modern misinterpretation of the old custom.

believed to have chosen for his temporary incarnation. When found, the man is taken to the altar of the god, where the mystery of incarnation takes place. Then the man becomes an object of veneration to his fellows, who implore him to protect the village against the plague.[1] The image of Apollo at Hylæ in Phocis was believed to impart superhuman strength. Sacred men, inspired by it, leaped down precipices, tore up huge trees by the roots, and carried them on their backs along the narrowest defiles.[2] The feats performed by inspired dervishes belong to the same class.

Thus far we have seen that the savage, failing to discern the limits of his ability to control nature, ascribes to himself and to all men certain powers which we should now call supernatural. Further, we have seen that over and above this general supernaturalism, some persons are supposed to be inspired for short periods by a divine spirit, and thus temporarily to enjoy the knowledge and power of the indwelling deity. From beliefs like these it is an easy step to the conviction that certain men are permanently possessed by a deity, or in some other undefined way are endued with so high a degree of supernatural powers as to be ranked as gods and to receive the homage of prayer and sacrifice. Sometimes these human gods are restricted to purely supernatural or spiritual functions. Sometimes they exercise supreme political power in addition. In the latter case they are kings as well as gods, and the government is a theocracy. I shall give examples of both.

In the Marquesas Islands there was a class of men who were deified in their life-time. They were sup-

---

[1] Moura, *Le Royaume du Cambodge*, i. 177 *sq.*   [2] Pausanias, x. 32, 6.

posed to wield a supernatural power over the elements ;
they could give abundant harvests or smite the ground
with barrenness ; and they could inflict disease or
death. Human sacrifices were offered to them to avert
their wrath. There were not many of them, at the
most one or two in each island. They lived in mystic
seclusion. Their powers were sometimes, but not
always, hereditary. A missionary has described one of
these human gods from personal observation. The
god was a very old man who lived in a large house
within an enclosure. In the house was a kind of altar,
and on the beams of the house and on the trees round
it were hung human skeletons, head down. No one
entered the enclosure, except the persons dedicated to
the service of the god ; only on days when human
victims were sacrificed might ordinary people penetrate
into the precinct. This human god received more
sacrifices than all the other gods ; often he would sit on
a sort of scaffold in front of his house and call for two
or three human victims at a time. They were always
brought, for the terror he inspired was extreme. He
was invoked all over the island, and offerings were sent
to him from every side.[1] Again, of the South Sea
Islands in general we are told that each island had a
man who represented or personified the divinity. Such
men were called gods, and their substance was confounded with that of the deity. The man-god was
sometimes the king himself ; oftener he was a priest
or subordinate chief.[2] Tanatoa, King of Raiatea, was
deified by a certain ceremony performed at the chief
temple. "As one of the divinities of his subjects,

---

[1] Vincendon-Dumoulin et Desgraz, *Iles Marquises*, pp. 226, 240 *sq.*

[2] Moerenhout, *Voyages aux Iles du Grand Océan*, i. 479 ; Ellis, *Polynesian Researches*, iii. 94.

therefore, the king was worshipped, consulted as an oracle and had sacrifices and prayers offered to him."[1] This was not an exceptional case. The kings of the island regularly enjoyed divine honours, being deified at the time of their accession.[2]   At his inauguration the king of Tahiti received a sacred girdle of red and yellow feathers, "which not only raised him to the highest earthly station, but identified him with their gods."[3]   The gods of Samoa generally appeared in animal form, but sometimes they were permanently incarnate in men, who gave oracles, received offerings (occasionally of human flesh), healed the sick, answered prayers, and so on.[4]   In regard to the old religion of the Fijians, and especially of the inhabitants of Somo-somo, it is said that "there appears to be no certain line of demarcation between departed spirits and gods, nor between gods and living men, for many of the priests and old chiefs are considered as sacred persons, and not a few of them will also claim to themselves the right of divinity. 'I am a god,' Tuikilakila would say; and he believed it too."[5]   In the Pelew Islands it is believed that every god can take possession of a man and speak through him.   The possession may be either temporary or permanent; in the latter case the chosen person is called a *korong*.   The god is free in his choice, so the position of *korong* is not hereditary. After the death of a *korong* the god is for some time unrepresented, until he suddenly makes his appearance in a new Avatar.   The person thus chosen gives signs

---

[1] Tyerman and Bennet, *Journal of Voyages and Travels in the South Sea Islands, China, India, etc.*, i. 524; cp. p. 529 *sq.*

[2] Tyerman and Bennet, *op. cit.* i. 529 *sq.*

[3] Ellis, *Polynesian Researches*, iii. 108.

[4] Turner, *Samoa*, pp. 37, 48, 57, 58, 59, 73.

[5] Hazlewood in Erskine's *Cruise among the Islands of the Western Pacific*, p. 246 *sq.* Cp. Wilkes's *Narrative of the U. S. Exploring Expedition*, iii. 87.

of the divine presence by behaving in a strange way ;
he gapes, runs about, and performs a number of senseless acts. At first people laugh at him, but his sacred
mission is in time recognised, and he is invited to
assume his proper position in the state. Generally
this position is a distinguished one and confers on him
a powerful influence over the whole community. In
some of the islands the god is political sovereign of
the land ; and hence his new incarnation, however
humble his origin, is raised to the same high rank, and
rules, as god and king, over all the other chiefs.[1] In
time of public calamity, as during war or pestilence,
some of the Molucca Islanders used to celebrate a festival of heaven. If no good result followed, they bought
a slave, took him at the next festival to the place of
sacrifice, and set him on a raised place under a certain
bamboo-tree. This tree represented heaven and had
been honoured as its image at previous festivals. The
portion of the sacrifice which had previously been
offered to heaven was now given to the slave, who ate
and drank it in the name and stead of heaven. Henceforth the slave was well treated, kept for the festivals
of heaven, and employed to represent heaven and
receive the offerings in its name.[2] In Tonquin every
village chooses its guardian spirit, often in the form of
an animal, as a dog, tiger, cat, or serpent. Sometimes
a living person is selected as patron-divinity. Thus a
beggar persuaded the people of a village that he was
their guardian spirit ; so they loaded him with honours
and entertained him with their best.[3] In India "every

---

[1] Kubary, "Die Religion der Pelauer,"
in Bastian's *Allerlei aus Volks-und
Menschenkunde*, i. 30 *sqq.*

[2] F. Valentyn, *Oud en nieuw Oost-
Indiën*, iii. 7 *sq.*

[3] Bastian, *Die Völker des östlichen
Asien*, iv. 383.

king is regarded as little short of a present god."[1]
The Indian law-book of Manu goes farther and says
that "even an infant king must not be despised from
an idea that he is a mere mortal; for he is a great
deity in human form."[2]   There is said to be a sect in
Orissa who worship the Queen of England as their
chief divinity.   And to this day in India all living
persons remarkable for great strength or valour or for
supposed miraculous powers run the risk of being
worshipped as gods.   Thus, a sect in the Punjaub
worshipped a deity whom they called Nikkal Sen.
This Nikkal Sen was no other than the redoubted
General Nicholson, and nothing that the general could
do or say damped the enthusiasm of his adorers.   The
more he punished them, the greater grew the religious
awe with which they worshipped him.[3]   Amongst the
Todas, a pastoral people of the Neilgherry Hills of
Southern India, the dairy is a sanctuary, and the milkman (*pâlâl*) who attends to it is a god.   On being
asked whether the Todas salute the sun, one of these
divine milkmen replied, "Those poor fellows do so,
but I," tapping his chest, "I, a god! why should I
salute the sun?"   Every one, even his own father, pros-
trates himself before the milkman, and no one would
dare to refuse him anything.   No human being, except
another milkman, may touch him; and he gives oracles
to all who consult him, speaking with the voice of
a god.[4]

The King of Iddah told the English officers of the
Niger Expedition, "God made me after his own

---

[1] Monier Williams, *Religious Life and Thought in India*, p. 259.
[2] *The Laws of Manu*, vii. 8, trans. by G. Bühler.

[3] Monier Williams, *op. cit.* p. 259 *sq.*
[4] Marshall, *Travels among the Todas*, pp. 136, 137; cp. pp. 141, 142; Metz, *Tribes of the Neilgherry Hills*, p. 19 *sqq.*

image; I am all the same as God; and He appointed me a king."[1]

Sometimes, at the death of the human incarnation, the divine spirit transmigrates into another man. In the kingdom of Kaffa, in Eastern Africa, the heathen part of the people worship a spirit called *Deòce*, to whom they offer prayer and sacrifice, and whom they invoke on all important occasions. This spirit is incarnate in the grand magician or pope, a person of great wealth and influence, ranking almost with the king, and wielding the spiritual, as the king wields the temporal, power. It happened that, shortly before the arrival of a Christian missionary in the kingdom, this African pope died, and the priests, fearing that the missionary would assume the position vacated by the deceased pope, declared that the *Deòce* had passed into the king, who henceforth, uniting the spiritual with the temporal power, reigned as god and king.[2] Before beginning to work at the salt-pans in a Laosian village, the workmen offer sacrifice to a local divinity. This divinity is incarnate in a woman and transmigrates at her death into another woman.[3] In Bhotan the spiritual head of the government is a person called the Dhurma Raja, who is supposed to be a perpetual incarnation of the deity. At his death the new incarnate god shows himself in an infant by the refusal of his mother's milk and a preference for that of a cow.[4] The Buddhist Tartars believe in a great number of living Buddhas, who officiate as Grand Lamas at the head of the most

---

[1] Allen and Thomson, *Narrative of the Expedition to the River Niger in* 1841, i. 288.

[2] G. Massaja, *I miei trentacinque anni di missione nell' alta Etiopia* (Rome and Milan, 1888), v. 53 *sq.*

[3] E. Aymonier, *Notes sur le Laos,* p. 141 *sq.*

[4] Robinson, *Descriptive Account of Assam,* p. 342 *sq.*; *Asiatic Researches,* xv. 146.

important monasteries. When one of these Grand Lamas dies his disciples do not sorrow, for they know that he will soon reappear, being born in the form of an infant. Their only anxiety is to discover the place of his birth. If at this time they see a rainbow they take it as a sign sent them by the departed Lama to guide them to his cradle. Sometimes the divine infant himself reveals his identity. " I am the Grand Lama," he says, " the living Buddha of such and such a temple. Take me to my old monastery. I am its immortal head." In whatever way the birthplace of the Buddha is revealed, whether by the Buddha's own avowal or by the sign in the sky, tents are struck, and the joyful pilgrims, often headed by the king or one of the most illustrious of the royal family, set forth to find and bring home the infant god. Generally he is born in Tibet, the holy land, and to reach him the caravan has often to traverse the most frightful deserts. When at last they find the child they fall down and worship him. Before, however, he is acknowledged as the Grand Lama whom they seek he must satisfy them of his identity. He is asked the name of the monastery of which he claims to be the head, how far off it is, and how many monks live in it ; he must also describe the habits of the deceased Grand Lama and the manner of his death. Then various articles, as prayer-books, tea-pots, and cups, are placed before him, and he has to point out those used by himself in his previous life. If he does so without a mistake his claims are admitted, and he is conducted in triumph to the monastery.[1] At the head of all the Lamas is the Dalai Lama of Lhasa, the Rome of Tibet. He is regarded as a living god

---

[1] Huc, *Souvenirs d'un Voyage dans la Tartarie et le Thibet*, i. 279 *sqq.* ed. 12mo.

and at death his divine and immortal spirit is born again in a child. According to some accounts the mode of discovering the Dalai Lama is similar to the method, already described, of discovering an ordinary Grand Lama. Other accounts speak of an election by lot. Wherever he is born, the trees and plants, it is said, put forth green leaves ; at his bidding flowers bloom. and springs of water rise ; and his presence diffuses heavenly blessings. His palace stands on a commanding height ; its gilded cupolas are seen sparkling in the sunlight for miles.[1]

Issuing from the sultry valleys upon the lofty plateau of the Colombian Andes, the Spanish conquerors were astonished to find, in contrast to the savage hordes they had left in the sweltering jungles below, a people enjoying a fair degree of civilisation, practising agriculture, and living under a government which Humboldt has compared to the theocracies of Tibet and Japan. These were the Chibchas, Muyscas, or Mozcas, divided into two kingdoms, with capitals at Bogota and Tunja, but united apparently in spiritual allegiance to the high pontiff of Sogamozo or Iraca. By a long and ascetic novitiate, this ghostly ruler was reputed to have acquired such sanctity that the waters and the rain obeyed him, and the weather depended on his will.[2] Weather kings are common in Africa. Thus the

---

[1] Huc, *op. cit.* ii. 279, 347 *sq.* ; Meiners, *Geschichte der Religionen*, i. 335 *sq.* ; Georgi, *Beschreibung aller Nationen des Russischen Reichs*, p. 415; A. Erman, *Travels in Siberia*, ii. 303 *sqq.* ; *Journal of the Roy. Geogr. Soc.*, xxxviii. (1868), 168, 169 ; *Proceedings of the Roy. Geogr. Soc.* N.S. vii. (1885) 67. In the *Journal Roy. Geogr. Soc.*, *l.c.*, the Lama in question is called the Lama Gûrû ; but the con-text shows that he is the great Lama of Lhasa.

[2] Alex. von. Humboldt, *Researches concerning the Institutions and Monuments of the Ancient Inhabitants of America*, ii. 106 *sqq.* ; Waitz, *Anthropologie der Naturvölker*, iv. 352 *sqq.*; J. G. Müller, *Geschichte der Amerikanischen Urreligionen*, p. 430 *sq.*; Martius, *Zur Ethnographie Amerikas*, p. 455 ; Bastian, *Die Culturländer des alten Amerika*, ii. 204 *sq.*

Waganda of Central Africa believe in a god of Lake Nyanza, who sometimes takes up his abode in a man or woman. The incarnate god is much feared by all the people, including the king and the chiefs. He is consulted as an oracle; by his word he can inflict or heal sickness, withhold rain, and cause famine. Large presents are made him when his advice is sought.[1] Often the king himself is supposed to control the weather. The king of Loango is honoured by his people "as though he were a god; and he is called Sambee and Pango, which mean god. They believe that he can let them have rain when he likes; and once a year, in December, which is the time they want rain, the people come to beg of him to grant it to them." On this occasion the king, standing on his throne, shoots an arrow into the air, which is supposed to bring on rain.[2] Much the same is said of the king of Mombaza.[3] The king of Quiteva, in Eastern Africa, ranks with the deity; "indeed, the Caffres acknowledge no other gods than their monarch, and to him they address those prayers which other nations are wont to prefer to heaven. . . . Hence these unfortunate beings, under the persuasion that their king is a deity, exhaust their utmost means and ruin themselves in gifts to obtain with more facility what they need. Thus, prostrate at his feet, they implore of him, when the weather long continues dry, to intercede with heaven that they may have rain; and when too much

---

[1] R. W. Felkin, "Notes on the Waganda Tribe of Central Africa," in *Proceedings of the Royal Society of Edinburgh*, xiii. 762; C. T. Wilson and R. W. Felkin, *Uganda and the Egyptian Soudan*, i. 206.
[2] "The Strange Adventures of Andrew Battel," in Pinkerton's *Voyages and* *Travels*, xvi. 330; Proyart, "History of Loango, Kakongo, and other Kingdoms in Africa," in Pinkerton, xvi. 577; Dapper, *Description de l'Afrique*, p. 335.
[3] Ogilby, *Africa*, p. 615; Dapper, *op. cit.* p. 400.

rain has fallen, that they may have fair weather ; thus, also, in case of winds, storms, and everything, they would either deprecate or implore."[1] Amongst the Barotse, a tribe on the upper Zambesi, " there is an old, but waning belief, that a chief is a demigod, and in heavy thunderstorms the Barotse flock to the chief's yard for protection from the lightning. I have been greatly distressed at seeing them fall on their knees before the chief, entreating him to open the water-pots of heaven and send rain upon their gardens. . . . The king's servants declare themselves to be invincible, because they are the servants of God (meaning *the king*)."[2] The chief of Mowat, New Guinea, is believed to have the power of affecting the growth of crops for good or ill, and of coaxing the *dugong* and turtle to come from all parts and allow themselves to be taken.[3]

Amongst the Antaymours of Madagascar the king is responsible for the growth of the crops and for every misfortune that befalls the people.[4] In many places the king is punished if rain does not fall and the crops do not turn out well. Thus, in some parts of West Africa, when prayers and offerings presented to the king have failed to procure rain, his subjects bind him with ropes and take him by force to the grave of his forefathers, that he may obtain from them the needed rain.[5] It appears that the Scythians also, when food was scarce, put their king in bonds.[6] The Banjars in

---

[1] Dos Santos, " History of Eastern Ethiopia," in Pinkerton, *Voyages and Travels*, xvi. 682, 687 *sq.*

[2] F. S. Arnot, *Garengauze ; or, Seven Years' Pioneer Mission Work in Central Africa*, London, N.D. (preface dated March 1889), p. 78.

[3] MS. notes by E. Beardmore.

[4] Waitz, *Anthropologie der Naturvölker*, ii. 439.

[5] Labat, *Relation historique de l'Ethiopie Occidentale*, ii. 172-176.

[6] Schol. on Apollonius Rhod. ii. 1248. καὶ Ἡρόδωρος ξένως περὶ τῶν δεσμῶν τοῦ Προμηθέως ταῦτα. Εἶναι· γὰρ αὐτὸν Σκυθῶν βασιλέα φησί · καὶ μὴ δυνάμενον παρέχειν τοῖς ὑπηκόοις τὰ ἐπιτήδεια, διὰ τὸν καλούμενον Ἀετὸν ποταμὸν ἐπικλύζειν τὰ πεδία, δεθῆναι ὑπὸ τῶν Σκυθῶν.

West Africa ascribe to their king the power of causing rain or fine weather. So long as the weather is fine they load him with presents of grain and cattle. But if long drought or rain threatens to spoil the crops, they insult and beat him till the weather changes.[1] When the harvest fails or the surf on the coast is too heavy to allow of fishing, the people of Loango accuse their king of a " bad heart " and depose him.[2] On the Pepper Coast the high priest or Bodio is responsible for the health of the community, the fertility of the earth, and the abundance of fish in the sea and rivers ; and if the country suffers in any of these respects the Bodio is deposed from his office.[3] So the Burgundians of old deposed their king if the crops failed.[4] Some peoples have gone further and killed their kings in times of scarcity. Thus, in the time of the Swedish king Domalde a mighty famine broke out, which lasted several years, and could be stayed by the blood neither of beasts nor of men. So, in a great popular assembly held at Upsala, the chiefs decided that king Domalde himself was the cause of the scarcity and must be sacrificed for good seasons. So they slew him and smeared with his blood the altars of the gods. Again, we are told that the Swedes always attributed good or bad crops to their kings as the cause. Now, in the reign of King Olaf, there came dear times and famine, and the people thought that the fault was the king's, because he was sparing in his sacrifices. So, mustering an army, they marched against him, surrounded

[1] H. Hecquard, *Reise an der Küste und in das Innere von West Afrika*, p. 78.

[2] Bastian, *Die Deutsche Expedition an der Loango-Küste*, i. 354, ii. 230.

[3] J. Leighton Wilson, *West Afrika*, p. 93 (German translation).

[4] Ammianus Marcellinus, xxviii. 5, 14.

his dwelling, and burned him in it, "giving him to Odin as a sacrifice for good crops."[1] In 1814, a pestilence having broken out among the reindeer of the Chukch, the Shamans declared that the beloved chief Koch must be sacrificed to the angry gods; so the chief's own son stabbed him with a dagger.[2] On the coral island of Niue, or Savage Island, in the South Pacific, there formerly reigned a line of kings. But as the kings were also high priests, and were supposed to make the food grow, the people became angry with them in times of scarcity and killed them; till at last, as one after another was killed, no one would be king, and the monarchy came to an end.[3] As in these cases the divine kings, so in ancient Egypt the divine beasts, were responsible for the course of nature. When pestilence and other calamities had fallen on the land, in consequence of a long and severe drought, the priests took the sacred animals secretly by night, and threatened them, but if the evil did not abate they slew the beasts.[4]

From this survey of the religious position occupied by the king in rude societies we may infer that the claim to divine and supernatural powers put forward by the monarchs of great historical empires like those of Egypt, Mexico, and Peru, was not the simple outcome of inflated vanity or the empty expression of a grovelling adulation; it was merely a survival and extension of the old savage apotheosis of living kings.

---

[1] Snorro Starleson, *Chronicle of the Kings of Norway* (trans. by S. Laing), saga i. chs. 18, 47. Cp. Liebrecht, *Zur Volkskunde*, p. 7; Scheffer, *Upsalia*, p. 137.

[2] C. Russwurm, "Aberglaube in Russland," in *Zeitschrift für Deutsche Mythologie und Sittenkunde*, iv. 162; Liebrecht, *op. cit.*, p. 15.

[3] Turner, *Samoa*, p. 304 *sq.*

[4] Plutarch, *Isis et Osiris*, 73.

Thus, for example, as children of the Sun the Incas of Peru were revered like gods; they could do no wrong, and no one dreamed of offending against the person, honour, or property of the monarch or of any of the royal race. Hence, too, the Incas did not, like most people, look on sickness as an evil. They considered it a messenger sent from their father the Sun to call his son to come and rest with him in heaven. Therefore the usual words in which an Inca announced his approaching end were these : " My father calls me to come and rest with him." They would not oppose their father's will by offering sacrifice for recovery, but openly declared that he had called them to his rest.[1] The Mexican kings at their accession took an oath that they would make the sun to shine, the clouds to give rain, the rivers to flow, and the earth to bring forth fruits in abundance.[2] By Chinese custom the emperor is deemed responsible if the drought be at all severe, and many are the self-condemnatory edicts on this subject published in the pages of the *Peking Gazette*. However it is rather as a high priest than as a god that the Chinese emperor bears the blame ; for in extreme cases he seeks to remedy the evil by personally offering prayers and sacrifices to heaven.[3] The Parthian monarchs of the Arsacid house styled themselves brothers of the sun and moon and were worshipped as deities. It was esteemed sacrilege to strike even a private member of the Arsacid family in a brawl.[4] The kings of Egypt were deified in their lifetime, and their worship was celebrated in special temples and by

---

[1] Garcilasso de la Vega, *First Part of the Royal Commentaries of the Yncas*, bk. ii. chs. 8 and 15 (vol. i. pp. 131, 155, Markham's Trans.)

[2] Bancroft, *Native Races of the Pacific States*, ii. 146.
[3] Dennys, *Folk-lore of China*, p. 125.
[4] Ammianus Marcellinus, xxiii. 6, § 5 and 6.

special priests. Indeed the worship of the kings sometimes cast that of the gods into the shade. Thus in the reign of Merenra a high official declared that he had built many holy places in order that the spirits of the king, the ever-living Merenra, might be invoked "more than all the gods."[1] The King of Egypt seems to have shared with the sacred animals the blame of any failure of the crops.[2] He was addressed as " Lord of heaven, lord of earth, sun, life of the whole world, lord of time, measurer of the sun's course, Tum for men, lord of well-being, creator of the harvest, maker and fashioner of mortals, bestower of breath upon all men, giver of life to all the host of gods, pillar of heaven, threshold of the earth, weigher of the equipoise of both worlds, lord of rich gifts, increaser of the corn" etc.[3] Yet, as we should expect, the exalted powers thus ascribed to the king differed in degree rather than in kind from those which every Egyptian claimed for himself. Tiele observes that "as every good man at his death became Osiris, as every one in danger or need could by the use of magic sentences assume the form of a deity, it is quite comprehensible how the king, not only after death, but already during his life, was placed on a level with the deity."[4]

Thus it appears that the same union of sacred

---

[1] C. P. Tiele, *History of the Egyptian Religion*, p. 103 *sq.* On the worship of the kings see also E. Meyer, *Geschichte des Altertums*, i. § 52 ; A. Erman, *Aegypten und aegyptisches Leben im Altertum*, p. 91 *sqq.*; V. von Strauss und Carnen, *Die altägyptischen Götter und Göttersagen*, p. 467 *sqq.*

[2] Ammianus Marcellinus, xxviii. 5, 14 ; Plutarch, *Isis et Osiris*, 73.

[3] V. von Strauss und Carnen, *op. cit.* p. 470.

[4] Tiele, *History of the Egyptian Religion*, p. 105. The Babylonian and Assyrian kings seem also to have been regarded as gods ; at least the oldest names of the kings on the monuments are preceded by a star, the mark for " god." But there is no trace in Babylon and Assyria of temples and priests for the worship of the kings. See Tiele, *Babylonisch - Assyrische Geschichte*, p. 492 *sq.*

functions with a royal title which meets us in the King
of the Wood at Nemi, the Sacrificial King at Rome and
the King Archon at Athens, occurs frequently outside
the limits of classical antiquity and is a common feature
of societies at all stages from barbarism to civilisation.
Further, it appears that the royal priest is often a king
in fact as well as in name, swaying the sceptre as well
as the crosier. All this confirms the tradition of the
origin of the titular and priestly kings in the republics
of ancient Greece and Italy. At least by showing
that the combination of spiritual and temporal power,
of which Graeco - Italian tradition preserved the
memory, has actually existed in many places, we have
obviated any suspicion of improbability that might
have attached to the tradition. Therefore we may
now fairly ask, May not the King of the Wood have
had an origin like that which a probable tradition
assigns to the Sacrificial King of Rome and the King
Archon of Athens? In other words, may not his
predecessors in office have been a line of kings whom
a republican revolution stripped of their political power,
leaving them only their religious functions and the
shadow of a crown? There are at least two reasons
for answering this question in the negative. One
reason is drawn from the abode of the priest of Nemi;
the other from his title, the King of the Wood. If
his predecessors had been kings in the ordinary
sense, he would surely have been found residing, like
the fallen kings of Rome and Athens, in the city of
which the sceptre had passed from him. This city
must have been Aricia, for there was none nearer.
But Aricia, as we have seen, was three miles off from
his forest sanctuary by the lake shore. If he reigned,
it was not in the city, but in the greenwood. Again

his title, King of the Wood, hardly allows us to suppose that he had ever been a king in the common sense of the word. More likely he was a king of nature, and of a special side of nature, namely, the woods from which he took his title. If we could find instances of what we may call departmental kings of nature, that is of persons supposed to rule over particular elements or aspects of nature, they would probably present a closer analogy to the King of the Wood than the divine kings we have been hitherto considering, whose control of nature is general rather than special. Instances of such departmental kings are not wanting.

On a hill at Bomma (the mouth of the Congo) dwells Namvulu Vumu, King of the Rain and Storm.[1] Of some of the tribes on the Upper Nile we are told that they have no kings in the common sense; the only persons whom they acknowledge as such are the Kings of the Rain, *Mata Kodou*, who are credited with the power of giving rain at the proper time, that is in the rainy season. Before the rains begin to fall at the end of March the country is a parched and arid desert; and the cattle, which form the people's chief wealth, perish for lack of grass. So, when the end of March draws on, each householder betakes himself to the King of the Rain and offers him a cow that he may make the rain to fall soon. If no shower falls, the people assemble and demand that the king shall give them rain; and if the sky still continues cloudless, they rip up his belly in which he is believed to keep the storms. Amongst the Bari tribe one of these Rain Kings made rain

---

[1] Bastian, *Die Deutsche Expedition an der Loango-Küste*, ii. 230.

by sprinkling water on the ground out of a hand-bell.[1]

Among tribes on the outskirts of Abyssinia a similar office exists and has been thus described by an observer. "The priesthood of the Alfai, as he is called by the Barea and Kunáma, is a remarkable one; he is believed to be able to make rain. This office formerly existed among the Algeds and appears to be still common to the Nuba negroes. The Alfai of the Bareas, who is also consulted by the northern Kunáma, lives near Tembádere on a mountain alone with his family. The people bring him tribute in the form of clothes and fruits, and cultivate for him a large field of his own. He is a kind of king, and his office passes by inheritance to his brother or sister's son. He is supposed to conjure down rain and to drive away the locusts. But if he disappoints the people's expectation and a great drought arises in the land, the Alfai is stoned to death, and his nearest relations are obliged to cast the first stone at him. When we passed through the country, the office of Alfai was still held by an old man; but I heard that rain-making had proved too dangerous for him and that he had renounced his office."[2]

In the backwoods of Cambodia live two mysterious sovereigns known as the King of the Fire and the King of the Water. Their fame is spread all over the south of the great Indo-Chinese peninsula; but only a faint echo of it has reached the West. No European, so far as is known, has ever seen them; and their very existence might have passed for a fable, were it not

---

[1] "Excursion de M. Brun-Rollet dans la région supérieure du Nil," *Bulletin de la Société de Géographie*, Paris, 1852,

pt. ii. p. 421 *sqq.*
[2] W. Munzinger, *Ostafrikanische Studien*, p. 474 (Schaffhausen, 1864).

that till a few years ago communications were regularly maintained between them and the King of Cambodia, who year by year exchanged presents with them. The Cambodian gifts were passed from tribe to tribe till they reached their destination; for no Cambodian would essay the long and perilous journey. The tribe amongst whom the Kings of Fire and Water reside is the Chréais or Jaray, a race with European features but a sallow complexion, inhabiting the forest-clad mountains and high plateaux which separate Cambodia from Annam. Their royal functions are of a purely mystic or spiritual order; they have no political authority; they are simple peasants, living by the sweat of their brow and the offerings of the faithful. According to one account they live in absolute solitude, never meeting each other and never seeing a human face. They inhabit successively seven towers perched upon seven mountains, and every year they pass from one tower to another. People come furtively and cast within their reach what is needful for their subsistence. The kingship lasts seven years, the time necessary to inhabit all the towers successively; but many die before their time is out. The offices are hereditary in one or (according to others) two royal families, who enjoy high consideration, have revenues assigned to them, and are exempt from the necessity of tilling the ground. But naturally the dignity is not coveted, and when a vacancy occurs, all eligible men (they must be strong and have children) flee and hide themselves. Another account, admitting the reluctance of the hereditary candidates to accept the crown, does not countenance the report of their hermit-like seclusion in the seven towers. For it represents the people as prostrating themselves before the mystic kings whenever they appear in public, it being thought that a terrible hurricane would burst over the country if this mark of homage were omitted.

The same report says that the Fire King, the more important of the two, and whose supernatural powers have never been questioned, officiates at marriages, festivals, and sacrifices in honour of the Yan. On these occasions a special place is set apart for him ; and the path by which he approaches is spread with white cotton cloths. A reason for confining the royal dignity to the same family is that this family is in possession of certain famous talismans which would lose their virtue or disappear if they passed out of the family. These talismans are three : the fruit of a creeper called *Cui*, gathered ages ago but still fresh and green ; a rattan, also very old and still not dry ; lastly a sword containing a Yan or spirit, who guards it constantly and works miracles with it. To this wondrous brand sacrifices of buffaloes, pigs, fowls, and ducks are offered for rain. It is kept swathed in cotton and silk ; and amongst the annual presents sent by the King of Cambodia were rich stuffs to wrap the sacred sword.

In return the Kings of Fire and Water sent him a huge wax candle and two calabashes, one full of rice and the other of sesame. The candle bore the impress of the Fire King's middle finger. Probably the candle was thought to contain the seed of fire, which the Cambodian monarch thus received once a year fresh from the Fire King himself. The holy candle was kept for sacred uses. On reaching the capital of Cambodia it was entrusted to the Brahmans, who laid it up beside the regalia, and with the wax made tapers which were burned on the altars on solemn days. As the candle was the special gift of the Fire King, we may conjecture that the rice and sesame were the special gift of the Water King. The latter was doubtless king of rain as well as of water, and the fruits of the earth were boons conferred by him on men. In times of calamity, as during plague, floods, and war, a little of this sacred rice and sesame was scattered on the ground "to appease the wrath of the maleficent spirits."[1]

These, then, are examples of what I have called departmental kings of nature. But it is a far cry to Italy from the forests of Cambodia and the sources of the Nile. And though Kings of Rain, Water and Fire have been found, we have still to discover a King of the Wood to match the Arician priest who bore that title. Perhaps we shall find him nearer home.

§ 4.—Tree-worship

In the religious history of the Aryan race in Europe the worship of trees has played an important part. Nothing could be more natural. For at the dawn of history Europe was covered with immense primeval forests, in which the scattered clearings must have appeared like islets in an ocean of green. Down to the first century before our era the Hercynian forest stretched eastward from

---

[1] J. Moura, Le Royaume du Cambodge, i. 432-436 ; Aymonier, "Notes sur les coutumes et croyances superstitieuses des Cambodgiens," in Cochin- chine Française, Excursions et Reconnaissances, No. 16, p. 172 sq. ; id., Notes sur le Laos, p. 60.

5959 76

the Rhine for a distance at once vast and unknown; Germans whom Caesar questioned had travelled for two months through it without reaching the end.[1] In our own country the wealds of Kent, Surrey, and Sussex are remnants of the great forest of Anderida, which once clothed the whole of the south eastern portion of the island. Westward it seems to have stretched till it joined another forest that extended from Hampshire to Devon. In the reign of Henry II the citizens of London still hunted the wild bull and the boar in the forest of Hampstead. Even under the later Plantagenets the royal forests were sixty-eight in number. In the forest of Arden it was said that down to modern times a squirrel might leap from tree to tree for nearly the whole length of Warwickshire.[2] The excavation of prehistoric pile-villages in the valley of the Po has shown that long before the rise and probably the foundation of Rome the north of Italy was covered with dense forests of elms, chestnuts, and especially of oaks.[3] Archaeology is here confirmed by history; for classical writers contain many references to Italian forests which have now disappeared.[4] In Greece the woods of the present day are a mere fraction of those which clothed great tracts in antiquity, and which at a more remote epoch may have spanned the Greek peninsula from sea to sea.[5]

From an examination of the Teutonic words for "temple" Grimm has made it probable that amongst

---

[1] Caesar, *Bell. Gall.* vi. 25.

[2] Elton, *Origins of English History*, pp. 3, 106 *sq.*, 224.

[3] W. Helbig, *Die Italiker in der Poebene*, p. 25 *sq.*

[4] H. Nissen, *Italische Landeskunde*, p. 431 *sqq.*

[5] Neumann und Partsch, *Physikalische Geographie von Griechenland*, p. 357 *sqq.*

the Germans the oldest sanctuaries were natural woods.[1] However this may be, tree-worship is well attested for all the great European families of the Aryan stock. Amongst the Celts the oak-worship of the Druids is familiar to every one.[2] Sacred groves were common among the ancient Germans, and tree-worship is hardly extinct amongst their descendants at the present day.[3] At Upsala, the old religious capital of Sweden, there was a sacred grove in which every tree was regarded as divine.[4] Amongst the ancient Prussians (a Slavonian people) the central feature of religion was the reverence for the sacred oaks, of which the chief stood at Romove, tended by a hierarchy of priests who kept up a perpetual fire of oak-wood in the holy grove.[5] The Lithuanians were not converted to Christianity till towards the close of the fourteenth century, and amongst them at the date of their conversion the worship of trees was prominent.[6] Proofs of the prevalence of tree-worship in ancient Greece and Italy are abundant.[7] Nowhere, perhaps, in the ancient world was this antique form of religion better preserved than in the heart of the great metropolis itself. In the Forum, the busy centre of Roman life, the sacred fig-tree of Romulus was worshipped down to the days of the empire, and the withering of its trunk was enough to spread consternation through the city.[8] Again, on the

---

[1] Grimm, *Deutsche Mythologie*,[4] i. 53 *sqq.*

[2] The *locus classicus* is Pliny, *Nat. Hist.* xvi. § 249 *sqq.*

[3] Grimm, *D. M.* i. 56 *sqq.*

[4] Adam of Bremen, *Descriptio Insul. Aquil.* p. 27.

[5] "Prisca antiquorum Prutenorum religio," in *Respublica sive Status Regni Poloniae, Lituaniae, Prussiae, Livoniae,* etc. (Elzevir, 1627), p. 321 *sq.* ; Dusburg, *Chronicon Prussiae,* ed. Hartknoch,

p. 79 ; Hartknoch, *Alt-und Neues Preussen,* p. 116 *sqq.*

[6] Mathias Michov, "De Sarmatia Asiana atque Europea," in *Novus Orbis regionum ac insularum veteribus incognitarum* (Paris, 1532), pp. 455 *sq.* 456 [wrongly numbered 445, 446] ; Martin Cromer, *De origine et rebus gestis Polonorum* (Basel, 1568), p. 241.

[7] See Bötticher, *Der Baumkultus der Hellenen.*

[8] Pliny, *Nat. Hist.* xv. § 77 ; Tacitus, *Ann.* xiii. 58.

slope of the Palatine Hill grew a cornel-tree which was esteemed one of the most sacred objects in Rome. Whenever the tree appeared to a passer-by to be drooping, he set up a hue and cry which was echoed by the people in the street, and soon a crowd might be seen running from all sides with buckets of water, as if (says Plutarch) they were hastening to put out a fire.[1]

But it is necessary to examine in some detail the notions on which tree-worship is based. To the savage the world in general is animate, and trees are no exception to the rule. He thinks that they have souls like his own and he treats them accordingly. Thus the Wanika in Eastern Africa fancy that every tree and especially every cocoa-nut tree has its spirit; "the destruction of a cocoa-nut tree is regarded as equivalent to matricide, because that tree gives them life and nourishment, as a mother does her child."[2] Siamese monks, believing that there are souls everywhere and that to destroy anything whatever is forcibly to dispossess a soul, will not break a branch of a tree "as they will not break the arm of an innocent person."[3] These monks, of course, are Buddhists. But Buddhist animism is not a philosophical theory. It is simply a common savage dogma incorporated in the system of an historical religion. To suppose with Benfey and others that the theories of animism and transmigration current among rude peoples of Asia are derived from Buddhism is to reverse the facts. Buddhism in this respect borrowed from savagery, not savagery from Buddhism. Again, the Dyaks ascribe souls to trees and do not dare to cut down an old tree. In some

[1] Plutarch, *Romulus*, 20.

[2] J. L. Krapf, *Travels, Researches, and Missionary Labours during an Eigh-* teen Years' *Residence in Eastern Africa*, p. 198.

[3] Loubere, *Historical Relation of the Kingdom of Siam*, p. 126.

places, when an old tree has been blown down, they set it up, smear it with blood, and deck it with flags "to appease the soul of the tree."[1] People in Congo place calabashes of palm-wine at the foot of certain trees for the trees to drink when they are thirsty.[2] In India shrubs and trees are formally married to each other or to idols.[3] In the North West Provinces of India a marriage ceremony is performed in honour of a newly-planted orchard; a man holding the Salagram represents the bridegroom, and another holding the sacred Tulsí (*Ocymum sanctum*) represents the bride.[4] On Christmas Eve German peasants used to tie fruit-trees together with straw ropes to make them bear fruit, saying that the trees were thus married.[5]

In the Moluccas when the clove-trees are in blossom they are treated like pregnant women. No noise must be made near them; no light or fire must be carried past them at night; no one must approach them with his hat on, but must uncover his head. These precautions are observed lest the tree should be frightened and bear no fruit, or should drop its fruit too soon, like the untimely delivery of a woman who has been frightened in her pregnancy.[6] So when the paddy (rice) is in bloom the Javanese say it is pregnant and make no noises (fire no guns, etc.) near

[1] Hupe "Over de godsdienst, zeden, enz. der Dajakker's" in *Tijdschrift voor Neêrland's Indië*, 1846, dl. iii. 158.

[2] Merolla, "Voyage to Congo," in Pinkerton's *Voyages and Travels*, xvi. 236.

[3] Monier Williams, *Religious Life and Thought in India*, p. 334 *sq.*

[4] Sir Henry M. Elliot and J. Beames, *Memoirs on the History etc. of the*

Races of the North Western Provinces of India, i. 233.

[5] *Die gestriegelte Rockenphilosophie* (Chemnitz, 1759), p. 239 *sq.*; U. Jahn, *Die deutsche Opfergebräuche bei Ackerbau und Viehzucht*, p. 214 *sqq.*

[6] Van Schmid, "Aanteekeningen, nopens de zeden, gewoonten en gebruiken, etc., der bevolking van de eilanden Saparoea, etc." in *Tijdschrift v. Neêrland's Indië*, 1843, dl. ii. 605; Bastian, *Indonesien*, i. 156.

the field, fearing that if they did so the crop would be all straw and no grain.[1] In Orissa, also, growing rice is "considered as a pregnant woman, and the same ceremonies are observed with regard to it as in the case of human females." [2]

Conceived as animate, trees are necessarily supposed to feel injuries done to them. When an oak is being felled " it gives a kind of shriekes or groanes, that may be heard a mile off, as if it were the genius of the oake lamenting. E. Wyld, Esq., hath heard it severall times." [3] The Ojebways "very seldom cut down green or living trees, from the idea that it puts them to pain, and some of their medicine-men profess to have heard the wailing of the trees under the axe." [4] Old peasants in some parts of Austria still believe that forest-trees are animate, and will not allow an incision to be made in the bark without special cause; they have heard from their fathers that the tree feels the cut not less than a wounded man his hurt. In felling a tree they beg its pardon.[5] So in Jarkino the woodman craves pardon of the tree he cuts down.[6] Again, when a tree is cut it is thought to bleed. Some Indians dare not cut a certain plant, because there comes out a red juice which they take for the blood of the plant.[7] In Samoa there was a grove of trees which no one dared cut. Once some strangers tried to do so, but blood flowed from the tree, and the sacrilegious strangers fell ill and died.[8] Till 1855 there was a sacred larch-tree at Nauders, in the Tyrol,

[1] Van Hoëvell; *Ambon en meer bepaaldelijk de Oeliasers*, p. 62.
[2] *The Indian Antiquary*, i. 170.
[3] J. Aubrey, *Remaines of Gentilisme*, p. 247.
[4] Peter Jones's *History of the Ojebway Indians*, p. 104.

[5] A. Peter, *Volksthümliches aus Österreichisch-Schlesien*, ii. 30.
[6] Bastian, *Indonesien*, i. 154; cp. *id.*, *Die Völker des östlichen Asien*, ii. 457 *sq.*, iii. 251 *sq.*, iv. 42 *sq.*
[7] Loubere, *Siam*, p. 126.
[8] Turner, *Samoa*, p. 63.

which was thought to bleed whenever it was cut;
moreover the steel was supposed to penetrate the
woodman's body to the same depth that it penetrated
the tree, and the wound on the tree and on the man's
body healed together.[1]

Sometimes it is the souls of the dead which are
believed to animate the trees. The Dieyerie tribe of
South Australia regard as very sacred certain trees,
which are supposed to be their fathers transformed;
hence they will not cut the trees down, and protest
against the settlers doing so.[2] Some of the Philippine
Islanders believe that the souls of their forefathers are
in certain trees, which they therefore spare. If obliged
to fell one of these trees they excuse themselves to it
by saying that it was the priest who made them fell it.[3]
In an Annamite story an old fisherman makes an incision in the trunk of a tree which has drifted ashore;
but blood flows from the cut, and it appears that an
empress with her three daughters, who had been
cast into the sea, are embodied in the tree.[4]
The story of Polydorus will occur to readers of
Virgil.

In these cases the spirit is viewed as incorporate in
the tree; it animates the tree and must suffer and die
with it. But, according to another and no doubt later
view, the tree is not the body, but merely the abode of
the tree-spirit, which can quit the injured tree as men
quit a dilapidated house. Thus when the Pelew
Islanders are felling a tree, they conjure the spirit of

---

[1] Mannhardt, *Baumkultus*, p. 35 *sq.*

[2] *Native Tribes of South Australia*, p. 280.

[3] Blumentritt, "Der Ahnencultus und die religiösen Anschauungen der Malaien des Philippinen-Archipels," in

Mittheilungen der Wiener Geogr. Gesellschaft, 1882, p. 165 *sq.*

[4] Landes, "Contes et légendes annamites," No. 9, in *Cochinchine Française, Excursions et Reconnaissances*, No. 20, p. 310.

the tree to leave it and settle on another.[1] The Pádams of Assam think that when a child is lost it has been stolen by the spirits of the wood. So they retaliate on the spirits by cutting down trees till they find the child. The spirits, fearing to be left without a tree in which to lodge, give up the child, and it is found in the fork of a tree.[2] Before the Katodis fell a forest-tree, they choose a tree of the same kind and worship it by presenting a cocoa-nut, burning incense, applying a red pigment, and begging it to bless the undertaking.[3] The intention, perhaps, is to induce the spirit of the former tree to shift its quarters to the latter. In clearing a wood, a Galeleze must not cut down the last tree till the spirit in it has been induced to go away.[4] The Mundaris have sacred groves which were left standing when the land was cleared, lest the sylvan gods, disquieted at the felling of the trees, should abandon the place.[5] The Miris in Assam are unwilling to break up new land for cultivation so long as there is fallow land available; for they fear to offend the spirits of the woods by cutting down trees unnecessarily.[6]

In Sumatra, so soon as a tree is felled, a young tree is planted on the stump; and some betel and a few small coins are also placed on it.[7] Here the purpose is unmistakable. The spirit of the tree is offered a new home in the young tree planted on the stump of the old one, and the offering of betel and money is meant

[1] Kubary in Bastian's *Allerlei aus Mensch-und Volkenkunde*, i. 52.

[2] Dalton, *Ethnology of Bengal*, p. 25; Bastian, *Völkerstämme am Brahmaputra*, p. 37.

[3] *Journal R. Asiatic Society*, vii. (1843) 29.

[4] Bastian, *Indonesien*, i. 17.

[5] Dalton, *Ethnology of Bengal*, pp. 186, 188; cp. Bastian, *Völkerstämme am Brahmaputra*, p. 9.

[6] Dalton, *op. cit.* p. 33; Bastian, *op. cit.* p. 16. Cp. W. Robertson Smith, *The Religion of the Semites*, i. 125.

[7] Van Hasselt, *Volksbeschrijving van Midden-Sumatra*, p. 156.

to compensate him for the disturbance he has suffered. So in the island of Chedooba, on felling a large tree, one of the woodmen was always ready with a green sprig, which he ran and placed on the middle of the stump the instant the tree fell.[1] For the same purpose German woodmen make a cross upon the stump while the tree is falling, in the belief that this enables the spirit of the tree to live upon the stump.[2]

Thus the tree is regarded, sometimes as the body, sometimes as merely the house of the tree-spirit; and when we read of sacred trees which may not be cut down because they are the seat of spirits, it is not always possible to say with certainty in which way the presence of the spirit in the tree is conceived. In the following cases, perhaps, the trees are conceived as the dwelling-place of the spirits rather than as their bodies. The old Prussians, it is said, believed that gods inhabited high trees, such as oaks, from which they gave audible answers to inquirers; hence these trees were not felled, but worshipped as the homes of divinities.[3] The great oak at Romove was the especial dwelling-place of the god; it was veiled with a cloth, which was, however, removed to allow worshippers to see the sacred tree.[4] The Battas of Sumatra have been known to refuse to cut down certain trees because they were

[1] *Handbook of Folk-lore*, p. 19 (proof).

[2] Mannhardt, *Baumkultus*, p. 83.

[3] Erasmus Stella, "De Borussiae antiquitatibus," in *Novus Orbis regionum ac insularum veteribus incognitarum*, p. 510; Lasiczki (Lasicius), "De diis Samagitarum caeterorumque Sarmatarum," in *Respublica sive Status Regni Poloniae, Lituaniae, Prussiae, Livoniae*, etc. (Elzevir, 1627), p. 299

sq. There is a good and cheap reprint of Lasiczki's work by W. Mannhardt in *Magazin herausgegeben von der Lettisch-Literärischen Gesellschaft*, xiv. 82 *sqq.* (Mitau, 1868).

[4] Simon Grünau, *Preussische Chronik*, ed. Perlbach (Leipzig 1876), p. 89; "Prisca antiquorum Prutenorum religio," in *Respublica sive Status Regni Poloniae* etc., p. 321.

the abode of mighty spirits which would resent the injury.[1] The Curka Coles of India believe that the tops of trees are inhabited by spirits which are disturbed by the cutting down of the trees and will take vengeance.[2] The Samogitians thought that if any one ventured to injure certain groves, or the birds or beasts in them, the spirits would make his hands or feet crooked.[3]

Even where no mention is made of wood-spirits, we may generally assume that when a grove is sacred and inviolable, it is so because it is believed to be either inhabited or animated by sylvan deities. In Livonia there is a sacred grove in which, if any man fells a tree or breaks a branch, he will die within the year.[4] The Wotjaks have sacred groves. A Russian who ventured to hew a tree in one of them fell sick and died next day.[5] Sacrifices offered at cutting down trees are doubtless meant to appease the wood-spirits. In Gilgit it is usual to sprinkle goat's blood on a tree of any kind before cutting it down.[6] Before thinning a grove a Roman farmer had to sacrifice a pig to the god or goddess of the grove.[7] The priestly college of the Arval Brothers at Rome had to make expiation when a rotten bough fell to the ground in the sacred grove, or when an old tree was blown down by a storm or dragged down by a weight of snow on its branches.[8]

When a tree comes to be viewed, no longer as the body of the tree-spirit, but simply as its dwelling-place which it can quit at pleasure, an important advance

---

[1] B. Hagen, " Beiträge zur Kenntniss der Battareligion," in *Tijdschrift voor Indische Taal-Land-en Volkenkunde*, xxviii. 530 *note*.

[2] Bastian, *Die Völker des östlichen Asien*, i. 134.

[3] Matthias Michov, in *Novus Orbis regionum ac insularum veteribus incognitarum*, p. 457.

[4] Grimm, *Deutsche Mythologie*,[4] i. 497 ; cp. ii. 540, 541.

[5] Max Buch, *Die Wotjäken*, p. 124.

[6] Biddulph, *Tribes of the Hindoo Koosh*, p. 116.

[7] Cato, *De agri cultura*, 139.

[8] Henzen, *Acta fratrum arvalium* (Berlin, 1874), p. 138.

has been made in religious thought. Animism is passing into polytheism. In other words, instead of regarding each tree as a living and conscious being, man now sees in it merely a lifeless, inert mass, tenanted for a longer or shorter time by a supernatural being who, as he can pass freely from tree to tree, thereby enjoys a certain right of possession or lordship over the trees, and, ceasing to be a tree-soul, becomes a forest god. As soon as the tree-spirit is thus in a measure disengaged from each particular tree, he begins to change his shape and assume the body of a man, in virtue of a general tendency of early thought to clothe all abstract spiritual beings in concrete human form. Hence in classical art the sylvan deities are depicted in human shape, their woodland character being denoted by a branch or some equally obvious symbol.[1] But this change of shape does not affect the essential character of the tree-spirit. The powers which he exercised as a tree-soul incorporate in a tree, he still continues to wield as a god of trees. This I shall now prove in detail. I shall show, first, that trees considered as animate beings are credited with the power of making the rain to fall, the sun to shine, flocks and herds to multiply, and women to bring forth easily ; and, second, that the very same powers are attributed to tree-gods conceived as anthropomorphic beings or as actually incarnate in living men.

First, then, trees or tree-spirits are believed to give rain and sunshine. When the missionary Jerome of Prague was persuading the heathen Lithuanians to fell their sacred groves, a multitude

---

[1] On the representations of Silvanus, the Roman wood-god, see Jordan in Preller's *Römische Mythologie,*[3] i. 393 *note ;* Baumeister, *Denkmäler des clas-* *sischen Altertums,* iii. 1665 *sq.* A good representation of Silvanus bearing a pine branch is given in the Sale Catalogue of H. Hoffmann, Paris, 1888, pt. ii.

of women besought the Prince of Lithuania to stop him, saying that with the woods he was destroying the house of god from which they had been wont to get rain and sunshine.[1] The Mundaris in Assam think if a tree in the sacred grove is felled, the sylvan gods evince their displeasure by withholding rain.[2] In Cambodia each village or province has its sacred tree, the abode of a spirit. If the rains are late, the people sacrifice to the tree.[3] To extort rain from the tree-spirit a branch is sometimes dipped in water, as we have seen above.[4] In such cases the spirit is doubtless supposed to be immanent in the branch, and the water thus applied to the spirit produces rain by a sort of sympathetic magic, exactly as we saw that in New Caledonia the rain-makers pour water on a skeleton, believing that the soul of the deceased will convert the water into rain.[5] There is hardly room to doubt that Mannhardt is right in explaining as a rain-charm the European custom of drenching with water the trees which are cut at certain popular festivals, as midsummer, Whitsuntide, and harvest.[6]

Again, tree-spirits make the crops to grow. Amongst the Mundaris every village has its sacred grove, and "the grove deities are held responsible for the crops, and are especially honoured at all the great agricultural festivals."[7] The negroes of the Gold Coast are in the habit of sacrificing at the foot of certain tall trees, and they think that if one of these

---

[1] Aeneas Sylvius, *Opera* (Bâle, 1571), p. 418 [wrongly numbered 420]; cp. Erasmus Stella, "De Borussiae antiquitatibus," in *Novus Orbis regionum ac insularum veteribus incognitarum*, p. 510.

[2] Dalton, *Ethnology of Bengal*, p. 186.

[3] Aymonier in *Excursions et Reconnaissances*, No. 16. p. 175 *sq.*

[4] See above, pp. 13, 21.

[5] Above, p. 16.

[6] Mannhardt, *B. K.* pp. 158, 159, 170, 197, 214, 351, 514.

[7] Dalton, *Ethnology of Bengal*, p. 188.

trees were felled, all the fruits of the earth would perish.[1] Swedish peasants stick a leafy branch in each furrow of their corn-fields, believing that this will ensure an abundant crop.[2] The same idea comes out in the German and French custom of the Harvest-May. This is a large branch or a whole tree, which is decked with ears of corn, brought home on the last waggon from the harvest-field, and fastened on the roof of the farmhouse or of the barn, where it remains for a year. Mannhardt has proved that this branch or tree embodies the tree-spirit conceived as the spirit of vegetation in general, whose vivifying and fructifying influence is thus brought to bear upon the corn in particular. Hence in Swabia the Harvest-May is fastened amongst the last stalks of corn left standing on the field; in other places it is planted on the corn-field and the last sheaf cut is fastened to its trunk.[3] The Harvest-May of Germany has its counterpart in the *eiresione* of ancient Greece.[4] The *eiresione* was a branch of olive or laurel, bound about with ribbons and hung with a variety of fruits. This branch was carried in procession at a harvest festival and was fastened over the door of the house, where it remained for a year. The object of preserving the Harvest-May or the *eiresione* for a year is that the life-giving virtue of the bough may foster the growth of the crops throughout the year. By the end of the year the virtue of the bough is supposed to be exhausted and it is replaced by a new one. Following a similar train of thought some of the Dyaks of Sarawak are

---

[1] Labat, *Voyage du Chevalier des Marchais en Guinée, Isles voisines, et à Cayenne* (Paris, 1730), i. 338.

[2] L. Lloyd, *Peasant Life in Sweden*, p. 266.

[3] Mannhardt, *B. K.* p. 190 *sqq.*

[4] Mannhardt, *A. W. F.* p. 212 *sqq.*

careful at the rice harvest to take up the roots of a certain bulbous plant, which bears a beautiful crown of white and fragrant flowers. These roots are preserved with the rice in the granary and are planted again with the seed-rice in the following season ; for the Dyaks say that the rice will not grow unless a plant of this sort be in the field.[1]

Customs like that of the Harvest-May appear to exist in India and Africa. At a harvest festival of the Lhoosai of S. E. India the chief goes with his people into the forest and fells a large tree, which is then carried into the village and set up in the midst. Sacrifice is offered, and spirits and rice are poured over the tree. The ceremony closes with a feast and a dance, at which the unmarried men and girls are the only performers.[2] Among the Bechuanas the hack-thorn is very sacred, and it would be a serious offence to cut a bough from it and carry it into the village during the rainy season. But when the corn is ripe in the ear the people go with axes, and each man brings home a branch of the sacred hack-thorn, with which they repair the village cattle-yard.[3] Many tribes of S. E. Africa will not cut down timber while the corn is green, fearing that if they did so, the crops would be destroyed by blight, hail, or early frost.[4]

Again, the fructifying power of the tree is put forth at seed-time as well as at harvest. Among the Aryan tribes of Gilgit, on the north-western frontier of India, the sacred tree is the *Chili*, a species of cedar (*Juniperus excelsa*). At the beginning of wheat-

---

[1] H. Low, *Sarawak*, p. 274.
[2] T. H. Lewin, *Wild Races of South-eastern India*, p. 270.
[3] J. Mackenzie, *Ten years north of the Orange River*, p. 385.
[4] Rev. J. Macdonald, MS. notes.

sowing the people receive from the Raja's granary a quantity of wheat, which is placed in a skin mixed with sprigs of the sacred cedar. A large bonfire of the cedar wood is lighted, and the wheat which is to be sown is held over the smoke. The rest is ground and made into a large cake, which is baked on the same fire and given to the ploughman.[1] Here the intention of fertilising the seed by means of the sacred cedar is unmistakable. In all these cases the power of fostering the growth of crops, and, in general, of cultivated plants, is ascribed to trees. The ascription is not unnatural. For the tree is the largest and most powerful member of the vegetable kingdom, and man is familiar with it before he takes to cultivating corn. Hence he naturally places the feebler and, to him, newer plant under the dominion of the older and more powerful.

Again, the tree-spirit makes the herds to multiply and blesses women with offspring. The sacred *Chili* or cedar of Gilgit was supposed to possess this virtue in addition to that of fertilising the corn. At the commencement of wheat-sowing three chosen unmarried youths, after undergoing daily washing and purification for three days, used to start for the mountain where the cedars grew, taking with them wine, oil, bread, and fruit of every kind. Having found a suitable tree they sprinkled the wine and oil on it, while they ate the bread and fruit as a sacrificial feast. Then they cut off the branch and brought it to the village, where, amid general rejoicing, it was placed on a large stone beside running water. "A goat was then sacrificed, its blood poured over the cedar branch, and a

---

[1] Biddulph, *Tribes of the Hindoo Koosh*, p. 103 *sq.*

wild dance took place, in which weapons were brandished about, and the head of the slaughtered goat was borne aloft, after which it was set up as a mark for arrows and bullet - practice. Every good shot was rewarded with a gourd full of wine and some of the flesh of the goat. When the flesh was finished the bones were thrown into the stream and a general ablution took place, after which every man went to his house taking with him a spray of the cedar. On arrival at his house he found the door shut in his face, and on his knocking for admission, his wife asked, ' What have you brought ? ' To which he answered, ' If you want children, I have brought them to you ; if you want food, I have brought it ; if you want cattle, I have brought them ; whatever you want, I have it.' The door was then opened and he entered with his cedar spray. The wife then took some of the leaves and pouring wine and water on them placed them on the fire, and the rest were sprinkled with flour and suspended from the ceiling. She then sprinkled flour on her husband's head and shoulders, and addressed him thus : ' Ai Shiri Bagerthum, son of the fairies, you have come from far ! ' *Shiri Bagerthum*, ' the dreadful king,' being the form of address to the cedar when praying for wants to be fulfilled. The next day the wife baked a number of cakes, and taking them with her, drove the family goats to the Chili stone. When they were collected round the stone, she began to pelt them with pebbles, invoking the Chili at the same time. According to the direction in which the goats ran off, omens were drawn as to the number and sex of the kids expected during the ensuing year. Walnuts and pomegranates were then placed on the Chili stone, the cakes were distributed and eaten, and the goats followed to pasture in whatever direction they showed a disposition to go. For five days afterwards this song was sung in all the houses :—

> ' Dread Fairy King, I sacrifice before you,
> How nobly do you stand ! you have filled up my house,
> You have brought me a wife when I had not one,
> Instead of daughters you have given me sons.
> You have shown me the ways of right,
> You have given me many children.' " [1]

Here the driving of the goats to the stone on which the cedar had been placed is clearly meant to impart to them the fertilising influence of the cedar. In Europe the May-tree (May-pole) is supposed to possess similar powers over both women and cattle. In some parts of Germany on the 1st of May the peasants set up May-trees at the doors of stables and byres, one May-tree for each horse and cow ; this is thought to make the cows yield much milk.[2] Camden says of the Irish, " They fancy a green bough of a tree, fastened on May-day against the house, will produce plenty of milk that summer." [3]

On the 2d of July some of the Wends used to set up an oak-tree in the middle of the village with an iron cock fastened to its top ; then they danced round it, and drove the cattle round it to make them thrive.[4]

Some of the Esthonians believe in a mischievous spirit called Metsik, who lives in the forest and has the weal of the cattle in his hands. Every year a new image of him is prepared. On an appointed day all the villagers assemble and. make a straw man, dress

---

[1] Biddulph, *op. cit.* p. 106 *sq.*

[2] Mannhardt, *B. K.* p. 161 ; E. Meier, *Deutsche Sagen, Sitten und Gebräuche aus Schwaben*, p. 397 ; A. Peter, *Volksthümliches aus Öster- reichisch-Schlesien*, ii. 286 ; Reinsberg-

Düringsfeld, *Fest-Kalendar aus Böh- men*, p. 210.

[3] Quoted by Brand, *Popular An- tiquities*, i. 227, Bohn's ed.

[4] Mannhardt, *B. K.* p. 174.

him in clothes, and take him to the common pasture land of the village. Here the figure is fastened to a high tree, round which the people dance noisily. On almost every day of the year prayer and sacrifice are offered to him that he may protect the cattle. Sometimes the image of Metsik is made of a corn-sheaf and fastened to a tall tree in the wood. The people perform strange antics before it to induce Metsik to guard the corn and the cattle.[1]

The Circassians regard the pear-tree as the protector of cattle. So they cut down a young pear-tree in the forest, branch it, and carry it home, where it is adored as a divinity. Almost every house has one such pear-tree. In autumn, on the day of the festival, it is carried into the house with great ceremony to the sound of music and amid the joyous cries of all the inmates, who compliment it on its fortunate arrival. It is covered with candles, and a cheese is fastened to its top. Round about it they eat, drink, and sing. Then they bid it good-bye and take it back to the courtyard, where it remains for the rest of the year, set up against the wall, without receiving any mark of respect.[2]

The common European custom of placing a green bush on May Day before the house of a beloved maiden probably originated in the belief of the fertilising power of the tree-spirit.[3] Amongst the Kara-Kirgiz barren women roll themselves on the ground under a solitary apple-tree, in order to obtain offspring.[4]

---

[1] Holzmayer, "Osiliana," *Verhandlungen der Estnischen Gesell. zu Dorpat*, vii. 10 *sq.*; Mannhardt, *B. K.* p. 407 *sq.*

[2] Potocki, *Voyage dans les steps d'Astrakhan et du Caucase* (Paris, 1829), i. 309.

[3] Mannhardt, *B. K.* p. 163 *sqq.* To his authorities add, for Sardinia, R. Tennant, *Sardinia and its Resources* (Rome and London, 1885), p. 185 *sq.*

[4] Radloff, *Proben der Volkslitteratur der nördlichen Türkischen Stämme*, v. 2.

Lastly, the power of granting to women an easy delivery at child-birth is ascribed to trees both in Sweden and Africa. In some districts of Sweden there was formerly a *bårdträd* or guardian-tree (lime, ash, or elm) in the neighbourhood of every farm. No one would pluck a single leaf of the sacred tree, any injury to which was punished by ill-luck or sickness. Pregnant women used to clasp the tree in their arms in order to ensure an easy delivery.[1] In some negro tribes of the Congo region pregnant women make themselves garments out of the bark of a certain sacred tree, because they believe that this tree delivers them from the dangers that attend child-bearing.[2] The story that Leto clasped a palm-tree and an olive-tree or two laurel-trees when she was about to give birth to Apollo and Artemis perhaps points to a similar Greek belief in the efficacy of certain trees to facilitate delivery.[3]

From this review of the beneficent qualities commonly ascribed to tree-spirits, it is easy to understand why customs like the May-tree or May-pole have prevailed so widely and figured so prominently in the popular festivals of European peasants. In spring or early summer or even on Midsummer Day, it was and still is in many parts of Europe the custom to go out to the woods, cut down a tree and bring it into the village, where it is set up amid general rejoicings. Or the people cut branches in the woods, and fasten them on every house. The intention of these customs is to bring home to the village, and to each house, the blessings which the tree-spirit has in its power to bestow.

---

[1] Mannhardt, *B. K.* p. 51 *sq.*

[2] Merolla, "Voyage to Congo," in Pinkerton's *Voyages and Travels*, xvi. 236 *sq.*

[3] Bötticher, *Der Baumkultus der Hellenen*, p. 30 *sq.*

Hence the custom in some places of planting a May-tree before every house, or of carrying the village May-tree from door to door, that every household may receive its share of the blessing. Out of the mass of evidence on this subject a few examples may be selected.

Sir Henry Piers, in his *Description of Westmeath*, writing in 1682 says: "On May-eve, every family sets up before their door a green bush, strewed over with yellow flowers, which the meadows yield plentifully. In countries where timber is plentiful, they erect tall slender trees, which stand high, and they continue almost the whole year ; so as a stranger would go nigh to imagine that they were all signs of ale-sellers, and that all houses were ale-houses."[1] In Northampton-shire a young tree ten or twelve feet high used to be planted before each house on May Day so as to appear growing.[2] "An antient custom, still retained by the Cornish, is that of decking their doors and porches on the 1st of May with green boughs of sycamore and hawthorn, and of planting trees, or rather stumps of trees, before their houses."[3] In the north of England it was formerly the custom for young people to rise very early on the morning of the 1st of May, and go out with music into the woods, where they broke branches and adorned them with nosegays and crowns of flowers. This done, they returned about sunrise and fastened the flower-decked branches over the doors and windows of their houses.[4] At Abingdon in Berkshire young people formerly went about in groups on May morning, singing a carol of which the following are some of the verses—

[1] Quoted by Brand, *Popular Antiquities*, i. 246 (ed. Bohn).

[2] Dyer, *British Popular Customs*, p. 254.

[3] Borlase, cited by Brand, *op. cit.* i. 222.

[4] Brand, *op. cit.* i. 212 *sq.*

" We've been rambling all the night ;
And sometime of this day ;
And now returning back again,
We bring a garland gay.

"A garland gay we bring you here ;
And at your door we stand ;
It is a sprout well budded out,
The work of our Lord's hand."[1]

At the villages of Saffron Walden and Debden
in Essex on the 1st of May little girls go about
in parties from door to door singing a song almost
identical with the above and carrying garlands ; a doll
dressed in white is usually placed in the middle of each
garland.[2] At Seven Oaks on May Day the children
carry boughs and garlands from house to house, begging
for pence. The garlands consist of two hoops inter-
laced crosswise, and covered with blue and yellow
flowers from the woods and hedges.[3] In some
villages of the Vosges Mountains on the first Sunday
of May young girls go in bands from house to
house, singing a song in praise of May, in which
mention is made of the " bread and meal that come in
May." If money is given them, they fasten a green
bough to the door ; if it is refused, they wish the family
many children and no bread to feed them.[4] In
Mayenne (France), boys who bore the name of
Maillotins used to go about from farm to farm on
the 1st of May singing carols, for which they received
money or a drink ; they planted a small tree or a branch
of a tree.[5]

On the Thursday before Whitsunday the Russian
villagers " go out into the woods, sing songs, weave

---

[1] Dyer, *Popular British Customs*, p. 233.
[2] Chambers, *Book of Days*, i. 578 ; Dyer, *op. cit.* p. 237 *sq.*
[3] Dyer, *op. cit.* p. 243.
[4] E. Cortet, *Fêtes religieuses*, p. 167 *sqq.*
[5] *Revue des Traditions populaires*, ii. 200.

garlands, and cut down a young birch-tree, which they dress up in woman's clothes, or adorn with many-coloured shreds and ribbons. After that comes a feast, at the end of which they take the dressed-up birch-tree, carry it home to their village with joyful dance and song, and set it up in one of the houses, where it remains as an honoured guest till Whitsunday. On the two intervening days they pay visits to the house where their 'guest' is ; but on the third day, Whitsunday, they take her to a stream and fling her into its waters," throwing their garlands after her. " All over Russia every village and every town is turned, a little before Whitsunday, into a sort of garden. Everywhere along the streets the young birch-trees stand in rows, every house and every room is adorned with boughs, even the engines upon the railway are for the time decked with green leaves."[1] In this Russian custom the dressing of the birch in woman's clothes shows how clearly the tree is conceived as personal ; and the throwing it into a stream is most probably a rain-charm. In some village of Altmark it was formerly the custom for serving-men, grooms, and cowherds to go from farm to farm at Whitsuntide distributing crowns made of birch-branches and flowers to the farmers ; these crowns were hung up in the houses and left till the following year.[2]

In the neighbourhood of Zabern in Alsace bands of people go about carrying May-trees. Amongst them is a man dressed in a white shirt, with his face blackened ; in front of him is carried a large May-tree, but each member of the band also carries a smaller one. One of the company carries a huge basket in which he

---

[1] Ralston, *Songs of the Russian People*, p. 234 *sq.*

[2] A. Kuhn, *Märkische Sagen und Märchen*, p. 315.

collects eggs, bacon, etc.[1] In some parts of Sweden on
the eve of May Day lads go about carrying each a
bunch of fresh-gathered birch twigs, wholly or partially
in leaf. With the village fiddler at their head they go
from house to house singing May songs ; the purport
of which is a prayer for fine weather, a plentiful
harvest, and worldly and spiritual blessings. One of
them carries a basket in which he collects gifts of
eggs and the like. If they are well received they
stick a leafy twig in the roof over the cottage door.[2]

But in Sweden midsummer is the season when
these ceremonies are chiefly observed. On the Eve
of St. John (23d June) the houses are thoroughly
cleansed and garnished with green boughs and
flowers. Young fir-trees are raised at the door-way
and elsewhere about the homestead ; and very often
small umbrageous arbours are constructed in the
garden. In Stockholm on this day a leaf-market is
held at which thousands of May-poles (*Maj Stänger*)
six inches to twelve feet high, decorated with leaves,
flowers, slips of coloured paper, gilt egg-shells, strung
on reeds, etc. are exposed for sale. Bonfires are lit
on the hills and the people dance round them and
jump over them. But the chief event of the day
is setting up the May-pole. This consists of a straight
and tall spruce-pine tree, stripped of its branches.
"At times hoops and at others pieces of wood, placed
crosswise, are attached to it at intervals ; whilst at
others it is provided with bows, representing so to
say, a man with his arms akimbo. From top to
bottom not only the 'Maj Stäng' (May-pole) itself,
but the hoops, bows, etc. are ornamented with leaves,

---

[1] Mannhardt, *B. K.* p. 162.   [2] L. Lloyd, *Peasant Life in Sweden*,
p. 235.

flowers, slips of various cloth, gilt egg-shells, etc. ;
and on the top of it is a large vane, or it may be a
flag." The raising of the May-pole, the decoration
of which is done by the village maidens, is an affair
of much ceremony; the people flock to it from all
quarters and dance round it in a great ring.[1] In
some parts of Bohemia also a May-pole or midsummer-
tree is erected on St. John's Eve. The lads fetch a
tall fir or pine from the wood and set it up on a
height, where the girls deck it with nosegays, garlands,
and red ribbons. Then they pile brushwood, dry
wood, and other combustible materials about the tree,
and, when darkness has fallen, set the whole on fire.
While the fire was burning the lads used to climb
up the tree and fetch down the garlands and ribbons
which the girls had fastened to it ; but as this led
to accidents, the custom has been forbidden. Sometimes the young people fling burning besoms into the
air, or run shouting down hill with them. When the
tree is consumed, the young men and their sweethearts
stand on opposite sides of the fire, and look at each
other through garlands and through the fire, to see
whether they will be true lovers and will wed. Then
they throw the garlands thrice across the smouldering
fire to each other. When the blaze has died down,
the couples join hands and leap thrice across the
glowing embers. The singed garlands are taken
home, and kept carefully in the house throughout
the year. Whenever a thunder-storm bursts, part of
the garlands are burned on the hearth ; and when
the cattle are sick or are calving, they get a portion
of the garlands to eat. The charred embers of the
bonfire are stuck in the cornfields and meadows and

---

[1] L. Lloyd, *op. cit.* p. 257 *sqq.*

on the roof of the house, to keep house and field from bad weather and injury. [1]

It is hardly necessary to illustrate the custom of setting up a village May-tree or May-pole on May Day. One point only—the renewal of the village May-tree—requires to be noticed. In England the village May-pole seems as a rule, at least in later times, to have been permanent, not renewed from year to year. [2] Sometimes, however, it was renewed annually. Thus, Borlase says of the Cornish people : " From towns they make incursions, on May-eve, into the country, cut down a tall elm, bring it into the town with rejoicings, and having fitted a straight taper pole to the end of it, and painted it, erect it in the most public part, and upon holidays and festivals dress it with garlands of flowers or ensigns and streamers." [3] An annual renewal seems also to be implied in the description by Stubbs, a Puritanical writer, of the custom of drawing home the May-pole by twenty or forty yoke of oxen. [4] In some parts of Germany and Austria the May-tree or Whitsuntide-tree is renewed annually, a fresh tree being felled and set up. [5]

We can hardly doubt that originally the practice everywhere was to set up a new May-tree every year. As the object of the custom was to bring in the fructifying spirit of vegetation, newly awakened in spring, the end would have been defeated if, instead of a living tree, green and sappy, an old withered one had been erected year after year or allowed to stand permanently. When, however, the meaning of the

[1] Reinsberg-Düringsfeld, *Fest-Kalendar aus Böhmen*, p. 308 *sq.*

[2] Hone, *Every-day Book*, i. 547 *sqq.* ; Chambers, *Book of Days*, i. 571.

[3] Quoted by Brand, *op. cit.* i. 237.

[4] *Id.*, *op. cit.* i. 235.

[5] Mannhardt, *B. K.* p. 169 *sq. note.*

custom had been forgotten, and the May-tree was regarded simply as a centre for holiday merrymaking,
people saw no reason for felling a fresh tree every
year, and preferred to let the same tree stand permanently, only decking it with fresh flowers on May
Day. But even when the May-pole had thus become a
fixture, the need of giving it the appearance of being a
green tree, not a dead pole, was sometimes felt. Thus
at Weverham in Cheshire "are two May-poles, which
are decorated on this day (May Day) with all due
attention to the ancient solemnity ; the sides are
hung with garlands, and the top terminated by a birch
or other tall slender tree with its leaves on ; the bark
being peeled, and the stem spliced to the pole, so as
to give the appearance of one tree from the summit."[1]
Thus the renewal of the May-tree is like the renewal
of the Harvest-May ; each is intended to secure a
fresh portion of the fertilising spirit of vegetation,
and to preserve it throughout the year. But whereas
the efficacy of the Harvest-May is restricted to
promoting the growth of the crops, that of the May-
tree or May-branch extends also, as we have seen,
to women and cattle. Lastly, it is worth noting that
the old May-tree is sometimes burned at the end
of the year. Thus in the district of Prague young
people break pieces off the public May-tree and
place them behind the holy pictures in their rooms,
where they remain till next May Day, and are then
burned on the hearth.[2] In Würtemberg the bushes
which are set up on the houses on Palm Sunday are
sometimes left there for a year and then burnt.[3] The

---

[1] Hone, *Every-day Book*, ii. 597 *sq.*
[2] Reinsberg-Düringsfeld, *Fest-Kalendar aus Böhmen*, p. 217 ; Mannhardt,
B. K. p. 566.
[3] Birlinger, *Volksthümliches aus
Schwaben*, ii. 74 *sq.* ; Mannhardt, *B.
K.* p. 566.

eiresione (the Harvest-May of Greece) was perhaps burned at the end of the year.[1]

So much for the tree-spirit conceived as incorporate or immanent in the tree. We have now to show that the tree-spirit is often conceived and represented as detached from the tree and clothed in human form, and even as embodied in living men or women. The evidence for this anthropomorphic representation of the tree-spirit is largely to be found in the popular customs of European peasantry.

There is an instructive class of cases in which the tree-spirit is represented simultaneously in vegetable form and in human form, which are set side by side as if for the express purpose of explaining each other. In these cases the human representative of the tree-spirit is sometimes a doll or puppet, sometimes a living person ; but whether a puppet or a person, it is placed beside a tree or bough ; so that together the person or puppet, and the tree or bough, form a sort of bilingual inscription, the one being, so to speak, a translation of the other. Here, therefore, there is no room left for doubt that the spirit of the tree is actually represented in human form. Thus in Bohemia, on the fourth Sunday in Lent, young people throw a puppet called Death into the water ; then the girls go into the wood, cut down a young tree, and fasten to it a puppet dressed in white clothes to look like a woman ; with this tree and puppet they go from house to house collecting gratuities and singing songs with the refrain—

" We carry Death out of the village,
We bring Summer into the village." [2]

---

[1] Aristophanes, *Plutus*, 1054 ; Mannhardt, *A. W. F.* p. 222 *sq.*

[2] Reinsberg-Düringsfeld, *Fest-Kalendar aus Böhmen*, p. 86 *sqq.* ; Mannhardt, *B. K.* p. 156.

Here, as we shall see later on, the "Summer" is the spirit of vegetation returning or reviving in spring. In some places in this country children go about asking for pence with some small imitations of May-poles, and with a finely dressed doll which they call the Lady of the May.[1] In these cases the tree and the puppet are obviously regarded as equivalent.

At Thann, in Alsace, a girl called the Little May Rose, dressed in white, carries a small May-tree, which is gay with garlands and ribbons. Her companions collect gifts from door to door, singing a song—

> " Little May Rose turn round three times,
> Let us look at you round and round !
> Rose of the May, come to the greenwood away,
> We will be merry all.
> So we go from the May to the roses."

In the course of the song a wish is expressed that those who give nothing may lose their fowls by the marten, that their vine may bear no clusters, their tree no nuts, their field no corn ; the produce of the year is supposed to depend on the gifts offered to these May singers.[2] Here and in the cases mentioned above, where children go about with green boughs on May Day singing and collecting money, the meaning is that with the spirit of vegetation they bring plenty and good luck to the house, and they expect to be paid for the service. In Russian Lithuania, on the 1st of May, they used to set up a green tree before the village. Then the rustic swains chose the prettiest girl, crowned her, swathed her in birch branches and set her beside the May-tree, where they danced, sang, and shouted

---

[1] Chambers, *Book of Days*, i. 573.   [2] Mannhardt, *B. K.* p. 312.

"O May! O May!"[1] In Brie (Isle de France) a May-tree is set up in the midst of the village; its top is crowned with flowers; lower down it is twined with leaves and twigs, still lower with huge green branches. The girls dance round it, and at the same time a lad wrapt in leaves and called Father May is led about.[2] In Bavaria, on the 2d of May, a *Walber* (?) tree is erected before a tavern, and a man dances round it, enveloped in straw from head to foot in such a way that the ears of corn unite above his head to form a crown. He is called the *Walber*, and used to be led in solemn procession through the streets, which were adorned with sprigs of birch.[3] In Carinthia, on St. George's Day (24th April), the young people deck with flowers and garlands a tree which has been felled on the eve of the festival. The tree is then carried in procession, accompanied with music and joyful acclamations, the chief figure in the procession being the Green George, a young fellow clad from head to foot in green birch branches. At the close of the ceremonies the Green George, that is an effigy of him, is thrown into the water. It is the aim of the lad who acts Green George to step out of his leafy envelope and substitute the effigy so adroitly that no one shall perceive the change. In many places, however, the lad himself who plays the part of Green George is ducked in a river or pond, with the express intention of thus ensuring rain to make the fields and meadows green in summer. In some places the cattle are crowned and driven from their stalls to the accompaniment of a song—

---

[1] Mannhardt, *B. K.* p. 313.

[2] *Ib.* p. 314.

[3] *Bavaria, Landes-und Volkskunde des Königreichs Bayern*, iii. 357; Mannhardt, *B. K.* p. 312 *sq.*

> " Green George we bring,
> Green George we accompany,
> May he feed our herds well,
> If not, to the water with him." [1]

Here we see that the same powers of making rain and fostering the cattle, which are ascribed to the tree-spirit regarded as incorporate in the tree, are also attributed to the tree-spirit represented by a living man.

An example of the double representation of the spirit of vegetation by a tree and a living man is reported from Bengal. The Oraons have a festival in spring while the sal trees are in blossom, because they think that at this time the marriage of earth is celebrated and the sal flowers are necessary for the ceremony. On an appointed day the villagers go with their priest to the Sarna, the sacred grove, a remnant of the old sál forest in which a goddess Sarna Burhi, or woman of the grove, is supposed to dwell. She is thought to have great influence on the rain; and the priest arriving with his party at the grove sacrifices to her five fowls, of which a morsel is given to each person present. Then they gather the sál flowers and return laden with them to the village. Next day the priest visits every house, carrying the flowers in a wide open basket. The women of each house bring out water to wash his feet as he approaches, and kneeling make him an obeisance. Then he dances with them and places some of the sál flowers over the door of the house and in the women's hair. No sooner is this done than the women empty their water-jugs over him, drenching him to the skin. A feast follows, and the young people, with sál flowers in their hair, dance all night on the village green.[2] Here, the equivalence of the flower-

---

[1] Mannhardt, *B. K.* p. 313 *sq.*   [2] Dalton, *Ethnology of Bengal*, p. 261.

bearing priest to the goddess of the flowering-tree
comes out plainly. For she is supposed to influence
the rain, and the drenching of the priest with water is,
doubtless, like the ducking of the Green George in
Bavaria, a rain-charm. Thus the priest, as if he were
the tree goddess herself, goes from door to door dis-
pensing rain and bestowing fruitfulness on each house,
but especially on the women.

Without citing more examples to the same effect,
we may sum up the result of the preceding paragraphs
in the words of Mannhardt. " The customs quoted
suffice to establish with certainty the conclusion that
in these spring processions the spirit of vegetation is
often represented both by the May-tree and in addition by a man dressed in green leaves or flowers or by
a girl similarly adorned. It is the same spirit which
animates the tree and is active in the inferior plants
and which we have recognised in the May-tree and
the Harvest-May. Quite consistently the spirit is also
supposed to manifest his presence in the first flower
of spring and reveals himself both in a girl representing a May-rose, and also, as giver of harvest, in the
person of the *Walber*. The procession with this
representative of the divinity was supposed to produce
the same beneficial effects on the fowls, the fruit-trees,
and the crops as the presence of the deity himself. In
other words, the mummer was regarded not as an
image but as an actual representative of the spirit of
vegetation ; hence the wish expressed by the attendants
on the May-rose and the May-tree that those who
refuse them gifts of eggs, bacon, etc. may have no share
in the blessings which it is in the power of the itinerant
spirit to bestow. We may conclude that these begging
processions with May-trees or May-boughs from door

to door ("bringing the May or the summer") had everywhere originally a serious and, so to speak, sacramental
significance; people really believed that the god of
growth was present unseen in the bough; by the procession he was brought to each house to bestow his
blessing. The names May, Father May, May Lady,
Queen of the May, by which the anthropomorphic spirit
of vegetation is often denoted, show that the conception of the spirit of vegetation is blent with a personification of the season at which his powers are most
strikingly manifested."[1]

Thus far we have seen that the tree-spirit or the
spirit of vegetation in general is represented either in
vegetable form alone, as by a tree, bough, or flower; or
in vegetable and human form simultaneously, as by a
tree, bough, or flower in combination with a puppet or
a living person. It remains to show that the representation of him by a tree, bough, or flower is sometimes
entirely dropped, while the representation of him by a
living person remains. In this case the representative
character of the person is generally marked by dressing him or her in leaves or flowers; sometimes too it
is indicated by the name he or she bears.

We saw that in Russia at Whitsuntide a birch-tree
is dressed in woman's clothes and set up in the house.
Clearly equivalent to this is the custom observed on
Whit-Monday by Russian girls in the district of Pinsk.
They choose the prettiest of their number, envelop
her in a mass of foliage taken from the birch-trees and
maples, and carry her about through the village. In a
district of Little Russia they take round a "poplar,"
represented by a girl wearing bright flowers in her hair.[2]

---

[1] Mannhardt, *B. K.* p. 315 *sq.*   [2] Ralston, *Songs of the Russian People*, p. 234.

In the Département de l'Ain (France) on the 1st of May eight or ten boys unite, clothe one of their number in leaves, and go from house to house begging.[1] At Whitsuntide in Holland poor women used to go about begging with a little girl called Whitsuntide Flower (*Pinxterbloem*, perhaps a kind of iris); she was decked with flowers and sat in a waggon. In North Brabant she wears the flowers from which she takes her name and a song is sung—

> " Whitsuntide Flower
> Turn yourself once round." [2]

In Ruhla (Thüringen) as soon as the trees begin to grow green in spring, the children assemble on a Sunday and go out into the woods, where they choose one of their playmates to be the Little Leaf Man. They break branches from the trees and twine them about the child till only his shoes peep out from the leafy mantle. Holes are made in it for him to see through, and two of the children lead the Little Leaf Man that he may not stumble or fall. Singing and dancing they take him from house to house, asking for gifts of food (eggs, cream, sausage, cakes). Lastly they sprinkle the Leaf Man with water and feast on the food they have collected.[3] In England the best-known example of these leaf-clad mummers is the Jack-in-the-Green, a chimney-sweeper who walks encased in a pyramidal-shaped framework of wicker-work, which is covered with holly and ivy, and surmounted by a crown of flowers and ribbons. Thus arrayed he dances on May Day at the head of a troop

---

[1] Mannhardt, *B. K.* p. 318.
[2] Mannhardt, *B. K.* p. 318; Grimm, *Deutsche Mythologie,*[4] ii. 657.
[3] Mannhardt, *B. K.* p. 320; Witzschel, *Sagen, Sitten und Gebräuche aus Thüringen,* p. 211.

of chimney-sweeps, who collect pence.[1] In some
parts also of France a young fellow is encased in a
wicker framework covered with leaves and is led
about.[2] In Frickthal (Aargau) a similar frame of
basketwork is called the Whitsuntide Basket. As
soon as the trees begin to bud, a spot is chosen in the
wood, and here the village lads make the frame with
all secrecy, lest others should forestall them. Leafy
branches are twined round two hoops, one of which
rests on the shoulders of the wearer, the other
encircles his calves ; holes are made for his eyes and
mouth ; and a large nosegay crowns the whole. In
this guise he appears suddenly in the village at the
hour of vespers, preceded by three boys blowing on
horns made of willow bark. The great object of his
supporters is to set up the Whitsuntide Basket beside
the village well, and to keep it and him there, despite
the efforts of the lads from neighbouring villages, who
seek to carry off the Whitsuntide Basket and set it
up at their own well.[3] In the neighbourhood of
Ertingen (Würtemberg) a masker of the same sort,
known as the Lazy Man (*Latzmann*), goes about the
village on Midsummer Day ; he is hidden under a
great pyramidal or conical frame of wicker-work, ten
or twelve feet high, which is completely covered with
sprigs of fir. He has a bell which he rings as he
goes, and he is attended by a suite of persons dressed
up in character—a footman, a colonel, a butcher, an
angel, the devil, the doctor, etc. They march in
Indian file and halt before every house, where each
of them speaks in character, except the Lazy Man,

[1] Mannhardt, *B. K.* p. 322 ; Hone, *Every-day Book*, i. 583 *sqq.* ; Dyer, *British Popular Customs*, p. 230 *sq.*

[2] Mannhardt, *B. K.* p. 323.

[3] *Ib.*

who says nothing. With what they get by begging from door to door they hold a feast.[1]

In the class of cases of which the above are specimens it is obvious that the leaf-clad person who is led about is equivalent to the May-tree, May-bough, or May-doll, which is carried from house to house by children begging. Both are representatives of the beneficent spirit of vegetation, whose visit to the house is recompensed by a present of money or food.

Often the leaf-clad person who represents the spirit of vegetation is known as the king or the queen; thus, for example, he or she is called the May King, Whitsuntide King, Queen of May, and so on. These titles, as Mannhardt observes, imply that the spirit incorporate in vegetation is a ruler, whose creative power extends far and wide.[2]

In a village near Salzwedel a May-tree is set up at Whitsuntide and the boys race to it; he who reaches it first is king; a garland of flowers is put round his neck and in his hand he carries a May-bush, with which, as the procession moves along, he sweeps away the dew. At each house they sing a song, wishing the inmates good luck, referring to the "black cow in the stall milking white milk, black hen on the nest laying white eggs," and begging a gift of eggs, bacon, etc.[3] In some villages of Brunswick at Whitsuntide a May King is completely enveloped in a May-bush. In some parts of Thüringen also they have a May King at Whitsuntide, but he is got up rather differently. A frame of wood is made in which

---

[1] Birlinger, *Volksthümliches aus Schwaben*, ii. 114 *sq.*; Mannhardt, *B. K.* p. 325.

[2] Mannhardt, *B. K.* p. 341 *sq.*

[3] Kuhn und Schwartz, *Norddeutsche Sagen, Märchen und Gebräuche*, p. 380.

a man can stand; it is completely covered with birch
boughs and is surmounted by a crown of birch and
flowers, in which a bell is fastened. This frame is
placed in the wood and the May King gets into it.
The rest go out and look for him, and when they have
found him they lead him back into the village to the
magistrate, the clergyman, and others, who have to
guess who is in the verdurous frame. If they guess
wrong, the May King rings his bell by shaking his
head, and a forfeit of beer or the like must be paid by
the unsuccessful guesser.[1] In some parts of Bohemia
on Whit-Monday the young fellows disguise themselves in tall caps of birch bark adorned with flowers.
One of them is dressed as a king and dragged on a
sledge to the village green, and if on the way they
pass a pool the sledge is always overturned into it.
Arrived at the green they gather round the king;
the crier jumps on a stone or climbs up a tree and
recites lampoons about each house and its inmates.
Afterwards the disguises of bark are stripped off and
they go about the village in holiday attire, carrying
a May-tree and begging. Cakes, eggs, and corn
are sometimes given them.[2] At Grossvargula, near
Langensalza, in last century a Grass King used to be
led about in procession at Whitsuntide. He was
encased in a pyramid of poplar branches, the top
of which was adorned with a royal crown of
branches and flowers. He rode on horseback with
the leafy pyramid over him, so that its lower end
touched the ground, and an opening was left in it
only for his face. Surrounded by a cavalcade of

[1] Kuhn und Schwartz, *op. cit.* p.
384 ; Mannhardt, *B. K.* p. 342.

[2] Reinsberg-Düringsfeld, *Fest-Kalendar aus Böhmen*, p. 260 *sq.* ;
Mannhardt, *B. K.* p. 342 *sq.*

young fellows, he rode in procession to the town hall, the parsonage, etc., where they all got a drink of beer. Then under the seven lindens of the neighbouring Sommerberg, the Grass King was stripped of his green casing; the crown was handed to the Mayor, and the branches were stuck in the flax fields in order to make the flax grow tall.[1] In this last trait the fertilising influence ascribed to the representative of the tree-spirit comes out clearly. In the neighbourhood of Pilsen (Bohemia) a conical hut of green branches, without any door, is erected at Whitsuntide in the midst of the village. To this hut rides a troop of village lads with a king at their head. He wears a sword at his side and a sugar-loaf hat of rushes on his head. In his train are a judge, a crier, and a personage called the Frog-flayer or Hangman. This last is a sort of ragged merryandrew, wearing a rusty old sword and bestriding a sorry hack. On reaching the hut the crier dismounts and goes round it looking for a door. Finding none, he says, "Ah, this is perhaps an enchanted castle ; the witches creep through the leaves and need no door." At last he draws his sword and hews his way into the hut, where there is a chair, on which he seats himself and proceeds to criticise in rhyme the girls, farmers, and farmservants of the neighbourhood. When this is over, the Frog-flayer steps forward and, after exhibiting a cage with frogs in it, sets up a gallows on which he hangs the frogs in a row.[2] In the neighbourhood of Plas the ceremony differs in some points. The king and his soldiers are completely clad in bark, adorned

---

[1] Mannhardt, *B. K.* p. 347 *sq.* ; Witzschel, *Sagen, Sitten und Gebräuche aus Thüringen*, p. 203.

[2] Reinsberg - Düringsfeld, *Fest-Kalendar aus Böhmen*, p. 253 *sqq.*

with flowers and ribbons; they all carry swords and ride horses, which are gay with green branches and flowers. While the village dames and girls are being criticised at the arbour, a frog is secretly pinched and poked by the crier till it quacks. Sentence of death is passed on the frog by the king; the hangman beheads it and flings the bleeding body among the spectators. Lastly, the king is driven from the hut and pursued by the soldiers.[1] The pinching and beheading of the frog are doubtless, as Mannhardt observes,[2] a rain-charm. We have seen[3] that some Indians of the Orinoco beat frogs for the express purpose of producing rain, and that killing a frog is a German rain-charm.

Often the spirit of vegetation in spring is represented by a queen instead of a king. In the neighbourhood of Libchowic (Bohemia), on the fourth Sunday in Lent, girls dressed in white and wearing the first spring flowers, as violets and daisies, in their hair, lead about the village a girl who is called the Queen and is crowned with flowers. During the procession, which is conducted with great solemnity, none of the girls may stand still, but must keep whirling round continually and singing. In every house the Queen announces the arrival of spring and wishes the inmates good luck and blessings, for which she receives presents.[4] In German Hungary the girls choose the prettiest girl to be their Whitsuntide Queen, fasten a towering wreath on her brow, and carry her singing through the streets. At every house they stop, sing old ballads, and receive presents.[5] In the

---

[1] Reinsberg-Düringsfeld, *Fest-Kalendar aus Böhmen*, p. 262; Mannhardt, *B. K.* p. 353 *sq.*

[2] *B. K.* p. 355.   [3] Above, p. 18.

[4] Reinsberg-Düringsfeld, *Fest-Kalendar aus Böhmen*, p. 93; Mannhardt, *B. K.* p. 344.

[5] Mannhardt, *B. K.* p. 343 *sq.*

south-east of Ireland on May Day the prettiest girl used to be chosen Queen of the district for twelve months. She was crowned with wild flowers ; feasting, dancing, and rustic sports followed, and were closed by a grand procession in the evening. During her year of office she presided over rural gatherings of young people at dances and merrymakings. If she married before next May Day her authority was at an end, but her successor was not elected till that day came round.[1] The May Queen is common in France [2] and familiar in England.

Again the spirit of vegetation is sometimes represented by a king and queen, a lord and lady, or a bridegroom and bride. Here again the parallelism holds between the anthropomorphic and the vegetable representation of the tree-spirit, for we have seen above that trees are sometimes married to each other.[3] In a village near Königgrätz (Bohemia) on Whit-Monday the children play the king's game, at which a king and a queen march about under a canopy, the queen wearing a garland, and the youngest girl carrying two wreaths on a plate behind them. They are attended by boys and girls called groom's men and bridesmaids, and they go from house to house collecting gifts.[4] Near Grenoble, in France, a king and queen are chosen on the 1st of May and are set on a throne for all to see.[5] At Headington, near Oxford, children used to carry garlands from door to door on

---

[1] Dyer, *British Popular Customs*, p. 270 *sq.*

[2] Mannhardt, *B. K.* p. 344 *sq.* ; Cortet, *Fêtes religieuses*, p. 160 *sqq.* ; Monnier, *Traditions populaires comparées*, p. 282 *sqq.* ; Bérenger-Féraud, *Réminiscences populaires de la Provence*, p. 1 *sqq.*

[3] Above, p. 60.

[4] Reinsberg-Düringsfeld, *Fest-Kalendar aus Böhmen*, p. 265 *sq.* ; Mannhardt, *B. K.* p. 422.

[5] Monnier, *Traditions populaires comparées*, p. 304; Mannhardt, *B. K.* p. 423.

May Day. Each garland was carried by two girls, and they were followed by a lord and lady—a boy and girl linked together by a white handkerchief, of which each held an end, and dressed with ribbons, sashes, and flowers. At each door they sang a verse—

> " Gentlemen and ladies,
>   We wish you happy May ;
>   We come to show you a garland,
>   Because it is May-day."

On receiving money the lord put his arm about his lady's waist and kissed her.[1] In some Saxon villages at Whitsuntide a lad and a lass disguise themselves and hide in the bushes or high grass outside the village. Then the whole village goes out with music "to seek the bridal pair." When they find the couple they all gather round them, the music strikes up, and the bridal pair is led merrily to the village. In the evening they dance. In some places the bridal pair is called the prince and the princess.[2]

In the neighbourhood of Briançon (Dauphiné) on May Day the lads wrap up in green leaves a young fellow whose sweetheart has deserted him or married another. He lies down on the ground and feigns to be asleep. Then a girl who likes him, and would marry him, comes and wakes him, and raising him up offers him her arm and a flag. So they go to the alehouse, where the pair lead off the dancing. But they must marry within the year, or they are treated as old bachelor and old maid, and are debarred the company of the young folk. The lad is called the bridegroom of the month of May (*le fiancé du mois de May*). In the alehouse he puts off his garment of leaves, out of

---

[1] Brand, *Popular Antiquities*, i. 233 *sq.* Bohn's ed. ; Mannhardt, *B. K.* p. 424.

[2] E. Sommer, *Sagen, Märchen und Gebräuche aus Sachsen und Thüringen*, p. 151 *sq.* ; Mannhardt, *B. K.* p. 431 *sq.*

which, mixed with flowers, his partner in the dance makes a nosegay, and wears it at her breast next day, when he leads her again to the alehouse.[1] Like this is a Russian custom observed in the district of Nerechta on the Thursday before Whitsunday. The girls go out into a birch-wood, wind a girdle or band round a stately birch, twist its lower branches into a wreath, and kiss each other in pairs through the wreath. The girls who kiss through the wreath call each other gossips. Then one of the girls steps forward, and mimicking a drunken man, flings herself on the ground, rolls on the grass, and feigns to go fast asleep. Another girl wakens the pretended sleeper and kisses him; then the whole bevy trips singing through the wood to twine garlands, which they throw into the water. In the fate of the garlands floating on the stream they read their own.[2] In this custom the rôle of the sleeper was probably at one time sustained by a lad. In these French and Russian customs we have a forsaken bridegroom, in the following a forsaken bride. On Shrove Tuesday the Slovenes of Oberkrain drag a straw puppet with joyous cries up and down the village; then they throw it into the water or burn it, and from the height of the flames they judge of the abundance of the next harvest. The noisy crew is followed by a female masker, who drags a great board by a string and gives out that she is a forsaken bride.[3]

Viewed in the light of what has gone before, the awakening of the forsaken sleeper in these ceremonies probably represents the revival of vegetation in spring. But it is not easy to assign their respective

---

[1] This custom was told to Mannhardt by a French prisoner in the war of 1870-71, B. K. p. 434.

[2] Mannhardt, B. K. p. 434 sq.

[3] Ib. p. 435.

rôles to the forsaken bridegroom and to the girl
who wakes him from his slumber.   Is the sleeper
the leafless forest or the bare earth of winter ?   Is
the girl who wakens him the fresh verdure or the
genial sunshine of spring ?   It is hardly possible, on
the evidence before us, to answer these questions.
The Oraons of Bengal, it may be remembered,
celebrate the marriage of earth in the springtime,
when the sal-tree is in blossom.   But from this we
can hardly argue that in the European ceremonies
the sleeping bridegroom is "the dreaming earth"
and the girl the spring blossoms.

In the Highlands of Scotland the revival of
vegetation in spring used to be graphically represented as follows.   On Candlemas day (2d February) in the Hebrides "the mistress and servants of
each family take a sheaf of oats, and dress it up in
women's apparel, put it in a large basket, and lay
a wooden club by it, and this they call Brüd's bed ;
and then the mistress and servants cry three times,
Brüd is come, Brüd is welcome.   This they do just
before going to bed, and when they rise in the
morning they look among the ashes, expecting to
see the impression of Brüd's club there ; which if
they do they reckon it a true presage of a good crop
and prosperous year, and the contrary they take as
an ill omen."[1]   The same custom is described by
another witness thus :   " Upon the night before
Candlemas it is usual to make a bed with corn and
hay, over which some blankets are laid, in a part of
the house near the door.   When it is ready, a person
goes out and repeats three times, . . . 'Bridget,

[1] Martin, " Description of the Western Islands of Scotland," in Pinkerton's
Voyages and Travels, iii. 613 ; Mannhardt, *B. K.* p. 436.

Bridget, come in; thy bed is ready.' One or more candles are left burning near it all night."[1]

Often the marriage of the spirit of vegetation in spring, though not directly represented, is implied by naming the human representative of the spirit "the Bride," and dressing her in wedding attire. Thus in some villages of Altmark at Whitsuntide, while the boys go about carrying a May-tree or leading a boy enveloped in leaves and flowers, the girls lead about the May Bride, a girl dressed as a bride with a great nosegay in her hair. They go from house to house, the May Bride singing a song in which she asks for a present, and tells the inmates of each house that if they give her something they will themselves have something the whole year through; but if they give her nothing they will themselves have nothing.[2] In some parts of Westphalia two girls lead a flower-crowned girl called "the Whitsuntide Bride" from door to door, singing a song in which they ask for eggs.[3] In Bresse in the month of May a girl called *la Mariée* is tricked out with ribbons and nosegays and is led about by a gallant. She is preceded by a lad carrying a green May-tree, and appropriate verses are sung.[4]

§ 5.—*Tree-worship in antiquity*

Such then are some of the ways in which the tree-spirit or the spirit of vegetation is represented

---

[1] *Scotland and Scotsmen in the Eighteenth Century*, from the MSS. of John Ramsay of Ochtertyre. Edited by Alex. Allardyce (Edinburgh, 1888), ii. 447.

[2] Kuhn, *Märkische Sagen und*

Märchen, p. 318 *sqq.* ; Mannhardt, *B. K.* p. 437.

[3] Mannhardt, *B. K.* p. 438.

[4] Monnier, *Traditions populaires comparées*, p. 283 *sq.* ; Cortet, *Fêtes religieuses*, p. 162 *sq.* ; Mannhardt, *B. K.* p. 439 *sq.*

in the customs of our European peasantry. From the remarkable persistence and similarity of such customs all over Europe we are justified in concluding that tree-worship was once an important element in the religion of the Aryan race in Europe, and that the rites and ceremonies of the worship were marked by great uniformity everywhere, and did not substantially differ from those which are still or were till lately observed by our peasants at their spring and midsummer festivals. For these rites bear internal marks of great antiquity, and this internal evidence is confirmed by the resemblance which the rites bear to those of rude peoples elsewhere.[1] Therefore it is hardly rash to infer, from this consensus of popular customs, that the Greeks and Romans, like the other Aryan peoples of Europe, once practised forms of tree-worship similar to those which are still kept up by our peasantry. In the palmy days of ancient civilisation, no doubt, the worship had sunk to the level of vulgar superstition and rustic merrymaking, as it has done among ourselves. We need not therefore be surprised that the traces of such popular rites are few and slight in ancient literature. They are not less so in the polite literature of modern Europe ; and the negative argument cannot be allowed to go for more in the one case than in the other. Enough, however, of positive evidence remains to confirm the presumption drawn from analogy. Much of this evidence has been collected and analysed with his usual learning and judgment by W. Mannhardt.[2] Here I shall content myself with citing certain Greek festivals which seem to be

---

[1] Above, pp. 69 *sqq.*, 85.   [2] See especially his *Antike Wald- und Feldkulte.*

the classical equivalents of an English May Day in the olden time.

Every few years the Boeotians of Plataea held a festival which they called the Little Daedala. On the day of the festival they went out into an ancient oak forest, the trees of which were of gigantic girth. Here they set some boiled meat on the ground, and watched the birds that gathered round it. When a raven was observed to carry off a piece of the meat and settle on an oak, the people followed it and cut down the tree. With the wood of the tree they made an image, dressed it as a bride, and placed it on a bullock-cart with a bridesmaid beside it. It seems then to have been drawn to the banks of the river Asopus and back to the town, attended by a piping and dancing crowd. After the festival the image was put away and kept till the celebration of the Great Daedala, which fell only once in sixty years. On this great occasion all the images that had accumulated from the celebrations of the Little Daedala were dragged on carts in solemn procession to the river Asopus, and then to the top of Mount Cithaeron. Here an altar had been constructed of square blocks of wood fitted together and sur- mounted by a heap of brushwood. Animals were sacrificed by being burned on the altar, and the altar itself, together with the images, were consumed by the flames. The blaze, we are told, rose to a prodigious height and was seen for many miles. To explain the origin of the festival it was said that once upon a time Hera had quarrelled with Zeus and left him in high dudgeon. To lure her back Zeus gave out that he was about to marry the nymph Plataea, daughter of the river Asopus. He caused a wooden image to be made, dressed and veiled as a bride, and conveyed on a bullock-cart. Transported with rage and jealousy, Hera flew to the cart, and tearing off the veil of the pretended bride, discovered the deceit that had been practised on her. Her rage was now changed to laughter, and she became reconciled to her husband Zeus.[1]

The resemblance of this festival to some of the European spring and midsummer festivals is tolerably close. We have seen that in Russia at Whitsuntide the villagers go out into the wood, fell a birch-tree, dress it in woman's clothes, and bring it back to the village with dance and song. On the third day it is thrown into the water.[2] Again, we have seen that in Bohemia on Midsummer Eve the village lads fell a tall fir or pine-tree in the wood and set it up on a height, where it is adorned with garlands, nosegays, and ribbons, and afterwards burnt.[3] The reason for burning the tree will appear afterwards; the custom itself is not uncommon in modern Europe. In some parts of the Pyrenees a tall and slender tree is cut down on May Day and kept till Midsummer Eve. It is then rolled to the top of a hill, set up, and burned.[4] In Angoulême on St. Peter's Day, 29th June, a tall leafy poplar is set up in the market-place and burned.[5] In Cornwall "there was formerly a great bonfire on midsummer-eve; a large summer pole was fixed in the centre, round which the fuel was heaped up. It had a large bush on the top of it."[6] In Dublin on May-morning boys used to go out and cut a May-bush, bring it back to town, and then burn it.[7]

---

[1] Pausanias, ix. 3 ; Plutarch, *ap.* Eusebius, *Praepar. Evang.* iii. 1 *sq.*
[2] Above, p. 76 *sq.*
[3] Above, p. 79.
[4] *B. K.* p. 177.
[5] *B. K.* p. 177 *sq.*
[6] Brand, *Popular Antiquities*, i. 318, Bohn's ed. ; *B. K.* p. 178.
[7] Hone, *Every-day Book*, ii. 595 *sq.* ; *B. K.* p. 178.

Probably the Boeotian festival belonged to the same class of rites. It represented the marriage of the powers of vegetation in spring or midsummer, just as the same event is represented in modern Europe by a King and Queen or a Lord and Lady of the May. In the Boeotian, as in the Russian, ceremony the tree dressed as a woman represents the English May-pole and May-queen in one. All such ceremonies, it must be remembered, are not, or at least were not originally, mere spectacular or dramatic exhibitions. They are magical charms designed to produce the effect which they dramatically represent. If the revival of vege- tation in spring is represented by the awakening of a sleeper, the representation is intended actually to quicken the growth of leaves and blossoms; if the marriage of the powers of vegetation is represented by a King and Queen of May, the idea is that the powers so represented will really be rendered more productive by the ceremony. In short, all these spring and midsummer festivals fall under the head of sym- pathetic magic. The event which it is desired to bring about is represented dramatically, and the very repre- sentation is believed to effect, or at least to contribute to, the production of the desired event. In the case of the Daedala the story of Hera's quarrel with Zeus and her sullen retirement may perhaps without strain- ing be interpreted as a mythical expression for a bad season and the failure of the crops. The same dis- astrous effects were attributed to the anger and seclusion of Demeter after the loss of her daughter Proserpine.[1] Now the institution of a festival is often explained by a mythical story of the occurrence upon a particular occasion of those very calamities which it is the real

---

[1] Pausanias, viii. 42.

object of the festival to avert; so that if we know the myth told to account for the historical origin of the festival, we can often infer from it the real intention with which the festival was celebrated. If, therefore, the origin of the Daedala was explained by a story of a failure of crops and consequent famine, we may infer that the real object of the festival was to prevent the occurrence of such disasters; and, if I am right in my interpretation of the festival, the object was supposed to be effected by a dramatic representation of the marriage of the divinities most concerned with the production of vegetation.[1] The marriage of Zeus and Hera was dramatically represented at annual festivals in various parts of Greece,[2] and it is at least a fair conjecture that the nature and intention of these ceremonies were such as I have assigned to the Plataean festival of the Daedala; in other words, that Zeus and Hera at these festivals were the Greek equivalents of the Lord and Lady of the May. Homer's glowing picture of Zeus and Hera couched on fresh hyacinths and crocuses,[3] like Milton's description of the dalliance of Zephyr and Aurora, "as he met her once a-Maying," was perhaps painted from the life.

Still more confidently may the same character be vindicated for the annual marriage at Athens of the

---

[1] Once upon a time the Wotjaks of Russia, being distressed by a series of bad harvests, ascribed the calamity to the wrath of one of their gods, *Keremet*, at being unmarried. So they went in procession to the sacred grove, riding on gaily-decked waggons, as they do when they are fetching home a bride. At the sacred grove they feasted all night, and next morning they cut in the grove a square piece of turf which they took home with them. "What they meant by this marriage ceremony," says the writer who reports it, "it is not easy to imagine. Perhaps, as Bechterew thinks, they meant to marry *Keremet* to the kindly and fruitful *mukylc̆ in*, the earth-wife, in order that she might influence him for good."—Max Buch, *Die Wotjäken, eine ethnologische Studie* (Stuttgart, 1882), p. 137.

[2] At Cnossus in Crete, Diodorus, v. 72; at Samos, Lactantius, *Instit.* i. 17; at Athens, Photius, *sv.* ἱερὸν γάμον; *Etymolog. Magn. sv.* ἱερομνήμονες, p. 468. 52.

[3] *Iliad*, xiv. 347 *sqq.*

Queen to Dionysus in the Flowery Month (*Anthes-terion*) of spring.[1] For Dionysus, as we shall see later on, was essentially a god of vegetation, and the Queen at Athens was a purely religious or priestly functionary.[2] Therefore at their annual marriage in spring he can hardly have been anything but a King, and she a Queen, of May. The women who attended the Queen at the marriage ceremony would correspond to the bridesmaids who wait on the May-queen.[3] Again, the story, dear to poets and artists, of the forsaken and sleeping Ariadne waked and wedded by Dionysus, resembles so closely the little drama acted by French peasants of the Alps on May Day[4] that, considering the character of Dionysus as a god of vegetation, we can hardly help regarding it as the description of a spring ceremony corresponding to the French one. In point of fact the marriage of Dionysus and Ariadne is believed by Preller to have been acted every spring in Crete.[5] His evidence, indeed, is inconclusive, but the view itself is probable. If I am right in instituting the comparison, the chief difference between the French and the Greek ceremonies must have been that in the former the sleeper was the forsaken bridegroom, in the latter the forsaken bride ; and the group of stars in the sky, in which fancy saw Ariadne's wedding-crown,[6] could only have been a translation to heaven of the garland worn by the Greek girl who played the Queen of May.

On the whole, alike from the analogy of modern

---

[1] Demosthenes, *Neaer.* § 73 *sqq.* p. 1369 *sq.*; Hesychius, *svv.* Διονύσου γάμος and γεραραί ; *Etymol. Magn. sv.* γεραίραι ; Pollux, viii. 108 ; Aug. Mommsen, *Heortologie*, p. 357 *sqq.*; Hermann, *Gottesdienstliche Alter-thümer*,[2] § 32. 15, § 58. 11 *sqq.*

[2] Above, p. 7.

[3] Above, p. 94.

[4] Above, p. 95 *sq.*

[5] Preller, *Griech. Mythol.*[3] i. 559.

[6] Hyginus, *Astronomica*, i. 5.

folk-custom and from the facts of ancient ritual and mythology, we are justified in concluding that the archaic forms of tree-worship disclosed by the spring and midsummer festivals of our peasants were practised by the Greeks and Romans in prehistoric times. Do then these forms of tree-worship help to explain the priesthood of Aricia, the subject of our inquiry? I believe they do. In the first place the attributes of Diana, the goddess of the Arician grove, are those of a tree-spirit or sylvan deity. Her sanctuaries were in groves, indeed every grove was her sanctuary,[1] and she is often associated with the wood-god Silvanus in inscriptions.[2] Like a tree-spirit, she helped women in travail, and in this respect her reputation appears to have stood high at the Arician grove, if we may judge from the votive offerings found on the spot.[3] Again, she was the patroness of wild animals;[4] just as in Finland the wood-god Tapio was believed to care for the wild creatures that roamed the wood, they being considered his cattle.[5] So, too, the Samogitians deemed the birds and beasts of the woods sacred, doubtless because they were under the protection of the god of the wood.[6] Again, there are indications that domestic cattle were protected by Diana,[7] as they certainly were supposed to be by Silvanus.[8] But we have seen that special influence over cattle is ascribed to wood-spirits; in Finland the herds enjoyed the protection of the wood-gods both while they were

---

[1] Servius on Virgil, *Georg.* iii. 332, *nam, ut diximus, et omnis quercus Jovi est consecrata, et omnis lucus Dianae.*

[2] Roscher's *Lexikon d. Griech u. Röm. Mythologie,* c. 1005.

[3] See above, p. 4. For Diana in this character, see Roscher, *op. cit.* c. 1007.

[4] Roscher, c. 1006 *sq.*

[5] Castren, *Finnische Mythologie,* p. 97.

[6] Mathias Michov, "De Sarmatia Asiana atque Europea," in *Novus Orbis regionum ac insularum veteribus incognitarum,* p. 457.

[7] Livy, i. 45; Plutarch, *Quaest. Rom.* 4.

[8] Virgil, *Aen.* viii. 600 *sq.*, with Servius's note.

in their stalls and while they strayed in the forest.[1]
Lastly, in the sacred spring which bubbled, and the
perpetual fire which seems to have burned in the
Arician grove,[2] we may perhaps detect traces of other
attributes of forest gods, the power, namely, to make
the rain to fall and the sun to shine.[3] This last attribute perhaps explains why Virbius, the companion
deity of Diana at Nemi, was by some believed to be
the sun.[4]

Thus the cult of the Arician grove was essentially
that of a tree-spirit or wood deity. But our examination of European folk-custom demonstrated that a tree-
spirit is frequently represented by a living person, who
is regarded as an embodiment of the tree-spirit and
possessed of its fertilising powers ; and our previous
survey of primitive belief proved that this conception of a god incarnate in a living man is common
among rude races. Further we have seen that the
living person who is believed to embody in himself the tree-spirit is often called a king, in which
respect, again, he strictly represents the tree-spirit.
For the sacred cedar of the Gilgit tribes is called,
as we have seen, " the Dreadful King " ;[5] and
the chief forest god of the Finns, by name Tapio,
represented as an old man with a brown beard, a high
hat of fir-cones and a coat of tree-moss, was styled the
Wood King, Lord of the Woodland, Golden King of
the Wood.[6] May not then the King of the Wood in
the Arician grove have been, like the King of May,
the Grass King, and the like, an incarnation of the
tree-spirit or spirit of vegetation ? His title, his sacred

---

[1] Castren, *op. cit.* p. 97 *sq.*
[2] Above, p. 4 *sq.*
[3] Above, p. 66 *sq.*   [4] Above, p. 6.
[5] Above, p. 71.
[6] Castren, *Finnische Mythologie*, pp. 92, 95.

office, and his residence in the grove all point to this conclusion, which is confirmed by his relation to the Golden Bough. For since the King of the Wood could only be assailed by him who had plucked the Golden Bough, his life was safe from assault so long as the bough or the tree on which it grew remained uninjured. In a sense, therefore, his life was bound up with that of the tree ; and thus to some extent he stood to the tree in the same relation in which the incorporate or immanent tree-spirit stands to it. The representation of the tree-spirit both by the King of the Wood and by the Golden Bough (for it will hardly be disputed that the Golden Bough was looked upon as a very special manifestation of the divine life of the grove) need not surprise us, since we have found that the tree-spirit is not unfrequently thus represented in double, first by a tree or a bough, and second by a living person.

On the whole then, if we consider his double character as king and priest, his relation to the Golden Bough, and the strictly woodland character of the divinity of the grove, we may provisionally assume that the King of the Wood, like the May King and his congeners of Northern Europe, was deemed a living incarnation of the tree-spirit. As such he would be credited with those miraculous powers of sending rain and sunshine, making the crops to grow, women to bring forth, and flocks and herds to multiply, which are popularly ascribed to the tree-spirit itself. The reputed possessor of powers so exalted must have been a very important personage, and in point of fact his influence appears to have extended far and wide. For[1] in the days when the champaign country around was

---

[1] *Historic. Roman. Fragm.* ed. Peter, p. 52 (first ed.)

still parcelled out among the petty tribes who composed the Latin League, the sacred grove on the Alban Mountain is known to have been an object of their common reverence and care. And just as the kings of Cambodia used to send offerings to the mystic Kings of Fire and Water far in the dim depths of the tropical forest, so, we may well believe, from all sides of the broad Latian plain the eyes and steps of Italian pilgrims turned to the quarter where, standing sharply out against the faint blue line of the Apennines or the deeper blue of the distant sea, the Alban Mountain rose before them, the home of the mysterious priest of Nemi, the King of the Wood.

CHAPTER II

" O liebe flüchtige Seele
Dir ist so bang und weh ! "
HEINE.

§ 1.—*Royal and priestly taboos*

IN the preceding chapter we saw that in early society the king or priest is often thought to be endowed with supernatural powers or to be an incarnation of a deity ; in consequence of which the course of nature is supposed to be more or less under his control, and he is held responsible for bad weather, failure of the crops, and similar calamities. Thus far it appears to be assumed that the king's power over nature, like that over his subjects and slaves, is exerted through definite acts of will ; and therefore if drought, famine, pestilence, or storms arise, the people attribute the misfortune to the negligence or guilt of their king, and punish him accordingly with stripes and bonds, or, if he remains obdurate, with deposition and death. Sometimes, however, the course of nature, while regarded as dependent on the king, is supposed to be partly independent of his will. His person is considered, if we may express it so, as the dynamical centre of the universe, from which lines of force radiate to all quarters of the heaven ; so that any motion of his—the turning of his head, the lifting of his hand — instantaneously affects and may seriously disturb some part of nature. He is the point of support on which hangs the balance of the world ; and the slightest irregularity on his part may over-throw the delicate equipoise. The greatest care must, therefore, be taken both by and of him ; and his whole life, down to its minutest details, must be so regulated that no act of his, voluntary or involuntary, may dis-arrange or upset the established order of nature. Of this class of monarchs the Mikado or Dairi, the spiritual emperor of Japan, is a typical example. He is an incarnation of the sun goddess, the deity who rules the universe, gods and men included ; once a year all the gods wait upon him and spend a month at his court. During that month, the name of which means "without gods," no one frequents the temples, for they are believed to be deserted.[1]

The following description of the Mikado's mode of life was written about two hundred years ago :[2]—

"Even to this day the princes descended of this family, more particularly those who sit on the throne, are looked upon as persons most holy in themselves, and as Popes by birth. And, in order to preserve these advantageous notions in the minds of their sub-jects, they are obliged to take an uncommon care of their sacred persons, and to do such things, which, examined according to the customs of other nations,

[1] *Manners and Customs of the Japan-ese in the Nineteenth Century. From recent Dutch Visitors to Japan, and the German of Dr. Ph. Fr. von Siebold* (London, 1841), p. 141 *sqq.*

[2] Kaempfer, " History of Japan," in Pinkerton's *Voyages and Travels,* vii. 716 *sq.*

would be thought ridiculous and impertinent.   It will
not be improper to give a few instances of it.   He
thinks that it would be very prejudicial to his dignity
and holiness to touch the ground with his feet; for this
reason, when he intends to go anywhere, he must
be carried thither on men's shoulders.   Much less will
they suffer that he should expose his sacred person to
the open air, and the sun is not thought worthy to
shine on his head.   There is such a holiness ascribed
to all the parts of his body, that he dares to cut off
neither his hair, nor his beard, nor his nails.   However, lest he should grow too dirty, they may clean
him in the night when he is asleep ; because, they say,
that which is taken from his body at that time hath
been stolen from him, and that such a theft doth not
prejudice his holiness or dignity.   In ancient times, he
was obliged to sit on the throne for some hours every
morning, with the imperial crown on his head, but to
sit altogether like a statue, without stirring either hands
or feet, head or eyes, nor indeed any part of his body,
because, by this means, it was thought that he could
preserve peace and tranquillity in his empire ; for if,
unfortunately, he turned himself on one side or the
other, or if he looked a good while towards any part
of his dominions, it was apprehended that war, famine,
fire, or some great misfortune was near at hand to
desolate the country.   But it having been afterwards
discovered that the imperial crown was the palladium
which by its mobility could preserve peace in the
empire, it was thought expedient to deliver his
imperial person, consecrated only to idleness and
pleasures, from this burthensome duty, and therefore
the crown is at present placed on the throne for some
hours every morning.   His victuals must be dressed

every time in new pots, and served at table in new dishes : both are very clean and neat, but made only of common clay ; that without any considerable expense they may be laid aside, or broken, after they have served once. They are generally broke, for fear they should come into the hands of laymen, for they believe religiously that if any layman should presume to eat his food out of these sacred dishes, it would swell and inflame his mouth and throat. The like ill effect is dreaded from the Dairi's sacred habits ; for they believe that if a layman should wear them, without the Emperor's express leave or command, they would occasion swellings and pains in all parts of his body." To the same effect an earlier account of the Mikado says : " It was considered as a shameful degradation for him even to touch the ground with his foot. The sun and moon were not even permitted to shine upon his head. None of the superfluities of the body were ever taken from him, neither his hair, his beard, nor his nails were cut. Whatever he eat was dressed in new vessels." [1]

Similar priestly or rather divine kings are found, at a lower level of barbarism, on the west coast of Africa. At Shark Point near Cape Padron, in Lower Guinea, lives the priestly king Kukulu, alone in a wood. He may not touch a woman nor leave his house ; indeed he may not even quit his chair, in which he is obliged to sleep sitting, for if he lay down no wind would arise and navigation would be stopped. He regulates storms, and in general maintains a wholesome and

---

[1] Caron, " Account of Japan," in Pinkerton's *Voyages and Travels*, vii. 613. Compare Varenius, *Descriptio regni Japoniae*, p. 11, *Nunquam attingebant (quemadmodum et hodie id observat) pedes ipsius terram : radiis Solis caput nunquam illustrabatur : in apertum aërem non procedebat*, etc.

equable state of the atmosphere.[1] In the kingdom of Congo (West Africa) there was a supreme pontiff called Chitomé or Chitombé, whom the negroes regarded as a god on earth and all powerful in heaven. Hence before they would taste the new crops they offered him the first-fruits, fearing that manifold misfortunes would befall them if they broke this rule. When he left his residence to visit other places within his jurisdiction, all married people had to observe strict continence the whole time he was out; for it was supposed that any act of incontinence would prove fatal to him. And if he were to die a natural death, they thought that the world would perish, and the earth, which he alone sustained by his power and merit, would immediately be annihilated.[2] Amongst the semibarbarous nations of the New World, at the date of the Spanish conquest, there were found hierarchies or theocracies like those of Japan. Some of these we have already noticed.[3] But the high pontiff of the Zapotecs in Southern Mexico appears to have presented a still closer parallel to the Mikado. A powerful rival to the king himself, this spiritual lord governed Yopaa, one of the chief cities of the kingdom, with absolute dominion. It is impossible, we are told, to over-rate the reverence in which he was held. He was looked on as a god whom the earth was not worthy to hold nor the sun to shine upon. He profaned his sanctity if he even touched the ground with his foot. The officers who bore his palanquin on their shoulders were members of the highest families; he hardly deigned to look on any-

---

[1] A. Bastian, *Die deutsche Expedition an der Loango-Küste*, i. 287 *sq.* ; cp. *id.*, p. 353 *sq.*

[2] Labat, *Relation historique de l'Ethiopie Occidentale*, i. 254 *sqq.*

[3] Above, pp. 44, 49.

thing around him ; and all who met him fell with their faces to the earth, fearing that death would overtake them if they saw even his shadow.   A rule of continence was regularly imposed on the Zapotec priests, especially upon the high pontiff; but "on certain days in each year, which were generally celebrated with feasts and dances, it was customary for the high priest to become drunk.   While in this state, seeming to belong neither to heaven nor to earth, one of the most beautiful of the virgins consecrated to the service of the gods was brought to him."   If the child she bore him was a son, he was brought up as a prince of the blood, and the eldest son succeeded his father on the pontifical throne.[1]   The supernatural powers attributed to this pontiff are not specified, but probably they resembled those of the Mikado and Chitomé.

Wherever, as in Japan and West Africa, it is supposed that the order of nature, and even the existence of the world, is bound up with the life of the king or priest, it is clear that he must be regarded by his subjects as a source both of infinite blessing and of infinite danger.   On the one hand, the people have to thank him for the rain and sunshine which foster the fruits of the earth, for the wind which brings ships to their coasts, and even for the existence of the earth beneath their feet.   But what he gives he can refuse ; and so close is the dependence of nature on his person, so delicate the balance of the system of forces whereof he is the centre, that the slightest irregularity on his part may set up a tremor which shall shake the earth to its foundations.   And

---

[1] Brasseur de Bourbourg, *Hist. des nations civilisées du Mexique et de l'Amérique-centrale*, iii. 29 *sq.* ; Bancroft, *Native Races of the Pacific States*, ii. 142 *sq.*

if nature may be disturbed by the slightest involuntary act of the king, it is easy to conceive the
convulsion which his death might occasion. The
death of the Chitomé, as we have seen, was thought
to entail the destruction of the world. Clearly, therefore, out of a regard for their own safety, which might
be imperilled by any rash act of the king, and still
more by his death, the people will exact of their king
or priest a strict conformity to those rules, the
observance of which is necessary for his own preservation, and consequently for the preservation of
his people and the world. The idea that early
kingdoms are despotisms in which the people exist
only for the sovereign, is wholly inapplicable to the
monarchies we are considering. On the contrary,
the sovereign in them exists only for his subjects;
his life is only valuable so long as he discharges the
duties of his position by ordering the course of nature
for his people's benefit. So soon as he fails to do so
the care, the devotion, the religious homage which
they had hitherto lavished on him, cease and are
changed into hatred and contempt; he is dismissed
ignominiously, and may be thankful if he escapes with
his life. Worshipped as a god by them one day, he
is killed by them as a criminal the next. But in this
changed behaviour of the people there is nothing capri-
cious or inconsistent. On the contrary, their conduct
is entirely of a piece. If their king is their god, he is
or should be also their preserver; and if he will not
preserve them, he must make room for another who
will. So long, however, as he answers their expecta-
tions, there is no limit to the care which they take of
him, and which they compel him to take of himself.
A king of this sort lives hedged in by a ceremonious

etiquette, a network of prohibitions and observances, of which the intention is not to contribute to his dignity, much less to his comfort, but to restrain him from conduct which, by disturbing the harmony of nature, might involve himself, his people, and the universe in one common catastrophe. Far from adding to his comfort, these observances, by trammelling his every act, annihilate his freedom and often render the very life, which it is their object to preserve, a burden and sorrow to him.

Of the supernaturally endowed kings of Loango it is said that the more powerful a king is, the more taboos is he bound to observe ; they regulate all his actions, his walking and his standing, his eating and drinking, his sleeping and waking.[1] To these restraints the heir to the throne is subject from infancy ; but as he advances in life the number of abstinences and ceremonies which he must observe increases, "until at the moment that he ascends the throne he is lost in the ocean of rites and taboos."[2] The kings of Egypt, as we have seen,[3] were worshipped as gods, and the routine of their daily life was regulated in every detail by precise and unvarying rules. " The life of the kings of Egypt," says Diodorus,[4] " was not like that of other monarchs who are irresponsible and may do just what they choose ; on the contrary, everything was fixed for them by law, not only their official duties, but even the details of their daily life. . . . The hours both of day and night were arranged at which the king had to do, not what he pleased, but what was prescribed for him. . . . For not only were the times

---

[1] Bastian, *Die deutsche Expedition an der Loango-Küste*, i. 355.

[2] Dapper, *Description de l'Afrique*, p. 336.

[3] P. 49 *sq.*   [4] *Bibl. Hist.* i. 70.

appointed at which he should transact public business or sit in judgment; but the very hours for his walking and bathing and sleeping with his wife, and, in short, performing every act of life, were all settled. Custom enjoined a simple diet; the only flesh he might eat was veal and goose, and he might only drink a prescribed quantity of wine." Of the taboos imposed on priests, the rules of life observed by the Flamen Dialis at Rome furnish a striking example. As the worship of Virbius at Nemi was conducted, as we have seen,[1] by a Flamen, who may possibly have been the King of the Wood himself, and whose mode of life may have resembled that of the Roman Flamen, these rules have a special interest for us. They were such as the following: The Flamen Dialis might not ride or even touch a horse, nor see an army under arms, nor wear a ring which was not broken, nor have a knot on any part of his garments; no fire except a sacred fire might be taken out of his house; he might not touch wheaten flour or leavened bread; he might not touch or even name a goat, a dog, raw meat, beans, and ivy; he might not walk under a vine; the feet of his bed had to be daubed with mud; his hair could be cut only by a free man and with a bronze knife, and his hair and nails when cut had to be buried under a lucky tree; he might not touch a dead body nor enter a place where one was burned; he might not see work being done on holy days; he might not be uncovered in the open air; if a man in bonds were taken into his house, he had to be unbound and the cords had to be drawn up through a hole in the roof and so let down into the street. His wife, the Flaminica, had to observe nearly the same rules, and others of her own

---

[1] P. 6.

besides. She might not ascend more than three steps of the kind of staircase called Greek; at a certain festival she might not comb her hair; the leather of her shoes might not be made from a beast that had died a natural death, but only from one that had been slain or sacrificed; if she heard thunder she was tabooed till she had offered an expiatory sacrifice.[1]

The burdensome observances attached to the royal or priestly office produced their natural effect. Either men refused to accept the office, which hence tended to fall into abeyance; or accepting it, they sank under its weight into spiritless creatures, cloistered recluses, from whose nerveless fingers the reigns of government slipped into the firmer grasp of men who were often content to wield the reality of sovereignty without its name. In some countries this rift in the supreme power deepened into a total and permanent separation of the spiritual and temporal powers, the old royal house retaining their purely religious functions, while the civil government passed into the hands of a younger and more vigorous race.

To take examples. We saw[2] that in Cambodia it is often necessary to force the kingships of Fire and Water upon the reluctant successors, and that in Savage Island the monarchy actually came to an end because at last no one could be induced to accept the dangerous distinction.[3] In some parts of West Africa, when the king dies, a family council is secretly held to determine his successor. He on whom the choice falls is suddenly seized, bound, and

---

[1] Aulus Gellius, x. 15; Plutarch, *Quaest. Rom.* 109-112; Pliny, *Nat. Hist.* xxviii. 146; Servius on Virgil, *Aen.* i. *vv.* 179, 448, iv. 518; Macrobius, *Saturn.* i. 16, 8 *sq.*; Festus, p. 161 A, ed. Müller. For more details see Marquardt, *Römische Staatsverwaltung*, iii.[2] 326 *sqq.*

[2] P. 54.

[3] P. 48.

thrown into the fetish-house, where he is kept in durance till he consents to accept the crown. Sometimes the heir finds means of evading the honour which it is sought to thrust upon him; a ferocious chief has been known to go about constantly armed, resolute to resist by force any attempt to set him on the throne.[1] The Mikados of Japan seem early to have resorted to the expedient of transferring the honours and burdens of supreme power to their infant children; and the rise of the Tycoons, long the temporal sovereigns of the country, is traced to the abdication of a certain Mikado in favour of his three-year-old son. The sovereignty having been wrested by a usurper from the infant prince, the cause of the Mikado was championed by Yoritomo, a man of spirit and conduct, who overthrew the usurper and restored to the Mikado the shadow, while he retained for himself the substance, of power. He bequeathed to his descendants the dignity he had won, and thus became the founder of the line of Tycoons. Down to the latter half of the sixteenth century the Tycoons were active and efficient rulers; but the same fate overtook them which had befallen the Mikados; entangled in the same inextricable web of custom and law, they degenerated into mere puppets, hardly stirring from their palaces and occupied in a perpetual round of empty ceremonies, while the real business of government was managed by the council of state.[2] In Tonquin the monarchy ran a similar course. Living like his predecessors in effeminacy and sloth, the king was driven from the throne by an ambitious adventurer named Mack, who from a fisherman had risen to be

---

[1] Bastian, *Die deutsche Expedition an der Loango-Küste*, i. 354 *sq.*; ii. 9, 11.

[2] *Manners and Customs of the Japanese*, pp. 199 *sqq.* 355 *sqq.*

Grand Mandarin. But the king's brother Tring put down the usurper and restored the king, retaining, however, for himself and his descendants the dignity of general of all the forces. Thenceforward the kings or *dovas*, though vested with the title and pomp of sovereignty, ceased to govern. While they lived secluded in their palaces, all real political power was wielded by the hereditary generals or *chovas*.[1] The custom regularly observed by the Tahitian kings of abdicating on the birth of a son, who was immediately proclaimed sovereign and received his father's homage, may perhaps have originated, like the similar custom occasionally practised by the Mikados, in a wish to shift to other shoulders the irksome burden of royalty; for in Tahiti as elsewhere the sovereign was subjected to a system of vexatious restrictions.[2] In Mangaia, another Polynesian island, religious and civil authority were lodged in separate hands, spiritual functions being discharged by a line of hereditary kings, while the temporal government was entrusted from time to time to a victorious war-chief, whose investiture, however, had to be completed by the king. To the latter were assigned the best lands, and he received daily offerings of the choicest food.[3] American examples of the partition of authority between an emperor and a pope have already been cited from the early history of Mexico and Colombia.[4]

---

[1] Richard, "History of Tonquin," in Pinkerton's *Voyages and Travels*, ix. 744 *sqq.*

[2] Ellis, *Polynesian Researches*, iii. 99 *sqq.* ed. 1836.

[3] Gill, *Myths and Songs of the South Pacific*, p. 293 *sqq.*   [4] Pp. 44, 113.

§ 2.—*The nature of the soul*

But if the object of the taboos observed by a divine king or priest is to preserve his life, the question arises, How is their observance supposed to effect this end? To understand this we must know the nature of the danger which threatens the king's life, and which it is the intention of the taboos to guard against. We must, therefore, ask : What does early man understand by death? To what causes does he attribute it? And how does he think it may be guarded against?

As the savage commonly explains the processes of inanimate nature by supposing that they are produced by living beings working in or behind the phenomena, so he explains the phenomena of life itself. If an animal lives and moves, it can only be, he thinks, because there is a little animal inside which moves it. If a man lives and moves, it can only be because he has a little man inside who moves him. The animal inside the animal, the man inside the man, is the soul. And as the activity of an animal or man is explained by the presence of the soul, so the repose of sleep or death is explained by its absence; sleep or trance being the temporary, death being the permanent absence of the soul. Hence if death be the permanent absence of the soul, the way to guard against it is either to prevent the soul from leaving the body, or, if it does depart, to secure that it shall return. The precautions adopted by savages to secure one or other of these ends take the form of prohibitions or taboos, which are nothing but rules intended to ensure either the continued presence or the return of the soul. In short, they are life-preservers or life-

guards.   These general statements will now be illustrated by examples.

Addressing some Australian blacks, a European
missionary said, "I am not one, as you think, but two."
Upon this they laughed.   " You may laugh as much
as you like," continued the missionary, " I tell you that
I am two in one ; this great body that you see is one ;
within that there is another little one which is not
visible.   The great body dies, and is buried, but the
little body flies away when the great one dies."   To
this some of the blacks replied, " Yes, yes.   We also
are two, we also have a little body within the breast."
On being asked where the little body went after death,
some said it went behind the bush, others said it went
into the sea, and some said they did not know.[1]   The
Hurons thought that the soul had a head and body,
arms and legs ; in short, that it was a complete little
model of the man himself.[2]   The Eskimos believe that
" the soul exhibits the same shape as the body it
belongs to, but is of a more subtle and ethereal nature."[3]
So exact is the resemblance of the mannikin to the
man, in other words, of the soul to the body, that, as
there are fat bodies and thin bodies, so there are fat
souls and thin souls ;[4] as there are heavy bodies and
light bodies, long bodies and short bodies, so there are
heavy souls and light souls, long souls and short souls.
The people of Nias (an island to the west of Sumatra)
think that every man, before he is born, is asked how
long or how heavy a soul he would like, and a soul of
the desired weight or length is measured out to him.

[1] *Journal of the Anthropological Institute*, vii. 282.
[2] *Relations des Jesuites*, 1634, p. 17; *id.*, 1636, p. 104; *id.*, 1639, p. 43 (Canadian reprint).
[3] H. Rink, *Tales and Traditions of the Eskimo*, p. 36.
[4] Gill, *Myths and Songs of the South Pacific*, p. 171.

The heaviest soul ever given out weighs about ten grammes. The length of a man's life is proportioned to the length of his soul; children who die young had short souls.[1] Sometimes, however, as we shall see, the human soul is conceived not in human but in animal form.

The soul is commonly supposed to escape by the natural openings of the body, especially the mouth and nostrils. Hence in Celebes they sometimes fasten fish-hooks to a sick man's nose, navel, and feet, so that if his soul should try to escape it may be hooked and held fast.[2] One of the "properties" of a Haida medicine-man is a hollow bone, in which he bottles up departing souls, and so restores them to their owners.[3] The Marquesans used to hold the mouth and nose of a dying man, in order to keep him in life, by preventing his soul from escaping.[4] When any one yawns in their presence the Hindus always snap their thumbs, believing that this will hinder the soul from issuing through the open mouth.[5] The Itonamas in South America seal up the eyes, nose, and mouth of a dying person, in case his ghost should get out and carry off other people.[6] In Southern Celebes, to prevent the escape of a woman's soul at childbirth, the nurse ties a band as tightly as possible round the body of the expectant mother.[7] And lest the soul of the babe should

---

[1] H. Sundermann, "Die Insel Nias und die Mission daselbst," in *Allgemeine Missions - Zeitschrift*, bd. xi. October 1884, p. 453.

[2] B. F. Matthes, *Over de Bissoes of heidensche priesters en priesteressen der Boeginezen*, p. 24.

[3] G. M. Dawson, "On the Haida Indians of the Queen Charlotte Islands," in *Geological Survey of Canada, Report of Progress for* 1878-1879, pp. 123 B, 139 B.

[4] Waitz, *Anthropologie der Naturvölker*, vi. 397 *sq.*

[5] *Panjab Notes and Queries*, ii. No. 665.

[6] D'Orbigny, *L'Homme Américain*, ii. 241; *Transact. Ethnol. Soc. of London*, iii. 322 *sq.*; Bastian, *Culturländer des alten Amerika*, i. 476.

[7] B. F. Matthes, *Bijdragen tot de Ethnologie van Zuid - Celebes*, p. 54.

escape and be lost as soon as it is born, the Alfoers of Celebes, when a birth is about to take place, are careful to close every opening in the house, even the keyhole; and they stop up every chink and cranny in the walls. Also they tie up the mouths of all animals inside and outside the house, for fear one of them might swallow the child's soul. For a similar reason all persons present in the house, even the mother herself, are obliged to keep their mouths shut the whole time the birth is taking place. When the question was put, Why they did not hold their noses also, lest the child's soul should get into one of them? the answer was that breath being exhaled as well as inhaled through the nostrils, the soul would be expelled before it could have time to settle down.[1]

Often the soul is conceived as a bird ready to take flight. This conception has probably left traces in most languages,[2] and it lingers as a metaphor in poetry. But what is metaphor to a modern European poet was sober earnest to his savage ancestor, and is still so to many people. The Malays carry out the conception in question to its practical conclusion. If the soul is a bird on the wing, it may be attracted by rice, and so prevented from taking its perilous flight. Thus in Java when a child is placed on the ground for the first time (a moment which uncultured people seem to regard as especially dangerous), it is put in a hencoop and the mother makes a clucking sound, as if she were calling hens.[3] Amongst the Battas of Sumatra, when a man returns from a dangerous enterprise, grains of rice are placed on his head, and these grains are

---

[1] Zimmermann, *Die Inseln des Indischen und Stillen Meeres*, ii. 386 *sq.*

[2] Cp. the Greek ποτάομαι, ἀναπτερόω, etc.

[3] G. A. Wilken, "Het animisme bij de volken van den Indischen Archipel," in *De Indische Gids*, June 1884, p. 944.

called *padiruma tondi*; that is, "means to make the soul
(*tondi*) stay at home." In Java also rice is placed on
the head of persons who have escaped a great danger
or have returned home unexpectedly after it had been
supposed that they were lost.[1] In Celebes they
think that a bridegroom's soul is apt to fly away at
marriage, so coloured rice is scattered over him to
induce it to stay. And, in general, at festivals in
South Celebes rice is strewed on the head of the
person in whose honour the festival is held, with the
object of detaining his soul, which at such times is
in especial danger of being lured away by envious
demons.[2]

The soul of a sleeper is supposed to wander away
from his body and actually to visit the very places of
which he dreams. But this absence of the soul has its
dangers, for if from any cause it should be permanently
detained away from the body, the person, deprived of
his soul, must die.[3] Many causes may detain the
sleeper's soul. Thus, his soul may meet the soul of
another sleeper and the two souls may fight ; if a
Guinea negro wakens with sore bones in the morning,
he thinks that his soul has been thrashed by another
soul in sleep.[4] Or it may meet the soul of a person
just deceased and be carried off by it ; hence in the
Aru Islands the inmates of a house will not sleep the
night after a death has taken place in it, because the
soul of the deceased is supposed to be still in the house

---

[1] Wilken, *l.c.*

[2] B. F. Matthes, *Bijdragen tot de Ethnologie van Zuid-Celebes*, p. 33 ; *id.*, *Over de Bissoes of heidensche priesters en priesteressen der Boeginezen*, p. 9 *sq.*; *id.*, *Makassaarsch-Hollandsch Woordenboek*, *svv. Koèrròe* and *soemàñgá*, pp. 41, 569. Of these two words, the former means the sound made in calling fowls, and the latter means the soul. The expression for the ceremonies described in the text is *ápakòerròe soemàñgá*.

[3] Shway Yoe, *The Burman, his Life and Notions*, ii. 100.

[4] J. L. Wilson, *West Afrika*, p. 162 *sq.* (German translation).

and they fear to meet it in a dream.[1]   Again, the soul
may be prevented by physical force from returning.
The Santals tell how a man fell asleep, and growing
very thirsty, his soul, in the form of a lizard, left his
body and entered a pitcher of water to drink. Just
then the owner of the pitcher happened to cover it;
so the soul could not return to the body and the man
died.   While his friends were preparing to burn the
body some one uncovered the pitcher to get water.
The lizard thus escaped and returned to the body,
which immediately revived; so the man rose up and
asked his friends why they were weeping.   They told
him they thought he was dead and were about to burn
his body.   He said he had been down a well to get
water but had found it hard to get out and had just
returned.   So they saw it all.[2]   A similar story is
reported from Transylvania as follows.   In the account
of a witch's trial at Mühlbach last century it is said
that a woman had engaged two men to work in her
vineyard.   After noon they all lay down to rest as
usual.   An hour later the men got up and tried to
waken the woman, but could not.   She lay motionless
with her mouth wide open.   They came back at sunset and still she lay like a corpse.   Just at that moment
a big fly came buzzing past, which one of the men
caught and shut up in his leathern pouch.   Then
they tried again to waken the woman but could not.
Afterwards they let out the fly; it flew straight into
the woman's mouth and she awoke.   On seeing

---

[1] J. G. F. Riedel, *De sluik-en
kroesharige rassen tusschen Selebes en
Papua*, p. 267.   For detention of
sleeper's soul by spirits and consequent
illness, see also Mason, quoted in
Bastian's *Die Völker des östlichen Asien*,
ii. 387 *note*.

[2] *Indian Antiquary*, 1878, vii.
273;   Bastian, *Völkerstämme am
Brahmaputra*, p. 127.   Similar story
(lizard form of soul not mentioned) told
by Hindus, *Panjab Notes and Queries*,
iii. No. 679.

this the men had no further doubt that she was a witch.[1]

It is a common rule with primitive people not to waken a sleeper, because his soul is away and might not have time to get back; so if the man wakened without his soul, he would fall sick. If it is absolutely necessary to waken a sleeper, it must be done very gradually, to allow the soul time to return.[2] In Bombay it is thought equivalent to murder to change the appearance of a sleeper, as by painting his face in fantastic colours or giving moustaches to a sleeping woman. For when the soul returns, it will not be able to recognise its body and the person will die.[3] The Servians believe that the soul of a sleeping witch often leaves her body in the form of a butterfly. If during its absence her body be turned round, so that her feet are placed where her head was before, the butterfly soul will not find its way back into her body through the mouth, and the witch will die.[4]

But in order that a man's soul should quit his body, it is not necessary that he should be asleep.

---

[1] E. Gerard, *The Land beyond the Forest*, ii. 27 *sq.* A similar story is told in Holland, J. W. Wolf, *Nederlandsche Sagen*, No. 251, p. 344 *sq.* The stories of Hermotimus and King Gunthram belong to the same class. In the latter the king's soul comes out of his mouth as a small reptile. The soul of Aristeas issued from his mouth in the form of a raven. Pliny, *Nat. Hist.* vii. § 174; Lucian, *Musc. Encom.* 7; Paulus, *Hist. Langobardorum*, iii. 34. In an East Indian story of the same type the sleeper's soul issues from his nose in the form of a cricket. Wilken in *De Indische Gids*, June 1884, p. 940. In a Swabian story a girl's soul creeps out of her mouth in the form of a white mouse. Birlinger, *Volksthümliches aus Schwaben*, i. 303.

[2] Shway Yoe, *The Burman*, ii. 103; Bastian, *Die Völker des östlichen Asien*, ii. 389; Blumentritt, "Der Ahnencultus und die religiösen Anschauungen der Malaien des Philippinen-Archipels," in *Mittheilungen d. Wiener Geogr. Gesellschaft*, 1882, p. 209; Riedel, *De sluik-en kroesharige rassen tusschen Selebes en Papua*, p. 440; *id.*, "Die Landschaft Dawan oder West-Timor," in *Deutsche Geographische Blätter*, x. 280.

[3] *Panjab Notes and Queries*, iii. No. 530.

[4] Ralston, *Songs of the Russian People*, p. 117 *sq.*

It may quit him in his waking hours, and then sickness or (if the absence is prolonged) death will be the result. Thus the Mongols sometimes explain sickness by supposing that the patient's soul is absent, and either does not care to return to its body or cannot find the way back. To secure the return of the soul it is therefore necessary on the one hand to make its body as attractive as possible, and on the other hand to show it the way home. To make the body attractive all the sick man's best clothes and most valued possessions are placed beside him ; he is washed, incensed, and made as comfortable as possible ; and all his friends march thrice round the hut calling out the sick man's name and coaxing his soul to return. To help the soul to find its way back a coloured cord is stretched from the patient's head to the door of the hut. The priest in his robes reads a list of the horrors of hell and the dangers incurred by souls which wilfully absent themselves from their bodies. Then turning to the assembled friends and the patient he asks, "Is it come ? " All answer Yes, and bowing to the returning soul throw seed over the sick man. The cord which guided the soul back is then rolled up and placed round the patient's neck, who must wear it for seven days without taking it off. No one may frighten or hurt him, lest his soul, not yet familiar with its body, should again take flight.[1] In an Indian story a king conveys his soul into the dead body of a Brahman, and a hunchback conveys his soul into the deserted body of the king. The hunchback is now king and the king is a Brahman. However,

---

[1] Bastian, *Die Seele und ihre Erscheinungwesen in der Ethnographie*, p. 36.

the hunchback is induced to show his skill by transferring his soul to the dead body of a parrot, and the
king seizes the opportunity to regain possession of
his own body.[1]   In another Indian story a Brahman
reanimates the dead body of a king by conveying
his own soul into it.   Meantime the Brahman's
body has been burnt, and his soul is obliged to remain
in the body of the king.[2]

The departure of the soul is not always voluntary.   It may be extracted from the body against its
will by ghosts, demons, or sorcerers.   Hence, when
a funeral is passing the house, the Karens of Burma
tie their children with a special kind of string to a
particular part of the house, in case the souls of
the children should leave their bodies and go into
the corpse which is passing.   The children are
kept tied in this way until the corpse is out of sight.[3]
And after the corpse has been laid in the grave, but
before the earth has been filled in, the mourners and
friends range themselves round the grave, each
with a bamboo split lengthwise in one hand and a
little stick in the other ; each man thrusts his bamboo
into the grave, and drawing the stick along the
groove of the bamboo points out to his soul that
in this way it may easily climb up out of the grave.
While the earth is being filled in, the bamboos are
kept out of the way, lest the souls should be in
them, and so should be inadvertently buried with
the earth as it is being thrown into the grave ; and
when the people leave the spot they carry away
the bamboos, begging their souls to come with

---

[1] *Pantschatantra*, Benfey, p. 124 *sqq.*
[2] *Katha Sarit Ságara*, trans. Taw-
ney, i. 21 *sq.*

[3] E. B. Cross, "On the Karens,"
in *Journal of the American Oriental
Society*, iv. 311.

them.[1] Further, on returning from the grave each Karen provides himself with three little hooks made of branches of trees, and calling his spirit to follow him, at short intervals, as he returns, he makes a motion as if hooking it, and then thrusts the hook into the ground. This is done to prevent the soul of the living from staying behind with the soul of the dead.[2] When a mother dies leaving a young baby, the Burmese think that the "butterfly" or soul of the baby follows that of the mother, and that if it is not recovered the child must die. So a wise woman is called in to get back the baby's soul. She places a mirror near the corpse, and on the mirror a piece of feathery cotton down. Holding a cloth in her open hands at the foot of the mirror, she with wild words entreats the mother not to take with her the "butterfly" or soul of her child, but to send it back. As the gossamer down slips from the face of the mirror she catches it in the cloth and tenderly places it on the baby's breast. The same ceremony is sometimes observed when one of two children that have played together dies, and is thought to be luring away the soul of its playmate to the spirit-land. It is sometimes performed also for a bereaved husband or wife.[3] In the Island of Keisar (East Indies) it is thought imprudent to go near a grave at night, lest the ghosts should catch and keep the soul of the passer-by.[4] The Key Islanders believe that the souls of their forefathers, angry at not receiving food, make people sick by detaining their souls. So they lay offerings of food

---

[1] A. R. M'Mahon, *The Karens of the Golden Chersonese*, p. 318.

[2] F. Mason, "Physical Character of the Karens," in *Journal of the Asiatic Society of Bengal*, 1866, pt. ii. p. 28 *sq.*

[3] C. J. S. F. Forbes, *British Burma*, p. 99 *sq.* ; Shway Yoe, *The Burman*, ii. 102 ; Bastian, *Die Völker des östlichen Asien*, ii. 389.

[4] Riedel, *De sluik-en kroesharige rassen tusschen Selebes en Papua*, p. 414.

on the grave and beg their ancestors to allow the soul of the sick to return or to drive it home speedily if it should be lingering by the way.[1]

In Bolang Mongondo, a district in the west of Celebes, all sickness is ascribed to the ancestral spirits who have carried off the patient's soul. The object therefore is to bring back the patient's soul and restore it to the sufferer. An eye-witness has thus described the attempted cure of a sick boy. The priestesses, who acted as physicians, made a doll of cloth and fastened it to the point of a spear, which an old woman held upright. Round this doll the priestesses danced, uttering charms, and chirruping as when one calls a dog. Then the old woman lowered the point of the spear a little, so that the priestesses could reach the doll. By this time the soul of the sick boy was supposed to be in the doll, having been brought into it by the incantations. So the priestesses approached it cautiously on tiptoe and caught the soul in the many-coloured cloths which they had been waving in the air. Then they laid the soul on the boy's head, that is, they wrapped his head in the cloth in which the soul was supposed to be, and stood still for some moments with great gravity, holding their hands on the patient's head. Suddenly there was a jerk, the priestesses whispered and shook their heads, and the cloth was taken off—the soul had escaped. The priestesses gave chase to it, running round and round the house, clucking and gesticulating as if they were driving hens into a poultry-yard. At last they recaptured the soul at the foot of the stair and restored it to its owner as before.[2]   Much in the same way an Australian

[1] Riedel, *op. cit.* p. 221 *sq*

[2] N. Ph. Wilken en J. A. Schwarz, "Het heidendom en de Islam in Bolaang Mongondou," in *Mededeelingen van wege het Nederlandsche Zendeling-genootschap*, 1867, xi. 263 *sq*.

medicine-man will sometimes bring the lost soul of a sick man into a puppet and restore it to the patient by pressing the puppet to his breast.[1] In Uea, one of the Loyalty Islands, the souls of the dead seem to have been credited with the power of stealing the souls of the living. For when a man was sick the soul-doctor would go with a large troop of men and women to the graveyard. Here the men played on flutes and the women whistled softly to lure the soul home. After this had gone on for some time they formed in procession and moved homewards, the flutes playing and the women whistling all the way, leading back the wandering soul and driving it gently along with open palms. On entering the patient's dwelling they commanded the soul in a loud voice to enter his body.[2] In Madagascar, when a sick man had lost his soul, his friends went to the family tomb, and making a hole in it, begged the soul of the patient's father to give them a soul for his son, who had none. So saying they clapped a bonnet on the hole, and folding up the soul in the bonnet, brought it to the patient, who put the bonnet on his head, and thus received a new soul or got back his old one.[3]

Often the abduction of a man's soul is set down to demons. The Annamites believe that when a man meets a demon and speaks to him, the demon inhales the man's breath and soul.[4] When a Dyak is about to leave a forest through which he has been walking alone, he never forgets to ask the demons to give him back his soul, for it may be that some forest-devil has

[1] James Dawson, *Australian Aborigines*, p. 57 *sq.*

[2] W. W. Gill, *Myths and Songs of the South Pacific*, p. 171 *sq.*

[3] G. A. Wilken, "Het animisme," in *De Indische Gids*, June 1884, p. 937.

[4] Landes, "Contes et légendes annamites," No. 76 in *Cochinchine Française, Excursions et Reconnaissances*, No. 23, p. 80.

carried it off. For the abduction of a soul may take place without its owner being aware of his loss, and it may happen either while he is awake or asleep.[1] In the Moluccas when a man is unwell it is thought that some devil has carried away his soul to the tree, mountain, or hill where he (the devil) dwells. A sorcerer having pointed out the devil's abode, the friends of the patient carry thither cooked rice, fruit, fish, raw eggs, a hen, a chicken, a silken robe, gold, armlets, etc. Having set out the food in order they pray, saying : "We come to offer to you, O devil, this offering of food, clothes, gold, etc. ; take it and release the soul of the patient for whom we pray. Let it return to his body and he who now is sick shall be made whole." Then they eat a little and let the hen loose as a ransom for the soul of the patient ; also they put down the raw eggs ; but the silken robe, the gold, and the armlets they take home with them. As soon as they are come to the house they place a flat bowl containing the offerings which have been brought back at the sick man's head, and say to him : "Now is your soul released, and you shall fare well and live to gray hairs on the earth."[2] A more modern account from the same region describes how the friend of the patient, after depositing his offerings on the spot where the missing soul is supposed to be, calls out thrice the name of the sick person, adding, "Come with me, come with me." Then he returns, making a motion with a cloth as if he had caught the soul in it. He must not look to right or left or speak a word to any one he meets, but must go straight to the patient's house. At the door he stands, and calling out the sick

---

[1] Perelaer, *Ethnographische Beschrijving der Dajaks*, p. 26 *sq.*

[2] Fr. Valentyn, *Oud en nieuw Oost-Indiën*, iii. 13 *sq.*

person's name, asks whether he is returned. Being answered from within that he is returned, he enters and lays the cloth in which he has caught the soul on the patient's throat, saying, "Now you are returned to the house." Sometimes a substitute is provided; a doll, dressed up in gay clothing and tinsel, is offered to the demon in exchange for the patient's soul with these words, "Give us back the ugly one which you have taken away and receive this pretty one instead."[1] Similarly the Mongols make up a horse of birch-bark and a doll, and invite the demon to take the doll instead of the patient and to ride away on the horse.[2]

Demons are especially feared by persons who have just entered on a new house. Hence at a house-warming among the Alfoers of Celebes the priest performs a ceremony for the purpose of restoring their souls to the inmates. He hangs up a bag at the place of sacrifice and then goes through a list of the gods. There are so many of them that this takes him the whole night through without stopping. In the morning he offers the gods an egg and some rice. By this time the souls of the household are supposed to be gathered in the bag. So the priest takes the bag, and holding it on the head of the master of the house says, "Here you have your soul—go (soul) to-morrow away again." He then does the same, saying the same words, to the housewife and all the other members of the family.[3] Amongst the same Alfoers one way of

---

[1] Van Schmidt, "Aanteekeningen, nopens de zeden, gewoonten en gebruiken, benevens de vooroordeelen en bijgelovigheden der bevolking van de eilanden Saparoea, Haroekoe, Noessa Laut, en van een gedeelte van de zuidkust van Ceram," in *Tijdschrift voor Neêrland's Indië*, 1843, dl. ii. 511 *sqq.*

[2] Bastian, *Die Seele*, p. 36 *sq.* ; J. G.

Gmelin, *Reise durch Sibirien*, ii. 359 *sq.*

[3] P. N. Wilken, "Bijdragen tot de kennis van de zeden en gewoonten der Alfoeren in de Minahassa," in *Mededeelingen van wege het Nederlandsche Zendelinggenootschap*, 1863, vii. 146 *sq.* Why the priest, after restoring the soul, tells it to go away again, is not clear.

recovering a sick man's soul is to let down a bowl by a belt out of a window and fish for the soul till it is caught in the bowl and hauled up.[1] Among the same people, when a priest is bringing back a sick man's soul which he has caught in a cloth, he is preceded by a girl holding the large leaf of a certain palm over his head as an umbrella to keep him and the soul from getting wet, in case it should rain ; and he is followed by a man brandishing a sword to deter other souls from any attempt at rescuing the captured soul.[2]

The Samoans tell how two young wizards, passing a house where a chief lay very sick, saw a company of gods from the mountain sitting in the doorway. They were handing from one to another the soul of the dying chief. It was wrapped in a leaf, and had been passed from the gods inside the house to those sitting in the doorway. One of the gods handed the soul to one of the wizards, taking him for a god in the dark, for it was night. Then all the gods rose up and went away ; but the wizard kept the chief's soul. In the morning some women went with a present of fine mats to fetch a famous physician. The wizards were sitting on the shore as the women passed, and they said to the women, "Give us the mats and we will heal him." So they went to the chief's house. He was very ill, his jaw hung down, and his end seemed near. But the wizards undid the leaf and let the soul into him again, and forthwith he brightened up and lived.[3]

The Battas of Sumatra believe that the soul of a

---

[1] Riedel, "De Minahasa in 1825," in *Tijdschrift voor Indische Taal-Land-en Volkenkunde*, xviii. 523.

[2] N. Graafland, *De Minahassa*, i. 327 *sq.*

[3] G. Turner, *Samoa*, p. 142 *sq.*

living man may transmigrate into the body of an animal. Hence, for example, the doctor is sometimes desired to extract the patient's soul from the body of a fowl, in which it has been hidden away by an evil spirit.[1]

Sometimes the lost soul is brought back in a visible shape. In Melanesia a woman knowing that a neighbour was at the point of death heard a rustling in her house, as of a moth fluttering, just at the moment when a noise of weeping and lamentation told her that the soul was flown. She caught the fluttering thing between her hands and ran with it, crying out that she had caught the soul. But though she opened her hands above the mouth of the corpse, it did not revive.[2] The Salish or Flathead Indians of Oregon believe that a man's soul may be separated for a time from his body without causing death and without the man being aware of his loss. It is necessary, however, that the lost soul should be soon found and restored to the man or he will die. The name of the man who has lost his soul is revealed in a dream to the medicine-man, who hastens to inform the sufferer of his loss. Generally a number of men have sustained a like loss at the same time; all their names are revealed to the medicine-man, and all employ him to recover their souls. The whole night long these soulless men go about the village from lodge to lodge, dancing and singing. Towards daybreak they go into a separate lodge, which is closed up so as to be

---

[1] J. B. Neumann, "Het Pane en Bila - stroomgebied op het eiland Sumatra," in *Tijdschrift van het Nederlandsch Aardrijkskundig Genootschap*, ii. de Serie, dl. iii., Afdeeling :

meer uitgebreide artikelen, No. 2 (1886), p. 302.

[2] Codrington, "Religious Beliefs and Practices in Melanesia," in *Journal of the Anthropological Institute*, x. 281.

totally dark. A small hole is then made in the roof,
through which the medicine-man, with a bunch of
feathers, brushes in the souls, in the shape of bits of
bone and the like, which he receives on a piece of
matting. A fire is next kindled, by the light of which
the medicine-man sorts out the souls. First he puts
aside the souls of dead people, of which there are
usually several; for if he were to give the soul of a
dead person to a living man, the man would die
instantly. Next he picks out the souls of all the
persons present, and making them all to sit down
before him, he takes the soul of each, in the shape of
a splinter of bone, wood, or shell, and placing it on
the owner's head, pats it with many prayers and
contortions till it descends into the heart and so
resumes its proper place.[1] In Amboina the sorcerer,
to recover a soul detained by demons, plucks a branch
from a tree, and waving it to and fro as if to catch
something, calls out the sick man's name. Returning
he strikes the patient over the head and body with
the branch, into which the lost soul is supposed to
have passed, and from which it returns to the patient.[2]
In the Babar Islands offerings for evil spirits are
laid at the root of a great tree (wokiorai), from which
a leaf is plucked and pressed on the patient's forehead
and breast; the lost soul, which is in the leaf, is thus
restored to its owner.[3] In some other islands of the
same seas, when a man returns ill and speechless from
the forest, it is inferred that the evil spirits which
dwell in the great trees have caught and kept his

---

[1] Horatio Hale, *U. S. Exploring
Expedition, Ethnography and Philology*,
p. 208 *sq.* Cp. Wilkes, *Narrative of the
U.S. Exploring Expedition* (London,
1845), iv. 448 *sq.*

[2] Riedel, *De sluik - en kroesharige
rassen tusschen Selebes en Papua*, p.
77 *sq.*

[3] *Ib.* p. 356 *sq.*

soul. Offerings of food are therefore left under a tree and the soul is brought home in a piece of wax.[1] Amongst the Dyaks of Sarawak the priest conjures the lost soul into a cup, where it is seen by the uninitiated as a lock of hair, but by the initiated as a miniature human being. This is supposed to be thrust by the priest into a hole in the top of the patient's head.[2] In Nias the sick man's soul is restored to him in the shape of a firefly, visible only to the sorcerer, who catches it in a cloth and places it on the forehead of the patient.[3]

Again, souls may be extracted from their bodies or detained on their wanderings not only by ghosts and demons but also by men, especially by sorcerers. In Fiji if a criminal refused to confess, the chief sent for a scarf with which "to catch away the soul of the rogue." At the sight, or even at the mention of the scarf the culprit generally made a clean breast. For if he did not, the scarf would be waved over his head till his soul was caught in it, when it would be carefully folded up and nailed to the end of a chief's canoe ; and for want of his soul the criminal would pine and die.[4] The sorcerers of Danger Island used to set snares for souls. The snares were made of stout cinet, about fifteen to thirty feet long, with loops on either side of different sizes, to suit the different sizes of souls ; for fat souls there were large loops, for thin souls there were small ones. When a man was sick against whom the sorcerers had a grudge, they set up these soul-

[1] Riedel, *op. cit.* p. 376.

[2] Spenser St. John, *Life in the Forests of the Far East*, i. 189. Sometimes the souls resemble cotton seeds (*ib.*) Cp. *id.* i. 183.

[3] Nieuwenhuisen en Rosenberg, "Ver-

slag omtrent het Eiland Nias," in *Verhandel. van het Batav. Genootsch. van Kunsten en Wetenschappen*, xxx. 116 ; Rosenberg, *Der Malayische Archipel*, p. 174.

[4] Williams, *Fiji and the Fijians*, i. 250.

snares near his house and watched for the flight of his soul. If in the shape of a bird or an insect it was caught in the snare the man would infallibly die.[1] Among the Sereres of Senegambia, when a man wishes to revenge himself on his enemy he goes to the *Fitaure* (chief and priest in one), and prevails on him by presents to conjure the soul of his enemy into a large jar of red earthenware, which is then deposited under a consecrated tree. The man whose soul is shut up in the jar soon dies.[2] Some of the Congo negroes think that enchanters can get possession of human souls, and enclosing them in tusks of ivory, sell them to the white man, who makes them work for him in his country under the sea. It is believed that very many of the coast labourers are men thus obtained ; so when these people go to trade they often look anxiously about for their dead relations. The man whose soul is thus sold into slavery will die "in due course, if not at the time."[3]

In Hawaii there were sorcerers who caught souls of living people, shut them up in calabashes, and gave them to people to eat. By squeezing a captured soul in their hands they discovered the place where people had been secretly buried.[4] Amongst the Canadian Indians, when a wizard wished to kill a man, he sent out his familiar spirits, who brought him the victim's soul in the shape of a stone or the like. The wizard struck the soul with a sword or an axe till it bled profusely, and as it bled the man to whom it belonged languished and died.[5] In Amboina if a doctor is con-

---

[1] Gill, *Myths and Songs of the South Pacific*, p. 171; *id.*, *Life in the Southern Isles*, p. 181 *sqq.*

[2] L. J. B. Bérenger-Féraud, *Les Peuplades de la Sénégambie* (Paris, 1879), p. 277.

[3] W. H. Bentley, *Life on the Congo* (London, 1887), p. 71.

[4] Bastian, *Allerlei aus Volks-und Menschenkunde* (Berlin, 1888), i. 119.

[5] *Relations des Jésuites*, 1637, p. 50.

vinced that a patient's soul has been carried away by a
demon beyond recovery, he seeks to supply its place
with a soul abstracted from another man. For this
purpose he goes by night to a house and asks, " Who's
there ? " If an inmate is incautious enough to answer,
the doctor takes up from before the door a clod of
earth, into which the soul of the person who replied is
believed to have passed. This clod the doctor lays
under the sick man's pillow, and performs certain ceremonies by which the stolen soul is conveyed into the
patient's body. Then as he goes home the doctor
fires two shots to frighten the soul from returning to
its proper owner.[1] A Karen wizard will catch the
wandering soul of a sleeper and transfer it to the
body of a dead man. The latter, therefore, comes to
life as the former dies. But the friends of the sleeper
in turn engage a wizard to steal the soul of another
sleeper, who dies as the first sleeper comes to life. In
this way an indefinite succession of deaths and resur-
rections is supposed to take place.[2]

The Indians of the Nass River, British Columbia,
think that a doctor may swallow his patient's soul by
mistake. A doctor who is believed to have done so
is made by the other doctors to stand over the patient,
while one of them thrusts his fingers down the doctor's
throat, another kneads him in the stomach with his
knuckles, and a third slaps him on the back. If the
soul is not in him after all, and if the same process has
been repeated upon all the doctors without success, it
is concluded that the soul must be in the head-doctor's
box. A party of doctors, therefore, waits upon him at

---

[1] Riedel, *De sluik-en kroesharige
rassen tusschen Selebes en Papua,* p.
78 *sq.*

[2] E. B. Cross, "On the Karens," in
*Journal of the American Oriental
Society,* iv. 307.

his house and requests him to produce his box. When he has done so and arranged its contents on a new mat, they take him and hold him up by the heels with his head in a hole in the floor. In this position they wash his head, and "any water remaining from the ablution is taken and poured upon the sick man's head."[1] Other examples of the recall and recovery of souls will be found referred to beneath.[2] But the spiritual dangers I have enumerated are not the only ones which beset the savage. Often he regards his shadow or reflection as his soul, or at all

[1] J. B. McCullagh in *The Church Missionary Gleaner*, xiv. No. 164 (August 1887), p. 91. The same account is copied from the "North Star" (Sitka, Alaska, December 1888), in *Journal of American Folk-lore*, ii. 74 *sq.* Mr. McCullagh's account (which is closely followed in the text) of the latter part of the custom is not quite clear. It would seem that failing to find the soul in the head-doctor's box it occurs to them that he may have swallowed it, as the other doctors were at first supposed to have done. With a view of testing this hypothesis they hold him up by the heels to empty out the soul ; and as the water with which his head is washed may possibly contain the missing soul, it is poured on the patient's head to restore the soul to him. We have already seen that the recovered soul is often conveyed into the sick person's head.

[2] Riedel, *De Topantunuasu of oorspronkelijke volksstammen van Central Selebes* (overgedrukt uit de *Bijdragen tot de Taal-Land-en Volkenkunde van Nederlandsch-Indië*, 5e volgr. i.), p. 17 ; Neumann, " Het Pane en Bila-stroomgebied," in *Tijdschrift van het Nederlandsch Aardrijkskundig Genootschap*, ii. de Serie, dl. iii., Afdeeling : meer uitgebreide artikelen, No. 2 (1886), p. 300 *sq.* ; Priklonski, "Die Jakuten," in Bastian's *Allerlei aus Volks-und Menschenkunde*, ii. 218 *sq.* ; Bastian, *Die Völker des östlichen Asien*, ii. 388, iii. 236 ; *id.*, *Völkerstämme am Brahmaputra*, p. 23 ; *id.*, "Hügelstämme Assam's," in *Verhandlungen d. Berlin. Gesell. f. Anthropol. Ethnol. und Urgeschichte*, 1881, p. 156 ; Shway Yoe, *The Burman*, i. 283 *sq.*, ii. 101 *sq.* ; Sproat, *Scenes and Studies of Savage Life*, p. 214 ; Doolittle, *Social Life of the Chinese*, p. 110 *sq.* (ed. Paxton Hood) ; T. Williams, *Fiji and the Fijians*, i. 242 ; E. B. Cross, "On the Karens," in *Journal of the American Oriental Society*, iv. 309 *sq.* ; A. W. Howitt, "On some Australian Beliefs," in *Journ. Anthrop. Instit.* xiii. 187 *sq.* ; *id.*, "On Australian Medicine Men," in *Journ. Anthrop. Inst.* xvi. 41 ; E. P. Houghton, "On the Land Dayaks of Upper Sarawak," in *Memoirs of the Anthropological Society of London*, iii. 196 *sq.* ; L. Dahle, "Sikidy and Vintana," in *Antananarivo Annual and Madagascar Annual*, xi. (1887) p. 320 *sq.* ; C. Leemius, *De Lapponibus Finmarchiae eorumque lingua, vita et religione pristina commentatio* (Copenhagen, 1767), p. 416 *sq.* Some time ago my friend Professor W. Robertson Smith suggested to me that the practice of hunting souls, which is denounced in Ezekiel xiii. 17 *sqq.* must have been akin to those described in the text.

events as a vital part of himself, and as such it is necessarily a source of danger to him. For if it is trampled upon, struck, or stabbed, he will feel the injury as if it were done to his person; and if it is detached from him entirely (as he believes that it may be) he will die. In the island of Wetar there are magicians who can make a man ill by stabbing his shadow with a pike or hacking it with a sword.[1] After Sankara had destroyed the Buddhists in India, it is said that he journeyed to Nepaul, where he had some difference of opinion with the Grand Lama. To prove his supernatural powers, he soared into the air. But as he mounted up, the Grand Lama, perceiving his shadow swaying and wavering on the ground, struck his knife into it and down fell Sankara and broke his neck.[2] In the Babar Islands the demons get power over a man's soul by holding fast his shadow, or by striking and wounding it.[3] There are stones in Melanesia on which, if a man's shadow falls, the demon of the stone can draw out his soul.[4] In Amboina and Uliase, two islands near the equator, and where, therefore, there is little or no shadow cast at noon, it is a rule not to go out of the house at mid-day, because it is supposed that by doing so a man may lose the shadow of his soul.[5] The Mangaians tell of a mighty warrior, Tukaitawa, whose strength waxed and waned with the length of his shadow. In the morning, when his shadow fell longest, his strength was greatest; but as the shadow shortened towards noon his strength ebbed with it, till exactly at noon it reached its lowest

---

[1] Riedel, *De sluik-en kroesharige rassen tusschen Selebes en Papua*, p. 440.
[2] Bastian, *Die Völker des östlichen Asien*, v. 455.

[3] Riedel, *op. cit.* p. 340.
[4] Codrington, "Religious Beliefs and Practices in Melanesia," in *Journ. Anthrop. Instit.* x. 281.
[5] Riedel, *op. cit.* p. 61.

point ; then, as the shadow stretched out in the afternoon, his strength returned. A certain hero discovered the secret of Tukaitawa's strength and slew
him at noon.[1] It is possible that even in lands outside
the tropics the fact of the diminished shadow at noon
may have contributed, even if it did not give rise, to
the superstitious dread with which that hour has been
viewed by various peoples, as by the Greeks, ancient
and modern, and by the Roumanians of Transylvania.[2]
In this fact, too, we may perhaps detect the reason
why noon was chosen by the Greeks as the hour for
sacrificing to the shadowless dead.[3] The ancients
believed that in Arabia if a hyaena trod on a man's
shadow it deprived him of the power of speech and
motion ; and that if a dog, standing on a roof in the
moonlight, cast a shadow on the ground and a hyaena
trod on it, the dog would fall down as if dragged with
a rope.[4] Clearly in these cases the shadow, if not
equivalent to the soul, is at least regarded as a living
part of the man or the animal, so that injury done to
the shadow is felt by the person or animal as if it were
done to his body. Whoever entered the sanctuary of
Zeus on Mount Lycaeus in Arcadia was believed to
lose his shadow and to die within the year.[5] Nowhere,
perhaps, does the equivalence of the shadow to the
life or soul come out more clearly than in some

---

[1] Gill, *Myths and Songs of the South Pacific*, p. 284 *sqq.*
[2] Bernard Schmidt, *Das Volksleben der Neugriechen*, pp. 94 *sqq.*, 119 *sq.* ; Grimm, *Deutsche Mythologie*,[4] ii. 972 ; Rochholz, *Deutscher Glaube und Brauch*, i. 62 *sqq.* ; E Gerard, *The Land beyond the Forest*, i. 331.
[3] Schol. on Aristophanes, *Ran.* 293.
[4] [Aristotle] *Mirab. Auscult.* 145 (157) ; *Geoponica*, xv. 1. In the latter passage, for καγάγει ἑαυτήν we must read κ. αὑτόν, an emendation neces-
sitated by the context, and confirmed by the passage of Damīrī quoted and translated by Bochart, *Hierozoicon*, i. c. 833, "*cum ad lunam calcat umbram canis, qui supra tectura est, canis ad eam* [scil. hyaenam] *decidit, et ea illum devorat.*" Cp. W. Robertson Smith, *The Religion of the Semites*, i. 122.
[5] Pausanias, viii. 38, 6 ; Polybius, xvi. 12, 7 ; Plutarch, *Quaest. Graec.* 39.

customs practised to this day in South-Eastern Europe. In modern Greece, when the foundation of a new building is being laid, it is the custom to kill a cock, a ram, or a lamb, and to let its blood flow on the foundation stone, under which the animal is afterwards buried. The object of the sacrifice is to give strength and stability to the building. But sometimes, instead of killing an animal, the builder entices a man to the foundation stone, secretly measures his body, or a part of it, or his shadow, and buries the measure under the foundation stone ; or he lays the foundation stone upon the man's shadow. It is believed that the man will die within the year.[1] The Bulgarians still observe a similar custom. If they cannot get a human shadow they measure the shadow of the first animal that comes that way.[2] The Roumanians of Transylvania think that he whose shadow is thus immured will die within forty days ; so persons passing by a building which is in course of erection may hear a warning cry, " Beware lest they take thy shadow ! " Not long ago there were still shadow-traders whose business it was to provide architects with the shadows necessary for securing their walls.[3] In these cases the measure of the shadow is looked on as equivalent to the shadow itself, and to bury it is to bury the life or soul of the man, who, deprived of it, must die. Thus the custom is a substitute for the old custom of immuring a living person in the walls, or crushing him under the foundation stone of a new building, in order to give strength and durability to the structure.

As some peoples believe a man's soul to be in his

---

[1] B. Schmidt, *Das Volksleben der Neugriechen*, p. 196 *sq.*

[2] Ralston, *Songs of the Russian People*, p. 127.

[3] W. Schmidt, *Das Jahr und seine Tage in Meinung und Brauch der Romänen Siebenbürgens*, p. 27 ; E. Gerard, *The Land beyond the Forest*, ii. 17 *sq.*

shadow, so other (or the same) peoples believe it to be in his reflection in water or a mirror. Thus "the Andamanese do not regard their shadows but their reflections (in any mirror) as their souls."[1] Some of the Fijians thought that man has two souls, a light one and a dark one; the dark one goes to Hades, the light one is his reflection in water or a mirror.[2] When the Motumotu of New Guinea first saw their likenesses in a looking-glass they thought that their reflections were their souls.[3] The reflection-soul, being external to the man, is exposed to much the same dangers as the shadow-soul. As the shadow may be stabbed, so may the reflection. Hence an Aztec mode of keeping sorcerers from the house was to leave a vessel of water with a knife in it behind the door. When a sorcerer entered he was so much alarmed at seeing his reflection in the water transfixed by a knife that he turned and fled.[4] The Zulus will not look into a dark pool because they think there is a beast in it which will take away their reflections, so that they die.[5] The Basutos say that crocodiles have the power of thus killing a man by dragging his reflection under water.[6] In Saddle Island (Melanesia) there is a pool "into which if any one looks he dies; the malignant spirit takes hold upon his life by means of his reflection on the water."[7]

---

[1] E. H. Mann, *Aboriginal Inhabitants of the Andaman Islands*, p. 94.

[2] Williams, *Fiji*, i. 241.

[3] James Chalmers, *Pioneering in New Guinea* (London, 1887), p. 170.

[4] Sahagun, *Histoire générale des choses de la Nouvelle-Espagne* (Paris, 1880), p. 314. The Chinese hang brass mirrors over the idols in their houses, because it is thought that evil spirits entering the house and seeing themselves in the mirrors will be scared away (*China Review*, ii. 164).

[5] Callaway, *Nursery Tales, Traditions, and Histories of the Zulus*, p. 342.

[6] Arbousset et Daumas, *Voyage d'exploration au Nord-est de la Colonie du Cap de Bonne-Espérance*, p. 12.

[7] Codrington, "Religious Beliefs and Practices in Melanesia," in *Journ. Anthrop. Instit.* x. 313.

We can now understand why it was a maxim both in ancient India and ancient Greece not to look at one's reflection in water, and why the Greeks regarded it as an omen of death if a man dreamed of seeing himself so reflected.[1] They feared that the water-spirits would drag the person's reflection (soul) under water, leaving him soulless to die. This was probably the origin of the classical story of the beautiful Narcissus, who pined and died in consequence of seeing his reflection in the water. The explanation that he died for love of his own fair image was probably devised later, after the old meaning of the story was forgotten. The same ancient belief lingers, in a faded form, in the English superstition that whoever sees a water-fairy must pine and die.

> "Alas, the moon should ever beam
> To show what man should never see !—
> I saw a maiden on a stream,
> And fair was she !
>
> "I staid to watch, a little space,
> Her parted lips if she would sing ;
> The waters closed above her face
> With many a ring.
>
> "I know my life will fade away,
> I know that I must vainly pine,
> For I am made of mortal clay,
> But she's divine ! "

Further, we can now explain the widespread custom of covering up mirrors or turning them to the wall after a death has taken place in the house. It is feared that the soul, projected out of the person in the shape of his reflection in the mirror, may be carried off by the ghost of the departed, which is commonly supposed to linger about the house till the burial. The custom

---

[1] *Fragmenta Philosoph. Graec.* ed. Mullach, i. 510; Artemidorus, *Onirocr.* ii. 7 ; *Laws of Manu,* iv. 38.

is thus exactly parallel to the Aru custom of not sleeping in a house after a death for fear that the soul, projected out of the body in a dream, may meet the ghost and be carried off by it.[1] In Oldenburg it is thought that if a person sees his image in a mirror after a death he will die himself. So all the mirrors in the house are covered up with white cloth.[2] In some parts of Germany after a death not only the mirrors but everything that shines or glitters (windows, clocks, etc.) is covered up,[3] doubtless because they might reflect a person's image. The same custom of covering up mirrors or turning them to the wall after a death prevails in England, Scotland, and Madagascar.[4] The Suni Mohammedans of Bombay cover with a cloth the mirror in the room of a dying man and do not remove it until the corpse is carried out for burial. They also cover the looking-glasses in their bedrooms before retiring to rest at night.[5] The reason why sick people should not see themselves in a mirror, and why the mirror in a sick-room is therefore covered up,[6] is also plain ; in time of sickness, when the soul might take flight so easily, it is particularly dangerous 'to project the soul out of the body by means of the reflection in a mirror. The rule is therefore precisely parallel to the rule observed by some peoples of not allowing sick people to sleep ;[7] for in sleep the soul is projected out of the body, and there is always a risk that it may not return. " In the opinion of the Raskolniks a mirror is an accursed thing, invented by

[1] See above, p. 125 *sq.*

[2] Wattke, *Der deutsche Volksaber-glaube,*[2] § 726.

[3] *Ib.*

[4] *Folk-lore Journal,* iii. 281 ; Dyer, *English Folk-lore,* p. 109 ; J. Napier, *Folk-lore, or Superstitious Beliefs in the West of Scotland,* p. 60 ; Ellis, *History of Madagascar,* i. 238 ; *Revue d'Ethnographie,* v. 215.

[5] *Panjáb Notes and Queries,* ii. 906.

[6] *Folk-lore Journal,* vi. 145 *sq.* ; *Panjab Notes and Queries,* ii., No. 378.

[7] *Journ. Anthrop. Inst.* xv. 82 *sqq.*

the devil,"¹ perhaps on account of the mirror's supposed power of drawing out the soul in the reflection and so facilitating its capture.

As with shadows and reflections, so with portraits ; they are often believed to contain the soul of the person portrayed. People who hold this belief are naturally loth to have their likenesses taken ; for if the portrait is the soul, or at least a vital part of the person portrayed, whoever possesses the portrait will be able to exercise a fatal influence over the original of it. Thus the Canelos Indians of South America think that their soul is carried away in their picture. Two of them having been photographed were so alarmed that they came back next day on purpose to ask if it were really true that their souls had been taken away.² When Mr. Joseph Thomson tried to photograph some of the Wa-teita in Eastern Africa, they imagined that he was a magician trying to get possession of their souls, and that if he got their likenesses they themselves would be entirely at his mercy.³ An Indian, whose portrait the Prince of Wied wished to get, refused to let himself be drawn, because he believed it would cause his death.⁴ The Mandans also thought that they would soon die if their portrait was in the hands of another ; they wished at least to have the artist's picture as a kind of antidote or guarantee.⁵ The same belief still lingers in various parts of Europe. Some old women in the Greek island of Carpathus were very angry a few years ago at having their likenesses drawn,

¹ Ralston, *Songs of the Russian People*, p. 117. The objection, however, may be merely Puritanical. Professor W. Robertson Smith informs me that the peculiarities of the Raskolniks are largely due to exaggerated Puritanism.

² A. Simson, " Notes on the Jívaros and Canelos Indians," in *Journ. Anthrop. Inst.* ix. 392.

³ J. Thomson, *Through Masai Land*, p. 86.

⁴ Maximilian Prinz zu Wied, *Reise in das Innere Nord-Amerika*, i. 417.

⁵ *Ib.* ii. 166.

thinking that in consequence they would pine and die.[1] Some people in Russia object to having their silhouettes taken, fearing that if this is done they will die before the year is out.[2] There are persons in the West of Scotland " who refuse to have their likeness taken lest it prove unlucky ; and give as instances the cases of several of their friends who never had a day's health after being photographed."[3]

§ 3.—*Royal and priestly taboos (continued)*

So much for the primitive conceptions of the soul and the dangers to which it is exposed. These conceptions are not limited to one people or country ; with variations of detail they are found all over the world, and survive, as we have seen, in modern Europe. Beliefs so deep-seated and so widespread must necessarily have contributed to shape the mould in which the early kingship was cast. For if every individual was at such pains to save his own soul from the perils which threatened it from so many sides, how much more carefully must *he* have been guarded upon whose life hung the welfare and even the existence of the whole people, and whom therefore it was the common interest of all to preserve ? Therefore we should expect to find the king's life protected by a system of precautions or safeguards still more numerous and minute than those which in primitive society every man adopts

[1] " A far-off Greek Island," *Black-wood's Magazine*, February 1886, p. 235.

[2] Ralston, *Songs of the Russian People*, p. 117.

[3] James Napier, *Folk-lore: or,* *Superstitious Beliefs in, the West of Scotland*, p. 142. For more examples of the same sort, see R. Andree, *Ethnographische Parallelen und Vergleiche*, Neue Folge (Leipzig, 1889), p. 18 *sqq.*

for the safety of his own soul. Now in point of fact
the life of the early kings is regulated, as we have seen
and shall see more fully presently, by a very exact
code of rules. May we not then conjecture that these
rules are the very safeguards which on *à priori* grounds
we expect to find adopted for the protection of the
king's life ? An examination of the rules themselves
confirms this conjecture. For from this it appears that
some of the rules observed by the kings are identical
with those observed by private persons out of regard
for the safety of their souls ; and even of those which
seem peculiar to the king, many, if not all, are most
readily explained on the hypothesis that they are
nothing but safeguards or lifeguards of the king. I
will now enumerate some of these royal rules or
taboos, offering on each of them such comments and
explanations as may serve to set the original intention
of the rule in its proper light.

As the object of the royal taboos is to isolate the
king from all sources of danger, their general effect
is to compel him to live in a state of seclusion,
more or less complete, according to the number and
stringency of the taboos he observes. Now of all
sources of danger none are more dreaded by the
savage than magic and witchcraft, and he suspects
all strangers of practising these black arts. To guard
against the baneful influence exerted voluntarily or
involuntarily by strangers is therefore an elementary
dictate of savage prudence. Hence before strangers
are allowed to enter a district, or at least before they
are permitted to mingle freely with the people of the
district, certain ceremonies are often performed by the
natives of the country for the purpose of disarming the
strangers of their magical powers, of counteracting the

baneful influence which is believed to emanate from them, or of disinfecting, so to speak, the tainted atmosphere by which they are supposed to be surrounded. Thus in the island of Nanumea (South Pacific) strangers from ships or from other islands were not allowed to communicate with the people until they all, or a few as representatives of the rest, had been taken to each of the four temples in the island, and prayers offered that the god would avert any disease or treachery which these strangers might have brought with them. Meat offerings were also laid upon the altars, accompanied by songs and dances in honour of the god. While these ceremonies were going on, all the people except the priests and their attendants kept out of sight. [1] On returning from an attempted ascent of the great African mountain Kilimanjaro, which is believed by the neighbouring tribes to be tenanted by dangerous demons, Mr. New and his party, as soon as they reached the border of the inhabited country, were disenchanted by the inhabitants, being sprinkled with "a professionally prepared liquor, supposed to possess the potency of neutralising evil influences, and removing the spell of wicked spirits." [2] In the interior of Yoruba (West Africa) the sentinels at the gates of towns often oblige European travellers to wait till nightfall before they admit them, the fear being that if the strangers were admitted by day the devils would enter behind them.[3] Amongst the Ot Danoms of Borneo it is the custom that strangers entering the territory should pay to

---

[1] Turner, *Samoa*, p. 291 *sq.*
[2] Charles New, *Life, Wanderings, and Labours in Eastern Africa*, p. 432. Cp. *ib.* pp. 400, 402. For the demons on Mt. Kilimanjaro, see also Krapf, *Travels, Researches* etc. *in Eastern Africa*, p. 192.
[3] Pierre Bouche, *La Côte des Esclaves et le Dahomey*, p. 133.

the natives a certain sum, which is spent in the sacrifice of animals (buffaloes or pigs) to the spirits of the land and water, in order to reconcile them to the presence of the strangers, and to induce them not to withdraw their favour from the people of the land, but to bless the rice-harvest, etc.[1] The men of a certain district in Borneo, fearing to look upon a European traveller lest he should make them ill, warned their wives and children not to go near him. These who could not restrain their curiosity killed fowls to appease the evil spirits and smeared themselves with the blood.[2] In Laos before a stranger can be accorded hospitality the master of the house must offer sacrifice to the ancestral spirits; otherwise the spirits would be offended and would send disease on the inmates.[3] In the Mentawej Islands when a stranger enters a house where there are children, the father or other member of the family takes the ornament which the children wear in their hair and hands it to the stranger, who holds it in his hands for a while and then gives it back to him. This is thought to protect the children from the evil effect which the sight of a stranger might have upon them.[4] At Shepherd's Isle Captain Moresby had to be disenchanted before he was allowed to land his boat's crew. When he leaped ashore a devil-man seized his right hand and waved a bunch of palm leaves over the captain's head. Then " he placed the leaves in my left hand, putting a small green twig into his mouth, still holding me fast, and then, as if with great effort, drew the twig from his mouth—this was extracting the evil

[1] C. A. L. M. Schwaner, *Borneo*, ii. 77.
[2] *Ib.* ii. 167.

[3] E. Aymonier, *Notes sur le Laos*, p. 196.
[4] Rosenberg, *Der Malayische Archipel*, p. 198.

spirit—after which he blew violently, as if to speed
it away. I now held a twig between my teeth, and
he went through the same process." Then the two
raced round a couple of sticks fixed in the ground
and bent to an angle at the top, which had leaves tied
to it. After some more ceremonies the devil-man
concluded by leaping to the level of Captain Moresby's
shoulders (his hands resting on the captain's shoulders)
several times, " as if to show that he had conquered
the devil, and was now trampling him into the earth." [1]
North American Indians " have an idea that strangers,
particularly white strangers, are ofttimes accompanied
by evil spirits. Of these they have great dread, as
creating and delighting in mischief. One of the duties
of the medicine chief is to exorcise these spirits.
I have sometimes ridden into or through a camp
where I was unknown or unexpected, to be confronted
by a tall, half-naked savage, standing in the middle
of the circle of lodges, and yelling in a sing-song,
nasal tone, a string of unintelligible words." [2] When
Crevaux was travelling in South America he entered
a village of the Apalai Indians. A few moments after
his arrival some of the Indians brought him a number
of large black ants, of a species whose bite is painful, fastened on palm leaves. Then all the people
of the village, without distinction of age or sex,
presented themselves to him, and he had to sting
them all with the ants on their faces, thighs, etc.
Sometimes when he applied the ants too tenderly they
called out " More! more!" and were not satisfied till
their skin was thickly studded with tiny swellings like
what might have been produced by whipping them

---

[1] Capt. John Moresby, *Discoveries and Surveys in New Guinea*, p. 102 *sq.*   [2] R. I. Dodge, *Our Wild Indians* (Hartford, Conn. ; 1886), p. 119.

with nettles.[1] The object of this ceremony is made plain by the custom observed in Amboina and Uliase of sprinkling sick people with pungent spices, such as ginger and cloves, chewed fine, in order by the prickling sensation to drive away the demon of disease which may be clinging to their persons.[2] With a similar intention some of the natives of Borneo and Celebes sprinkle rice upon the head or body of a person supposed to be infested by dangerous spirits; a fowl is then brought, which, by picking up the rice from the person's head or body, removes along with it the spirit or ghost which is clinging like a burr to his skin. This is done, for example, to persons who have attended a funeral, and who may therefore be supposed to be infested by the ghost of the deceased.[3] Similarly Basutos, who have carried a corpse to the grave, have their hands scratched with a knife from the tip of the thumb to the tip of the forefinger, and magic stuff is rubbed into the wound,[4] for the purpose, no doubt, of removing the ghost which may be adhering to their skin. The people of Nias carefully scrub and scour the weapons and clothes which they buy, in order to efface all connection between the things and the persons from whom they bought them.[5] It is probable that the same dread of strangers, rather than any desire to do them honour, is the motive of certain ceremonies which are sometimes observed at their reception, but of which the intention is not directly

[1] J. Crevaux, *Voyages dans l'Amérique du Sud*, p. 300.

[2] Riedel, *De sluik-en kroesharige rassen tusschen Selebes en Papua*, p. 78.

[3] Perelaer, *Ethnographische Beschrijving der Dajaks*, pp. 44, 54, 252; Matthes, *Bijdragen tot de Ethnologie van Zuid-Celebes*, p. 49.

[4] H. Grützner, "Ueber die Gebräuche der Basutho," in *Verhandl. d. Berlin. Gesell. f. Anthropologie*, etc. 1877, p. 84 *sq.*

[5] Nieuwenhuisen en Rosenberg, "Verslag omtrent het eiland Nias," in *Verhandel. v. h. Batav. Genootsch. v. Kunsten en Wetenschappen*, xxx. 26.

stated. In Afghanistan and in some parts of Persia the traveller, before he enters a village, is frequently received with a sacrifice of animal life or food, or of fire and incense. The recent Afghan Boundary Mission, in passing by villages in Afghanistan, was often met with fire and incense.[1] Sometimes a tray of lighted embers is thrown under the hoofs of the traveller's horse, with the words, "You are welcome."[2] On entering a village in Central Africa Emin Pasha was received with the sacrifice of two goats; their blood was sprinkled on the path and the chief stepped over the blood to greet Emin.[3] Amongst the Eskimos of Cumberland Inlet, when a stranger arrives at an encampment, the sorcerer goes out to meet him. The stranger folds his arms and inclines his head to one side, so as to expose his cheek, upon which the sorcerer deals a terrible blow, sometimes felling him to the ground. Next the sorcerer in his turn presents his cheek and receives a buffet from the stranger. Then they kiss each other, the ceremony is over, and the stranger is hospitably received by all.[4] Sometimes the dread of strangers and their magic is too great to allow of their reception on any terms. Thus when Speke arrived at a certain village the natives shut their doors against him, "because they had never before seen a white man nor the tin boxes that the men were carrying : 'Who knows,' they said, 'but that these very boxes are the plundering Watuta transformed and come to kill us? You cannot be admitted.' No

[1] *Journal of the Anthropological Society of Bombay*, i. 35.

[2] E. O'Donovan, *The Merv Oasis* (London, 1882), ii. 58.

[3] *Emin Pasha in Central Africa*, being a Collection of his Letters and Journals (London, 1888), p. 107.

[4] *Narrative of the Second Arctic Expedition made by Charles F. Hall.* Edited by Prof. J. G. Nourse, U.S.N. (Washington, 1879), p. 269 *note*.

persuasion could avail with them, and the party had to proceed to the next village."[1]

The fear thus entertained of alien visiters is often mutual. Entering a strange land, the savage feels that he is treading enchanted ground, and he takes steps to guard against the demons that haunt it and the magical arts of its inhabitants. Thus on going to a strange land the Maoris performed certain ceremonies to make it *noa* (common), lest it might have been previously *tapu* (sacred).[2] When Baron Miklucho-Maclay was approaching a village on the Maclay Coast of New Guinea, one of the natives who accompanied him broke a branch from a tree and going aside whispered to it for a while; then going up to each member of the party, one after another, he spat something upon his back and gave him some blows with the branch. Lastly, he went into the forest and buried the branch under withered leaves in the thickest part of the jungle. This ceremony was believed to protect the party against all treachery and danger in the village they were approaching.[3] The idea probably was that the malignant influences were drawn off from the persons into the branch and buried with it in the depths of the forest. In Australia, when a strange tribe has been invited into a district and is approaching the encampment of the tribe which owns the land, "the strangers carry lighted bark or burning sticks in their hands, for the purpose, they say, of clearing and purifying the air."[4] So when two Greek armies were

---

[1] J. A. Grant, *A Walk across Africa*, p. 104 *sq.*

[2] E. Shortland, *Traditions and Superstitions of the New Zealanders*, p. 103.

[3] N. von Miklucho-Maclay, "Eth-

nologische Bemerkungen über die Papuas der Maclay - Küste in Neu-Guinea," in *Natuurkundig Tijdschrift voor Nederlandsch Indie*, xxxvi. 317 *sq.*

[4] Brough Smyth, *Aborigines of Victoria*, i. 134.

advancing to the onset, sacred men used to march in front of each, bearing lighted torches, which they flung into the space between the hosts and then retired unmolested.[1]

Again, it is thought that a man who has been on a journey may have contracted some magic evil from the strangers with whom he has been brought into contact. Hence on returning home, before he is readmitted to the society of his tribe and friends, he has to undergo certain purificatory ceremonies. Thus the Bechuanas "cleanse or purify themselves after journeys by shaving their heads, etc., lest they should have contracted from strangers some evil by witchcraft or sorcery."[2] In some parts of Western Africa when a man returns home after a long absence, before he is allowed to visit his wife, he must wash his person with a particular fluid, and receive from the sorcerer a certain mark on his forehead, in order to counteract any magic spell which a stranger woman may have cast on him in his absence, and which might be communicated through him to the women of his village.[3] Two Hindoo ambassadors, who had been sent to England by a native prince and had returned to India, were considered to have so polluted themselves by contact with strangers that nothing but being born again could restore them to purity. "For the purpose of regeneration it is directed to make an image of pure gold of the female power of nature, in the shape either of a woman or of a cow. In this statue the person to be regenerated is enclosed, and dragged through the

---

[1] Scholiast on Euripides, *Phoeniss.* 1377. These men were sacred to the war-god (Ares), and were always spared in battle.

[2] John Campbell, *Travels in South Africa, being a Narrative of a Second Journey in the Interior of that Country,* ii. 205.

[3] Ladislaus Magyar, *Reisen in Süd-Afrika,* p. 203.

usual channel.   As a statue of pure gold and of proper
dimensions would be too expensive, it is sufficient to
make an image of the sacred *Yoni,* through which the
person to be regenerated is to pass." Such an image
of pure gold was made at the prince's command, and
his ambassadors were born again by being dragged
through it.[1]   When Damaras return home after a long
absence, they are given a small portion of the fat of
particular animals which is supposed to possess certain
virtues.[2]   In some of the Moluccas, when a brother or
young blood-relation returns from a long journey, a
young girl awaits him at the door with a *caladi* leaf in
her hand and water in the leaf.   She throws the water
over his face and bids him welcome.[3]   The natives of
Savage Island (South Pacific) invariably killed, not
only all strangers in distress who were drifted to their
shores, but also any of their own people who had gone
away in a ship and returned home.   This was done
out of dread of disease.   Long after they began to
venture out to ships they would not immediately use
the things they obtained from them, but hung them up
in quarantine for weeks in the bush.[4]

When precautions like these are taken on behalf
of the people in general against the malignant influence
supposed to be exercised by strangers, we shall not be
surprised to find that special measures are adopted to
protect the king from the same insidious danger.   In
the middle ages the envoys who visited a Tartar Khan
were obliged to pass between two fires before they
were admitted to his presence, and the gifts they
brought were also carried between the fires.   The

[1] *Asiatick Researches,* vi. 535 *sq.* ed.
4to (p. 537 *sq.* ed. 8vo).
[2] C. J. Andersson, *Lake Ngami,* p.
223.

[3] François Valentyn, *Oud en nieuw
Oost-Indiën,* iii. 16.
[4] Turner, *Samoa,* p. 305 *sq.*

reason assigned for the custom was that the fire purged away any magic influence which the strangers might mean to exercise over the Khan.[1] When subject chiefs come with their retinues to visit Kalamba (the most powerful chief of the Bashilange in the Congo Basin) for the first time or after being rebellious, they have to bathe, men and women together, in two brooks on two successive days, passing the nights in the open air in the market-place. After the second bath they proceed, entirely naked, to the house of Kalamba, who makes a long white mark on the breast and forehead of each of them. Then they return to the market-place and dress, after which they undergo the pepper ordeal. Pepper is dropped into the eyes of each of them, and while this is being done the sufferer has to make a confession of all his sins, to answer all questions that may be put to him, and to take certain vows. This ends the ceremony, and the strangers are now free to take up their quarters in the town for as long as they choose to remain.[2] At Kilema, in Eastern Africa, when a stranger arrives, a medicine is made out of a certain plant or a tree fetched from a distance, mixed with the blood of a sheep or goat. With this mixture the stranger is besmeared or besprinkled before he is admitted to the presence of the king.[3] The King of Monomotapa (South-East Africa) might not wear any foreign stuffs for fear of their being poisoned.[4] The

[1] De Plano Carpini, *Historia Mongolorum quos nos Tartaros appellamus*, ed. D'Avezac (Paris, 1838), cap. iii. § iii. p. 627, cap. ult. § i. x. p. 744, and Appendix, p. 775 : "Travels of William de Rubriquis into Tartary and China," in Pinkerton's *Voyages and Travels*, vii. 82 *sq.*

[2] Paul Pogge, "Bericht über die Station Mukenge," in *Mittheilungen der Afrikanischen Gesellschaft in Deutschland*, iv. (1883-1885) 182 *sq.*

[3] J. L. Krapf, *Travels, Researches, and Missionary Labours during an Eighteen Years' Residence in Eastern Africa*, p. 252 *sq.*

[4] Dapper, *Description de l'Afrique*, p. 391.

King of Kakongo (West Africa) might not possess or even touch European goods, except metals, arms, and articles made of wood and ivory. Persons wearing foreign stuffs were very careful to keep at a distance from his person, lest they should touch him.[1] The King of Loango might not look upon the house of a white man.[2]

In the opinion of savages the acts of eating and drinking are attended with special danger ; for at these times the soul may escape from the mouth, or be extracted by the magic arts of an enemy present. Precautions are therefore taken to guard against these dangers. Thus of the Battas of Sumatra it is said that " since the soul can leave the body, they always take care to prevent their soul from straying on occasions when they have most need of it. But it is only possible to prevent the soul from straying when one is in the house. At feasts one may find the whole house shut up, in order that the soul (*tondi*) may stay and enjoy the good things set before it."[3] In Fiji persons who suspected others of plotting against them avoided eating in their presence, or were careful to leave no fragment of food behind.[4] The Zafimanelo in Madagascar lock their doors when they eat, and hardly any one ever sees them eating.[5] The Warua will not allow any one to see them eating and drinking, being doubly particular that no person of the opposite

[1] Proyart, "History of Loango, Kakongo," etc., in Pinkerton's *Voyages and Travels*, xvi. 583 ; Dapper, *op. cit.* p. 340 ; J. Ogilby, *Africa* (London, 1670), p. 521. Cp. Bastian, *Die deutsche Expedition an der Loango-Küste*, i. 288.

[2] Bastian, *op. cit.* i. 268 *sq.*

[3] J. B. Neumann, "Het Pane-en Bila-Stroomgebied op het eiland Sumatra," in *Tijdschrift van het Nederlandsch Aardrijkskundig Genootschap*, ii. de Serie, dl. iii., Afdeeling : meer uitgebreide artikelen, No. 2, p. 300.

[4] Th. Williams, *Fiji and the Fijians*, i. 249.

[5] J. Richardson, "Tanala Customs, Superstitions and Beliefs," in *The Antananarivo Annual and Madagascar Magazine*, No. ii. p. 219.

sex shall see them doing so. " I had to pay a man to let me see him drink ; I could not make a man let a woman see him drink." When offered a drink of *pombe* they often ask that a cloth may be held up to hide them whilst drinking. Further, each man and woman must cook for themselves ; each person must have his own fire.[1] If these are the ordinary precautions taken by common people, the precautions taken by kings are extraordinary. The King of Loango may not be seen eating or drinking by man or beast under pain of death. A favourite dog having broken into the room where the king was dining, the king ordered it to be killed on the spot. Once the king's own son, a boy of twelve years old, inadvertently saw the king drink. Immediately the king ordered him to be finely apparelled and feasted, after which he commanded him to be cut in quarters, and carried about the city with a proclamation that he had seen the king drink. " When the king has a mind to drink, he has a cup of wine brought ; he that brings it has a bell in his hand, and as soon as he has delivered the cup to the king he turns his face from him and rings the bell, on which all present fall down with their faces to the ground, and continue so till the king has drank. . . . His eating is much in the same style, for which he has a house on purpose, where his victuals are set upon a bensa or table : which he goes to and shuts the door ; when he has done, he knocks and comes out. So that none ever see the king eat or drink. For it is believed that if any one should, the king shall immediately die." [2] The rules

---

[1] Lieut. Cameron, *Across Africa*, ii. 71 (ed. 1877) ; *id.*, in *Journ. Anthrop. Inst.* vi. 173.

[2] " Adventures of Andrew Battel," in Pinkerton's *Voyages and Travels*,

xvi. 330 ; Dapper, *Description de l'Afrique*, p. 330 ; Bastian, *Die deutsche Expedition an der Loango-Küste*, i. 262 *sq.*; R. F. Burton, *Abeokuta and the Cameroons Mountains*, i. 147.

observed by the neighbouring King of Kakongo were similar ; it was thought that the king would die if any of his subjects were to see him drink.[1]   It is a capital offence to see the King of Dahomey at his meals. When he drinks in public, as he does on extraordinary occasions, he hides himself behind a curtain, or hand-kerchiefs are held up round his head, and all the people throw themselves with their faces to the earth.[2]   Any one who saw the Muato Jamwo (a great potentate in the Congo Basin) eating or drinking would certainly be put to death.[3]   When the King of Tonga ate all the people turned their backs to him.[4]   In the palace of the Persian kings there were two dining-rooms opposite each other ; in one of them the king dined, in the other his guests.   He could see them through a curtain on the door, but they could not see him.   Generally the king took his meals alone ; but sometimes his wife or some of his sons dined with him.[5]

In these cases, however, the intention may perhaps be to hinder evil influences from entering the body rather than to prevent the escape of the soul.   To the former rather than to the latter motive is to be ascribed the custom observed by some African sultans of veiling their faces.   The Sultan of Darfur wraps up his face with a piece of white muslin, which goes round his head several times, covering his mouth and nose first, and then his forehead, so that only his eyes are visible.   The same custom of veiling the face as a mark of sovereignty is said to be observed in other

[1] Proyart's " History of Loango, Kakongo," etc., in Pinkerton's *Voyages and Travels*, xvi. 584.

[2] J. L. Wilson, *West Afrika*, p. 148 (German trans.) ; John Duncan, *Travels in Western Africa*, i. 222. Cp. W. W. Reade, *Savage Africa*, p. 543.

[3] Paul Pogge, *Im Reiche des Muato Jamwo* (Berlin, 1880), p. 231.

[4] Capt. James Cook, *Voyages*, v. 374 (ed. 1809).

[5] Heraclides Cumanus in Athenaeus, iv. 145 B-D.

parts of Central Africa.[1] The Sultan of Wadai always speaks from behind a curtain; no one sees his face except his intimates and a few favoured persons.[2] Amongst the Touaregs of the Sahara all the men (but not the women) keep the lower part of their face, especially the mouth, veiled constantly; the veil is never put off, not even in eating or sleeping.[3] In Samoa a man whose family god was the turtle might not eat a turtle, and if he helped a neighbour to cut up and cook one he had to wear a bandage tied over his mouth, lest an embryo turtle should slip down his throat, grow up, and be his death.[4] In West Timor a speaker holds his right hand before his mouth in speaking lest a demon should enter his body, and lest the person with whom he converses should harm the speaker's soul by magic.[5] In New South Wales for some time after his initiation into the tribal mysteries, a young blackfellow (whose soul at this time is in a critical state) must always cover his mouth with a rug when a woman is present.[6] Popular expressions in the language of civilised peoples, such as to have one's heart in one's mouth, show how natural is the idea that the life or soul may escape by the mouth or nostrils.[7]

[1] Mohammed Ibn-Omar el Tounsy, *Voyage au Darfour* (Paris, 1845), p. 203; *Travels of an Arab Merchant* [Mohammed Ibn-Omar el Tounsy] *in Soudan*, abridged from the French (of Perron) by Bayle St. John, p. 91 *sq.*

[2] Mohammed Ibn-Omar el Tounsy, *Voyage au Ouadây* (Paris, 1851), p. 375.

[3] H. Duveyrier, *Exploration du Sahara. Les Touareg du Nord*, p. 391 *sq.*; Reclus, *Nouvelle Géographie Universelle*, xi. 838 *sq.*; James Richardson, *Travels in the Great Desert of Sahara*, ii. 208. Amongst the Arabs men sometimes veiled their faces. Wellhausen, *Reste Arabischen Heidentumes*, p. 146.

[4] Turner, *Samoa*, p. 67 *sq.*

[5] Riedel, "Die Landschaft Dawan oder West-Timor," in *Deutsche Geographische Blätter*, x. 230.

[6] A. W. Howitt, "On some Australian Ceremonies of Initiation," in *Journ. Anthrop. Inst.* xiii. 456.

[7] Compare μόνον οὐκ ἐπὶ τοῖς χείλεσι τὰς ψυχὰς ἔχοντας Dio Chrysostomus, *Orat.* xxxii. i. 417, ed. Dindorf; *mihi anima in naso esse, stabam tanquam mortuus*, Petronius, *Sat.* 62; *in primis labris animam habere*, Seneca, *Natur Quaest.* iii. praef. 16.

By an extension of the like precaution kings are sometimes forbidden ever to leave their palaces ; or, if they are allowed to do so, their subjects are forbidden to see them abroad. We have seen that the priestly king at Shark Point, West Africa, may never quit his house or even his chair, in which he is obliged to sleep sitting.[1] After his coronation the King of Loango is confined to his palace, which he may not leave.[2] The King of Ibo (West Africa) "does not step out of his house into the town unless a human sacrifice is made to propitiate the gods : on this account he never goes out beyond the precincts of his premises."[3] The kings of Aethiopia were worshipped as gods, but were mostly kept shut up in their palaces.[4] The kings of Sabaea (Sheba), the spice country of Arabia, were not allowed to go out of their palaces ; if they did so, the mob stoned them to death.[5] But at the top of the palace there was a window with a chain attached to it. If any man deemed he had suffered wrong, he pulled the chain, and the king perceived him and called him in and gave judgment.[6] So to this day the kings of Corea, whose persons are sacred and receive "honours almost divine," are shut up in their palace from the age of twelve or fifteen ; and if a suitor wishes to obtain justice of the king he sometimes lights a great bonfire on a mountain facing the palace; the king sees the fire and informs himself of the case.[7] The

---

[1] See above, p. 112.
[2] Bastian, *Die Loango-Küste*, i. 263. However, a case is recorded in which he marched out to war (*ib.* i. 268 *sq.*)
[3] S Crowther and J. C. Taylor, *The Gospel on the Banks of the Niger*, p. 433. On p. 379 mention is made of the king's "annual appearance to the public," but this may have taken place within "the precincts of his premises."

[4] Strabo, xvii. 2, 2, σέβονται δ' ὡς θεοὺς τοὺς βασιλέας, κατακλείστους ὄντας καὶ οἰκουροὺς τὸ πλέον.
[5] Strabo, xvi. 4, 19 ; Diodorus Siculus, iii. 47.
[6] Heraclides Cumanus in Athenaeus, 517 B.C.
[7] Ch. Dallet, *Histoire de l'Église de Corée* (Paris, 1874), i. xxiv - xxvi. The king sometimes, though rarely,

King of Tonquin was permitted to appear abroad twice or thrice a year for the performance of certain religious ceremonies; but the people were not allowed to look at him. The day before he came forth notice was given to all the inhabitants of the city and country to keep from the way the king was to go; the women were obliged to remain in their houses and durst not show themselves under pain of death, a penalty which was carried out on the spot if any one disobeyed the order, even through ignorance. Thus the king was invisible to all but his troops and the officers of his suite.[1] In Mandalay a stout lattice-paling, six feet high and carefully kept in repair, lined every street in the walled city and all those in the suburbs through which the king was likely at any time to pass. Behind this paling, which stood two feet or so from the houses, all the people had to stay when the king or any of the queens went out. Any one who was caught outside it by the beadles after the procession had started was severely handled, and might think himself lucky if he got off with a beating. No one was supposed to look through the holes in the lattice-work, which were besides partly stopped up with flowering shrubs.[2]

Again, magic mischief may be wrought upon a man through the remains of the food he has partaken of, or the dishes out of which he has eaten. Thus the Narrinyeri in South Australia think that if a man eats of the sacred animal (totem) of his tribe, and an enemy gets hold of a portion of the flesh, the latter

---

leaves his palace. When he does so, notice is given beforehand to the people. All doors must be shut and each householder must kneel before his threshold with a broom and a dust-pan in his hand. All windows, especially the upper ones, must be sealed with slips of paper, lest some one should look down upon the king. W. E. Griffis, *Corea, the Hermit Nation*, p. 222.

[1] Richard, "History of Tonquin," in Pinkerton's *Voyages and Travels*, ix. 746.

[2] Shway Yoe, *The Burman*, i. 308 *sq.*

can make it grow in the inside of the eater, and so cause his death. Therefore when a man eats of his totem he is careful to eat it all or else to conceal or destroy the remains.[1] In Tana, one of the New Hebrides, people bury or throw into the sea the leavings of their food, lest these should fall into the hands of the disease - makers. For if a disease-maker finds the remnants of a meal, say the skin of a banana, he picks it up and burns it slowly in the fire. As it burns the person who ate the banana falls ill and sends to the disease-maker, offering him presents if he will stop burning the banana skin.[2] Hence no one may touch the food which the King of Loango leaves upon his plate; it is buried in a hole in the ground. And no one may drink out of the king's vessel.[3] Similarly no man may drink out of the same cup or glass with the King of Fida (in Guinea); " he hath always one kept particularly for himself; and that which hath but once touched another's lips he never uses more, though it be made of metal that may be cleansed by fire."[4] Amongst the Alfoers of Celebes there is a priest called the *Leleen*, whose duty appears to be to make the rice grow. His functions begin about a month before the rice is sown, and end after the crop is housed. During this time he has to observe certain taboos; amongst others he may not eat or drink with any one else, and he may drink out of no vessel but his own.[5]

We have seen that the Mikado's food was cooked

---

[1] *Native Tribes of South Australia,* p. 63 ; Taplin, " Notes on the mixed races of Australia," in *Journ. Anthrop. Inst.* iv. 53.

[2] Turner, *Samoa,* p. 320 *sq.*

[3] Dapper, *Description de l'Afrique,* p. 330.

[4] Bosman's "Guinea," in Pinkerton's *Voyages and Travels,* xvi. 487.

[5] P. N. Wilken, " Bijdragen tot de kennis van de zeden en gewoonten der Alfoeren in de Minahassa," in *Mededeelingen van wege het Nederlandsche Zendelinggenootschap,* xi. (1863) 126.

every day in new pots and. served up in new dishes ;
both pots and dishes were of common clay, in order
that they might be broken or laid aside after they had
been once used. They were generally broken, for it
was believed that if any one else ate his food out of
these sacred dishes his mouth and throat would become swollen and inflamed. The same ill effect was
thought to be experienced by any one who should
wear the Mikado's clothes without his leave ; he would
have swellings and pains all over his body.[1] In the
evil effects thus supposed to follow upon the use of
the Mikado's vessels or clothes we see that other side
of the divine king's or god-man's character to which
attention has been already called. The divine person
is a source of danger as well as of blessing ; he must
not only be guarded, he must also be guarded against.
His sacred organism, so delicate that a touch may
disorder it, is also electrically charged with a powerful
spiritual force which may discharge itself with fatal
effect on whatever comes in contact with it. Hence
the isolation of the man-god is quite as necessary for
the safety of others as for his own. His divinity is a
fire, which, under proper restraints, confers endless
blessings, but, if rashly touched or allowed to break
bounds, burns and destroys what it touches.
Hence the disastrous effects supposed to attend a
breach of taboo ; the offender has thrust his hand into
the divine fire, which shrivels up and consumes him
on the spot. To take an example from the taboo we
are considering. It happened that a New Zealand
chief of high rank and great sanctity had left the
remains of his dinner by the wayside. A slave, a

---

[1] Kaempfer's " History of Japan," in Pinkerton's *Voyages and Travels*, vii. 717.

stout, hungry fellow, coming up after the chief had gone, saw the unfinished dinner, and ate it up without asking questions. Hardly had he finished when he was informed by a horror-stricken spectator that the food of which he had eaten was the chief's. "I knew the unfortunate delinquent well. He was remarkable for courage, and had signalised himself in the wars of the tribe. . . . No sooner did he hear the fatal news than he was seized by the most extraordinary convulsions and cramp in the stomach, which never ceased till he died, about sundown the same day. He was a strong man, in the prime of life, and if any pakeha [European] freethinker should have said he was not killed by the *tapu* [taboo] of the chief, which had been communicated to the food by contact, he would have been listened to with feelings of contempt for his ignorance and inability to understand plain and direct evidence." [1] This is not a solitary case. A Maori woman having eaten of some fruit, and being afterwards told that the fruit had being taken from a tabooed place, exclaimed that the spirit of the chief whose sanctity had been thus profaned would kill her. This was in the afternoon, and next day by twelve o'clock she was dead. [2] An observer who knows the Maoris well, says, "Tapu [taboo] is an awful weapon. I have seen a strong young man die the same day he was tapued; the victims die under it as though their strength ran out as water." [3] A Maori chief's tinder-box was once the means of killing several persons; for having been lost by him, and found by some men who used it to

---

[1] *Old New Zealand*, by a Pakeha Maori (London, 1884), p. 96 *sq.*

[2] W. Brown, *New Zealand and its Aborigines* (London, 1845), p. 76.

For more examples of the same kind see *ib.* p. 77 *sq.*

[3] E. Tregear, "The Maoris of New Zealand," in *Journ. Anthrop. Inst.* xix. 100.

light their pipes, they died of fright on learning to
whom it had belonged. So too the garments of a high
New Zealand chief will kill any one else who wears
them. A chief was observed by a missionary to
throw down a precipice a blanket which he found too
heavy to carry. Being asked by the missionary why
he did not leave it on a tree for the use of a future
traveller, the chief replied that "it was the fear of its
being taken by another which caused him to throw
it where he did, for if it were worn, his tapu" (*i.e.*
his spiritual power communicated by contact to the
blanket and through the blanket to the man) "would
kill the person." [1]

No wonder therefore that the savage should rank
these human divinities amongst what he regards as the
dangerous classes, and should impose exactly the same
restraints upon the one as upon the other. For instance, those who have defiled themselves by touching
a dead body are regarded by the Maoris as in a
very dangerous state, and are sedulously shunned and
isolated. But the taboos observed by and towards
these defiled persons (*e.g.* they may not touch food
with their hands, and the vessels used by them may
not be used by other people) are identical with those
observed by and towards sacred chiefs.[2] And, in
general, the prohibition to use the dress, vessels, etc.,
of certain persons and the effects supposed to follow
an infraction of the rule are exactly the same whether
the persons to whom the things belong are sacred or
what we might call unclean and polluted. As the
garments which have been touched by a sacred chief

---

[1] R. Taylor, *Te Ika a Maui: or,
New Zealand and its Inhabitants,*[2]
p. 164.

[2] A. S. Thomson, *The Story of New
Zealand,* i. 101 *sqq.*; *Old New Zealand,*
by a Pakeha Maori, pp. 94, 104 *sqq.*

kill those who handle them, so do the things which have been touched by a menstruous woman. An Australian blackfellow, who discovered that his wife had lain on his blanket at her menstrual period, killed her and died of terror himself within a fortnight.[1] Hence Australian women at these times are forbidden under pain of death to touch anything that men use. They are also secluded at child-birth, and all vessels used by them during their seclusion are burned.[2] Amongst some of the Indians of North America also women at menstruation are forbidden to touch men's utensils, which would be so defiled by their touch that their subsequent use would be attended by certain mischief or misfortune.[3] Amongst the Eskimo of Alaska no one will willingly drink out of the same cup or eat out of the same dish that has been used by a woman at her confinement until it has been purified by certain incantations.[4] Amongst some of the Tinneh Indians of North America the dishes out of which girls eat during their seclusion at puberty "are used by no other person, and wholly devoted to their own use."[5] Again amongst some Indian tribes of North America men who have slain enemies are considered to be in a state of uncleanness, and will not eat or drink out of any dish or smoke out of any pipe but their own for a considerable time after the slaughter, and no one will willingly use their dishes or pipes. They live in a kind of seclusion during this time, at the end of which all

---

[1] *Journ. Anthrop. Inst.* ix. 458.

[2] W. Ridley, "Report on Australian Languages and Traditions," in *Journ. Anthrop. Inst.* ii. 268.

[3] Alexander Mackenzie, *Voyages from Montreal through the Continent of North America*, cxxiii.

[4] *Report of the International Polar Expedition to Point Barrow, Alaska* (Washington, 1885), p. 46.

[5] "Customs of the New Caledonian Women," in *Journ. Anthrop. Inst.* vii. 206.

the dishes and pipes used by them during their seclusion are burned.[1] Amongst the Kafirs, boys at circumcision live secluded in a special hut, and when they are healed all the vessels which they had used during their seclusion and the boyish mantles which they had hitherto worn are burned together with the hut.[2] When a young Indian brave is out on the war-path for the first time the vessels he eats and drinks out of must be touched by no one else.[3]

Thus the rules of ceremonial purity observed by divine kings, chiefs, and priests, by homicides, women at child-birth, and so on, are in some respects alike. To us these different classes of persons appear to differ totally in character and condition; some of them we should call holy, others we might pronounce unclean and polluted. But the savage makes no such moral distinction between them; the conceptions of holiness and pollution are not yet differentiated in his mind. To him the common feature of all these persons is that they are dangerous and in danger, and the danger in which they stand and to which they expose others is what we should call spiritual or supernatural, that is, imaginary. The danger, however, is not less real because it is imaginary; imagination acts upon man as really as does gravitation, and may kill him as certainly as a dose of prussic acid. To seclude these persons from the rest of the world so that the dreaded spiritual danger shall neither reach them, nor spread from them, is the object of the taboos which they have to observe.

[1] S. Hearne, *A Journey from Prince of Wales's Fort in Hudson's Bay to the Northern Ocean*, p. 204 *sqq.*
[2] L. Alberti, *De Kaffers* (Amsterdam, 1810), p. 76 *sq.* ; H. Lichten-
stein, *Reisen im südlichen Afrika*, i. 427.
[3] *Narrative of the Captivity and Adventures of John Tanner* (London, 1830), p. 122.

These taboos act, so to say, as electrical insulators to preserve the spiritual force with which these persons are charged from suffering or inflicting harm by contact with the outer world.[1]

No one was allowed to touch the body of the King or Queen of Tahiti;[2] and no one may touch the King of Cambodia, for any purpose whatever, without his express command. In July 1874 the king was thrown from his carriage and lay insensible on the ground, but not one of his suite dared to touch him; a European coming to the spot carried the injured monarch to his palace.[3] No one may touch the King of Corea; and if he deigns to touch a subject, the spot touched becomes sacred, and the person thus honoured must wear a visible mark (generally a cord of red silk) for the rest of his life. Above all, no iron may touch the king's body. In 1800 King Tieng-tsong-tai-oang died of a tumour in the back, no one dreaming of employing the lancet, which would probably have saved his life. It is said that one king suffered terribly from an abscess in the lip, till his physician called in a jester, whose antics made the king laugh heartily, and so the abscess burst.[4] Roman and Sabine priests might not be shaved with iron but only with bronze razors or shears;[5] and whenever an iron graving-tool was brought into the sacred grove of the Arval Brothers at Rome for the purpose of cutting an inscription in stone, an expiatory sacrifice of a lamb and a pig was offered, which was repeated when the graving-tool was removed from the

---

[1] On the nature of taboo, see especially W. Robertson Smith, *Religion of the Semites*, i. 142 *sqq.* 427 *sqq.*

[2] Ellis, *Polynesian Researches*, iii. 102.

[3] J. Moura, *Le Royaume du Cambodge*, i. 226.

[4] Ch. Dallet, *Histoire de l'Église de Corée,* i. xxiv. *sq.*; Griffis, *Corea, the Hermit Nation*, p. 219.

[5] Macrobius, *Sat.* v. 19, 13; Servius on Virgil, *Aen.* i. 448; Joannes Lydus, *De mens.* i. 31.

grove.[1] In Crete sacrifices were offered to Menedemus without the use of iron, because, it was said,
Menedemus had been killed by an iron weapon in the
Trojan war.[2] The Archon of Plataeae might not touch
iron ; but once a year, at the annual commemoration
of the men who fell at the battle of Plataeae, he was
allowed to carry a sword wherewith to sacrifice a bull.[3]
To this day a Hottentot priest never uses an iron
knife, but always a sharp splint of quartz in sacrificing
an animal or circumcising a lad.[4] Amongst the Moquis
of Arizona stone knives, hatchets, etc., have passed
out of common use, but are retained in religious ceremonies.[5] Negroes of the Gold Coast remove all iron
or steel from their person when they consult their
fetish.[6] The men who made the need-fire in Scotland
had to divest themselves of all metal.[7] In making the
clavie (a kind of Yule-tide fire-wheel) at Burghead, no
hammer may be used ; the hammering must be done
with a stone.[8] Amongst the Jews no iron tool was
used in building the temple at Jerusalem or in making
an altar.[9] The old wooden bridge (*Pons Sublicius*) at
Rome, which was considered sacred, was made and
had to be kept in repair without the use of iron or
bronze.[10] It was expressly provided by law that the
temple of Jupiter Liber at Furfo might be repaired

---

[1] *Acta Fratrum Arvalium*, ed. Henzen, pp. 128-135 ; Marquardt, *Römische
Staatsverwaltung*, iii.[2](*Das Sacralwesen*),
p. 459 *sq.*
[2] Callimachus, referred to by the Old
Scholiast on Ovid, *Ibis*. See Callimachus, ed. Blomfield, p. 216 ; Lobeck,
Aglaophamus, p. 686.
[3] Plutarch, *Aristides*, 21. This
passage I owe to Mr. W. Wyse.
[4] Theophilus Hahn, *Tsuni - Goam,
the Supreme Being of the Khoi-Khoi*,
p. 22.

[5] J. G. Bourke, *The Snake Dance of
the Moquis of Arizona*, p. 178 *sq.*
[6] C. F. Gordon Cumming, *In the
Hebrides* (ed. 1883), p. 195.
[7] James Logan, *The Scottish Gael*
(ed. Alex. Stewart), ii. 68 *sq.*
[8] C. F. Gordon Cumming, *In the
Hebrides*, p. 226 ; E. J. Guthrie, *Old
Scottish Customs*, p. 223.
[9] 1 Kings vi. 7 ; Exodus xx. 25.
[10] Dionysius Halicarn. *Antiquit.
Roman.* iii. 45, v. 24 ; Plutarch, *Numa*,
9 ; Pliny, *Nat. Hist.* xxxvi. § 100.

with iron tools.[1] The council chamber at Cyzicus was constructed of wood without any iron nails, the beams being so arranged that they could be taken out and replaced.[2] The late Raja Vijyanagram, a member of the Viceroy's Council, and described as one of the most enlightened and estimable of Hindu princes, would not allow iron to be used in the construction of buildings within his territory, believing that its use would inevitably be followed by small-pox and other epidemics.[3]

This superstitious objection to iron perhaps dates from that early time in the history of society when iron was still a novelty, and as such was viewed by many with suspicion and dislike. For everything new is apt to excite the awe and dread of the savage. "It is a curious superstition," says a recent pioneer in Borneo, "this of the Dusuns, to attribute anything —whether good or bad, lucky or unlucky—that happens to them to something novel which has arrived in their country. For instance, my living in Kindram has caused the intensely hot weather we have experienced of late."[4] The first introduction of iron ploughshares into Poland having been followed by a succession of bad harvests, the farmers attributed the badness of the crops to the iron ploughshares, and discarded them for the old wooden ones.[5] The general dislike of innovation, which always makes itself strongly felt in the sphere of religion, is sufficient by itself to

---

[1] *Acta Fratrum Arvalium*, ed. Henzen, p. 132; *Corpus Inscriptionum Latinarum*, i. No. 603.

[2] Pliny, *l.c.*

[3] *Indian Antiquary*, x. (1881) 364.

[4] Frank Hatton, *North Borneo* (1886), p. 233.

[5] Alexand. Guagninus, "De ducatu Samogitiae," in *Respublica sive Status Regni Poloniae, Lituaniae, Prussiae, Livoniae* etc. (Elzevir, 1627), p. 276; Johan. Lasicius, "De diis Samogitarum caeterorumque Sarmatum," in *Respublica*, etc. (*ut supra*), p. 294 (p. 84 ed. Mannhardt, in *Magazin herausgeg. von der Lettisch - Literär. Gesellsch.* bd. xiv.)

account for the superstitious aversion to iron entertained by kings and priests and attributed by them
to the gods; possibly this aversion may have been
intensified in places by some such accidental cause as
the series of bad seasons which cast discredit on iron
ploughshares in Poland. But the disfavour in which
iron is held by the gods and their ministers has another
side. The very fact that iron is deemed obnoxious to
spirits furnishes men with a weapon which may be
turned against the spirits when occasion serves. As
their dislike of iron is supposed to be so great that
they will not approach persons and things protected
by the obnoxious metal, iron may obviously be employed
as a charm for banning ghosts and other dangerous
spirits. And it often is so used. Thus when Scotch
fishermen were at sea, and one of them happened
to take the name of God in vain, the first man who
heard him called out "Cauld airn," at which every
man of the crew grasped the nearest bit of iron and
held it between his hands for a while.[1] In Morocco
iron is considered a great protection against demons;
hence it is usual to place a knife or dagger under
a sick man's pillow.[2] In India "the mourner who
performs the ceremony of putting fire into the dead
person's mouth carries with him a piece of iron: it
may be a key or a knife, or a simple piece of iron, and
during the whole time of his separation (for he is
unclean for a certain time, and no one will either touch
him or eat or drink with him, neither can he change
his clothes[3]) he carries the piece of iron about with

---

[1] E. J. Guthrie, *Old Scottish Customs*,
p. 149; Ch. Rogers, *Social Life in Scotland* (London, 1886), iii. 218.

[2] A. Leared, *Morocco and the Moors*,
p. 273.

[3] The reader may observe how closely
the taboos laid upon mourners resemble
those laid upon kings. From what has
gone before the reason of the resemblance is obvious.

him to keep off the evil spirit. In Calcutta the Bengali
clerks in the Government Offices used to wear a small
key on one of their fingers when they had been chief
mourners."[1] In the north-east of Scotland immediately
after a death had taken place, a piece of iron, such as
a nail or a knitting-wire, used to be stuck into all the
meal, butter, cheese, flesh, and whisky in the house,
"to prevent death from entering them." The neglect
of this precaution is said to have been closely followed
by the corruption of the food and drink; the whisky
has been known to become as white as milk.[2] When
iron is used as a protective charm after a death, as in
these Hindu and Scotch customs, the spirit against
which it is directed is the ghost of the deceased.[3]

There is a priestly king to the north of Zengwih in
Burma, revered by the Sotih as the highest spiritual
and temporal authority, into whose house no weapon
or cutting instrument may be brought.[4] This rule
may perhaps be explained by a custom observed by
various peoples after a death; they refrain from the
use of sharp instruments so long as the ghost of the
deceased is supposed to be near, lest they should
wound it. Thus after a death the Roumanians of
Transylvania are careful not to leave a knife lying
with the sharp edge uppermost as long as the corpse
remains in the house, "or else the soul will be
forced to ride on the blade."[5] For seven days

---

[1] *Panjab Notes and Queries*, iii. No.
282.
[2] Walter Gregor, *The Folk-lore of
the North-East of Scotland*, p. 206.
[3] This is expressly said in *Panjab
Notes and Queries*, iii. No. 846. On
iron as a protective charm see also
Liebrecht, *Gervasius von Tilbury*, p.
99 *sqq.*; *id.*, *Zur Volkskunde*, p. 311;
L. Strackerjan, *Aberglaube und Sagen*

aus dem Herzogthum Oldenburg, § 233;
Wattke, *Der deutsche Volksaberglaube²*, §
414 *sq.*; Tylor, *Primitive Culture*, i. 140;
Mannhardt, *Der Baumkultus*, 132 *note*.
[4] Bastian, *Die Völker des östlichen
Asien*, i. 136.
[5] E. Gerard, *The Land beyond the
Forest*, i. 312; W. Schmidt, *Das Jahr
und seine Tage in Meinung und Brauch
der Romänen Siebenbürgens*, p. 40.

after a death, the corpse being still in the house, the Chinese abstain from the use of knives and needles, and even of chopsticks, eating their food with their fingers.[1] Amongst the Innuit (Eskimos) of Alaska for four days after a death the women in the village do no sewing, and for five days the men do not cut wood with an axe.[2] On the third, sixth, ninth, and fortieth days after the funeral the old Prussians and Lithuanians used to prepare a meal, to which, standing at the door, they invited the soul of the deceased. At these meals they sat silent round the table and used no knives, and the women who served up the food were also without knives. If any morsels fell from the table they were left lying there for the lonely souls that had no living relations or friends to feed them. When the meal was over the priest took a broom and swept the souls out of the house, saying, " Dear souls, ye have eaten and drunk. Go forth, go forth."[3] In cutting the nails and combing the hair of a dead prince in South Celebes only the back of the knife and of the comb may be used.[4] The Germans say that a knife should not be left edge upwards, because God and the spirits dwell there, or because it will cut the face of God and the angels.[5] We can now understand why no cutting instrument may be taken into the house of the Burmese pontiff. Like so many priestly kings, he is probably regarded as divine,

---

[1] J. H. Gray, *China*, i. 288.

[2] W. H. Dall, *Alaska and its Resources*, p. 146; *id.* in *American Naturalist*, xii. 7.

[3] Jo. Meletius, "De religione et sacrificiis veterum Borussorum," in *De Russorum Muscovitarum et Tartarorum religione, sacrificiis, nuptiarum, funerum ritu* (Spires, 1582), p. 263; Hartknoch, *Alt und neues Preussen* (Frankfort and Leipzig, 1684), p. 187 *sq.*

[4] B. F. Matthes, *Bijdragen tot de Ethnologie van Zuid-Celebes*, p. 136.

[5] Tettau und Temme, *Die Volkssagen Ostpreussens, Litthauens und Westpreussens*, p. 285; Grimm, *Deutsche Mythologie*,[4] iii. 454; cp. *id.* pp. 441, 469; Grohmann, *Aberglauben und Gebräuche aus Böhmen und Mähren*, p. 198.

and it is therefore right that his sacred spirit should not be exposed to the risk of being cut or wounded whenever it quits his body to hover invisible in the air or to fly on some distant mission.

We have seen that the Flamen Dialis was forbidden to touch or even name raw flesh.[1] In the Pelew Islands when a raid has been made on a village and a head carried off, the relations of the slain man are tabooed and have to submit to certain observances in order to escape the wrath of his ghost. They are shut up in the house, touch no raw flesh, and chew beetel over which an incantation has been uttered by the exorcist. After this the ghost of the slaughtered man goes away to the enemy's country in pursuit of his murderer.[2] The taboo is probably based on the common belief that the soul or spirit of the animal is in the blood. As tabooed persons are believed to be in a perilous state—for example, the relations of the slain man are liable to the attacks of his indignant ghost—it is especially necessary to isolate them from contact with spirits ; hence the prohibition to touch raw meat. But as usual the taboo is only the special enforcement in particular circumstances of a general rule ; in other words, its observance is particularly enjoined in circumstances which are supposed especially to call for its application, but apart from such special circumstances the prohibition is also observed, though less strictly, as an ordinary rule of life. Thus some of the Esthonians will not taste blood because they believe that it contains the animal's soul, which would enter the body of the person who

[1] Plutarch, *Quaest. Rom.* 110; Aulus Gellius, x. 15, 12.

[2] J. Kubary, *Die socialen Einricht-ungen der Pelauer* (Berlin, 1885), p. 126 *sq.*

tasted the blood.[1]   Some Indian tribes of North America, "through a strong principle of religion, abstain in the strictest manner from eating the blood of any animal, as it contains the life and spirit of the beast." These Indians "commonly pull their new-killed venison (before they dress it) several times through the smoke and flame of the fire, both by the way of a sacrifice and to consume the blood, life, or animal spirits of the beast, which with them would be a most horrid abomination to eat."[2]   Many of the Slave, Hare, and Dogrib Indians scruple to taste the blood of game ; hunters of the former tribes collect the blood in the animal's paunch and bury it in the snow.[3] Jewish hunters poured out the blood of the game they had killed and covered it up with dust. They would not taste the blood, believing that the soul or life of the animal was in the blood, or actually was the blood.[4]   The same belief was held by the Romans,[5] and is shared by the Arabs,[6] and by some of the Papuan tribes of New Guinea.[7]

It is a common rule that royal blood must not be shed upon the ground. Hence when a king or one of his family is to be put to death a mode of execution is devised by which the royal blood shall not be spilt upon the earth. About the year 1688 the generalis-simo of the army rebelled against the King of Siam and put him to death "after the manner of royal criminals, or as princes of the blood are treated when

---

[1] F. J. Wiedemann, *Aus dem inneren und äussern Leben der Ehsten* (St. Petersburg, 1876), pp. 448, 478.

[2] James Adair, *History of the American Indians*, pp. 134, 117.

[3] E. Petitot, *Monographie des Dènè-Dindjié*, p. 76.

[4] Leviticus xvii. 10-14. The Hebrew word translated "life" in the English version of verse 11 means also "soul" (marginal note in the Revised Version). Cp. Deuteronomy xii. 23-25.

[5] Servius on Virgil, *Aen.* v. 79 ; cp. *id.* on *Aen.* iii. 67.

[6] J. Wellhausen, *Reste Arabischen Heidentumes*, p. 217.

[7] A. Goudswaard, *De Papoewa's van de Geelvinksbaai* (Schiedam, 1863), p. 77.

convicted of capital crimes, which is by putting them into a large iron caldron, and pounding them to pieces with wooden pestles, because none of their royal blood must be spilt on the ground, it being, by their religion, thought great impiety to contaminate the divine blood by mixing it with earth."[1] Other Siamese modes of executing a royal person are starvation, suffocation, stretching him on a scarlet cloth and thrusting a billet of odoriferous "saunders wood" into his stomach,[2] or lastly, sewing him up in a leather sack with a large stone and throwing him into the river; sometimes the sufferer's neck is broken with sandal-wood clubs before he is thrown into the water.[3] When Kublai Khan defeated and took his uncle Nayan, who had rebelled against him, he caused Nayan to be put to death by being wrapt in a carpet and tossed to and fro till he died, "because he would not have the blood of his Line Imperial spilt upon the ground or exposed in the eye of Heaven and before the Sun."[4] "Friar Ricold mentions the Tartar maxim : 'One Khan will put another to death to get possession of the throne, but he takes great care that the blood be not spilt. For they say that it is highly improper that the blood of the Great Khan should be spilt upon the ground; so they cause the victim to be smothered somehow or other.' The like feeling prevails at the court of Burma, where a peculiar mode of execution without bloodshed is reserved for princes of the blood."[5] In Tonquin the ordinary mode of execution is beheading, but persons of

---

[1] Hamilton's "Account of the East Indies," in Pinkerton's *Voyages and Travels*, viii. 469. Cp. W. Robertson Smith, *Religion of the Semites*, i. 349, note 2.

[2] De la Loubere, *A New Historical*

Account of the Kingdom of Siam (London, 1693), p. 104 *sq.*

[3] Pallegoix, *Description du Royaume Thai ou Siam*, i. 271, 365 *sq.*

[4] Marco Polo, trans. by Col. H. Yule (2d ed. 1875), i. 335.

[5] Col. H. Yule on Marco Polo, *l.c.*

the blood royal are strangled.[1] In Ashantee the blood of none of the royal family may be shed; if one of them is guilty of a great crime he is drowned in the river Dah.[2] In Madagascar the blood of nobles might not be shed; hence when four Christians of that class were to be executed they were burned alive.[3] When a young king of Uganda comes of age all his brothers are burnt except two or three, who are preserved to keep up the succession.[4] The reluctance to shed royal blood seems to be only a particular case of a general reluctance to shed blood or at least to allow it to fall on the ground. Marco Polo tells us that in his day persons found on the streets of Cambaluc (Pekin) at unseasonable hours were arrested, and if found guilty of a misdemeanour were beaten with a stick. " Under this punishment people sometimes die, but they adopt it in order to eschew bloodshed, for their *Bacsis* say that it is an evil thing to shed man's blood."[5] When Captain Christian was shot by the Manx Government at the Restoration in 1660, the spot on which he stood was covered with white blankets, that his blood might not fall on the ground.[6] Amongst some primitive peoples, when the blood of a tribesman has to be shed it is not suffered to fall upon the ground, but is received upon the bodies of his fellow tribesmen. Thus in some Australian tribes boys who are being circumcised are laid on a platform, formed by the living bodies of the tribesmen;[7] and when a boy's tooth

[1] Baron's "Description of the Kingdom of Tonqueen," in Pinkerton's *Voyages and Travels*, ix. 691.

[2] T. E. Bowdich, *Mission from Cape Coast Castle to Ashantee* (London, 1873), p. 207.

[3] Sibree, *Madagascar and its People*, p. 430.

[4] C. T. Wilson and R. W. Felkin, *Uganda and the Egyptian Soudan*, i. 200.

[5] Marco Polo, i. 399, Yule's translation, 2d ed.

[6] Sir Walter Scott, note 2 to *Peveril of the Peak*, ch. v.

[7] *Native Tribes of South Australia*,

is knocked out as an initiatory ceremony, he is seated on the shoulders of a man, on whose breast the blood flows and may not be wiped away.[1] When Australian blacks bleed each other as a cure for headache, and so on, they are very careful not to spill any of the blood on the ground, but sprinkle it on each other.[2] We have already seen that in the Australian ceremony for making rain the blood which is supposed to imitate the rain is received upon the bodies of the tribesmen.[3] In South Celebes at child-birth a female slave stands under the house (the houses being raised on posts above the ground) and receives in a basin on her head the blood which trickles through the bamboo floor.[4] The unwillingness to shed blood is extended by some peoples to the blood of animals. When the Wanika in Eastern Africa kill their cattle for food, "they either stone or beat the animal to death, so as not to shed the blood."[5] Amongst the Damaras cattle killed for food are suffocated, but when sacrificed they are speared to death.[6] But like most pastoral tribes in Africa, both the Wanika and Damaras very seldom kill their cattle, which are indeed commonly invested with a kind of sanctity.[7] In killing an animal for food the Easter Islanders do not shed its blood, but stun it

p. 230; E. J. Eyre, *Journals of Expeditions of Discovery into Central Australia,* ii. 335; Brough Smyth, *Aborigines of Victoria,* i. 75 *note.*

[1] Collins, *Account of the English Colony of New South Wales* (London, 1798), p. 580.

[2] *Native Tribes of South Australia,* p. 224 *sq.* ; Angas, *Savage Life and Scenes in Australia and New Zealand,* i. 110 *sq.*

[3] Above, p. 20.

[4] B. F. Matthes, *Bijdragen tot de Ethnologie van Zuid-Celebes,* p. 53.

[5] Lieut. Emery, in *Journal of the R. Geogr. Soc.* iii. 282.

[6] Ch. Andersson, *Lake Ngami,* p. 224.

[7] Ch. New, *Life, Wanderings, and Labours in Eastern Africa,* p. 124; Francis Galton, "Domestication of Animals," in *Transactions of the Ethnolog. Soc. of London,* iii. 135. On the original sanctity of domestic animals, see above all W. Robertson Smith, *The Religion of the Semites,* i. 263 *sqq.,* 277 *sqq.*

or suffocate it in smoke.[1]　The explanation of the reluctance to shed blood on the ground is probably to be found in the belief that the soul is in the blood, and that therefore any ground on which it may fall necessarily becomes taboo or sacred. In New Zealand anything upon which even a drop of a high chief's blood chances to fall becomes taboo or sacred to him. For instance, a party of natives having come to visit a chief in a fine new canoe, the chief got into it, but in doing so a splinter entered his foot, and the blood trickled on the canoe, which at once became sacred to him. The owner jumped out, dragged the canoe ashore opposite the chief's house, and left it there. Again, a chief in entering a missionary's house knocked his head against a beam, and the blood flowed. The natives said that in former times the house would have belonged to the chief.[2]　As usually happens with taboos of universal application, the prohibition to spill the blood of a tribesman on the ground applies with peculiar stringency to chiefs and kings, and is observed in their case long after it has ceased to be observed in the case of others.

We have seen that the Flamen Dialis was not allowed to walk under a trellised vine.[3]　The reason for this prohibition was perhaps as follows. It has been shown that plants are considered as animate beings which bleed when cut, the red juice which exudes from some plants being regarded as the blood of the plant.[4] The juice of the grape is therefore naturally conceived as the blood of the vine.[5]　And since, as we have just

[1] L. Linton Palmer, " A Visit to Easter Island," in *Journ. R. Geogr. Soc.* xl. (1870) 171.

[2] R. Taylor, *Te Ika a Maui; or, New Zealand and its Inhabitants*,[2] p. 164 *sq.*

[3] Plutarch, *Quaest. Rom.* 112; Aulus Gellius, x. 15, 13.

[4] Above, p. 61 *sq.*

[5] Cp. W. Robertson Smith, *op. cit.* p. 213 *sq.*

seen, the soul is often believed to be in the blood, the juice of the grape is regarded as the soul, or as containing the soul, of the vine. This belief is strengthened by the intoxicating effects of wine. For, according to primitive notions, all abnormal mental states, such as intoxication or madness, are caused by the entrance of a spirit into the person; such mental states, in other words, are regarded as forms of possession or inspiration. Wine, therefore, is considered on two distinct grounds as a spirit or containing a spirit; first because, as a red juice, it is identified with the blood of the plant, and second because it intoxicates or inspires. Therefore if the Flamen Dialis had walked under a trellised vine, the spirit of the vine, embodied in the clusters of grapes, would have been immediately over his head and might have touched it, which for a person like him in a state of permanent taboo[1] would have been highly dangerous. This interpretation of the prohibition will be made probable if we can show, first, that wine has been actually viewed by some peoples as blood and intoxication as inspiration produced by drinking the blood; and, second, that it is often considered dangerous, especially for tabooed persons, to have either blood or a living person over their heads.

With regard to the first point, we are informed by Plutarch that of old the Egyptian kings neither drank wine nor offered it in libations to the gods, because they held it to be the blood of beings who had once fought against the gods, the vine having sprung from their rotting bodies; and the frenzy of intoxication was explained by the supposition that the drunken man was

---

[1] *Dialis cotidie feriatus est*, Aulus Gellius, x. 15, 16.

filled with the blood of the enemies of the gods.[1] The Aztecs regarded *pulque* or the wine of the country as bad, on account of the wild deeds which men did under its influence. But these wild deeds were believed to be the acts, not of the drunken man, but of the wine-god by whom he was possessed and inspired ; and so seriously was this theory of inspiration held that if any one spoke ill of or insulted a tipsy man, he was liable to be punished for disrespect to the wine-god incarnate in his votary. Hence, says Sahagun, it was believed, not without ground, that the Indians intoxicated themselves on purpose to commit with impunity crimes for which they would certainly have been punished if they had committed them sober.[2] Thus it appears that on the primitive view intoxication or the inspiration produced by wine is exactly parallel to the inspiration produced by drinking the blood of animals.[3] The soul or life is in the blood, and wine is the blood of the vine. Hence whoever drinks the blood of an animal is inspired with the soul of the animal or of the god, who, as we have seen,[4] is often supposed to enter into the animal before it is slain ; and whoever drinks wine drinks the blood, and so receives into himself the soul or spirit, of the god of the vine.

With regard to the second point, the fear of passing under blood or under a living person, we are told that some of the Australian blacks have a dread of passing under a leaning tree or even under the rails of a fence. The reason they give is that a woman may

---

[1] Plutarch, *Isis et Osiris*, c. 6. A myth apparently akin to this has been preserved in some native Egyptian writings. See Ad. Erman, *Aegypten und aegyptisches Leben im Altertum*, p. 364.

[2] Bernardino de Sahagun, *Histoire générale des choses de la Nouvelle-Espagne*, traduite par Jourdanet et Siméon (Paris, 1880), p. 46 *sq.*

[3] See above, p. 34 *sq.*

[4] P. 35.

have been upon the tree or fence, and some blood from her may have fallen on it and might fall from it on them.[1] In Ugi, one of the Solomon Islands, a man will never, if he can help it, pass under a tree which has fallen across the path, for the reason that a woman may have stepped over it before him.[2] Amongst the Karens of Burma "going under a house, especially if there are females within, is avoided; as is also the passing under trees of which the branches extend downwards in a particular direction, and the but-end of fallen trees, etc."[3] The Siamese think it unlucky to pass under a rope on which women's clothes are hung, and to avert evil consequences the person who has done so must build a chapel to the earth-spirit.[4]

Probably in all such cases the rule is based on a fear of being brought into contact with blood, especially the blood of women. From a like fear a Maori will never lean his back against the wall of a native house.[5] For the blood of women is believed to have disastrous effects upon males. In the Encounter Bay tribe of South Australia boys are warned that if they see the blood of women they will early become gray-headed and their strength will fail prematurely.[6] Men of the Booandik tribe think that if they see the blood of their women they will not be able to fight against their enemies and will be killed; if the sun dazzles their eyes at a fight, the first woman they afterwards meet is sure to get a blow from their club.[7] In the

---

[1] E. M. Curr, *The Australian Race* (Melbourne and London, 1887), iii. 179.

[2] H. B. Guppy, *The Solomon Islands and their Natives* (London, 1887), p. 41.

[3] E. B. Cross, "On the Karens," in *Journal of the American Oriental Society*, iv. (1854) 312.

[4] Bastian, *Die Völker des östlichen Asien*, iii. 230.

[5] For the reason see Shortland, *Traditions and Superstitions of the New Zealanders*, pp. 112 *sq.*, 292.

[6] *Native Tribes of South Australia*, p. 186.

[7] Mrs. James Smith, *The Booandik Tribe*, p. 5.

island of Wetar it is thought that if a man or a lad comes upon a woman's blood he will be unfortunate in war and other undertakings, and that any precautions he may take to avoid the misfortune will be vain.[1] The people of Ceram also believe that men who see women's blood will be wounded in battle.[2] Similarly the Ovahereró (Damaras) of South Africa think that if they see a lying-in woman shortly after child-birth they will become weaklings and will be shot when they go to war.[3] It is an Esthonian belief that men who see women's blood will suffer from an eruption on the skin.[4]

Again, the reason for not passing under dangerous objects, like a vine or women's blood, is a fear that they may come in contact with the head; for among primitive people the head is peculiarly sacred. The special sanctity attributed to it is sometimes explained by a belief that it is the seat of a spirit which is very sensitive to injury or disrespect. Thus the Karens suppose that a being called the *tso* resides in the upper part of the head, and while it retains its seat no harm can befall the person from the efforts of the seven *Kelahs*, or personified passions. "But if the *tso* becomes heedless. or weak certain evil to the person is the result. Hence the head is carefully attended to, and all possible pains are taken to provide such dress and attire as will be pleasing to the *tso*."[5] The Siamese think that a spirit called *Khuan*, or *Chom Kuan*, dwells in the human head, of which it is the

---

[1] Riedel, *De sluik-en kroesharige rassen tusschen Selebes en Papua*, p. 450.

[2] Riedel, *op. cit.* p. 139 ; cp. *id.* p. 209.

[3] E. Dannert, "Customs of the Ovaherero at the Birth of a Child," in (South African) *Folk-lore Journal*, ii. 63.

[4] F. J. Wiedemann, *Aus dem innern und äussern Leben der Ehsten*, p. 475.

[5] E. B. Cross, "On the Karens," in *Journal of the American Oriental Society*, iv. 311 *sq.*

guardian spirit. The spirit must be carefully protected from injury of every kind; hence the act of shaving or cutting the hair is accompanied with many ceremonies. The *Khuan* is very sensitive on points of honour, and would feel mortally insulted if the head in which he resides were touched by the hand of a stranger. When Dr. Bastian, in conversation with a brother of the king of Siam, raised his hand to touch the prince's skull in order to illustrate some medical remarks he was making, a sullen and threatening murmur bursting from the lips of the crouching courtiers warned him of the breach of etiquette he had committed, for in Siam there is no greater insult to a man of rank than to touch his head. If a Siamese touch the head of another with his foot, both of them must build chapels to the earth-spirit to avert the omen. Nor does the guardian spirit of the head like to have the hair washed too often; it might injure or incommode him. It was a grand solemnity when the king of Burmah's head was washed with water taken from the middle of the river. Whenever the native professor, from whom Dr. Bastian took lessons in Burmese at Mandalay, had his head washed, which took place as a rule once a month, he was generally absent for three days together, that time being consumed in preparing for, and recovering from, the operation of head-washing. Dr. Bastian's custom of washing his head daily gave rise to much remark.[1]

Again, the Burmese think it an indignity to have any one, especially a woman, over their heads, and for this reason Burmese houses have never more than one story. The houses are raised on posts above the ground, and whenever anything fell through the floor

[1] Bastian, *Die Völker des östlichen Asien*, ii. 256, iii. 71, 230, 235 *sq.*

Dr. Bastian had always difficulty in persuading a servant to fetch it from under the house. In Rangoon a priest, summoned to the bedside of a sick man, climbed up a ladder and got in at the window rather than ascend the staircase, to reach which he must have passed under a gallery. A pious Burman of Rangoon, finding some images of Buddha in a ship's cabin, offered a high price for them, that they might not be degraded by sailors walking over them on the deck.[1] Similarily the Cambodians esteem it a grave offence to touch a man's head ; some of them will not enter a place where anything whatever is suspended over their heads ; and the meanest Cambodian would never consent to live under an inhabited room. Hence the houses are built of one story only ; and even the Government respects the prejudice by never placing a prisoner in the stocks under the floor of a house, though the houses are raised high above the ground.[2] The same superstition exists amongst the Malays ; for an early traveller reports that in Java people "wear nothing on their heads, and say that nothing must be on their heads . . . and if any person were to put his hand upon their head they would kill him ; and they do not build houses with storeys, in order that they may not walk over each other's heads."[3] It is also found in full force throughout Polynesia. Thus of Gattanewa, a Marquesan chief, it is said that "to touch the top of his head, or any thing which had been on his head was sacrilege. To pass over his head

[1] Bastian, *op. cit.* ii. 150 ; Sangermano, *Description of the Burmese Empire* (Rangoon, 1885), p. 131; C. F. S. Forbes, *British Burma*, p. 334 ; Shway Yoe, *The Burman*, i. 91.

[2] J. Moura, *Le Royaume du Cambodge*, i. 178, 388.

[3] Duarte Barbosa, *Description of the Coasts of East Africa and Malabar in the beginning of the Sixteenth Century* (Hakluyt Society, 1866), p. 197.

was an indignity never to be forgotten. Gattanewa, nay, all his family, scorned to pass a gateway which is ever closed, or a house with a door; all must be as open and free as their unrestrained manners. He would pass under nothing that had been raised by the hand of man, if there was a possibility of getting round or over it. Often have I seen him walk the whole length of our barrier, in preference to passing between our water-casks; and at the risk of his life scramble over the loose stones of a wall, rather than go through the gateway."[1] Marquesan women have been known to refuse to go on the decks of ships for fear of passing over the heads of chiefs who might be below.[2] But it was not the Marquesan chiefs only whose heads were sacred; the head of every Marquesan was taboo, and might neither be touched nor stepped over by another; even a father might not step over the head of his sleeping child.[3] No one was allowed to be over the head of the king of Tonga.[4] In Hawaii (the Sandwich Islands) if a man climbed upon a chief's house or upon the wall of his yard, he was put to death; if his shadow fell on a chief, he was put to death; if he walked in the shadow of a chief's house with his head painted white or decked with a garland or wetted with water, he was put to death.[5] In Tahiti any one who stood over the king or queen, or passed his hand over their heads, might be put to death.[6] Until certain rites were performed over it, a Tahitian infant was

[1] David Porter, *Journal of a Cruise made to the Pacific Ocean in the U.S. Frigate Essex* (New York, 1822), ii. 65.

[2] Vincendon-Dumoulin et Desgraz, *Iles Marquises*, p. 262.

[3] Langsdorff, *Reise um die Welt*, i. 115 *sq.*

[4] Capt. James Cook, *Voyages*, v. 427 (ed. 1809).

[5] Jules Remy, *Ka Mooolelo Hawaii, Histoire de l'Archipel Havaiien* (Paris and Leipzig, 1862), p. 159.

[6] Ellis, *Polynesian Researches*, iii. 102.

especially taboo ; whatever touched the child's head, while it was in this state, became sacred and was deposited in a consecrated place railed in for the purpose at the child's house.   If a branch of a tree touched the child's head, the tree was cut down ; and if in its fall it injured another tree so as to penetrate the bark, that tree also was cut down as unclean and unfit for use.   After the rites were performed, these special taboos ceased ; but the head of a Tahitian was always sacred, he never carried anything on it, and to touch it was an offence.[1]   The head of a Maori chief was so sacred that "if he only touched it with his fingers, he was obliged immediately to apply them to his nose, and snuff up the sanctity which they had acquired by the touch, and thus restore it to the part from whence it was taken."[2]   In some circumstances the tabooed person is forbidden to touch his head at all.   Thus in North America, Tinneh girls at puberty, Creek lads during the year of their initiation into manhood, and young braves on their first war-path, are forbidden to scratch their heads with their fingers, and are provided with a stick for the purpose.[3]   But to return to the Maoris. On account of the sacredness of his head "a chief could not blow the fire with his mouth, for the breath being sacred, communicated his sanctity to it, and a brand might be taken by a slave, or a man of another tribe, or the fire might be used for other purposes,

---

[1] James Wilson, *A Missionary Voyage to the Southern Pacific Ocean* (London, 1799), p. 354 *sq.*

[2] R. Taylor, *Te Ika a Maui : or, New Zealand and its Inhabitants*, p. 165.

[3] "Customs of the New Caledonian Women," in *Journ. Anthrop. Inst.* vii. 206 ; B. Hawkins, "Sketch of the Creek Country," in *Collections of the Georgia Historical Society*, iii. pt. i. (Savannah, 1848), p. 78 ; A. S. Gatschet, *Migration Legend of the Creek Indians*, i. 185 ; *Narrative of the Captivity and Adventures of John Tanner* (London, 1830), p. 122 ; Kohl, *Kitschi-Gami*, ii. 168.

such as cooking, and so cause his death."[1] It is a crime for a sacred person in New Zealand to leave his comb, or anything else which has touched his head, in a place where food has been cooked, or to suffer another person to drink out of any vessel which has touched his lips. Hence when a chief wishes to drink he never puts his lips to the vessel, but holds his hands close to his mouth so as to form a hollow, into which water is poured by another person, and thence is allowed to flow into his mouth. If a light is needed for his pipe, the burning ember taken from the fire must be thrown away as soon as it is used ; for the pipe becomes sacred because it has touched his mouth ; the coal becomes sacred because it has touched the pipe ; and if a particle of the sacred cinder were replaced on the common fire, the fire would also become sacred and could no longer be used for cooking.[2] Some Maori chiefs, like other Polynesians, object to go down into a ship's cabin from fear of people passing over their heads.[3] Dire misfortune was thought by the Maoris to await those who entered a house where any article of animal food was suspended over their heads. "A dead pigeon, or a piece of pork hung from the roof was a better protection from molestation than a sentinel."[4] If I am right, the reason for the special objection to having animal food over the head is the fear of bringing the sacred head into contact with the spirit

[1] R. Taylor, l.c.

[2] E. Shortland, The Southern Districts of New Zealand, p. 293; id., Traditions and Superstitions of the New Zealanders, p. 107, sq.

[3] J. Dumont D'Urville, Voyage autour du Monde et à la recherche de La Pérouse, exécuté sous son commandement sur la corvette Astrolabe. Histoire du Voyage, ii. 534.

[4] R. A. Cruise, Journal of a Ten Months' Residence in New Zealand (London, 1823), p. 187; Dumont D'Urville, op. cit. ii. 533; E. Shortland, The Southern Districts of New Zealand (London, 1851), p. 30.

of the animal ; just as the reason why the Flamen Dialis might not walk under a vine was the fear of bringing his sacred head into contact with the spirit of the vine.

When the head was considered so sacred that it might not even be touched without grave offence, it is obvious that the cutting of the hair must have been a delicate and difficult operation. The difficulties and dangers which, on the primitive view, beset the operation are of two kinds. There is first the danger of disturbing the spirit of the head, which may be injured in the process and may revenge itself upon the person who molests him. Secondly, there is the difficulty of disposing of the shorn locks. For the savage believes that the sympathetic connection which exists between himself and every part of his body continues to exist even after the physical connection has been severed, and that therefore he will suffer from any harm that may befall the severed parts of his body, such as the clippings of his hair or the parings of his nails. Accordingly he takes care that these severed portions of himself shall not be left in places where they might either be exposed to accidental injury or fall into the hands of malicious persons who might work magic on them to his detriment or death. Such dangers are common to all, but sacred persons have more to fear from them than ordinary people, so the precautions taken by them are proportionately stringent. The simplest way of evading the danger is of course not to cut the hair at all ; and this is the expedient adopted where the danger is thought to be more than usually great. The Frankish kings were not allowed to cut their hair.[1] A Haida medicine-man may neither cut

---

[1] Agathias i. 3 ; Grimm, *Deutsche Rechtsalterthümer*, p. 239 *sqq.*

nor comb his hair, so it is always long and tangled.[1] Amongst the Alfoers of Celebes the *Leleen* or priest who looks after the rice-fields may not cut his hair during the time that he exercises his special functions, that is, from a month before the rice is sown until it is housed.[2] In Ceram men do not cut their hair : if married men did so, they would lose their wives ; if young men did so, they would grow weak and enervated.[3] In Timorlaut, married men may not cut their hair for the same reason as in Ceram, but widowers and men on a journey may do so after offering a fowl or a pig in sacrifice.[4] Here men on a journey are specially permitted to cut their hair ; but elsewhere men travelling abroad have been in the habit of leaving their hair uncut until their return. The reason for the latter custom is probably the danger to which, as we have seen, a traveller is believed to be exposed from the magic arts of the strangers amongst whom he sojourns ; if they got possession of his shorn hair, they might work his destruction through it. The Egyptians on a journey kept their hair uncut till they returned home.[5] "At Tâif when a man returned from a journey his first duty was to visit the Rabba and poll his hair."[6] The custom of keeping the hair unshorn during a dangerous expedition seems to have been observed, at least occasionally, by the Romans.[7] Achilles kept unshorn his yellow hair,

---

[1] G. M. Dawson "On the Haida Indians of the Queen Charlotte Islands," in *Geological Survey of Canada, Report of Progress for* 1878-79, p. 123 B.

[2] P. N. Wilken, " Bijdragen tot de kennis van de zeden en gewoonten der Alfoeren in de Minahassa," in *Mededeelingen van wege het Nederlandsche Zendelinggenootschap*, vii. (1863) p. 126.

[3] Riedel, *De sluik-en kroesharige*

rassen tusschen Selebes en Papua, p. 137. [4] Riedel, *op. cit.* p. 292 *sq.*

[5] Diodorus Siculus, i. 18.

[6] W. Robertson Smith, *Kinship and Marriage in Early Arabia*, p. 152 *sq.*

[7] Valerius Flaccus, *Argonaut.* i. 378 *sq.* :—

" *Tectus et Eurytion servato colla capillo,
Quem pater Aonias reducem tondebit ad
    aras.*"

because his father had vowed to offer it to the river Sperchius if ever his son came home from the wars beyond the sea.[1] Again, men who have taken a vow of vengeance sometimes keep their hair unshorn till they have fulfilled their vow. Thus of the Marquesans we are told that "occasionally they have their head entirely shaved, except one lock on the crown, which is worn loose or put up in a knot. But the latter mode of wearing the hair is only adopted by them when they have a solemn vow, as to revenge the death of some near relation, etc. In such case the lock is never cut off until they have fulfilled their promise."[2] Six thousand Saxons once swore that they would not cut their hair nor shave their beards until they had taken vengeance on their enemies.[3] On one occasion a Hawaiian taboo is said to have lasted thirty years "during which the men were not allowed to trim their beards, etc."[4] While his vow lasted, a Nazarite might not have his hair cut : "All the days of the vow of his separation there shall no razor come upon his head."[5] Possibly in this case there was a special objection to touching the tabooed man's head with iron. The Roman priests, as we have seen, were shorn with bronze knives. The same feeling probably gave rise to the European rule that a child's nails should not be cut during the first year, but that if it is absolutely necessary to shorten them they should be bitten off by the mother or nurse.[6] For

[1] Homer, *Iliad*, xxiii. 141 *sqq.*

[2] D. Porter, *Journal of a Cruise made to the Pacific Ocean*, ii. 120.

[3] Paulus Diaconus, *Hist. Langobard.* iii. 7.

[4] Ellis, *Polynesian Researches*, iv. 387.

[5] Numbers vi. 5.

[6] J. A. E. Köhler, *Volksbrauch*, etc. *im Voigtlande*, p. 424 ; W. Henderson, *Folk-lore of the Northern Counties*, p. 16 *sq.*; F. Panzer, *Beitrag zur deutschen Mythologie*, i. 258 ; Zingerle, *Sitten, Bräuche und Meinungen des Tiroler Volkes*,[2] Nos. 46, 72 ; J. W. Wolf, *Beiträge zur deutschen Mythologie*, i. 208 (No. 45), 209 (No. 53) ; Knoop, *Volkssagen, Erzählungen*, etc. *aus dem*

in all parts of the world a young child is believed to be especially exposed to supernatural dangers, and particular precautions are taken to guard it against them ; in other words, the child is under a number of taboos, of which the rule just mentioned is one. "Among Hindus the usual custom seems to be that the nails of a first-born child are cut at the age of six months. With other children a year or two is allowed to elapse."[1] The Slave, Hare, and Dogrib Indians of North America do not cut the nails of female children till they are four years of age.[2] In some parts of Germany it is thought that if a child's hair is combed in its first year the child will be unlucky ;[3] or that if a boy's hair is cut before his seventh year he will have no courage.[4]

But when it is necessary to cut the hair, precautions are taken to lessen the dangers which are supposed to attend the operation. Amongst the Maoris many spells were uttered at hair-cutting ; one, for example, was spoken to consecrate the obsidian knife with which the hair was cut ; another was pronounced to avert the thunder and lightning which hair-cutting was believed to cause.[5] "He who has had his hair cut is in the immediate charge of the Atua (spirit) ; he is removed from the contact and society of

---

östlichen Hinterpommern, p. 157 (No. 23) ; E. Veckenstedt, *Wendische Sagen, Märchen und abergläubische Gebräuche*, p. 445 ; J. Haltrich, *Zur Volkskunde der Siebenbürger Sachsen*, p. 313 ; E. Krause, "Abergläubische Kuren u. sonstiger Aberglaube in Berlin," *Zeitschrift für Ethnologie*, xv. 84.

[1] *Panjab Notes and Queries*, ii. No. 1092.

[2] G. Gibbs, "Notes on the Tinneh or Chepewyan Indians of British and Russian America," in *Annual Report of the Smithsonian Institution*, 1866,

p. 305 ; W. Dall, *Alaska and its Resources*, p. 202. The reason alleged by the Indians (that if the girls' nails were cut sooner the girls would be lazy and unable to embroider in porcupine quill-work) is probably a late invention, like the reasons assigned in Europe for the similar custom (the commonest being that the child would become a thief).

[3] Knoop, *l.c.*

[4] Wolf, *Beiträge zur deutschen Mythologie*, i. 209 (No. 57).

[5] R. Taylor, *New Zealand and its Inhabitants*, p. 206 *sqq.*

his family and his tribe; he dare not touch his food himself; it is put into his mouth by another person; nor can he for some days resume his accustomed occupations or associate with his fellow men."[1] The person who cuts the hair is also tabooed; his hands having been in contact with a sacred head, he may not touch food with them or engage in any other employment; he is fed by another person with food cooked over a sacred fire. He cannot be released from the taboo before the following day, when he rubs his hands with potato or fern root which has been cooked on a sacred fire; and this food having been taken to the head of the family in the female line and eaten by her, his hands are freed from the taboo. In some parts of New Zealand the most sacred day of the year was that appointed for hair-cutting; the people assembled in large numbers on that day from all the neighbourhood.[2] It is an affair of state when the king of Cambodia's hair is cut. The priests place on the barber's fingers certain old rings set with large stones, which are supposed to contain spirits favourable to the kings, and during the operation the Brahmans keep up a noisy music to drive away the evil spirits.[3] The hair and nails of the Mikado could only be cut while he was asleep,[4] perhaps because his soul being then absent from his body, there was less chance of injuring it with the shears.

But even when the hair and nails have been safely cut, there remains the difficulty of disposing of them,

---

[1] Richard A. Cruise, *Journal of a Ten Months' Residence in New Zealand,* p. 283 *sq.* Cp. Dumont D'Urville, *Voyage autour du Monde et à la recherche de La Pérouse. Histoire du Voyage* (Paris, 1832), ii. 533.

[2] E. Shortland, *Traditions and Superstitions of the New Zealanders,* p. 108 *sqq.* ; Taylor, *l.c.*

[3] J. Moura, *Le Royaume du Cambodge,* i. 226 *sq.*

[4] See above, p. 111.

for their owner believes himself liable to suffer from
any harm that may befall them.   Thus, an Australian girl, sick of a fever, attributed her illness to
the fact that some months before a young man had
come behind her and cut off a lock of her hair ; she
was sure he had buried it and that it was rotting.
" Her hair," she said, " was rotting somewhere, and
her *Marm-bu-la* (kidney fat) was wasting away, and
when her hair had completely rotted, she would die."[1]
A Marquesan chief told Lieutenant Gamble that he
was extremely ill, the Happah tribe having stolen a
lock of his hair and buried it in a plantain leaf for
the purpose of taking his life.   Lieut. Gamble argued
with him, but in vain ; die he must unless the hair
and the plantain leaf were brought back to him ; and
to obtain them he had offered the Happahs the
greater part of his property.   He complained of ex-
cessive pain in the head, breast and sides.[2]   When
an Australian blackfellow wishes to get rid of his
wife, he cuts off a lock of her hair in her sleep, ties
it to his spear-thrower, and goes with it to a
neighbouring tribe, where he gives it to a friend.
His friend sticks the spear-thrower up every night
before the camp fire, and when it falls down it is a
sign that his wife is dead.[3]   The way in which the
charm operates was explained to Mr. Howitt by a
Mirajuri man.   " You see," he said, " when a blackfellow doctor gets hold of something belonging to a
man and roasts it with things, and sings over it, the
fire catches hold of the smell of the man, and that
settles the poor fellow." [4]   In Germany it is a common

[1] Brough Smyth, *Aborigines of
Victoria*, i. 468 *sq.*
[2] D. Porter, *Journal of a Cruise made
to the Pacific Ocean*, ii. 188.

[3] J. Dawson, *Australian Aborigines*,
p. 36.
[4] A. W. Howitt, "On Australian
Medicine-men," in *Journ. Anthrop. Inst.*

notion that if birds find a person's cut hair, and build
their nests with it, the person will suffer from headache ;[1] sometimes it is thought that he will have an
eruption on the head.[2] Again it is thought that cut
or combed out hair may disturb the weather by
producing rain and hail, thunder and lightning.
We have seen that in New Zealand a spell was
uttered at hair-cutting to avert thunder and lightning. In the Tirol, witches are supposed to use
cut or combed out hair to make hail-stones or
thunder-storms with.[3] Thlinket Indians have been
known to attribute stormy weather to the fact that
a girl had combed her hair outside of the house.[4]
The Romans seem to have held similar views, for
it was a maxim with them that no one on ship-
board should cut his hair or nails except in a storm,[5]
that is, when the mischief was already done. In
West Africa, when the Mani of Chitombe or Jumba
died, the people used to run in crowds to the corpse
and tear out his hair, teeth, and nails, which they kept
as a rain-charm, believing that otherwise no rain
would fall. The Makoko of Anzikos begged the
missionaries to give him half their beards as a rain-

xvi. 27. Cp. E. Palmer, "Notes on
some Australian Tribes," in *Journ.
Anthrop. Inst.* xiii. 293 ; James
Bonwick, *Daily Life of the Tasmanians*,
p. 178 ; James Chalmers, *Pioneering in
New Guinea*, p. 187 ; J. S. Polack,
*Manners and Customs of the New
Zealanders*, i. 282 ; Bastian, *Die
Völker des östlichen Asien*, iii. 270 ;
Langsdorff, *Reise um die Welt*, i. 134 *sq.*
A. S. Thomson, *The Story of New
Zealand*, i. 79, 116 *sq.* ; Ellis, *Poly-
nesian Researches*, i. 364 ; Zingerle,
*Sitten, Bräuche und Meinungen des
Tiroler Volkes*,[2] No. 178.

[1] Meier, *Deutsche Sagen, Sitten und
Gebräuche aus Schwaben*, p. 509; Panzer,
Beitrag zur deutschen Mythologie, i.
258 ; J. A. E. Köhler, *Volksbrauch*
etc. *im Voigtlande*, p. 425 ; A. Witzschel,
*Sagen, Sitten und Gebräuche aus Thür-
ingen*, p. 282 ; Zingerle, *op. cit.* No. 180;
Wolf, *Beiträge zur deutschen Mythologie*,
i. 224 (No. 273).

[2] Zingerle, *op. cit.* No. 181.

[3] Zingerle, *op. cit.* Nos. 176, 179.

[4] A. Krause, *Die Tlinkit-Indianer*.
(Jena, 1885), p. 300.

[5] Petronius, *Sat.* 104.

charm.[1] In some Victorian tribes the sorcerer used to burn human hair in time of drought; it was never burned at other times for fear of causing a deluge of rain. Also when the river was low, the sorcerer would place human hair in the stream to increase the supply of water.[2]

To preserve the cut hair and nails from injury and from the dangerous uses to which they may be put by sorcerers, it is necessary to deposit them in some safe place. Hence the natives of the Maldives carefully keep the cuttings of their hair and nails and bury them, with a little water, in the cemeteries; "for they would not for the world tread upon them nor cast them in the fire, for they say that they are part of their body and demand burial as it does; and, indeed, they fold them neatly in cotton; and most of them like to be shaved at the gates of temples and mosques."[3] In New Zealand the severed hair was deposited on some sacred spot of ground "to protect it from being touched accidentally or designedly by any one."[4] The shorn locks of a chief were gathered with much care and placed in an adjoining cemetery.[5] The Tahitians buried the cuttings of their hair at the temples.[6] The cut hair and nails of the Flamen Dialis were buried under a lucky tree.[7] The hair of the Vestal virgins was hung upon an ancient lotus-tree.[8] In Germany

[1] Bastian, *Die deutsche Expedition an der Loango-Küste*, i. 231 *sq.*; *id.*, *Ein Besuch in San Salvador*, p. 117.

[2] W. Stanbridge, "On the Aborigines of Victoria," in *Transact. Ethnolog. Soc. of London*, i. 300.

[3] François Pyrard, *Voyages to the East Indies, the Maldives, the Moluccas, and Brazil.* Translated by Albert Gray (Hakluyt Society, 1887), i. 110 *sq.*

[4] Shortland, *Traditions and Superstitions of the New Zealanders*, p. 110.

[5] Polack, *Manners and Customs of the New Zealanders*, i. 38 *sq.*

[6] James Wilson, *A Missionary Voyage to the Southern Pacific Ocean*, p. 355.

[7] Aulus Gellius, x. 15, 15.

[8] Pliny, *Nat. Hist.* xvi. 235; Festus, *s.v. capillatam vel capillarem arborem.*

the clippings of hair used often to be buried under an elder-bush.[1] In Oldenburg cut hair and nails are wrapt in a cloth which is deposited in a hole in an elder-tree three days before the new moon; the hole is then plugged up.[2] In the West of Northumberland it is thought that if the first parings of a child's nails are buried under an ash-tree, the child will turn out a fine singer.[3] In Amboina before a child may taste sago-pap for the first time, the father cuts off a lock of the child's hair which he buries under a sago palm.[4] In the Aru Islands, when a child is able to run alone, a female relation cuts off a lock of its hair and deposits it on a banana-tree.[5] In the island of Roti it is thought that the first hair which a child gets is not his own and that, if it is not cut off, it will make him weak and ill. Hence, when the child is about a month old, his hair is cut off with much ceremony. As each of the friends who are invited to the ceremony enters the house he goes up to the child, cuts off a little of its hair and drops it into a cocoa-nut shell full of water. Afterwards the father or another relation takes the hair and packs it into a little bag made of leaves, which he fastens to the top of a palm-tree. Then he gives the leaves of the palm a good shaking, climbs down, and goes home without speaking to any one.[6] Indians of the Yukon territory, Alaska, do not throw away their cut hair and nails, but tie them up in little bundles and place them in the crotches of trees or anywhere where they will

[1] Wuttke, *Der deutsche Volksaber-glaube,*[2] § 464.

[2] W. Mannhardt, *Germanische My-then,* p. 630.

[3] W. Henderson, *Folk-lore of the Northern Counties,* p. 17.

[4] Riedel, *De sluik-en kroesharige rassen tusschen Selebes en Papua,* p. 74.
[5] Riedel, *op. cit.* p. 265.
[6] G. Heijmering "Zeden en gewoonten op het eiland Rottie," in *Tijdschrift voor Neêrland's Indië* (1843), dl. ii. 634-637.

not be disturbed by animals. For "they have a superstition that disease will follow the disturbance of such remains by animals."[1] The clipped hair and nails are often buried in any secret place, not necessarily in a temple or cemetery or under a tree, as in the cases already mentioned. In Swabia it is said that cut hair should be buried in a place where neither sun nor moon shines, therefore in the ground, under a stone, etc.[2] In Danzig it is buried in a bag under the threshold.[3] In Ugi, one of the Solomon Islands, men bury their hair lest it should fall into the hands of an enemy who would make magic with it and so bring sickness or calamity on them.[4] The Zend Avesta directs that the clippings of hair and the parings of nails shall be placed in separate holes, and that three, six, or nine furrows shall be drawn round each hole with a metal knife.[5] In the Gṛihya-Sûtras it is provided that the hair cut from a child's head at the end of the first, third, fifth, or seventh year shall be buried in the earth at a place covered with grass or in the neighbourhood of water.[6] The Madi or Moru tribe of Central Africa bury the parings of their nails in the ground.[7] The Kafirs carry still further this dread of allowing any portion of themselves to fall into the hands of an enemy; for not only do they bury their cut hair and nails in a sacred place, but when one of them cleans the head of another he preserves the insects which he

---

[1] W. Dall, *Alaska and its Resources*, p. 54; F. Whymper, "The Natives of the Youkon River," in *Transact. Ethnolog. Soc. of London*, vii. 174.

[2] E. Meier, *Deutsche Sagen, Sitten und Gebräuche aus Schwaben*, p. 509.

[3] W. Mannhardt, *Germanische Mythen*, p. 630.

[4] H. B. Guppy, *The Solomon Islands and their Natives*, p. 54.

[5] Fargaard, xvii.

[6] *Grihya-Sûtras*, translated by H. Oldenberg (Oxford, 1886), vol. i. p. 57.

[7] R. W. Felkin, "Notes on the Madi or Moru tribe of Central Africa," in *Proceedings of the Royal Society of Edinburgh*, xii. (1882-84) p. 332.

finds, "carefully delivering them to the person to
whom they originally appertained, supposing, according to their theory, that as they derived their support
from the blood of the man from whom they were
taken, should they be killed by another the blood
of his neighbour would be in his possession, thus
placing in his hands the power of some superhuman
influence."[1] Amongst the Wanyoro of Central Africa
all cuttings of the hair and nails are carefully stored
under the bed and afterwards strewed about among
the tall grass.[2] In North Guinea they are carefully
hidden (it is not said where) "in order that they may
not be used as a fetish for the destruction of him to
whom they belong.[3] In Bolang Mongondo (Celebes)
the first hair cut from a child's head is kept in a
young cocoa-nut, which is commonly hung on the front
of the house, under the roof.[4]

Sometimes the severed hair and nails are preserved, not to prevent them from falling into the
hands of a magician, but that the owner may have
them at the resurrection of the body, to which some
races look forward. Thus the Incas of Peru "took
extreme care to preserve the nail-parings and the
hairs that were shorn off or torn out with a comb;
placing them in holes or niches in the walls, and if
they fell out, any other Indian that saw them picked
them up and put them in their places again. I very
often asked different Indians, at various times, why

---

[1] A. Steedman, *Wanderings and
Adventures in the Interior of Southern
Africa* (London, 1835), i. 266.

[2] *Emin Pasha in Central Africa,
being a Collection of his Letters and
Journals* (London, 1888), p. 74.

[3] J. L. Wilson, *West Afrika*, p.
159 (German trans.)

[4] N. P. Wilken en J. A. Schwarz,
"Allerlei over het land en volk van
Bolaang Mongondou," in *Mededeelingen
van wege het Nederlandsche Zendelinggenootschap*, xi. (1867) p. 322.

they did this, in order to see what they would say,
and they all replied in the same words, saying, ' Know
that all persons who are born must return to life'
(they have no word to express resuscitation), 'and
the souls must rise out of their tombs with all that
belonged to their bodies. We, therefore, in order
that we may not have to search for our hair and
nails at a time when there will be much hurry and
confusion, place them in one place, that they may
be brought together more conveniently, and, whenever it is possible, we are also careful to spit in one
place.'"[1] In Chile this custom of stuffing the shorn
hair into holes in the wall is still observed, it being
thought the height of imprudence to throw the hair
away.[2] Similarly the Turks never throw away the
parings of their nails, but carefully keep them in
cracks of the walls or of the boards, in the belief
that they will be needed at the resurrection.[3] Some
of the Esthonians keep the parings of their finger
and toe nails in their bosom, in order to have them
at hand when they are asked for them at the day
of judgment.[4] The Fors of Central Africa object to
cut any one else's nails, for should the part cut off
be lost and not delivered into its owner's hands, it
will have to be made up to him somehow or other
after death. The parings are buried in the ground.[5]
To spit upon the hair before throwing it away is
thought in some parts of Europe sufficient to prevent

[1] Garcilasso de la Vega, *First part
of the Royal Commentaries of the Yncas*,
bk. ii. ch. 7 (vol. i. p. 127, Markham's
translation).
[2] *Mélusine*, 1878, c. 583 *sq.*
[3] *The People of Turkey*, by a Con-
sul's daughter and wife, ii. 250.
[4] Boecler-Kreutzwald, *Der Ehsten*

*abergläubische Gebräuche, Weisen und
Gewohnheiten*, p. 139; F. J. Wiedemann, *Aus dem innern und äussern
Leben der Ehsten*, p. 491.
[5] R. W. Felkin, "Notes on the
For tribe of Central Africa," in *Proceedings of the Royal Society of Edinburgh*, xiii. (1884-86) p. 230.

its being used by witches.[1] Spitting as a protective charm is well known.

Some people burn their loose hair to save it from falling into the power of sorcerers. This is done by the Patagonians and some of the Victorian tribes.[2] The Makololo of South Africa either burn it or bury it secretly,[3] and the same alternative is sometimes adopted by the Tirolese.[4] Cut and combed out hair is burned in Pomerania and sometimes at Liége.[5] In Norway the parings of nails are either burned or buried, lest the elves or the Finns should find them and make them into bullets wherewith to shoot the cattle.[6] This destruction of the hair or nails plainly involves an inconsistency of thought. The object of the destruction is avowedly to prevent these severed portions of the body from being used by sorcerers. But the possibility of their being so used depends upon the supposed sympathetic connection between them and the man from whom they were severed. And if this sympathetic connection still exists, clearly these severed portions cannot be destroyed without injury to the man.

Before leaving this subject, on which I have perhaps dwelt too long, it may be well to call attention to the motive assigned for cutting a young child's hair in Roti.[7] In that island the first hair is regarded as a danger to the child, and its removal is intended to avert the danger. The reason of this may be that as a

---

[1] Zingerle, *Sitten, Bräuche und Meinungen des Tiroler Volkes*,[2] Nos. 176, 580; *Mélusine*, 1878, c. 79.

[2] Musters, "On the Races of Patagonia," in *Journ. Anthrop. Inst.* i. 197; J. Dawson, *Australian Aborigines*, p. 36.

[3] David Livingstone, *Narrative of Expedition to the Zambesi*, p. 46 *sq.*

[4] Zingerle, *op. cit.* Nos. 177, 179, 180.

[5] M. Jahn, *Hexenwesen und Zauberei in Pommern*, p. 15; *Mélusine*, 1878, c. 79.

[6] E. H. Meyer, *Indogermanische Mythen*, ii. *Achilleis* (Berlin, 1887); p. 523.

[7] Above, p. 201.

young child is almost universally supposed to be in a
tabooed or dangerous state, it is necessary, in removing
the taboo, to destroy the separable parts of the child's
body on the ground that they are infected, so to say,
by the virus of the taboo and as such are dangerous.
The cutting of the child's hair would thus be exactly
parallel to the destruction of the vessels which have
been used by a tabooed person.[1] This view is borne
out by a practice, observed by some Australians, of
burning off part of a woman's hair after childbirth as
well as burning every vessel which has been used by
her during her seclusion.[2] Here the burning of the
woman's hair seems plainly intended to serve the same
purpose as the burning of the vessels used by her ; and
as the vessels are burned because they are believed to be
tainted with a dangerous infection, so, we must suppose,
is also the hair. We can, therefore, understand the
importance attached by many peoples to the first cutting of a child's hair and the elaborate ceremonies by
which the operation is accompanied.[3] Again, we can
understand why a man should poll his head after a
journey.[4] For we have seen that a traveller is often
believed to contract a dangerous infection from
strangers and that, therefore, on his return home he is
obliged to submit to various purificatory ceremonies
before he is allowed to mingle freely with his own
people.[5] On my hypothesis the polling of the hair is
simply one of these purificatory or disinfectant ceremonies. The cutting of the hair after a vow may
have the same meaning. It is a way of ridding the

[1] Above, pp. 167, 169 *sqq.*

[2] W. Ridley, " Report on Australian
Languages and Traditions," in *Journ.
Anthrop. Inst.* ii. 268.

[3] See G. A. Wilken, *Ueber das Haar-*

*opfer und einige andere Trauerge-
bräuche bei den Völkern Indonesiens,* p.
94 *sqq.* ; H. Ploss, *Das Kind in Brauch
und Sitte der Völker,*[2] i. 289 *sqq.*

[4] Above, p. 194.　[5] Above, p. 157 *sq.*

man of what has been infected by the dangerous state of taboo, sanctity, or uncleanness (for all these are only different expressions for the same primitive conception) under which he laboured during the continuance of the vow. Similarly at some Hindu places of pilgrimage on the banks of rivers men who have committed great crimes or are troubled by uneasy consciences have every hair shaved off by professional barbers before they plunge into the sacred stream, from which " they emerge new creatures, with all the accumulated guilt of a long life effaced." [1]

As might have been expected, the superstitions of the savage cluster thick about the subject of food; and he abstains from eating many animals and plants, wholesome enough in themselves, but which for one reason or another he considers would prove dangerous or fatal to the eater. Examples of such abstinence are too familiar and far too numerous to quote. But if the ordinary man is thus deterred by superstitious fear from partaking of various foods, the restraints of this kind which are laid upon sacred or tabooed persons, such as kings and priests, are still more numerous and stringent. We have already seen that the Flamen Dialis was forbidden to eat or even name several plants and animals, and that the flesh diet of the Egyptian kings was restricted to veal and goose.[2] The *Gangas* or fetish priests of the Loango Coast are forbidden to eat or even see a variety of animals and fish, in consequence of which their flesh diet is extremely limited; often they live only on herbs and roots, though they may drink fresh blood.[3] The heir to the throne of

---

[1] Monier Williams, *Religious Thought and Life in India*, p. 375.

[2] Above, p. 117.

[3] Bastian, *Die deutsche Expedition* an der *Loango-Küste*, ii. 170. The blood may be drunk by them as a medium of inspiration. See above, p. 34 *sq.*

Loango is forbidden from infancy to eat pork; from early childhood he is interdicted the use of the *cola* fruit in company; at puberty he is taught by a priest not to partake of fowls except such as he has himself killed and cooked; and so the number of taboos goes on increasing with his years.[1] In Fernando Po the king after installation is forbidden to eat *cocco* (*arum acaule*), deer, and porcupine, which are the ordinary foods of the people.[2] Amongst the Murrams of Manipur (a district of Eastern India, on the border of Burma), "there are many prohibitions in regard to the food, both animal and vegetable, which the chief should eat, and the Murrams say the chief's post must be a very uncomfortable one."[3] To explain the ultimate reason why any particular food is prohibited to a whole tribe or to certain of its members would commonly require a far more intimate knowledge of the history and beliefs of the tribe than we possess. The general motive of such prohibitions is doubtless the same which underlies the whole taboo system, namely, the conservation of the tribe and the individual.

It would be easy to extend the list of royal and priestly taboos, but the above may suffice as specimens. To conclude this part of our subject it only remains to state summarily the general conclusions to which our inquiries have thus far conducted us. We have seen that in savage or barbarous society there are often found men to whom the superstition of their fellows ascribes a controlling influence over the general course of nature. Such men are accordingly adored and treated as gods. Whether these human divinities

---

[1] Dapper, *Description de l'Afrique*, p. 336.
[2] T. J. Hutchinson, *Impressions of Western Africa* (London, 1858), p. 198.

[3] G. Watt (quoting Col. W. J. M'Culloch), "The Aboriginal Tribes of Manipur," in *Journ. Anthrop. Inst.* xvi. 360.

also hold temporal sway over the lives and fortunes of their fellows, or whether their functions are purely spiritual and supernatural, in other words, whether they are kings as well as gods or only the latter, is a distinction which hardly concerns us here. Their supposed divinity is the essential fact with which we have to deal. In virtue of it they are a pledge and guarantee to their worshippers of the continuance and orderly succession of those physical phenomena upon which mankind depends for subsistence. Naturally, therefore, the life and health of such a god-man are matters of anxious concern to the people whose welfare and even existence are bound up with his; naturally. he is constrained by them to conform to such rules as the wit of early man has devised for averting the ills to which flesh is heir, including the last ill, death. These rules, as an examination of them has shown, are nothing but the maxims with which, on the primitive view, every man of common prudence must comply if he would live long in the land. But while in the case of ordinary men the observance of the rules is left to the choice of the individual, in the case of the god-man it is enforced under penalty of dismissal from his high station, or even of death. For his worshippers have far too great a stake in his life to allow him to play fast and loose with it. Therefore all the quaint superstitions, the old-world maxims, the venerable saws which the ingenuity of savage philosophers elaborated long ago, and which old women at chimney corners still impart as treasures of great price to their descendants gathered round the cottage fire on winter evenings—all these antique fancies clustered, all these cobwebs of the brain were spun about the path of the old king, the human god, who, immeshed in them like

a fly in the toils of a spider, could hardly stir a limb
for the threads of custom, "light as air but strong as
links of iron," that crossing and recrossing each other
in an endless maze bound him fast within a network of
observances from which death or deposition alone
could release him.

To students of the past the life of the old kings
and priests thus teems with instruction. In it was
summed up all that passed for wisdom when the
world was young. It was the perfect pattern after
which every man strove to shape his life ; a faultless
model constructed with rigorous accuracy upon the
lines laid down by a barbarous philosophy. Crude and
false as that philosophy may seem to us, it would be
unjust to deny in the merit of logical consistency.
Starting from a conception of the vital principle as a
tiny being or soul existing in, but distinct and separable from, the living being, it deduces for the practical
guidance of life a system of rules which in general
hangs well together and forms a fairly complete and
harmonious whole. The flaw—and it is a fatal one—
of the system lies not in its reasoning, but in its premises ; in its conception of the nature of life, not in
any irrelevancy of the conclusions which it draws from
that conception. But to stigmatise these premises as
ridiculous because we can easily detect their falseness,
would be ungrateful as well as unphilosophical. We
stand upon the foundation reared by the generations
that have gone before, and we can but dimly realise
the painful and prolonged efforts which it has cost
humanity to struggle up to the point, no very exalted
one after all, which we have reached. Our gratitude
is due to the nameless and forgotten toilers, whose
patient thought and active exertions have largely made

us what we are. The amount of new knowledge
which one age, certainly which one man, can add to
the common store is small, and it argues stupidity or
dishonesty, besides ingratitude, to ignore the heap
while vaunting the few grains which it may have been
our privilege to add to it. There is indeed little
danger at present of undervaluing the contributions
which modern times and even classical antiquity have
made to the general advancement of our race. But
when we pass these limits, the case is different.
Contempt and ridicule or abhorrence and denunciation
are too often the only recognition vouchsafed to the
savage and his ways. Yet of the benefactors whom
we are bound thankfully to commemorate, many, perhaps most, were savages. For when all is said and
done our resemblances to the savage are still far more
numerous than our differences from him ; and what we
have in common with him, and deliberately retain as
true and useful, we owe to our savage forefathers who
slowly acquired by experience and transmitted to us by
inheritance those seemingly fundamental ideas which
we are apt to regard as original and intuitive. We
are like heirs to a fortune which has been handed
down for so many ages that the memory of those who
built it up is lost, and its possessors for the time being
regard it as having been an original and unalterable
possession of their race since the beginning of the
world. But reflection and inquiry should satisfy us
that to our predecessors we are indebted for much of
what we thought most our own, and that their errors
were not wilful extravagances or the ravings of insanity,
but simply hypotheses, justifiable as such at the time
when they were propounded, but which a fuller experience has proved to be inadequate. It is only by the

successive testing of hypotheses and rejection of the false that truth is at last elicited. After all, what we call truth is only the hypothesis which is found to work best. Therefore in reviewing the opinions and practices of ruder ages and races we shall do well to look with leniency upon their errors as inevitable slips made in the search for truth, and to give them the benefit of that indulgence which we may one day stand in need of ourselves : *cum excusatione itaque veteres audiendi sunt.*

CHAPTER III

"Sed adhuc supersunt aliae superstitiones, quarum secreta pandenda sunt, . . . ut et in istis profanis religionibus sciatis mortes esse hominum consecratas."—FIRMICUS MATERNUS, *De errore profanarum religionum*, c. 6.

§ 1.—*Killing the divine king*

LACKING the idea of eternal duration primitive man naturally supposes the gods to be mortal like himself. The Greenlanders believed that a wind could kill their most powerful god, and that he would certainly die if he touched a dog. When they heard of the Christian God, they kept asking if he *never* died, and being informed that he did not, they were much surprised and said that he must be a very great god indeed.[1] In answer to the inquiries of Colonel Dodge, a North American Indian stated that the world was made by the Great Spirit. Being asked which Great Spirit he meant, the good one or the bad one, "Oh, neither of *them*," replied he, "the Great Spirit that made the world is dead long ago. He could not possibly have lived as long as this."[2] A tribe in the Philippine Islands told the Spanish conquerors that the grave of

---

[1] Meiners, *Geschichte der Religionen*, i. 48.

[2] R. I. Dodge, *Our Wild Indians*, p. 112.

the Creator was upon the top of Mount Cabunian.[1] Heitsi-eibib, a god or divine hero of the Hottentots, died several times and came to life again. His graves are generally to be met with in narrow passes between mountains.[2] The grave of Zeus, the great god of Greece, was shown to visiters in Crete as late as about the beginning of our era.[3] The body of Dionysus was buried at Delphi beside the golden statue of Apollo, and his tomb bore the inscription, "Here lies Dionysus dead, the son of Semele."[4] According to one account, Apollo himself was buried at Delphi; for Pythagoras is said to have carved an inscription on his tomb, setting forth how the god had been killed by the python and buried under the tripod.[5] Cronus was buried in Sicily,[6] and the graves of Hermes, Aphrodite, and Ares were shown in Hermopolis, Cyprus, and Thrace.[7]

If the great invisible gods are thus supposed to die, it is not to be expected that a god who dwells in the flesh and blood of a man should escape the same fate. Now primitive peoples, as we have seen, sometimes believe that their safety and even that of the world is bound up with the life of one of these god-men or human incarnations of the divinity. Naturally, therefore, they take the utmost care of his life, out of a regard for their own. But no amount of care and precaution will prevent the man-god from growing old and feeble and at last dying. His worshippers have

[1] Blumentritt, "Der Ahnencultus und die relig. Anschauungen der Malaien des Philippinen - Archipels," in *Mittheilungen d. Wiener Geogr. Gesellschaft*, 1882, p. 198.

[2] Theophilus Hahn, *Tsuni - Goam, the Supreme Being of the Khoi-Khoi*, pp. 56, 69.

[3] Diodorus, iii. 61; Pomponius Mela, ii. 7, 112; Minucius Felix, *Octavius*, 21.

[4] Plutarch, *Isis et Osiris*, 35; Philochorus, *Fragm.* 22, in Müller's *Fragm. Hist. Graec.* i. p. 387.

[5] Porphyry, *Vit. Pythag.* 16.

[6] Philochorus, *Fr.* 184, in *Fragm. Hist. Graec.* ii. p. 414.

[7] Lobeck, *Aglaophamus*, p. 574 *sq.*

to lay their account with this sad necessity and to meet it as best they can. The danger is a formidable one ; for if the course of nature is dependent on the man-god's life, what catastrophes may not be expected from the gradual enfeeblement of his powers and their final extinction in death ? There is only one way of averting these dangers. The man-god must be killed as soon as he shows symptoms that his powers are beginning to fail, and his soul must be transferred to a vigorous successor before it has been seriously impaired by the threatened decay. The advantages of thus putting the man-god to death instead of allowing him to die of old age and disease are, to the savage, obvious enough. For if the man-god dies what we call a natural death, it means, according to the savage, that his soul has either voluntarily departed from his body and refuses to return, or more commonly that it has been extracted or at least detained in its wanderings by a demon or sorcerer.[1] In any of these cases the soul of the man-god is lost to his worshippers ; and with it their prosperity is gone and their very existence endangered. Even if they could arrange to catch the soul of the dying god as it left his lips or his nostrils and so transfer it to a successor, this would not effect their purpose ; for, thus dying of disease, his soul would necessarily leave his body in the last stage of weakness and exhaustion, and as such it would continue to drag out a feeble existence in the body to which it might be transferred. Whereas by killing him his worshippers could, in the first place, make sure of catching his soul as it escaped and transferring it to a suitable successor ; and, in the second place, by killing him before his natural force

---

[1] See above, p. 121 *sqq.*

was abated, they would secure that the world should not fall into decay with the decay of the man-god. Every purpose, therefore, was answered, and all dangers averted by thus killing the man-god and transferring his soul, while yet at its prime, to a vigorous successor.

Some of the reasons for preferring a violent death to the slow death of old age or disease are obviously as applicable to common men as to the man-god. Thus the Mangaians think that "the spirits of those who die a natural death are excessively feeble and weak, as their bodies were at dissolution ; whereas the spirits of those who are slain in battle are strong and vigorous, their bodies not having been reduced by disease."[1] Hence, men sometimes prefer to kill themselves or to be killed before they grow feeble, in order that in the future life their souls may start fresh and vigorous as they left their bodies, instead of decrepit and worn out with age and disease. Thus in Fiji, "self-immolation is by no means rare, and they believe that as they leave this life, so they will remain ever after. This forms a powerful motive to escape from decrepitude, or from a crippled condition, by a voluntary death."[2] Or, as another observer of the Fijians puts it more fully, "the custom of voluntary suicide on the part of the old men, which is among their most extraordinary usages, is also connected with their superstitions respecting a future life. They believe that persons enter upon the delights of their elysium with the same faculties, mental and physical, that they possess at the hour of death, in short, that the spiritual life commences where the corporeal existence terminates.

---

[1] Gill, *Myths and Songs of the South Pacific*, p. 163.

[2] Ch. Wilkes, *Narrative of the U.S. Exploring Expedition* (London, 1845), iii. 96.

With these views, it is natural that they should desire to pass through this change before their mental and bodily powers are so enfeebled by age as to deprive them of their capacity for enjoyment. To this motive must be added the contempt which attaches to physical weakness among a nation of warriors, and the wrongs and insults which await those who are no longer able to protect themselves. When therefore a man finds his strength declining with the advance of age, and feels that he will soon be unequal to discharge the duties of this life, and to partake in the pleasures of that which is to come, he calls together his relations, and tells them that he is now worn out and useless, that he sees they are all ashamed of him, and that he has determined to be buried." So on a day appointed they meet and bury him alive.[1] In Vaté (New Hebrides) the aged were buried alive at their own request. It was considered a disgrace to the family of an old chief if he was not buried alive.[2] Of the Kamants, a Jewish tribe in Abyssinia, it is reported that "they never let a person die a natural death, but if any of their relatives is nearly expiring, the priest of the village is called to cut his throat; if this be omitted, they believe that the departed soul has not entered the mansions of the blessed."[3]

But it is with the death of the god-man—the divine king or priest—that we are here especially concerned. The people of Congo believed, as we have seen, that if their pontiff the Chitomé were to die a natural death,

---

[1] *U.S. Exploring Expedition, Ethnology and Philology*, by H. Hale (Philadelphia, 1846), p. 65. Cp. Th. Williams, *Fiji and the Fijians*, i. 183; J. E. Erskine, *Journal of a Cruise among the Islands of the Western Pacific*, p. 248.

[2] Turner, *Samoa*, p. 335.

[3] Martin Flad, *A Short Description of the Falasha and Kamants in Abyssinia*, p. 19.

the world would perish, and the earth, which he alone sustained by his power and merit, would immediately be annihilated. Accordingly when he fell ill and seemed likely to die, the man who was destined to be his successor entered the pontiff's house with a rope or a club and strangled or clubbed him to death.[1] The Ethiopian kings of Meroe were worshipped as gods ; but whenever the priests chose, they sent a messenger to the king, ordering him to die, and alleging an oracle of the gods as their authority for the command. This command the kings always obeyed down to the reign of Ergamenes, a contemporary of Ptolemy II, King of Egypt. Having received a Greek education which emancipated him from the superstitions of his countrymen, Ergamenes ventured to disregard the command of the priests, and, entering the Golden Temple with a body of soldiers, put the priests to the sword.[2] In the kingdom of Unyoro in Central Africa, custom still requires that as soon as the king falls seriously ill or begins to break up from age, he shall be killed by his own wives ; for, according to an old prophecy, the throne will pass away from the dynasty in the event of the king dying a natural death.[3] When the king of Kibanga, on the Upper Congo, seems near his end, the sorcerers put a rope round his neck, which they draw gradually tighter till he dies.[4] It seems to have been a Zulu custom to put the king to death as soon as he began to have wrinkles or gray hairs. At least this seems implied in the following

[1] J. B. Labat, *Relation historique de l'Ethiopie Occidentale*, i. 260 *sq.* ; W. Winwood Reade, *Savage Africa*, p. 362.
[2] Diodorus Siculus, iii. 6 ; Strabo, xvii. 2, 3.
[3] *Emin Pasha in Central Africa*, being a Collection of his Letters and Journals (London, 1888), p. 91.
[4] P. Guillemé, " Credenze religiose dei Negri di Kibanga nell' Alto Congo," in *Archivio per lo studio delle tradizioni popolari*, vii. (1888) p. 231.

passage, written by one who resided for some time at
the court of the notorious Zulu tyrant Chaka, in the
early part of this century : " The extraordinary violence
of the king's rage with me was mainly occasioned by
that absurd nostrum, the hair oil, with the notion of
which Mr. Farewell had impressed him as being a
specific for removing all indications of age. From the
first moment of his having heard that such a preparation was attainable, he evinced a solicitude to procure
it, and on every occasion never forgot to remind us of
his anxiety respecting it ; more especially on our
departure on the mission his injunctions were
particularly directed to this object. It will be seen
that it is one of the barbarous customs of the Zoolas in
their choice or election of their kings that he must
neither have wrinkles nor gray hairs, as they are both
distinguishing marks of disqualification for becoming
a monarch of a warlike people. It is also equally
indispensable that their king should never exhibit
those proofs of having become unfit and incompetent
to reign ; it is therefore important that they should conceal these indications so long as they possibly can.
Chaka had become greatly apprehensive of the approach
of gray hairs; which would at once be the signal for him
to prepare to make his exit from this sublunary world,
it being always followed by the death of the monarch."[1]

   The custom of putting kings to death as soon as they
suffered from any personal defect prevailed two centuries
ago in the Kafir kingdoms of Sofala, to the north of the
present Zululand. These kings of Sofala, as we have
seen,[2] were regarded as gods by their people, being en-
treated to give rain or sunshine, according as each might

---

[1] Nathaniel Isaacs, *Travels and Adventures in Eastern Africa*, i. p. 295 *sq.*, cp.
pp. 232, 290 *sq.*   [2] Above, p. 45 *sq.*

be wanted. Nevertheless a slight bodily blemish, such as the loss of a tooth, was considered a sufficient cause for putting one of these god-men to death, as we learn from the following passage of an old historian. " Contiguous to the domains of the Quiteva [the king of the country bordering on the river Sofala], are those of another prince called Sedanda. This prince becoming afflicted with leprosy, resolved on following implicitly the laws of the country, and poisoning himself, conceiving his malady to be incurable, or at least that it would render him so loathsome in the eyes of his people that they would with difficulty recognise him. In consequence he nominated his successor, holding as his opinion that sovereigns who should serve in all things as an example to their people ought to have no defect whatever, even in their persons ; that when any defects may chance to befall them they cease to be worthy of life and of governing their dominions ; and preferring death in compliance with this law to life, with the reproach of having been its violator. But this law was not observed with equal scrupulosity by one of the Quitevas, who, having lost a tooth and feeling no disposition to follow the practice of his predecessors, published to the people that he had lost a front tooth, in order that when they might behold, they yet might be able to recognise him ; declaring at the same time that he was resolved on living and reigning as long as he could, esteeming his existence requisite for the welfare of his subjects. He at the same time loudly condemned the practice of his predecessors, whom he taxed with imprudence, nay, even with madness, for having condemned themselves to death for casual accidents to their persons, confessing plainly that it would be with much regret, even when the course of nature should bring him to his end, that he should submit to die. He observed, moreover, that no reasonable being, much less a monarch, ought to anticipate the scythe of time ; and, abrogating this mortal law, he ordained that all his successors, if sane, should follow the precedent he gave, and the new law established by him." [1]

This King of Sofala was, therefore, a bold reformer like Ergamenes, King of Ethiopia. We may conjecture that the ground for putting the Ethiopian kings to death was, as in the case of the Zulu and Sofala kings, the appearance on their person of any bodily defect or sign of decay ; and that the oracle which the priests alleged as the authority for the royal execution was to the effect that great calamities would result from the reign of a king who had any blemish on his body; just as an oracle warned Sparta against a "lame reign," that is, the reign of a lame king.[2] This conjecture is confirmed by the fact that the kings of Ethiopia were chosen for their size, strength, and beauty long before the custom of killing them was abolished.[3] To this day the Sultan of Wadâi must have no obvious bodily defect, and a king of Angoy cannot be crowned if he has a single blemish, such as a broken or filed tooth or the scar of an old wound.[4] It is only natural, therefore, to suppose, especially

[1] Dos Santos, " History of Eastern Ethiopia " (published at Paris in 1684), in Pinkerton's *Voyages and Travels*, xvi. 684.

[2] Plutarch, *Agesilaus*, 3.

[3] Herodotus, iii. 20 ; Aristotle, *Politics*, iv. 4, 4 ; Athenaeus, xiii. p. 566. According to Nicolaus Damascenus (*Fr.* 142, in *Fragm. Historic. Graecor.* ed. C. Müller, iii. p. 463), the handsomest and bravest man was only raised to the throne when the king had no heirs, the heirs being the sons of his sisters. But this limitation is not mentioned by the other authorities. Among the Gordioi the fattest man was chosen king ; among the Syrakoi, the tallest, or the man with the longest head. Zenobius, v. 25.

[4] G. Nachtigal, *Saharâ und Sûdân* (Leipzig, 1889), iii. 225 ; Bastian, *Die deutsche Expedition an der Loango-Küste*, i. 220.

with the other African examples before us, that any
bodily defect or symptom of old age appearing on the
person of the Ethiopian monarch was the signal for
his execution. At a later time it is recorded that if
the King of Ethiopia became maimed in any part of his
body all his courtiers had to suffer the same mutila-
tion.[1] But this rule may perhaps have been instituted
at the time when the custom of killing the king for
any personal defect was abolished ; instead of compel-
ling the king to die because, *e.g.*, he had lost a tooth,
all his subjects would be obliged to lose a tooth,
and thus the invidious superiority of the subjects
over the king would be cancelled. A rule of this
sort is still observed in the same region at the
court of the Sultans of Darfur. When the Sultan
coughs, every one makes the sound *ts ts* by striking
the tongue against the root of the upper teeth ; when
he sneezes, the whole assembly utters a sound like the
cry of the jeko ; when he falls off his horse, all his
followers must fall off likewise ; if any one of them
remains in the saddle, no matter how high his
rank, he is laid on the ground and beaten.[2] At the
court of the King of Uganda in Central Africa, when
the king laughs, every one laughs ; when he sneezes,
every one sneezes ; when he has a cold, every one
pretends to have a cold ; when he has his hair cut, so
has every one.[3] At the court of Boni in Celebes it is
a rule that whatever the king does all the courtiers
must do. If he stands, they stand ; if he sits, they sit ;

---

[1] Strabo, xvii. 2, 3 ; Diodorus, iii. 7.

[2] Mohammed Ebn- Omar El-Tounsy,
Voyage au Darfour (Paris, 1845), p.
162 *sq.* ; *Travels of an Arab Merchant
in Soudan*, abridged from the French
by Bayle St. John (London, 1854), p.

78 ; *Bulletin de la Société de Géographie*
(Paris) IVme Série, iv. (1852) p. 539 *sq.*

[3] R. W. Felkin, "Notes on the
Waganda Tribe of Central Africa," in
*Proceedings of the Royal Society of
Edinburgh*, xiii. (1884-1886) p. 711.

if he falls off his horse, they fall off their horses ; if
he bathes, they bathe, and passers-by must go into the
water in the dress, good or bad, which they happen to
have on.[1]   But to return to the death of the divine
man. The old Prussians acknowledged as their supreme
lord a ruler who governed them in the name of the
gods, and was known as God's Mouth (*Kirwaido*).
When he felt himself weak and ill, if he wished to leave
a good name behind him, he had a great heap made of
thorn-bushes and straw, on which he mounted and delivered a long sermon to the people, exhorting them to
serve the gods and promising to go to the gods and
speak for the people.   Then he took some of the perpetual fire which burned in front of the holy oak-tree,
and lighting the pile with it burned himself to death.[2]

In the cases hitherto described, the divine king
or priest is suffered by his people to retain office
until some outward defect, some visible symptom of
failing health or advancing age warns them that he
is no longer equal to the discharge of his divine
duties ; but not until such symptoms have made
their appearance is he put to death.   Some peoples,
however, appear to have thought it unsafe to wait for
even the slightest symptom of decay and have preferred to kill the king while he was still in the full
vigour of life.   Accordingly, they have fixed a term
beyond which he might not reign, and at the close of
which he must die, the term fixed upon being short
enough to exclude the probability of his degenerat-
ing physically in the interval.   In some parts of
Southern India the period fixed was twelve years.

[1] *Narrative of events in Borneo and
Celebes, from the Journals of James
Brooke, Esq., Rajah of Sarawak.*   By
Captain R. Mundy, i. 134.

[2] Simon Grunau, *Preussische Chronik*, herausgegeben von Dr. M. Perlbach (Leipzig, 1876), i. p. 97.

Thus, according to an old traveller, in the province of Quilacare " There is a Gentile house of prayer, in which there is an idol which they hold in great account, and every twelve years they celebrate a great feast to it, whither all the Gentiles go as to a jubilee. This temple possesses many lands and much revenue ; it is a very great affair. This province has a king over it ; who has not more than twelve years to reign from jubilee to jubilee. His manner of living is in this wise, that is to say, when the twelve years are completed, on the day of this feast there assemble together innumerable people, and much money is spent in giving food to Bramans. The king has a wooden scaffolding made, spread over with silken hangings ; and on that day he goes to bathe at a tank with great ceremonies and sound of music, after that he comes to the idol and prays to it, and mounts on to the scaffolding, and there before all the people he takes some very sharp knives and begins to cut off his nose, and then his ears and his lips and all his members and as much flesh of himself as he can ; and he throws it away very hurriedly until so much of his blood is spilled that he begins to faint, and then he cuts his throat himself. And he performs this sacrifice to the idol ; and whoever desires to reign other twelve years, and undertake this martyrdom for love of the idol, has to be present looking on at this ; and from that place they raise him up as king." [1]

Formerly the Samorin or King of Calicut, on the Malabar coast, had also to cut his throat in public at the end of a twelve years' reign. But towards the end of the seventeenth century the rule had been

---

[1] Barbosa, *A Description of the Coasts of East Africa and Malabar in the beginning of the Sixteenth Century* (Hakluyt Society, 1866), p. 172 *sq.*

modified as follows : " A new custom is followed by the modern Samorins, that jubilee is proclaimed throughout his dominions, at the end of twelve years, and a tent is pitched for him in a spacious plain, and a great feast is celebrated for ten or twelve days, with mirth and jollity, guns firing night and day, so at the end of the feast any four of the guests that have a mind to gain a crown by a desperate action, in fighting their way through 30 or 40,000 of his guards, and kill the Samorin in his tent, he that kills him succeeds him in his empire. In anno 1695, one of those jubilees happened, and the tent pitched near Pennany, a sea-port of his, about fifteen leagues to the southward of Calicut. There were but three men that would venture on that desperate action, who fell in, with sword and target among the guard, and, after they had killed and wounded many were themselves killed. One of the desperados had a nephew of fifteen or sixteen years of age, that kept close by his uncle in the attack on the guards, and, when he saw him fall, the youth got through the guards into the tent, and made a stroke at his Majesty's head, and had certainly despatched him, if a large brass lamp which was burning over his head, had not marred the blow ; but, before he could make another he was killed by the guards ; and, I believe, the same Samorin reigns yet. I chanced to come that time along the coast and heard the guns for two or three days and nights successively." [1]

In some places it appears that the people could not trust the king to remain in full bodily and mental vigour for more than a year ; hence at the end of a year's reign he was put to death, and a new king

---

[1] Alex. Hamilton, " A new Account of the East Indies," in Pinkerton's *Voyages and Travels*, viii. 374.

appointed to reign in his turn a year, and suffer death at the end of it. At least this is the conclusion to which the following evidence points. According to the historian Berosus, who as a Babylonian priest spoke with ample knowledge, there was annually celebrated in Babylon a festival called the Sacaea. It began on the 16th day of the month Lous, and lasted for five days. During these five days masters and servants changed places, the servants giving orders and the masters obeying them. A prisoner condemned to death was dressed in the king's robes, seated on the king's throne, allowed to issue whatever commands he pleased, to eat, drink, and enjoy himself, and to lie with the king's concubines. But at the end of the five days he was stripped of his royal robes, scourged, and crucified.[1] This custom might perhaps have been explained as merely a grim jest perpetrated in a season of jollity at the expense of an unhappy criminal. But one circumstance—the leave given to the mock king to enjoy the king's concubines—is decisive against this interpretation. Considering the jealous seclusion of

---

[1] Athenaeus, xiv. p. 639 C; Dio Chrysostom, *Orat.* iv. p. 69 *sq.* (vol. i. p. 76, ed. Dindorf). Dio. Chrysostom does not mention his authority, but it was probably either Berosus or Ctesias. Though the execution of the mock king is not mentioned in the passage of Berosus cited by Athenaeus, the omission is probably due to the fact that the mention of it was not germane to Athenaeus's purpose, which was simply to give a list of festivals at which masters waited on their servants. That the ζωγάνης was put to death is further shown by Macrobius, *Sat.* iii. 7, 6, "*Animas vero sacratorum hominum quos † zanas Graeci vocant, dis debitas aestimabant,*" where for *zanas* we should probably read ζωγάνας with Liebrecht, in *Philologus,* xxii. 710, and

Bachofen, *Die Sage von Tanaquil,* p. 52, *note* 16. The custom, so far as appears from our authorities, does not date from before the Persian domination in Babylon; but probably it was much older. In the passage of Dio Chrysostom ἐκρέμασαν should be translated "crucified" (or "impaled"), not "hung." It is strange that this, the regular, sense of κρεμάννυμι, as applied to executions, should not be noticed even in the latest edition of Liddell and Scott's *Greek Lexicon.* Hanging, though a mode of suicide, was not a mode of execution in antiquity either in the east or west. In one of the passages cited by L. and S. for the sense "to hang" (Plutarch, *Caes.* 2), the context proves that the meaning is "to crucify."

an oriental despot's harem we may be quite certain that permission to invade it would never have been granted by the despot, least of all to a condemned criminal, except for the very gravest cause. This cause could hardly be other than that the condemned man was about to die in the king's stead, and that to make the substitution perfect it was necessary he should enjoy the full rights of royalty during his brief reign. There is nothing surprising in this substitution. The rule that the king must be put to death either on the appearance of any symptom of bodily decay or at the end of a fixed period is certainly one which, sooner or later, the kings would seek to abolish or modify. We have seen that in Ethiopia and Sofala the rule was boldly set aside by enlightened monarchs ; and that in Calicut the old custom of killing the king at the end of twelve years was changed into a permission granted to any one at the end of the twelve years' period to attack the king, and, in the event of killing him, to reign in his stead ; though, as the king took care at these times to be surrounded by his guards, the permission was little more than a form. Another way of modifying the stern old rule is seen in the Babylonian custom just described. When the time drew near for the king to be put to death (in Babylon this appears to have been at the end of a single year's reign) he abdicated for a few days, during which a temporary king reigned and suffered in his stead. At first the temporary king may have been an innocent person, possibly a member of the king's own family; but with the growth of civilisation the sacrifice of an innocent person would be revolting to the public sentiment, and accordingly a condemned criminal would be invested with the brief and fatal sovereignty. In the sequel we shall find other examples of a dying criminal representing a dying god. For we must not forget that the king is slain in his character of a god, his death and resurrection, as the only means of perpetuating the divine life unimpaired, being deemed necessary for the salvation of his people and the world.

In some places this modified form of the old custom has been further softened down. The king still abdicates annually for a short time and his place is filled by a more or less nominal sovereign ; but at the close of his short reign the latter is no longer killed, though sometimes a mock execution still survives as a memorial of the time when he was actually put to death. To take examples. In the month of Méac (February) the King of Cambodia annually abdicated for three days. During this time he performed no act of authority, he did not touch the seals, he did not even receive the revenues which fell due. In his stead there reigned a temporary king called Sdach Méac, that is, King February. The office of temporary king was hereditary in a family distantly connected with the royal house, the sons succeeding the fathers and the younger brothers the elder brothers, just as in the succession to the real sovereignty. On a favourable day fixed by the astrologers the temporary king was conducted by the mandarins in triumphal procession. He rode one of the royal elephants, seated in the royal palanquin, and escorted by soldiers who, dressed in appropriate costumes, represented the neighbouring peoples of Siam, Annam, Laos, and so on. Instead of the golden crown he wore a peaked white cap, and his regalia, instead of being of gold encrusted with diamonds, were of rough wood. After paying homage to the real king, from whom he received the sovereignty for three days, together with all the revenues accruing during that time (though this last custom has been omitted for some time), he moved in procession round the palace and through the streets of the capital. On the third day, after the usual procession, the temporary king gave orders that the elephants should trample under foot the "mountain of rice," which was a scaffold of bamboo surrounded by sheaves of rice. The people gathered up the rice, each man taking home a little with him to secure a good harvest. Some of it was also taken to the king, who had it cooked and presented to the monks.[1]

In Siam on the sixth day of the moon in the sixth month (the end of April) a temporary king is appointed, who for three days enjoys the royal prerogatives, the real king remaining shut up in his palace. This temporary king sends his numerous satellites in all directions to seize and confiscate whatever they can find in the bazaar and open shops; even the ships and junks which arrive in harbour during the three days are confiscated to him and must be redeemed. He goes to a field in the middle of the city, whither is brought a gilded plough drawn by gaily-decked oxen. After the plough has been anointed and the oxen rubbed with incense, the mock king traces nine furrows with the plough, followed by aged dames of the palace scattering the first seed of the season. As soon as the nine furrows are drawn, the crowd of spectators rushes in and scrambles for the seed which has just been sown, believing that, mixed with the seed-rice, it will ensure a plentiful crop. Then the oxen are unyoked, and

---

[1] E. Aymonier, *Notice sur le Cambodge*, p. 61 ; J. Moura, *Le Royaume du Cambodge*, i. 327 *sq.* For the connection of the temporary king's family with the royal house, see Aymonier, *op. cit.* p. 36 *sq.*

rice, maize, sesame, sago, bananas, sugar-cane, melons, etc. are set before them; whatever they eat first will, it is thought, be dear in the year following, though some people interpret the omen in the opposite sense. During this time the temporary king stands leaning against a tree with his right foot resting on his left knee. From standing thus on one foot he is popularly known as King Hop; but his official title is Phaya Phollathep, "Lord of the Heavenly Hosts."[1] He is a sort of Minister of Agriculture; all disputes about fields, rice, and so on, are referred to him. There is moreover another ceremony in which he personates the king. It takes place in the second month (which falls in the cold season) and lasts three days. He is conducted in procession to an open place opposite the Temple of the Brahmans, where there are a number of poles dressed like May-poles, upon which the Brahmans swing. All the while that they swing and dance, the Lord of the Heavenly Hosts has to stand on one foot upon a seat which is made of bricks plastered over, covered with a white cloth, and hung with tapestry. He is supported by a wooden frame with a gilt canopy, and two Brahmans stand one on each side of him. The dancing Brahmans carry buffalo horns with which they draw water from a large copper caldron and sprinkle it on the people; this is supposed to bring good luck, causing the people to dwell in peace and quiet, health and prosperity. The time during which the Lord of the Heavenly Hosts has to stand on one foot is about three hours. This is thought " to prove the dispositions of the Devattas and spirits." If he lets his foot down

---

[1] Pallegoix, *Description du Royaume Thai ou Siam*, i. 250; Bastian, *Die Völker des östlichen Asien*, iii. 305-309, 526-528; Turpin, *History of Siam*, in Pinkerton's *Voyages and Travels*, ix. 581 *sq.* Bowring (*Siam*, i. 158 *sq.*) copies, as usual, from Pallegoix.

"he is liable to forfeit his property and have his family enslaved by the king; as it is believed to be a bad omen, portending destruction to the state, and instability to the throne. But if he stand firm he is believed to have gained a victory over evil spirits, and he has moreover the privilege, ostensibly at least, of seizing any ship which may enter the harbour during these three days, and taking its contents, and also of entering any open shop in the town and carrying away what he chooses." [1]

In Upper Egypt on the first day of the solar year by Coptic reckoning, that is on 10th September, when the Nile has generally reached its highest point, the regular government is suspended for three days and every town chooses its own ruler. This temporary lord wears a sort of tall fool's cap and a long flaxen beard, and is enveloped in a strange mantle. With a wand of office in his hand and attended by men disguised as scribes, executioners, etc., he proceeds to the Governor's house. The latter allows himself to be deposed; and the mock king, mounting the throne, holds a tribunal, to the decisions of which even the governor and his officials must bow. After three days the mock king is condemned to death; the envelope or shell in which he was encased is committed to the flames, and from its ashes the Fellah creeps forth. [2]

Sometimes the temporary king occupies the throne, not annually, but once for all at the beginning of each reign. Thus in the kingdom of Jambi (in Sumatra) it is the custom that at the beginning of a new reign a man of the people should occupy the throne and

---

[1] Lieut. Col. James Low, "On the Laws of Muung Thai or Siam," in *Journal of the Indian Archipelago*, i. (Singapore, 1847) p. 339; Bastian, *Die Völker des östlichen Asien*, iii. 98, 314, 526 *sq.*

[2] C. B. Klunzinger, *Bilder aus Oberägypten, der Wüste und dem Rothen Meere*, p. 180 *sq.*

exercise the royal prerogatives for a single day. The origin of the custom is explained by a tradition that there were once five royal brothers, the four elder of whom all declined the crown on the ground of various bodily defects, leaving it to their youngest brother. But the eldest occupied the throne for one day, and reserved for his descendants a similar privilege at the beginning of every reign. Thus the office of temporary king is hereditary in a family akin to the royal house.[1] In Bilaspur it seems to be the custom, after the death of a Rajah, for a Brahman to eat rice out of the dead Rajah's hand, and then to occupy the throne for a year. At the end of the year the Brahman receives presents and is dismissed from the territory, being forbidden apparently to return. " The idea seems to be that the spirit of the Rájá enters into the Bráhman who eats the *khír* (rice and milk) out of his hand when he is dead, as the Brahman is apparently carefully watched during the whole year, and not allowed to go away." The same or a similar custom is believed to obtain among the hill states about Kángrá.[2] At the installation of a prince of Carinthia a peasant, in whose family the office was hereditary, ascended a marble stone which stood surrounded by meadows in a spacious valley ; on his right stood a black mother-cow, on his left an ugly mare. A rustic crowd gathered about him. Then the future prince, dressed as a peasant and carrying a shepherd's staff, drew near, attended by courtiers and magistrates. On perceiving him the peasant called out, " Who is this whom I see coming so proudly along ? " The people answered, " The

[1] J. W. Boers, "Oud volksgebruik in het Rijk van Jambi," in *Tijdschrift voor Neêrland's Indië*, iii. (1840), dl. i. 372 *sqq.*
[2] *Panjab Notes and Queries*, i. 674.

prince of the land." The peasant was then prevailed on to surrender the marble seat to the prince on condition of receiving sixty pence, the cow and mare, and exemption from taxes. But before yielding his place he gave the prince a light blow on the cheek.[1]

Some points about these temporary kings deserve to be specially noticed before we pass to the next branch of the evidence. In the first place, the Cambodian and Siamese examples bring clearly out the fact that it is especially the divine or supernatural functions of the king which are transferred to his temporary substitute. This appears from the belief that by keeping up his foot the temporary king of Siam gained a victory over the evil spirits; whereas by letting it down he imperilled the existence of the state. Again, the Cambodian ceremony of trampling down the "mountain of rice," and the Siamese ceremony of opening the ploughing and sowing, are charms to produce a plentiful harvest, as appears from the belief that those who carry home some of the trampled rice or of the seed sown will thereby secure a good crop. But the task of making the crops grow, thus deputed to the temporary kings, is one of the supernatural functions regularly supposed to be dischaŕged by kings in primitive society. The rule that the mock king must stand on one foot upon a raised seat in the rice-field was perhaps originally meant as a charm to make the crop grow high; at least this was the object of a similar ceremony observed by the old Prussians. The tallest girl, standing on one foot upon a seat, with her lap full of cakes, a cup of brandy in her right hand and a piece of elm-bark

---

[1] Aeneas Sylvius, *Opera* (Bâle, 1571), p. 409 *sq.*; Grimm, *Deutsche Rechtsalterthümer*, p. 253. According to Grimm (who does not refer to Aeneas Sylvius) the cow and mare stood beside the prince, not the peasant.

or linden-bark in her left, prayed to the god Waizganthos that the flax might grow as high as she
was standing. Then, after draining the cup, she had
it refilled, and poured the brandy on the ground as
an offering to Waizganthos, and threw down the cakes
for his attendant sprites. If she remained steady on
one foot throughout the ceremony, it was an omen
that the flax crop would be good; but if she let her
foot down, it was feared that the crop might fail.[1]
The gilded plough with which the Siamese mock king
opens the ploughing may be compared with the bronze
ploughs which the Etruscans employed at the ceremony of founding cities;[2] in both cases the use of
iron was probably forbidden on superstitious grounds.[3]

Another point to notice about these temporary
kings is that in two places (Cambodia and Jambi)
they come of a stock which is believed to be akin
to the royal family. If the view here taken of the
origin of these temporary kingships is correct, the fact
that the temporary king is sometimes of the same race
as the real king admits of a ready explanation. When
the king first succeeded in getting the life of another
accepted as a sacrifice in lieu of his own, he would
have to show that the death of that other would serve
the purpose quite as well as his own would have done.
Now it was as a god that the king had to die; therefore the substitute who died for him had to be invested,
at least for the occasion, with the divine attributes of
the king. This, as we have just seen, was certainly
the case with the temporary kings of Siam and Cam-

---

[1] Lasicius, "De diis Samagitarum
caeterorumque Sarmatarum," in *Respublica sive Status Regni Poloniae,
Lituaniae, Prussiae, Livoniae*, etc.
(Elzevir, 1627), p. 306 *sq.*; *id.* edited

by W. Mannhardt in *Magazin herausgegeben von der Lettisch-Literärischen
Gesellschaft*, xiv. 91 *sq.*
[2] Macrobius, *Saturn.* v. 19, 13.
[3] See above, p. 172 *sqq.*

bodia; they were invested with the supernatural
functions, which in an earlier stage of society were
the special attributes of the king. But no one could
so well represent the king in his divine character as
his son, who might be supposed to share the divine
afflatus of his father. No one, therefore, could so
appropriately die for the king and, through him, for
the whole people, as the king's son. There is evidence
that amongst the Semites of Western Asia (the very
region where the redemption of the king's life by the
sacrifice of another comes out so unmistakably in
the Sacaean festival) the king, in a time of national
danger, sometimes gave his own son to die as a
sacrifice for the people. Thus Philo of Byblus,
in his work on the Jews, says: " It was an ancient
custom in a crisis of great danger that the ruler of a
city or nation should give his beloved son to die for
the whole people, as a ransom offered to the avenging
demons; and the children thus offered were slain with
mystic rites. So Cronus, whom the Phoenicians call
Israel, being king of the land and having an only-
begotten son called Jeoud (for in the Phoenician tongue
Jeoud signifies ' only-begotten '), dressed him in royal
robes and sacrificed him upon an altar in a time of war,
when the country was in great danger from the enemy."[1]
When the King of Moab was besieged by the Israelites
and hard beset, he took his eldest son, who should
have reigned in his stead, and offered him for a burnt
offering on the wall.[2] But amongst the Semites the
practice of sacrificing their children was not confined
to kings. In times of great calamity, such as
pestilence, drought, or defeat in war, the Phoenicians

---

[1] Philo of Byblus, quoted by Eusebius, *Praepar. Evang.* i. 10, 29 *sq.*
[2] 2 Kings iii. 27.

used to sacrifice one of their dearest to Baal. " Phoenician history," says an ancient writer, "is full of such
sacrifices."[1] When the Carthaginians were defeated
and besieged by Agathocles, they ascribed their disasters to the wrath of Baal; for whereas in former
times they had been wont to sacrifice to him their own
children, they had latterly fallen into the habit of buy-
ing children and rearing them to be victims. So, to
appease the angry god, two hundred children of the
noblest families were picked out for sacrifice, and the
tale of victims was swelled by not less than three
hundred more who volunteered to die for the father-
land. They were sacrificed by being placed, one by
one, on the sloping hands of the brazen image, from
which they rolled into a pit of fire.[2] If an aristocracy
thus adopted the practice of sacrificing other people's
children instead of their own, kings may very well
have followed or set the example. A final mitigation
of the custom would be the substitution of condemned
criminals for innocent victims. Such a substitution
is known to have taken place in the human sacrifices
annually offered in Rhodes to Baal.[3]

The custom of sacrificing children, especially the
first born, is not peculiarly Semitic. In some tribes
of New South Wales the first-born child of every
woman was eaten by the tribe as part of a religious
ceremony.[4] The Indians of Florida sacrificed their
first-born male children.[5] Amongst the people of
Senjero in Eastern Africa we are told that many
families "must offer up their first-born sons as sacri-

---

[1] Porphyry, *De abstin.* ii. 56.

[2] Diodorus, xx. 14.

[3] Porphyry, *De abstin.* ii. 54.

[4] Brough Smyth, *Aborigines of Victoria*, ii. 311.

[5] Strachey, *Historie of travaille into Virginia Britannia* (Hakluyt Society), p. 84.

fices, because once upon a time, when summer and winter were jumbled together in a bad season, and the fruits of the earth would not ripen, the sooth-sayers enjoined it. At that time a great pillar of iron is said to have stood at the entrance of the capital, which by the advice of the soothsayers was broken down by order of the king, upon which the seasons bécame regular again. To avert the recurrence of such a confusion of the seasons, the soothsayers are reported to have enjoined the king to pour human blood once a year on the base of the broken shaft of the pillar, and also upon the throne. Since then certain families are obliged to deliver up their first-born sons, who are sacrificed at an appointed time."[1] The heathen Russians often sacrificed their first-born to the god Perun.[2]

The condemnation and pretended death by fire of the mock king in Egypt is probably a reminiscence of a real custom of burning him. Evidence of a practice of burning divine personages will be forth-coming later on. In Bilaspur the expulsion of the Brahman who had occupied the king's throne for a year is perhaps a substitute for putting him to death.

The explanation here given of the custom of killing divine persons assumes, or at least is readily combined with, the idea that the soul of the slain divinity is transmitted to his successor. Of this trans-mission I have no direct proof; and so far a link in

---

[1] J. L. Krapf, *Travels, Researches, and Missionary Labours during an Eighteen Years' Residence in Eastern Africa*, p. 69 *sq.* Dr. Krapf, who reports the custom at second hand, thinks that the existence of the pillar may be doubted, but that the rest of the story harmonises well enough with African superstition.

[2] F. J. Mone, *Geschichte des Heid-enthums im nördlichen Europa*, i. 119.

the chain of evidence is wanting. But if I cannot prove by actual examples this succession to the soul of the slain god, it can at least be made probable that such a succession was supposed to take place. For it has been already shown that the soul of the incarnate deity is often supposed to transmigrate at death into another incarnation;[1] and if this takes place when the death is a natural one, there seems no reason why it should not take place when the death is a violent one. Certainly the idea that the soul of a dying person may be transmitted to his successor is perfectly familiar to primitive peoples. In Nias the eldest son usually succeeds his father in the chieftainship. But if from any bodily or mental defect the eldest son is incapacitated from ruling, the father determines in his life-time which of his sons shall succeed him. In order, however, to establish his right of succession it is necessary that the son upon whom his father's choice falls shall catch in his mouth or in a bag the last breath, and with it the soul, of the dying chief. For whoever catches his last breath is chief equally with the appointed successor. Hence the other brothers, and sometimes also strangers, crowd round the dying man to catch his soul as it passes. The houses in Nias are raised above the ground on posts, and it has happened that when the dying man lay with his face on the floor, one of the candidates has bored a hole in the floor and sucked in the chief's last breath through a bamboo tube. When the chief has no son, his soul is caught in a bag, which is fastened to an image made to represent the deceased; the

---

[1] Above, p. 42 *sqq.*

soul is then believed to pass into the image.[1] Amongst the Takilis or Carrier Indians of North-West America, when a corpse is burned the priest pretends to catch the soul of the deceased in his hands, which he closes with many gesticulations. He then communicates the captured soul to the dead man's successor by throwing his hands towards and blowing upon him. The person to whom the soul is thus communicated takes the name and rank of the deceased. On the death of a chief the priest thus fills a responsible and influential position, for he may transmit the soul to whom he will, though, doubtless, he generally follows the regular line of succession.[2] Algonkin women who wished to become mothers flocked to the side of a dying person in the hope of receiving and being impregnated by the passing soul. Amongst the Seminoles of Florida when a woman died in childbed the infant was held over her face to receive her parting spirit.[3] The Romans caught the breath of dying friends in their mouths, and so received into themselves the soul of the departed.[4] The same custom is said to be still practised in Lancashire.[5] We may therefore fairly suppose that when the divine king or priest is put to death his spirit is believed to pass into his successor.

[1] Nieuwenhuisen en Rosenberg, "Verslag omtrent het eiland Nias," in *Verhandelingen van het Batav. Genootschap van Kunsten en Wetenschappen*, xxx. 85; Rosenberg, *Der Malayische Archipel*, p. 160; Chatelin, "Godsdienst en bijgeloof der Niassers," in *Tijdschrift voor Indische Taal-Land-en Volkenkunde*, xxvi. 142 *sq.*; Sundermann, "Die Insel Nias und die Mission daselbst," in *Allgemeine Missions-Zeitschrift*, xi. 445.

[2] Ch. Wilkes, *Narrative of the U.S. Exploring Expedition* (London, 1845), iv. 453; *U.S. Exploring Expedition, Ethnography and Philology*, by H. Hale, p. 203.

[3] D. G. Brinton, *Myths of the New World*, p. 270 *sq.*

[4] Servius on Virgil, *Aen.* iv. 685; Cicero, *In Verr.* ii. 5, 45; K. F. Hermann, *Griech. Privatalterthümer*, ed. Blumner, p. 362 *note* 1.

[5] Harland and Wilkinson, *Lancashire Folk-lore*, p. 7 *sq.*

§ 2.—*Killing the tree-spirit*

It remains to ask what light the custom of killing the divine king or priest sheds upon the subject of our inquiry. In the first chapter we saw reason to suppose that the King of the Wood was regarded as an incarnation of the tree-spirit or of the spirit of vegetation, and that as such he would be endowed, in the belief of his worshippers, with a supernatural power of making the trees to bear fruit, the crops to grow, and so on. His life must therefore have been held very precious by his worshippers, and was probably hedged in by a system of elaborate precautions or taboos like those by which, in so many places, the life of the god-man has been guarded against the malignant influence of demons and sorcerers. But we have seen that the very value attached to the life of the man-god necessitates his violent death as the only means of preserving it from the inevitable decay of age. The same reasoning would apply to the King of the Wood ; he too had to be killed in order that the divine spirit, incarnate in him, might be transferred in unabated vigour to his successor. The rule that he held office till a stronger should slay him might be supposed to secure both the preservation of his divine life in full vigour and its transference to a suitable successor as soon as that vigour began to be impaired. For so long as he could maintain his position by the strong hand, it might be inferred that his natural force was not abated ; whereas his defeat and death at the hands of another proved that his strength was beginning to fail and that it was time his divine life should be lodged in a less dilapidated tabernacle. This explanation of the rule that the King of the Wood had to be slain by his successor at least renders that rule perfectly intelligible. Moreover it is countenanced by the analogy of the Chitombé, upon whose life the existence of the world was supposed to hang, and who was therefore slain by his successor as soon as he showed signs of breaking up. Again, the terms on which in later times the King of Calicut held office are identical with those attached to the office of King of the Wood, except that whereas the former might be assailed by a candidate at any time, the King of Calicut might only be attacked once every twelve years. But as the leave granted to the King of Calicut to reign so long as he could defend himself against all comers was a mitigation of the old rule which set a fixed term to his life, so we may conjecture that the similar permission granted to the King of the Wood was a mitigation of an older custom of putting him to death at the end of a set period. In both cases the new rule gave to the god-man at least a chance for his life, which under the old rule was denied him ; and people probably reconciled themselves to the change by reflecting that so long as the god-man could maintain himself by the sword against all assaults, there was no reason to apprehend that the fatal decay had set in.

The conjecture that the King of the Wood was formerly put to death at the expiry of a set term, without being allowed a chance for his life, will be confirmed if evidence can be adduced of a custom of periodically killing his counterparts, the human representatives of the tree-spirit, in Northern Europe. Now in point of fact such a custom has left unmis-

595976

takable traces of itself in the rural festivals of the peasantry. To take examples.

In Lower Bavaria the Whitsuntide representative of the tree-spirit—the *Pfingstl* as he was called—was clad from top to toe in leaves and flowers. On his head he wore a high pointed cap, the ends of which rested on his shoulders, only two holes being left in it for his eyes. The cap was covered with water flowers and surmounted with a nosegay of peonies. The sleeves of his coat were also made of water-plants, and the rest of his body was enveloped in alder and hazel leaves. On each side of him marched a boy holding up one of the *Pfingstl's* arms. These two boys carried drawn swords, and so did most of the others who formed the procession. They stopped at every house where they hoped to receive a present ; and the people, in hiding, soused the leaf-clad boy with water. All rejoiced when he was well drenched. Finally he waded into the brook up to his middle ; whereupon one of the boys, standing on the bridge, pretended to cut off his head.[1] At Wurmlingen in Swabia a score of young fellows dress themselves on Whit-Monday in white shirts and white trousers, with red scarves round their waists and swords hanging from the scarves. They ride on horse-back into the wood, led by two trumpeters blowing their trumpets. In the wood they cut down leafy oak branches, in which they envelop from head to foot him who was the last of their number to ride out of the village. His legs, however, are encased separately, so that he may be able to mount his horse again. Further, they give him a long artificial neck, with an

---

[1] Fr. Panzer, *Beitrag zur deutschen Mythologie*, i. 235 *sq.* ; W. Mannhardt, *Baumkultus*, p. 320 *sq.*

artificial head and a false face on the top of it.   Then
a May-tree is cut, generally an aspen or beech about
ten feet high ; and being decked with coloured
handkerchiefs and ribbons it is entrusted to a special
" May-bearer."   The cavalcade then returns with
music and song to the village.   Amongst the personages who figure in the procession are a Moorish king
with a sooty face and a crown on his head, a Dr.
Iron-Beard, a corporal, and an executioner.   They
halt on the village green, and each of the characters
makes a speech in rhyme.   The executioner announces
that the leaf-clad man has been condemned to death
and cuts off his false head.   Then the riders race to
the May-tree, which has been set up a little way off.
The first man who succeeds in wrenching it from the
ground as he gallops past keeps it with all its decorations.   The ceremony is observed every second or
third year.[1]

In Saxony and Thüringen there is a Whitsuntide
ceremony called "chasing the Wild Man out of the
bush," or "fetching the Wild Man out of the wood."
A young fellow is enveloped in leaves or moss and
called the Wild Man.   He hides in the wood and the
other lads of the village go out to seek him.   They
find him, lead him captive out of the wood, and fire at
him with blank muskets.   He falls like dead to the
ground, but a lad dressed as a doctor bleeds him, and
he comes to life again.   At this they rejoice and
binding him fast on a waggon take him to the village,
where they tell all the people how they have caught the
Wild Man.   At every house they receive a gift.[2]   In

---

[1] E. Meier, *Deutsche Sagen, Sitten und Gebräuche aus Schwaben*, pp. 409-419 ; W. Mannhardt, *Baumkultus*, p. 349 *sq.*

[2] E. Sommer, *Sagen, Märchen und Gebräuche aus Sachsen und Thüringen*, p. 154 *sq.* ; W. Mannhardt, *Baumkultus*, p. 335 *sq.*

the Erzgebirge the following custom was annually observed at Shrovetide about the beginning of the
seventeenth century. Two men disguised as Wild
Men, the one in brushwood and moss, the other
in straw, were led about the streets, and at last taken
to the market-place, where they were chased up and
down, shot and stabbed. Before falling they reeled
about with strange gestures and spirted blood on the
people from bladders which they carried. When they
were down, the huntsmen placed them on boards
and carried them to the alehouse, the miners march-
ing beside them and winding blasts on their ·min-
ing tools as if they had taken a noble head of
game.[1] A very similar Shrovetide custom is still
observed in the neighbourhood of Schluckenau
(Bohemia). A man dressed up as a Wild Man is
chased through several streets till he comes to a narrow
lane across which a cord is stretched. He stumbles
over the cord and, falling to the ground, is overtaken
and caught by his pursuers. The executioner runs up
and stabs with his sword a bladder filled with blood
which the Wild Man wears round his body ; so the
Wild Man dies, while a stream of blood reddens the
ground. Next day a straw-man, made up to look like
the Wild Man, is placed on a litter, and, accompanied
by a great crowd, is taken to a pool into which it is
thrown by the executioner. The ceremony is called
" burying the Carnival." [2]

In Semic (Bohemia) the custom of beheading the
King is observed on Whit-Monday. A troop of
young people disguise themselves ; each is girt with
a girdle of bark and carries a wooden sword and a

---

[1] W. Mannhardt, *Baumkultus*, p. 336.
[2] Reinsberg - Düringsfeld, *Fest-Kal-* ender *aus Böhmen*, p. 61 ; W. Mannhardt, *Baumkultus*, p. 336 *sq.*

trumpet of willow-bark. The King wears a robe of tree-bark adorned with flowers, on his head is a crown of bark decked with flowers and branches, his feet are wound about with ferns, a mask hides his face, and for a sceptre he has a hawthorn switch in his hand. A lad leads him through the village by a rope fastened to his foot, while the rest dance about, blow their trumpets, and whistle. In every farmhouse the King is chased round the room, and one of the troop, amid much noise and outcry, strikes with his sword a blow on the King's robe of bark till it rings again. Then a gratuity is demanded.[1] The ceremony of decapitation, which is here somewhat slurred over, is carried out with a greater semblance of reality in other parts of Bohemia. Thus in some villages of the Königgrätz district on Whit-Monday the girls assemble under one lime-tree and the young men under another, all dressed in their best and tricked out with ribbons. The young men twine a garland for the Queen and the girls for the King. When they have chosen the King and Queen they all go in procession, two and two, to the alehouse, from the balcony of which the crier proclaims the names of the King and Queen. Both are then invested with the insignia of their dignity and are crowned with the garlands, while the music plays up. Then some one gets on a bench and accuses the King of various offences, such as ill-treating the cattle. The King appeals to witnesses and a trial ensues, at the close of which the judge, who carries a white wand as his badge of office, pronounces a verdict of "guilty" or "not guilty." If the verdict is "guilty" the judge breaks his wand, the

---

[1] Reinsberg-Düringsfeld, *Fest-Kalender aus Böhmen*, p. 263; W. Mannhardt, *Baumkultus*, p. 343.

King kneels on a white cloth, all heads are bared, and a soldier sets three or four hats, one above the other, on the King's head. The judge then pronounces the word "guilty" thrice in a loud voice, and orders the crier to behead the King. The crier obeys by striking off the King's hats with his wooden sword.[1]

But perhaps, for our purpose, the most instructive of these mimic executions is the following Bohemian one, which has been in part described already.[2] In some places of the Pilsen district (Bohemia) on Whit-Monday the King is dressed in bark, ornamented with flowers and ribbons; he wears a crown of gilt paper and rides a horse, which is also decked with flowers. Attended by a judge, an executioner and other characters, and followed by a train of soldiers, all mounted, he rides to the village square, where a hut or arbour of green boughs has been erected under the May-trees, which are firs, freshly cut, peeled to the top, and dressed with flowers and ribbons. After the dames and maidens of the village have been criticised and a frog beheaded, in the way already described, the cavalcade rides to a place previously determined upon, in a straight, broad street. Here they draw up in two lines and the King takes to flight. He is given a short start and rides off at full speed, pursued by the whole troop. If they fail to catch him he remains King for another year, and his companions must pay his score at the alehouse in the evening. But if they overtake and catch him he is scourged with hazel rods or beaten with the wooden swords and compelled to dismount. Then the executioner asks, "Shall I behead this King?" The answer is given, "Behead him;" the executioner

---

[1] Reinsberg-Düringsfeld, *Fest-Kalender aus Böhmen*, p. 269 *sq.*
[2] See above, p. 92 *sq.*

brandishes his axe, and with the words, "One, two, three, let the King headless be!" he strikes off the King's crown. Amid the loud cries of the bystanders the King sinks to the ground ; then he is laid on a bier and carried to the nearest farmhouse.[1]

In the personages who are thus slain in mimicry it is impossible not to recognise representatives of the tree-spirit or spirit of vegetation, as he is supposed to manifest himself in spring. The bark, leaves, and flowers in which the actors are dressed, and the season of the year at which they appear, show that they belong to the same class as the Grass King, King of the May, Jack-in-the-Green, and other representatives of the vernal spirit of vegetation which we examined in the first chapter. As if to remove any possible doubt on this head, we find that in two cases[2] these slain men are brought into direct connection with May-trees, which are (as we have seen) the impersonal, as the May King, Grass King, etc., are the personal representatives of the tree-spirit. The drenching of the *Pfingstl* with water and his wading up to the middle into the brook are, therefore, no doubt rain-charms like those which have been already described.[3]

But if these personages represent, as they certainly do, the spirit of vegetation in spring, the question arises, Why kill them ? What is the object of slaying the spirit of vegetation at any time and above all in spring, when his services are most wanted ? The only answer to this question seems to be given in the explanation already proposed of the custom of killing the divine king or priest. The divine life, incarnate in a material and mortal body, is liable

---

[1] Reinsberg-Düringsfeld, *Fest-Kalender aus Böhmen*, p. 264 *sq.* ; W. Mannhardt, *Baumkultus*, p. 353 *sq.*   [2] See pp. 243, 246.   [3] See p. 15 *sqq.*

to be tainted and corrupted by the weakness of the frail medium in which it is for a time enshrined; and if it is to be saved from the increasing enfeeblement which it must necessarily share with its human incarnation as he advances in years, it must be detached from him before, or at least as soon as, he exhibits signs of decay, in order to be transferred to a vigorous successor. This is done by killing the old representative of the god and conveying the divine spirit from him to a new incarnation. The killing of the god, that is, of his human incarnation, is, therefore, only a necessary step to his revival or resurrection in a better form. Far from being an extinction of the divine spirit, it is only the beginning of a purer and stronger manifestation of it. If this explanation holds good of the custom of killing divine kings and priests in general, it is still more obviously applicable to the custom of annually killing the representative of the tree-spirit or spirit of vegetation in spring. For the decay of vegetation in winter is readily interpreted by primitive man as an enfeeblement of the spirit of vegetation; the spirit has (he thinks) grown old and weak and must therefore be renovated by being slain and brought to life in a younger and fresher form. Thus the killing of the representative of the tree-spirit in spring is regarded as a means to promote and quicken the growth of vegetation. For the killing of the tree-spirit is associated always (we must suppose) implicitly, and sometimes explicitly also, with a revival or resurrection of him in a more youthful and vigorous form. Thus in the Saxon and Thüringen custom, after the Wild Man has been shot he is brought to life again by a doctor;[1] and in the Wurmlingen ceremony there

---

[1] See p. 243.

figures a Dr. Iron-Beard, who probably once played a similar part; certainly in another spring ceremony (to be described presently) Dr. Iron-Beard pretends to restore a dead man to life. But of this revival or resurrection of the god we shall have more to say anon.

The points of similarity between these North European personages and the subject of our inquiry —the King of the Wood or priest of Nemi—are sufficiently striking. In these northern maskers we see kings, whose dress of bark and leaves, along with the hut of green boughs and the fir-trees under which they hold their court, proclaim them unmistakably as, like their Italian counterpart, Kings of the Wood. Like him they die a violent death; but like him they may escape from it for a time by their bodily strength and agility; for in several of these northern customs the flight and pursuit of the king is a prominent part of the ceremony, and in one case at least if the king can out-run his pursuers he retains his life and his office for another year. In this last case, in fact, the king holds office on condition of running for his life once a year, just as the King of Calicut in later times held office on condition of defending his life against all comers once every twelve years, and just as the priest of Nemi held office on condition of defending himself against any assault at any time. In all these cases the life of the god-man is prolonged on condition of showing, in a severe physical contest of fight or flight, that his bodily strength is not decayed, and that, therefore, the violent death, which sooner or later is inevitable, may for the present be postponed. With regard to flight it is noticeable that flight figured conspicuously both in the legend and the practice of the King of the Wood. He had to be a runaway slave (*fugitivus*) in memory of the flight of Orestes, the traditional founder of the worship ; hence the Kings of the Wood are described by an ancient writer as "both strong of hand and fleet of foot."[1] Perhaps if we knew the ritual of the Arician grove fully we might find that the king was allowed a chance for his life by flight, like his Bohemian brother. We may conjecture that the annual flight of the priestly king at Rome (*regifugium*)[2] was at first a flight of the same kind ; in other words, that he was originally one of those divine kings who are either put to death after a fixed period or allowed to prove by the strong hand or the fleet foot that their divinity is vigorous and unimpaired. One more point of resemblance may be noted between the Italian King of the Wood and his northern counterparts. In Saxony and Thüringen the representative of the tree-spirit, after being killed, is brought to life again by a doctor. This is exactly what legend affirmed to have happened to the first King of the Wood at Nemi, Hippolytus or Virbius, who after he had been killed by his horses was restored to life by the physician Aesculapius.[3] Such a legend tallies well with the theory that the slaying of the King of the Wood was only a step to his revival or resurrection in his successor.

It has been assumed that the mock killing of the Wild Man and of the King in North European folk-custom is a modern substitute for an ancient custom of killing them in earnest. Those who best know the tenacity of life possessed by folk-custom and its tendency, with the growth of civilisation, to dwindle from solemn ritual into mere pageant and pastime, will be

---

[1] Above, p. 4. [2] Marquardt, *Römische Staatsverwaltung*, iii.[2] 323 *sq.*
[3] See above, p. 6.

least likely to question the truth of this assumption. That human sacrifices were commonly offered by the ancestors of the civilised races of North Europe (Celts, Teutons, and Slavs) is certain.[1] It is not, therefore, surprising that the modern peasant should do in mimicry what his forefathers did in reality. We know as a matter of fact that in other parts of the world mock human sacrifices have been substituted for real ones. Thus Captain Bourke was informed by an old chief that the Indians of Arizona used to offer human sacrifices at the Feast of Fire when the days are shortest. The victim had his throat cut, his breast opened, and his heart taken out by one of the priests. This custom was abolished by the Mexicans, but for a long time afterwards a modified form of it was secretly observed as follows. The victim, generally a young man, had his throat cut, and blood was allowed to flow freely; but the medicine-men sprinkled "medicine" on the gash, which soon healed up, and the man recovered.[2] So in the ritual of Artemis at Halae in Attica, a man's throat was cut and the blood allowed to gush out, but he was not killed.[3] At the funeral of a chief in Nias slaves are sacrificed; a little of their hair is cut off, and then they are beheaded. The victims are generally purchased for the purpose, and their number is proportioned to the wealth and power of the deceased. But if the number required is excessively great or cannot be procured, some of the chief's own slaves undergo a sham sacrifice. They are told, and believe, that

[1] Caesar, *Bell. Gall.* vi. 16; Adam of Bremen, *Descript. Insul. Aquil.* c. 27; Olaus Magnus, iii. 6; Grimm, *Deutsche Mythologie*,[4] i. 35 *sqq.*; Mone, *Geschichte des nordischen Heidenthums*, i. 69, 119, 120, 149, 187 *sq.*

[2] J. G. Bourke, *Snake Dance of the Moquis of Arizona*, p. 196 *sq.*

[3] Euripides, *Iphig. in Taur.* 1458 *sqq.*

they are about to be decapitated ; their heads are placed on a log and their necks struck with the back of a sword. The fright drives some of them crazy.[1] When a Hindoo has killed or ill-treated an ape, a bird of prey of a certain kind, or a cobra capella, in the presence of the worshippers of Vishnu, he must expiate his offence by the pretended sacrifice and resurrection of a human being. An incision is made in the victim's arm, the blood flows, he grows faint, falls, and feigns to die. Afterwards he is brought to life by being sprinkled with blood drawn from the thigh of a worshipper of Vishnu. The crowd of spectators is fully convinced of the reality of this simulated death and resurrection.[2] Sometimes the mock sacrifice is carried out, not on a living person but on an image. Thus an Indian law-book, the *Calica Puran*, prescribes that when the sacrifice of lions, tigers, or human beings is required, an image of a lion, tiger, or man shall be made with butter, paste, or barley meal, and sacrificed instead.[3] Some of the Gonds of India formerly offered human sacrifices ; they now sacrifice straw-men instead.[4] Colonel Dalton was told that in some of their villages the Bhagats (Hindooised Oraons) "annually make an image of a man in wood, put clothes and ornaments on it, and present it before the altar of a Mahádeo. The person who officiates as priest on the occasion says : ' O, Mahádeo, we sacrifice this man to you according to ancient customs. Give us rain in due season, and a

---

[1] Nieuwenhuisen en Rosenberg, "Verslag omtrent het eiland Nias," in *Verhandelingen van het Batav. Genootsch. van Kunsten en Wetenschappen*, xxx. 43.

[2] J. A. Dubois, *Moeurs, Institutions et Cérémonies des Peuples de l'Inde*, i. 151 *sq.*

[3] " The Rudhirádhyáyă, or sanguinary chapter," translated from the *Calica Puran* by W. C. Blaquiere, in *Asiatick Researches*, v. 376 (8vo. ed. London, 1807).

[4] Dalton, *Ethnology of Bengal*, p. 281.

plentiful harvest.' Then with one stroke of the axe
the head of the image is struck off, and the body is
removed and buried." [1]

§ 3.—*Carrying out Death*

Thus far I have offered an explanation of the
rule which required that the priest of Nemi should be
slain by his successor. The explanation claims to be
no more than probable ; our scanty knowledge of the
custom and of its history forbids it to be more. But
its probability will be augmented in proportion to
the extent to which the motives and modes of thought
which it assumes can be proved to have operated in
primitive society. Hitherto the god with whose
death and resurrection we have been chiefly concerned has been the tree-god. Tree-worship may
perhaps be regarded (though this is a conjecture)
as occupying an intermediate place in the history
of religion, between the religion of the hunter and
shepherd on the one side, whose gods are mostly
animals, and the religion of the husbandman on the
other hand, in whose worship the cultivated plants
play a leading part. If then I can show that the custom
of killing the god and the belief in his resurrection originated, or at least existed, in the hunting and pastoral
stage of society, when the slain god was an animal, and
survived into the agricultural stage, when the slain god
was the corn or a human being representing the corn,
the probability of my explanation will have been con-
siderably increased. This I shall attempt to do in
the remainder of this chapter, in the course of which

---

[1] Dalton, *Ethnology of Bengal*, p. 258 *sq.*

I hope to clear up some obscurities which still remain, and to answer some objections which may have suggested themselves to the reader.

We start from the point at which we left off—the spring customs of European peasantry. Besides the ceremonies already described there are two kindred sets of observances in which the simulated death of a divine or supernatural being is a leading feature. These observances are commonly known as " Burying the Carnival," and " Driving or carrying out Death." Both customs are chiefly practised, or at least best known, on German and Slavonic ground. The former custom is observed on the last day of the Carnival, namely, Shrove Tuesday (*Fastnacht*), or on the first day of Lent, namely, Ash Wednesday. The latter custom is commonly observed on the Fourth Sunday in Lent, which hence gets the name of Dead Sunday (*Todtensonntag*); but in some places it is observed a week earlier ; in others again, as amongst the Czechs of Bohemia, a week later. Originally the date of the celebration of the " Carrying out Death " appears not to have been fixed, but to have depended on the appearance of the first swallow or of some other natural phenomenon.[1] A Bohemian form of the custom of " Burying the Carnival " has been already described.[2] The following Swabian form is obviously similar. In the neighbourhood of Tübingen on Shrove Tuesday a straw-man, called the Shrovetide Bear, is made up ; he is dressed in a pair of old trousers, and a

---

[1] Grimm, *Deutsche Mythologie*,[4] ii. 645 ; K. Haupt, *Sagenbuch der Lausitz*, ii. 58 ; Reinsberg - Düringsfeld, *Fest - Kalender aus Böhmen*, p. 86 *sq.* ; *id.*, *Das festliche Jahr*, p. 77 *sq.* The Fourth Sunday in Lent is also known as Mid-Lent, because it falls in the middle of Lent, or as *Laetare* from the first word of the liturgy for the day. In the Roman Calendar it is the Sunday of the Rose, *Domenica rosae*.

[2] See p. 244.

fresh black-pudding or two squirts filled with blood are inserted in his neck. After a formal condemnation he is beheaded, laid in a coffin, and on Ash Wednesday is buried in the churchyard. This is called " Burying the Carnival" ("*die Fastnacht vergraben* ").[1] Amongst some of the Saxons of Transylvania the Carnival is hung. Thus at Braller on Ash Wednesday or Shrove Tuesday two white and two chestnut horses draw a sledge on which is placed a straw-man swathed in a white cloth ; beside him is a cart-wheel which is kept turning round. Two lads disguised as old men follow the sledge lamenting. The rest of the village lads, mounted on horseback and decked with ribbons, accompany the procession, which is headed by two girls crowned with evergreen and drawn in a waggon or sledge. A trial is held under a tree, at which lads disguised as soldiers pronounce sentence of death. The two old men try to rescue the straw-man and to fly with him, but to no purpose ; he is caught by the two girls and handed over to the executioner, who hangs him on a tree. In vain the old men try to climb up the tree and take him down ; they always tumble down, and at last in despair they throw themselves on the ground and weep and howl for the hanged man. An official then makes a speech in which he declares that the Carnival was condemned to death because he had done them harm, by wearing out their shoes and making them tired and sleepy.[2] At the " Burial of Carnival " in Lechrain, a man dressed as a woman in black clothes is carried on a litter or bier by four men ; he is lamented over by men disguised as

---

[1] E. Meier, *Deutsche Sagen, Sitten und Gebraüche aus Schwaben*, p. 371.

[2] J. Haltrich, *Zur Volkskunde der Siebenbürger Sachsen* (Wien, 1885), p. 284 *sq.*

women in black clothes, then thrown down before the village dung-heap, drenched with water, buried in the dung-heap, and covered with straw.[1] Similarly in Schörzingen, near Schömberg, the "Carnival (Shrovetide) Fool" was carried all about the village on a bier, preceded by a man dressed in white, and followed by a devil who was dressed in black and carried chains, which he clanked. One of the train collected gifts. After the procession the Fool was buried under straw and dung.[2] In Rottweil the "Carnival Fool" is made drunk on Ash Wednesday and buried under straw amid loud lamentation.[3] In Wurmlingen the Fool is represented by a young fellow enveloped in straw, who is led about the village by a rope as a "Bear" on Shrove Tuesday and the preceding day. He dances to the flute. Then on Ash Wednesday a straw-man is made, placed on a trough, carried out of the village to the sound of drums and mournful music, and buried in a field.[4] In Altdorf and Weingarten on Ash Wednesday the Fool, represented by a straw-man, is carried about and then thrown into the water to the accompaniment of melancholy music. In other villages of Swabia the part of fool is played by a live person, who is thrown into the water after being carried about in procession.[5] At Balwe, in Westphalia, a straw-man is made on Shrove Tuesday and thrown into the river amid rejoicings. This is called, as usual, "Burying the Carnival."[6] On the evening of Shrove Tuesday, the Esthonians make a

[1] Leoprechting, *Aus dem Lechrain*, p. 162 *sqq.* ; Mannhardt, *Baumkultus*, p. 411.

[2] E. Meier, *Deutsche Sagen, Sitten und Gebräuche aus Schwaben* p. 374 ; cp. Birlinger, *Volksthümliches aus Schwaben*, ii. 55.

[3] E. Meier, *op. cit.* p. 372.

[4] E. Meier, *op. cit.* p. 373.

[5] E. Meier, *op. cit.* pp. 373, 374.

[6] A. Kuhn, *Sagen, Gebräuche und Märchen aus Westfalen*, ii. 130.

straw figure called *metsik* or " wood-spirit ;" one year
it is dressed with a man's coat and hat, next year with
a hood and a petticoat.   This figure is stuck on a long
pole, carried across the boundary of the village with
loud cries of joy, and fastened to the top of a tree in
the wood.   The ceremony is believed to be a protection against all kinds of misfortune.[1]   Sometimes the
resurrection of the pretended dead person is enacted.
Thus, in some parts of Swabia, on Shrove Tuesday
Dr. Iron-Beard professes to bleed a sick man, who
thereupon falls as dead to the ground ; but the doctor
at last restores him to life by blowing air into him
through a tube.[2]   In the Harz mountains, when Carnival is over, a man is laid on a baking-trough and
carried with dirges to a grave ; but in the grave, instead of the man, a glass of brandy is placed.   A
speech is delivered and then the people return to the
village-green or meeting-place, where they smoke the
long clay pipes which are distributed at funerals.   On
the morning of Shrove Tuesday in the following year
the brandy is dug up and the festival begins by every
one tasting the brandy which, as the phrase goes, has
come to life again.[3]

The ceremony of "Carrying out Death" presents
much the same features as "Burying the Carnival ;"
except that the figure of Death is oftener drowned
or burned than buried, and that the carrying out of
Death is generally followed by a ceremony, or at least
accompanied by a profession, of bringing in Summer,
Spring, or Life.   Thus, in some villages of Thüringen
on the Fourth Sunday of Lent, the children used to
carry a puppet of birchen twigs through the village,

---

[1] F. J. Wiedemann, *Aus dem inneren und äusseren Leben der Ehsten*, p. 353.

[2] E. Meier, *op. cit.* p. 374.
[3] H. Pröhle, *Harzbilder*, p. 54.

and then threw it into a pool, while they sang, "We carry the old Death out behind the herdsman's old house; we have got Summer, and Kroden's (?) power is destroyed."[1] In one village of Thüringen (Dobschwitz near Gera), the ceremony of "Driving out Death" is still annually observed on the 1st of March. The young people make up a figure of straw or the like materials, dress it in old clothes which they have begged from the houses in the village, and carry it out and throw it into the river. On returning to the village they announce the fact to the people, and receive eggs and other victuals as a reward. In other villages of Thüringen, in which the population was originally Slavonic, the carrying out of the puppet is accompanied with the singing of a song, which begins, "Now we carry Death out of the village and Spring into the village."[2] In Bohemia the children go out with a straw-man, representing Death, to the end of the village, where they burn it, singing—

> "Now carry we Death out of the village,
> The new Summer into the village,
> Welcome dear Summer,
> Green little corn!"[3]

At Tabor (Bohemia) the figure of Death is carried out of the town and flung from a high rock into the water, while they sing—

> "Death swims on the water,
> Summer will soon be here,
> We carried Death away for you,
> We brought the Summer.
> And do thou, O holy Marketa,
> Give us a good year
> For wheat and for rye."[4]

---

[1] Aug. Witzschel, *Sagen, Sitten und Gebräuche aus Thüringen*, p. 193.
[2] Witzschel, *op. cit.* p. 199.

[3] Grimm, *Deutsche Mythologie*,[4] ii. 642.
[4] Reinsberg-Düringsfeld, *Fest-Kalender aus Böhmen*, p. 90 *sq.*

In other parts of Bohemia they carry Death to the end of the village, singing—

> " We carry Death out of the village,
> And the New Year into the village.
> Dear Spring, we bid you welcome,
> Green grass, we bid you welcome."

Behind the village they erect a pyre, on which they burn the straw figure, reviling and scoffing at it the while. Then they return, singing—

> " We have carried away Death,
> And brought Life back.
> He has taken up his quarters in the village,
> Therefore sing joyous songs." [1]

At Nürnberg, girls of seven to eighteen years of age, dressed in their best, carry through the streets a little open coffin in which is a doll, hidden under a shroud. Others carry a beech branch, with an apple fastened to it for a head, in an open box. They sing, " We carry Death into the water, it is well," or, " We carry Death into the water, carry him in and out again." [2]

The effigy of Death is often regarded with fear and treated with marks of hatred and contempt. In Lusatia the figure is sometimes made to look in at the window of a house, and it is believed that some one in the house will die within the year unless his life is redeemed by the payment of money. [3] Again, after throwing the effigy away, the bearers sometimes run home lest Death should follow them ; and if one of them falls in running, it is believed that he will die within the year. [4] At Chrudim, in Bohemia, the

---

[1] Reinsberg - Düringsfeld, *op. cit.* p. 91.
[2] Grimm, *Deutsche Mythologie*,[4] ii. 639 *sq.* ; Mannhardt, *Baumkultus*, p. 412.

[3] Grimm, *op. cit.* ii. 644 ; K. Haupt, *Sagenbuch der Lausitz*, ii. 55.
[4] Grimm, *op. cit.* ii. 640, 643.

figure of Death is made out of a cross, with a head and mask stuck at the top, and a shirt stretched out on it. On the Fifth Sunday in Lent the boys take this effigy to the nearest brook or pool, and standing in a line throw it into the water. Then they all plunge in after it; but as soon as it is caught no one more may enter the water. The boy who did not enter the water or entered it last will die within the year, and he is obliged to carry the Death back to the village. The effigy is then burned.[1] On the other hand it is believed that no one will die within the year in the house out of which the figure of Death has been carried;[2] and the village out of which Death has been driven is sometimes supposed to be protected against sickness and plague.[3] In some villages of Austrian Silesia on the Saturday before Dead Sunday an effigy is made of old clothes, hay, and straw, for the purpose of driving Death out of the village. On Sunday the people, armed with sticks and straps, assemble before the house where the figure is lodged. Four lads then draw the effigy by cords through the village amid exultant shouts, while all the others beat it with their sticks and straps. On reaching a field which belongs to a neighbouring village they lay down the figure, cudgel it soundly, and scatter the fragments over the field. The people believe that the village from which Death has been thus carried out will be safe from any infectious disease for the whole year.[4] In Slavonia the figure of Death is cudgelled and then

---

[1] Vernalecken, *Mythen und Bräuche des Volkes in Oesterreich*, p. 294 *sq.*; Reinsberg-Düringsfeld, *Fest - Kalender aus Böhmen*, p. 90.

[2] Grimm, *Deutsche Mythologie*,[4] ii. 640.

[3] J. A. E. Köhler, *Volksbrauch, Aberglauben, Sagen und andre alte Ueberlieferungen im Voigtlande*, p. 171.

[4] Reinsberg-Düringsfeld, *Das festliche Jahr*, p. 80.

rent in two.[1]   In Poland the effigy, made of hemp and
straw, is flung into a pool or swamp with the words,
" The devil take thee." [2]
    The custom of " sawing the Old Woman," which is
or used to be observed in Italy and Spain on the Fourth
Sunday in Lent, is doubtless, as Grimm supposes,
merely another form of the custom of "carrying out
Death." A great hideous figure representing the oldest
woman of the village was dragged out and sawn in
two, amid a prodigious noise made with cow-bells, pots
and pans, etc.[3]   In Palermo the ceremony used to be
still more realistic.   At Mid-Lent an old woman was
drawn through the streets on a cart, attended by two
men dressed in the costume of the *Compagnia de'*
Bianchi, a society or religious order whose function it
was to attend and console prisoners condemned to
death.   A scaffold was erected in a public square ; the
old woman mounted it, and two mock executioners
proceeded, amid a storm of huzzas and hand-clapping,
to saw through her neck or rather through a bladder
of blood which had been previously fitted to her neck.
The blood gushed out and the old woman pretended
to swoon and die.   The last of these mock executions
took place in 1737.[4]   At Florence, during the fifteenth
and sixteenth centuries, the Old Woman was represented by a figure stuffed with walnuts and dried figs
and fastened to the top of a ladder.   At Mid-Lent this
effigy was sawn through the middle under the *Loggie*
of the Mercato Nuovo, and as the dried fruits tumbled
out they were scrambled for by the crowd.   A trace of
the custom is still to be seen in the practice, observed

[1] Ralston, *Songs of the Russian*
People, p. 211.   [2] *Ib.* p. 210.
[3] Grimm, *Deutsche Mythologie*,[4] ii.
652 ; H. Usener, "Italische Mythen,"

in *Rheinisches Museum*, N. F. xxx.
(1875) p. 191 *sq.*
[4] G. Pitrè, *Spettacoli e feste popolari*
siciliane (Palermo, 1881), p. 207 *sq.*

by urchins, of secretly pinning paper ladders to the shoulders of women of the lower classes who happen to show themselves in the streets on the morning of Mid-Lent.[1] A similar custom is observed by urchins in Rome; and at Naples on the 1st of April boys cut strips of cloth into the shape of saws, smear them with gypsum, and strike passers-by with their "saws" on the back, thus imprinting the figure of a saw upon their clothes.[2] At Montalto in Calabria boys go about at Mid-Lent with little saws made of cane and jeer at old people, who therefore generally stay indoors on that day. The Calabrian women meet together at this time and feast on figs, chestnuts, honey, etc.; this they call "sawing the Old Woman"—a reminiscence probably of a custom like the old Florentine one.[3]

In Barcelona on the day in question boys run about the streets, some with saws, others with billets of wood, others again with cloths in which they collect gratuities. They sing a song in which it is said that they are looking for the oldest woman of the city for the purpose of sawing her in two in honour of Mid-Lent; at last, pretending to have found her, they saw something in two and burn it. A like custom is found amongst the South Slavs. In Lent the Croats tell their children that at noon an old woman is being sawn in two outside the gates; and in Carniola also the saying is current that at Mid-Lent an old woman is taken out of the village and sawn in two. The North Slavonian expression for keeping Mid-Lent is *bábu rezati*, that is, "sawing the Old Wife."[4]

---

[1] *Archivio per lo studio delle tradizioni popolari*, iv. (1885) p. 294 *sq.*

[2] H. Usener, *op. cit.* p. 193.

[3] Vincenzo Dorsa, *La tradizione greco-latina negli usi e nelle credenze popolari della Calabria citeriore* (Cosenza, 1884), p. 43 *sq.*

[4] Grimm, *Deutsche Mythologie*,[4] ii. 652; H. Usener, "Italische Mythen," in *Rheinisches Museum*, N. F. xxx. 1875) p. 191 *sq.*

In the preceding ceremonies the return of Spring, Summer, or Life, as a sequel to the expulsion of Death, is only implied or at most announced. In the following ceremonies it is plainly enacted. In some parts of Bohemia the effigy of Death is buried at sunset ; then the girls go out into the wood and cut down a young tree with a green crown, hang a doll dressed as a woman on it, deck the whole with green, red, and white ribbons, and march in procession with their *Líto* (Summer) into the village, collecting gifts and singing—

> " We carried Death out of the village,
> We are carrying Summer into the village."[1]

In many Silesian villages the figure of Death, after being treated with respect, is stripped of its clothes and flung with curses into the water, or torn in pieces in a field. Then a fir-tree adorned with ribbons, coloured egg-shells, and motley bits of cloth, is carried through the streets by boys who collect pennies and sing—

> " We have carried Death out,
> We are bringing the dear Summer back,
> The Summer and the May
> And all the flowers gay." [2]

At Eisenach on the Fourth Sunday in Lent young people used to fasten a straw-man, representing Death, to a wheel, which they trundled to the top of a hill. Then setting fire to the figure they allowed it and the wheel to roll downhill. Next they cut a tall fir-tree, tricked it out with ribbons, and set it up in the plain. The men then climbed the tree to fetch down the

---

[1] Reinsberg-Düringsfeld, *Fest-Kalender aus Böhmen*, p. 89 *sq.* ; W. Mannhardt, *Baumkultus*, p. 156. This custom has been already referred to. See p. 82.

[2] Reinsberg-Düringsfeld, *Das festliche Jahr*, p. 82 ; Philo vom Walde, *Schlesien in Sage und Brauch* (N.D. preface dated 1883), p. 122.

ribbons.[1]   In Upper Lusatia the figure of Death, made
of straw and rags, is dressed in a veil furnished by the
last bride and a shirt furnished by the house in which
the last death occurred.   Thus arrayed the figure is
stuck on the end of a long pole and carried at full speed
by the tallest and strongest girl, while the rest pelt the
effigy with sticks and stones.   Whoever hits it will be
sure to live through the year.   In this way Death is
carried out of the village and thrown into the water or
over the boundary of the next village.   On their way
home each one breaks a green branch and carries it
gaily with him till he reaches the village, when he
throws it away.   Sometimes the young people of the
next village, upon whose land the figure has been
thrown, run after them and hurl it back, not wishing
to have Death among them.   Hence the two parties
occasionally come to blows.[2]

In these cases Death is represented by the puppet
which is thrown away, Summer or Life by the branches
or trees which are brought back.   But sometimes a
new potency of life seems to be attributed to the image
of Death itself, and by a kind of resurrection it becomes
the instrument of the general revival.   Thus in some
parts of Lusatia women alone are concerned in carrying out Death, and suffer no male to meddle with it.
Attired in mourning, which they wear the whole day,
they make a puppet of straw, clothe it in a white shirt,
and give it a broom in one hand and a scythe in the
other.   Singing songs and pursued by urchins throwing stones, they carry the puppet to the village boundary, where they tear it in pieces.   Then they cut down

[1] Witzschel,   *Sagen,   Sitten   und   Gebräuche aus Thüringen*, p. 192 *sq.*

[2] Grimm, *Deutsche Mythologie*,[4] ii.

643 *sq.* ;   K. Haupt, *Sagenbuch der Lausitz*, ii. 54 *sq.* ;   Mannhardt, *Baum-kultus*, p. 412 *sq.* ;   Ralston, *Songs of the Russian People*, p. 211.

a fine tree, hang the shirt on it, and carry it home singing.[1] On the Feast of Ascension the Saxons of a village near Hermanstadt (Transylvania) observe the ceremony of "carrying out Death" in the following manner. After forenoon church all the school-girls repair to the house of one of their number, and there dress up the Death. This is done by tying a threshed-out corn-sheaf into the rough semblance of a head and body, while the arms are simulated by a broomstick stuck horizontally. The figure is dressed in the Sunday clothes of a village matron. It is then displayed at the window that all people may see it on their way to afternoon church. As soon as vespers are over the girls seize the effigy and, singing a hymn, carry it in procession round the village. Boys are excluded from the procession. After the procession has traversed the village from end to end, the figure is taken to another house and stripped of its attire; the naked straw bundle is then thrown out of the window to the boys, who carry it off and fling it into the nearest stream. This is the first act of the drama. In the second, one of the girls is solemnly invested with the clothes and ornaments previously worn by the figure of Death, and, like it, is led in procession round the village to the singing of the same hymns as before. The ceremony ends with a feast at the house of the girl who acted the chief part; as before, the boys are excluded. "According to popular belief, it is allowed to eat fruit only after this day, as now the 'Death,' that is, the unwholesomeness—has been expelled from them. Also the river in which the Death has been drowned may now be considered fit for public bathing. If this ceremony be neglected in the

---

[1] Grimm, *op. cit.* ii. 644 ; K. Haupt, *op. cit.* ii. 55.

village where it is customary, such neglect is supposed
to entail death to one of the young people, or loss of
virtue to a girl."[1]

In the first of these two ceremonies the tree which
is brought home after the destruction of the figure of
Death is plainly equivalent to the trees or branches
which, in the preceding customs, were brought back
as representatives of Summer or Life, after Death had
been thrown away or destroyed. But the transference
of the shirt worn by the effigy of Death to the tree
clearly indicates that the tree is a kind of revivification, in a new form, of the destroyed effigy.[2] This
comes out also in the Transylvanian custom ; the
dressing of a girl in the clothes worn by the Death, and
the leading her about the village to the same songs
which had been sung when the Death was being carried
about, show that she is intended to be a kind of resuscitation of the being whose effigy has just been
destroyed. These examples therefore suggest that the
Death whose demolition is represented in these ceremonies cannot be regarded as the purely destructive
agent which we understand by Death. If the tree
which is brought back as an embodiment of the reviving vegetation of spring is clothed in the shirt worn by
the Death which has been just destroyed, the object
certainly cannot be to check and counteract the revival
of vegetation ; it can only be to foster and promote it.
Therefore the being which has just been destroyed—
the so-called Death—must be supposed to be endowed
with a vivifying and quickening influence, which it can
communicate to the vegetable and even the animal
world. This ascription of a life-giving virtue to the

---

[1] E. Gerard, *The Land beyond the Forest*, ii. 47-49.

[2] This is also the view taken of the custom by Mannhardt, *Baumkultus*, p. 419.

figure of Death is put beyond a doubt by the custom, observed in some places, of taking pieces of the straw effigy of Death and placing them in the fields to make the crops grow, or in the manger to make the cattle thrive. Thus in Spachendorf (Austrian Silesia) the figure of Death made of straw, brushwood, and rags, is carried out with wild songs to an open place outside the village and there burned, and while it is burning a general struggle takes place for the pieces, which are pulled out of the flames with bare hands. Each one who secures a fragment of the effigy ties it to a branch of the largest tree in his garden, or buries it in his field, in the belief that this causes the crops to grow better.[1] In the Troppau district (Austrian Silesia) the straw figure which the boys make on the Fourth Sunday in Lent is dressed by the girls in woman's clothes and hung with ribbons, necklace, and garlands. Attached to a long pole it is carried out of the village, followed by a troop of young people of both sexes, who alternately frolic, lament, and sing songs. Arrived at its destination—a field outside the village—the figure is stripped of its clothes and ornaments ; then the crowd rushes on it and tears it to bits, scuffling for the fragments. Every one tries to get a wisp of the straw of which the effigy was made, because such a wisp, placed in the manger, is believed to make the cattle thrive.[2] Or the straw is put in the hens' nest, it being supposed that this prevents the hens from carrying away their eggs, and makes them brood much better.[3] The same attribution of a fertilising power to the figure of Death appears in the belief that

[1] Vernalecken, *Mythen und Bräuche des Volkes in Oesterreich*, p. 293 *sq.*

[2] Reinsberg-Düringsfeld, *Das fest-liche Jahr*, p. 82.

[3] Philo vom Walde, *Schlesien in Sage und Brauch*, p. 122.

if the bearers of the figure, after throwing it away, meet cattle and strike them with their sticks, this will render the cattle prolific.[1] Perhaps the sticks had been previously used to beat the Death,[2] and so had acquired the fertilising power ascribed to the effigy. In Leipzig at Mid-Lent men and women of the lowest class used to carry through all the streets a straw effigy of Death, which they exhibited to young wives, and finally threw into the river, alleging that this made young wives fruitful, cleansed the city, and averted the plague and other sickness from the inhabitants for that year.[3]

It seems hardly possible to separate from the May-trees the trees or branches which are brought into the village after the destruction of the Death. The bearers who bring them in profess to be bringing in the Summer;[4] therefore the trees obviously represent the Summer; and the doll which is sometimes attached to the Summer-tree is a duplicate representative of the Summer, just as the May is sometimes represented at the same time by a May-tree and a May Lady.[5] Further, the Summer-trees are adorned like May-trees with ribbons, etc.; like May-trees, when large, they are planted in the ground and climbed up; and like May-trees, when small, they are carried from door to door by boys or girls singing songs and collecting money.[6] And as if to demonstrate the identity of the two sets of customs the bearers of the Summer-tree sometimes announce that they are bringing in the Summer

---

[1] Grimm, *Deutsche Mythologie*,[4] ii. 640 *sq.* [2] See above, p. 260.
[3] K. Schwenk, *Die Mythologie der Slawen*, p. 217 *sq.*
[4] Above, p. 263.

[5] See above, pp. 83, 263.
[6] Above, p. 263, and Grimm, *Deutsche Mythologie*,[4] ii. 644; Reinsberg-Düringsfeld, *Fest-Kalender aus Böhmen*, p. 87 *sq.*

and the May.[1]　The customs, therefore, of bringing
in the May and bringing in the Summer are essentially
the same; and the Summer-tree is merely another
form of the May-tree, the only distinction (besides
that of name) being in the time at which they are
respectively brought in; for while the May-tree is
usually fetched in on the 1st of May or at Whitsuntide, the Summer-tree is fetched in on the Fourth
Sunday in Lent.　Therefore, if the explanation here
adopted of the May-tree (namely, that it is an embodiment of the tree-spirit or spirit of vegetation) is
correct, the Summer-tree must likewise be an embodiment of the tree-spirit or spirit of vegetation.　But
we have seen that the Summer-tree is in some cases
a revivification of the effigy of Death.　It follows,
therefore, that in these cases the effigy called Death
must be an embodiment of the tree-spirit or spirit of
vegetation.　This inference is confirmed, first, by
the vivifying and fertilising influence which the fragments of the effigy of Death are believed to exercise
both on vegetable and on animal life;[2] for this influence, as we saw in the first chapter, is supposed
to be a special attribute of the tree-spirit.　It is
confirmed, secondly, by observing that the effigy of
Death is sometimes composed of birchen twigs, of
the branch of a beech-tree, of a threshed-out corn-
sheaf, or of hemp;[3] and that sometimes it is hung
on a little tree and so carried about by girls collecting money,[4] just as is done with the May-tree and
the May Lady, and with the Summer-tree and the

---

[1] Above, p. 263.

[2] See above, p. 266 *sqq.*

[3] Above, pp. 257, 259, 265; and Grimm, *D. M.*[4] ii. 643.

[4] Reinsberg-Düringsfeld, *Fest-Kalen-der aus Böhmen*, p. 88.　Sometimes the effigy of Death (without a tree) is carried round by boys who collect gratuities.　Grimm, *D. M.*[4] ii. 644.

doll attached to it. In short we are driven to regard the expulsion of Death and the bringing in of Summer as, in some cases at least, merely another form of that death and resuscitation of the spirit of vegetation in spring which we saw enacted in the killing and resurrection of the Wild Man.[1] The burial and resurrection of the Carnival is probably another way of expressing the same idea. The burying of the representative of the Carnival under a dung-heap is natural, if he is supposed to possess a quickening and fertilising influence like that ascribed to the effigy of Death. By the Esthonians, indeed, the straw figure which is carried out of the village in the usual way on Shrove Tuesday is not called the Carnival, but the Wood-spirit (*Metsik*), and the identity of it with the wood-spirit is further shown by fixing it to the top of a tree in the wood, where it remains for a year, and is besought almost daily with prayers and offerings to protect the herds; for like a true wood-spirit the *Metsik* is a patron of cattle. Sometimes the *Metsik* is made of sheafs of corn.[2] Therefore, we may fairly conjecture that the names Carnival, Death, and Summer, are comparatively late and inadequate expressions for the beings personified or embodied in the customs described. The very abstractness of the names bespeaks a modern origin; the personification of times and seasons like the Carnival and Summer, or of an abstract notion like death, is hardly primitive. But the ceremonies themselves bear the stamp of a dateless antiquity; therefore we can hardly help supposing that in their origin the

[1] Above, p. 243.
[2] Wiedemann, *Aus dem inneren und äusseren Leben der Ehsten*, p. 353; Holzmayer, " Osiliana," in *Verhandlungen der gelehrten Estnischen Gesellschaft zu Dorpat*, vii. Heft 2, p. 10 *sq.*; W. Mannhardt, *Baumkultus*, p. 407 *sq.*

ideas which they embodied were of a more simple and concrete order. The conception of a tree, perhaps of a particular kind of tree (for some savages have no word for tree in general), or even of an individual tree, is sufficiently concrete to supply a basis from which by a gradual process of generalisation the wider conception of a spirit of vegetation might be reached. But this general conception of vegetation would readily be confounded with the season in which it manifests itself; hence the substitution of Spring, Summer, or May for the tree-spirit or spirit of vegetation would be easy and natural. Again the concrete notion of the dying tree or dying vegetation would by a similar process of generalisation glide into a notion of death in general; so that instead of the carrying out of the dying or dead vegetation in spring (as a preliminary to its revival) we should in time get a carrying out of Death itself. The view that in these spring ceremonies Death meant originally the dying or dead vegetation of winter has the high support of W. Mannhardt; and he confirms it by the analogy of the name Death as applied to the spirit of the ripe corn. Commonly the spirit of the ripe corn is conceived, not as dead, but as old, and hence it goes by the name of the Old Man or the Old Woman. But in some places the last sheaf cut at harvest, which is generally believed to be the seat of the corn spirit, is called "the Dead One;" children are warned against entering the corn-fields because Death sits in the corn; and, in a game played by Saxon children in Transylvania at the maize harvest, Death is represented by a child completely covered with maize leaves.[1]

---

[1] W. Mannhardt, *Baumkultus*, pp. 417-421.

The supposition that behind the conceptions of
Death, Carnival, Summer, etc., as embodied in
these spring ceremonies, there lurk older and more
concrete notions is to a certain extent countenanced
by the fact that in Russia funeral ceremonies like
those of "Burying the Carnival" and "Carrying
out Death" are celebrated under the names, not
of Death or the Carnival, but of certain mythic
figures, Kostrubonko, Kostroma, Kupalo, Lada, and
Yarilo. These Russian ceremonies are observed both
in spring and at midsummer. Thus "in Little Russia
it used to be the custom at Eastertide to celebrate the
funeral of a being called Kostrubonko, the deity of the
spring. A circle was formed of singers who moved
slowly around a girl who lay on the ground as if dead,
and as they went they sang—

> ' Dead, dead is our Kostrubonko !
> Dead, dead is our dear one ! '

until the girl suddenly sprang up, on which the chorus
joyfully exclaimed—

> ' Come to life, come to life has our Kostrubonko !
> Come to life, come to life has our dear one ! ' " [1]

On the Eve of St. John (Midsummer Eve) a figure of
Kupalo is made of straw and "is dressed in woman's
clothes, with a necklace and a floral crown. Then
a tree is felled, and, after being decked with ribbons,
is set up on some chosen spot. Near this tree, to
which they give the name of Marena [Winter or
Death], the straw figure is placed, together with a
table, on which stand spirits and viands. Afterwards
a bonfire is lit, and the young men and maidens jump
over it in couples, carrying the figure with them. On

---

[1] Ralston, *Songs of the Russian People*, p. 221.

the next day they strip the tree and the figure of their ornaments, and throw them both into a stream."[1]   On St. Peter's Day (29th June) or on the following Sunday, "the Funeral of Kostroma" or of Lada or of Yarilo is celebrated in Russia.   In the Governments of Penza and Simbirsk the "funeral" used to be represented as follows.   A bonfire was kindled on the 28th of June, and on the next day the maidens chose one of their number to play the part of Kostroma.   Her companions saluted her with deep obeisances, placed her on a board, and carried her to the bank of a stream. There they bathed her in the water, while the oldest girl made a basket of lime-tree bark and beat it like a drum.   Then they returned to the village and ended the day with processions, games, and dances.[2]   In the Murom district, Kostroma was represented by a straw figure dressed in woman's clothes and flowers.   This was laid in a trough and carried with songs to the bank of a lake or river.   Here the crowd divided into two sides, of which the one attacked and the other defended the figure.   At last the assailants gained the day, stripped the figure of its dress and ornaments, tore it in pieces, trod the straw of which it was made under foot, and flung it into the stream ; while the defenders of the figure hid their faces in their hands and pretended to bewail the death of Kostroma.[3]   In the district of Kostroma the burial of Yarilo was celebrated on the 29th or 30th of June.   The people chose an old man and gave him a small coffin containing a Priapus-like figure representing Yarilo.   This he carried out of the town, followed by women chanting

---

[1] Ralston, *op. cit.* p. 241.
[2] Ralston, *op. cit.* p. 243 *sq.*; W. Mannhardt, *Baumkultus*, p. 414.

[3] W. Mannhardt, *Baumkultus*, p. 414 *sq.*; Ralston, *op. cit.* p. 244.

dirges and expressing by their gestures grief and despair. In the open fields a grave was dug, and into it the figure was lowered amid weeping and wailing, after which games and dances were begun, "calling to mind the funeral games celebrated in old times by the pagan Slavonians."[1] In Little Russia the figure of Yarilo was laid in a coffin and carried through the streets after sunset surrounded by drunken women, who kept repeating mournfully, " He is dead! he is dead!" The men lifted and shook the figure as if they were trying to recall the dead man to life. Then they said to the women, " Women, weep not. I know what is sweeter than honey." But the women continued to lament and chant, as they do at funerals. " Of what was he guilty ? He was so good. He will arise no more. O how shall we part from thee ? What is life without thee ? Arise, if only for a brief hour. But he rises not, he rises not." At last the Yarilo was buried in a grave.[2]

These Russian customs are plainly of the same nature as those which in Austria and Germany are known as " Burying the Carnival" and " Carrying out Death." Therefore if my interpretation of the latter is right, the Russian Kostroma, Yarilo, etc. must also have been originally embodiments of the spirit of vegetation, and their death must have been regarded as a necessary preliminary to their revival. The revival as a sequel to the death is enacted in the first of the ceremonies described, the death and resurrection of Kostrubonko. The reason why in some of these Russian ceremonies the death of the spirit of vegetation is celebrated at midsummer may

[1] Ralston, *op. cit.* p. 245 ; W. Mannhardt, *Baumkultus*, p. 416.
[2] W. Mannhardt, *l.c.* ; Ralston, *l.c.*

be that the decline of summer is dated from Midsummer Day, after which the days begin to shorten,
and the sun sets out on his downward journey—

> " To the darksome hollows
> Where the frosts of winter lie."

Such a turning-point of the year, when vegetation
might be thought to share the incipient though still
almost imperceptible decay of summer, might very
well be chosen by primitive man as a fit moment for
resorting to those magic ceremonies by which he
hopes to stay the decline, or at least to ensure the
revival, of plant life.

But while the death of vegetation appears to have
been represented in all, and its revival in some, of these
spring and midsummer ceremonies, there are features
in some of them which can hardly be explained on
this hypothesis alone.   The solemn funeral, the lamentations, and the mourning attire, which often characterise
these ceremonies, are indeed appropriate at the death
of the beneficent spirit of vegetation.   But what shall
we say of the glee with which the effigy is often carried
out, of the sticks and stones with which it is assailed,
and the taunts and curses which are hurled at
it ?   What shall we say of the dread of the effigy
evinced by the haste with which the bearers scamper
home as soon as they have thrown it away, and by
the belief that some one must soon die in any house
into which it has looked ?   This dread might perhaps be explained by a belief that there is a certain
infectiousness in the dead spirit of vegetation which
renders its approach dangerous.   But this explanation,
besides being rather strained, does not cover the rejoicings which often attend the carrying out of Death.

We must therefore recognise two distinct and seemingly opposite features in these ceremonies; on the one hand, sorrow for the death, and affection and respect for the dead ; on the other hand, fear and hatred of the dead, and rejoicings at his death. How the former of these features is to be explained I have attempted to show; how the latter came to be so closely associated with the former is a question which I shall try to answer in the sequel.

Before we quit these European customs to go farther afield, it will be well to notice that occasionally the expulsion of Death or of a mythic being is conducted without any visible representative of the personage expelled. Thus at Königshain, near Görlitz (Silesia), all the villagers, young and old, used to go out with straw torches to the top of a neighbouring hill, called *Todtenstein* (Death-stone), where they lit their torches, and so returned home singing, "We have driven out Death, we are bringing back Summer."[1] In Albania young people light torches of resinous wood on Easter Eve, and march in procession through the village brandishing them. At last they throw the torches into the river, saying, "Ha, Kore, we fling you into the river, like these torches, that you may return no more." Some say that the intention of the ceremony is to drive out winter ; but Kore is conceived as a malignant being who devours children.[2]

In the Kânagrâ district, India, there is a custom observed by young girls in spring which closely resembles some of the European spring ceremonies just described. It is called the *Ralî Ka melâ*, or

---

[1] Grimm, *Deutsche Mythologie*,⁴ ii. 644. [2] J. G. von Hahn, *Albanesische Studien*, i. 160.

fair of Rali, the *Rali* being a small painted earthen image of Siva or Pârvatî. It lasts through most of Chet (March-April) up to the Sankrânt of Bai-sâkh (April), and is in vogue all over the Kânagrâ district. Its celebration is entirely confined to young girls. On a morning in March all the young girls of the village take small baskets of *dûb* grass and flowers to a certain fixed spot, where they throw them in a heap. Round this heap they stand in a circle and sing. This goes on every day for ten days, till the heap of grass and flowers has reached a fair height. Then they cut in the jungle two branches having three prongs at one end, and place them, prongs downwards, over the heap of flowers, so as to make two tripods or pyramids. On the single uppermost points of these branches they get an image-maker to construct two clay images, one to represent Siva, and the other Pârvatî. The girls then divide themselves into two parties, one for Siva and one for Pârvatî, and marry the images in the usual way, leaving out no part of the ceremony. After the marriage they have a feast, the cost of which is defrayed by contributions solicited from their parents. Then at the next Sankrânt (Baisâkh) they all go together to the riverside, throw the images into a deep pool, and weep over the place, as though they were performing funeral obsequies. The boys of the neighbourhood often annoy them by diving after the images, bringing them up, and waving them about while the girls are crying over them. The object of the fair is said to be to secure a good husband.[1]

That in this Indian ceremony the deities Siva and Pârvatî are conceived as spirits of vegetation seems to

---

[1] Captain R. C. Temple, in *Indian Antiquary*, xi. (1882) p. 297 *sq.*

be proved by the fact that their images are placed on branches over a heap of grass and flowers. Here, as often in European folk-custom, the divinities of vegetation are represented in duplicate, by plants and by puppets. The marriage of these Indian deities in spring corresponds to the European ceremonies in which the marriage of the vernal spirits of vegetation is represented by the King and Queen of May, the May Bride, Bridegroom of the May, etc.[1] The throwing of the images into the water, and the mourning for them, are the equivalents of the European customs of throwing the dead spirit of vegetation (under the name of Death, Yarilo, Kostroma, etc.) into the water and lamenting over it. Again, in India, as often in Europe, the rite is performed exclusively by females. The notion that the ceremony was effective for procuring husbands to the girls can be explained by the quickening and fertilising influence which the spirit of vegetation is believed to exert upon human and animal, as well as upon vegetable life.[2]

§ 4.—*Adonis*

But it is in Egypt and Western Asia that the death and resurrection of vegetation appear to have been most widely celebrated with ceremonies like those of modern Europe. Under the names of Osiris, Adonis, Thammuz, Attis, and Dionysus, the Egyptians, Syrians, Babylonians, Phrygians, and Greeks represented the decay and revival of vegetation with rites which, as the ancients themselves recognised,

---

[1] See above, p. 94 *sqq.*   [2] Above, p. 70 *sqq.*

were substantially the same, and which find their parallels in the spring and midsummer customs of our European peasantry. The nature and worship of these deities have been discussed at length by many learned writers ; all that I propose to do is to sketch those salient features in their ritual and legends which seem to establish the view here taken of their nature. We begin with Adonis or Thammuz.

The worship of Adonis was practised by the Semitic peoples of Syria, from whom it was borrowed by the Greeks as early at least as the fifth century before Christ. The name Adonis is the Phoenician *Adon*, "lord."[1] He was said to have been a fair youth, beloved by Aphrodite (the Semitic Astarte), but slain by a boar in his youthful prime. His death was annually lamented with a bitter wailing, chiefly by women ; images of him, dressed to resemble corpses, were carried out as to burial and then thrown into the sea or into springs ;[2] and in some places his revival was celebrated on the following day.[3] But the ceremonies varied somewhat both in the manner and the season of their celebration in different places. At Alexandria images of Adonis and Aphrodite were displayed on two couches ; beside them were set ripe fruits of all kinds, cakes, plants growing in flower pots, and green bowers twined with anise. The marriage of the lovers was celebrated one day, and on the next the image of Adonis was borne by women attired as mourners, with streaming hair and bared breasts, to

---

[1] Baudissin, *Studien zur semitischen Religionsgeschichte*, i. 299 ; W. Mannhardt, *Antike Wald-und Feldkulte*, p. 274.

[2] Plutarch, *Alcibiades*, 18 ; Zenobius, *Centur.* i. 49 ; Theocritus, xv. 132 *sq.* ; Eustathius on Homer, *Od.* xi. 590.

[3] Besides Lucian (cited below) see Jerome, *Comment. in Ezechiel.* viii. 14, *in qua* (*solemnitate*) *plangitur quasi mortuus, et postea reviviscens, canitur atque laudatur . . . interfectionem et resurrectionem Adonidis planctu et gaudio prosequens.*

the sea-shore and committed to the waves.[1] The date at which this Alexandrian ceremony was observed is not expressly stated ; but from the mention of the ripe fruits it has been inferred that it took place in late summer.[2] At Byblus the death of Adonis was annually mourned with weeping, wailing, and beating of the breast ; but next day he was believed to come to life again and ascend up to heaven in the presence of his worshippers.[3] This celebration appears to have taken place in spring ; for its date was determined by the discoloration of the river Adonis, and this has been observed by modern travellers to occur in spring. At that season the red earth washed down from the mountains by the rain tinges the water of the river and even the sea for a great way with a blood-red hue, and the crimson stain was believed to be the blood of Adonis, annually wounded to death by the boar on Mount Lebanon.[4] Again, the red anemone[5] was said to have sprung from the blood of Adonis ; and as the anemone blooms in Syria about Easter, this is a fresh proof that the festival of Adonis, or at least one of his festivals, was celebrated in spring. The name of the flower is probably derived from Naaman ("darling"), which seems to have been an epithet of Adonis. The Arabs still call the anemone "wounds of the Naaman."[6]

---

[1] Theocritus, xv.

[2] W. Mannhardt, *op. cit.* p. 277.

[3] Lucian, *De dea Syria*, 6. The words ἐς τὸν ἠέρα πέμπουσι imply that the ascension was supposed to take place in the presence, if not before the eyes, of the worshipping crowds.

[4] Lucian, *op. cit.* 8. The discoloration of the river and the sea was observed by Maundrell on ¹⁷/₁₈th March ¹⁶⁹⁶/₁₆₉₇. See his "Journey from Aleppo to Jerusalem," in Bohn's *Early Travels in Palestine*, edited by Thomas Wright,

p. 411. Renan observed the discoloration at the beginning of February ; Baudissin, *Studien*, i. 298 (referring to Renan, *Mission de Phénicie*, p. 283). Milton's lines will occur to most readers.

[5] Ovid, *Metam.* x. 735, compared with Bion i. 66. The latter, however, makes the anemone spring from the tears, as the rose from the blood of Adonis.

[6] W. Robertson Smith, "Ctesias and the Semiramis legend," in *English Historical Review*, April 1887, following Lagarde.

The resemblance of these ceremonies to the Indian and European ceremonies previously described is obvious. In particular, apart from the somewhat doubtful date of its celebration, the Alexandrian ceremony is almost identical with the Indian. In both of them the marriage of two divinities, whose connection with vegetation seems indicated by the fresh plants with which they are surrounded, is celebrated in effigy, and the effigies are afterwards mourned over and thrown into the water.[1] From the similarity of these customs to each other and to the spring and midsummer customs of modern Europe we should naturally expect that they all admit of a common explanation. Hence, if the explanation here adopted of the latter is correct, the ceremony of the death and resurrection of Adonis must also have been a representation of the decay and revival of vegetation. The inference thus based on the similarity of the customs is confirmed by the following features in the legend and ritual of Adonis. His connection with vegetation comes out at once in the common story of his birth. He was said to have been born from a myrrh-tree, the bark of which bursting, after a ten months' gestation, allowed the lovely infant to come forth. According to some, a boar rent the bark with his tusk and so opened a passage for the babe. A faint rationalistic colour was given to the legend by saying that his mother was a woman named Myrrh, who had been turned into a myrrh-tree soon after she had conceived the child.[2] Again the story that Adonis

---

[1] In the Alexandrian ceremony, however, it appears to have been the image of Adonis only which was thrown into the sea.

[2] Apollodorus, *Biblioth.* iii. 14, 4;

Schol. on Theocritus, i. 109; Antoninus Liberalis, 34; Tzetzes on Lycophron, 829; Ovid, *Metam.* x. 489 *sqq.*; Servius on Virgil, *Aen.* v. 72, and on *Bucol.* x. 18; Hyginus, *Fab.* 58, 164;

spent half, or according to others a third, of the
year in the lower world and the rest of it in the
upper world,[1] is explained most simply and naturally by supposing that he represented vegetation,
especially the corn, which lies buried in the earth
half the year and reappears above ground the
other half. Certainly of the annual phenomena of
nature there is none which suggests so obviously
the idea of a yearly death and resurrection as the
disappearance and reappearance of vegetation in
autumn and spring. Adonis has been taken for the
sun; but there is nothing in the sun's annual course
within the temperate and tropical zones to suggest
that he is dead for half or a third of the year and
alive for the other half or two-thirds. He might,
indeed, be conceived as weakened in winter,[2] but
dead he could not be thought to be; his daily reappearance contradicts the supposition. Within the
arctic circle, where the sun annually disappears for a
continuous period of from twenty-four hours to six
months, according to the latitude, his annual death
and resurrection would certainly be an obvious idea;
but no one has suggested that the Adonis worship
came from those regions. On the other hand the
annual death and revival of vegetation is a conception
which readily presents itself to men in every stage of
savagery and civilisation; and the vastness of the
scale on which this yearly decay and regeneration

Fulgentius, iii. 8. The word Myrrha
or Smyrna is borrowed from the
Phoenician (Liddell and Scott, *Greek
Lexicon*, *s.v.* σμύρνα). Hence the
mother's name, as well as the son's,
was taken directly from the Semites.

[1] Schol. on Theocritus, iii. 48;
Hyginus, *Astronom.* ii. 7; Lucian,
Dialog. deor. xi. 1; Cornutus, *De
natura deorum*, 28, p. 163 *sq.* ed.
Osannus; Apollodorus, iii. 14, 4.

[2] Thus, after the autumnal equinox
the Egyptians celebrated the "nativity
of the sun's walking-sticks," because, as
the sun declined daily in the sky, and his
heat and light diminished, he was supposed to need a staff with which to support his steps. Plutarch, *Isis et Osiris*, 52.

takes place, together with man's intimate dependence
on it for subsistence, combine to render it the
most striking annual phenomenon in nature, at least
within the temperate zones. It is no wonder that a
phenomenon so important, so striking, and so universal
should, by suggesting similar ideas, have given rise
to similar rites in many lands. We may, therefore,
accept as probable an explanation of the Adonis worship which accords so well with the facts of nature
and with the analogy of similar rites in other lands,
and which besides is countenanced by a considerable
body of opinion amongst the ancients themselves.[1]

The character of Thammuz or Adonis as a corn-
spirit comes out plainly in an account of his festival
given by an Arabic writer of the tenth century.
In describing the rites and sacrifices observed at the
different seasons of the year by the heathen Syrians of
Harran, he says :—" Thammuz (July). In the middle
of this month is the festival of el-Bûgât, that is, of the
weeping women, and this is the Tâ-uz festival, which
is celebrated in honour of the god Tâ-uz. The women
bewail him, because his lord slew him so cruelly,
ground his bones in a mill, and then scattered them to

[1] Schol. on Theocritus, iii. 48,
ὁ Ἄδωνις, ἤγουν ὁ σῖτος ὁ σπειρόμενος,
ἐξ μῆνας ἐν τῇ γῇ ποιεῖ ἀπὸ τῆς σπορᾶς,
καὶ ἐξ μῆνας ἔχει αὐτὸν ἡ Ἀφροδίτη,
τουτέστιν ἡ εὐκρασία τοῦ ἀέρος. καὶ
ἐκτότε λαμβάνουσιν αὐτὸν οἱ ἄνθρωποι.
Jerome on Ezech. c. viii. 14. Eadem
gentilitas hujuscemodi fabulas poetarum,
quae habent turpitudinem, interpretatur
subtiliter interfectionem et resurrectionem
Adonidis planctu et gaudio prosequens:
quorum alterum in seminibus, quae
moriuntur in terra, alterum in segeti-
bus, quibus mortua semina renas-
cuntur, ostendi putat. Ammianus Marcellinus, xix. 1, 11, in sollemnibus
Adonidis sacris, quod simulacrum
aliquod esse frugum adultarum religiones
mysticae docent. Id. xxii. 9, 15, amato
Veneris, ut fabulae fingunt, apri dente
ferali deleto, quod in adulto flore sec-
tarum est indicium frugum. Clemens
Alexandr. Hom. 6, 11 (quoted by
W. Mannhardt, Antike Wald-und
Feldkulte, p. 281), λάμβανουσι δὲ καὶ
Ἀδῶνιν εἰς ὡραίους καρπούς. Etymolog.
Magn. Ἄδωνις κύριον· δύναται καὶ ὁ
καρπὸς εἶναι ἄδωνις· οἷον ἀδώνειος καρπός,
ἀρέσκων. Eusebius, Praepar. Evang.
iii. 11, 9, Ἄδωνις τῆς τῶν τελείων
καρπῶν ἐκτομῆς σύμβολον.

the wind. The women (during this festival) eat
nothing which has been ground in a mill, but limit
their diet to steeped wheat, sweet vetches, dates,
raisins, and the like."[1] Thammuz (of which Tâ-uz is
only another form of pronunciation) is here like Burns's
John Barleycorn—

> " They wasted, o'er a scorching flame,
> The marrow of his bones ;
> But a miller us'd him worst of all,
> For he crush'd him between two stones."[2]

But perhaps the best proof that Adonis was a
deity of vegetation is furnished by the gardens of
Adonis, as they were called. These were baskets or
pots filled with earth, in which wheat, barley, lettuces,
fennel, and various kinds of flowers were sown and
tended for eight days, chiefly or exclusively by women.
Fostered by the sun's heat, the plants shot up rapidly,
but having no root withered as rapidly away, and at
the end of eight days were carried out with the images
of the dead Adonis, and flung with them into the sea
or into springs.[3] At Athens these ceremonies were
observed at midsummer. For we know that the fleet
which Athens fitted out against Syracuse, and by the destruction of which her power was permanently crippled,
sailed at midsummer, and by an ominous coincidence
the sombre rites of Adonis were being celebrated at
the very time. As the troops marched down to the
harbour to embark, the streets through which they

---

[1] D. Chwolsohn, *Die Ssabier und
der Ssabismus*, ii. 27 ; *id.*, *Ueber
Tammûz und die Menschenverehrung
bei den alten Babyloniern*, p. 38.

[2] The comparison is due to Felix
Liebrecht (*Zur Volkskunde*, p. 259).

[3] For the authorities see W. Mann
hardt, *Antike Wald-und Feldkulte*, p.
279, *note* 2, and p. 280, *note* 2 ; to
which add Diogenianus, i. 14 ; Plutarch,
De sera num. vind. 17. Women
only are mentioned as planting the
gardens of Adonis by Plutarch, *l.c.*;
Julian, *Convivium*, p. 329 ed. Span-
heim (p. 423 ed. Hertlein) ; Eustathius
on Homer, *Od.* xi. 590. On the other
hand Diogenianus, *l.c.* says φυτεύοντες
ἢ φυτεύουσαι.

passed were lined with coffins and corpse-like effigies, and the air was rent with the noise of women wailing for the dead Adonis. The circumstance cast a gloom over the sailing of the most splendid armament that Athens ever sent to sea.[1]

These gardens of Adonis are most naturally interpreted as representatives of Adonis or manifestations of his power; they represented him, true to his original nature, in vegetable form, while the images of him, with which they were carried out and cast into the water, represented him in his later anthropomorphic form. All these Adonis ceremonies, if I am right, were originally intended as charms to promote the growth and revival of vegetation; and the principle by which they were supposed to produce this effect was sympathetic magic. As was explained in the first chapter, primitive people suppose that by representing or mimicking the effect which they desire to produce they actually help to produce it ; thus by sprinkling water they make rain, by lighting a fire they make sunshine, and so on. Similarly by mimicking the growth of crops, they hope to insure a good harvest. The rapid growth of the wheat and barley in the gardens of Adonis was intended to make the corn shoot up; and the throwing of the gardens and of the images into the water was a charm to secure a due supply of fertilising rain.[2] The same, I take it, was the object of throwing the

---

[1] Plutarch, *Alcibiades*, 18; *id.*, *Nicias*, 13. The date of the sailing of the fleet is given by Thucydides, vi. 30, θέρους μεσοῦντος ἤδη.

[2] In hot southern countries like Egypt and the Semitic regions of Western Asia, where vegetation depends chiefly or entirely upon irrigation, the purpose of the charm is doubtless to secure a plentiful flow of water in the streams. But as the ultimate object and the charms for securing it are the same in both cases, it has not been thought necessary always to point out the distinction.

effigies of Death and the Carnival into water in the corresponding ceremonies of modern Europe. We have seen that the custom of drenching a leaf-clad person (who undoubtedly personifies vegetation) with water is still resorted to in Europe for the express purpose of producing rain.[1] Similarly the custom of throwing water on the last corn cut at harvest, or on the person who brings it home (a custom observed in Germany and France, and till quite lately in England and Scotland), is in some places practised with the avowed intent to procure rain for the next year's crops. Thus in Wallachia and amongst the Roumanians of Transylvania, when a girl is bringing home a crown made of the last ears of corn cut at harvest, all who meet her hasten to throw water on her, and two farm-servants are placed at the door for the purpose ; for they believe that if this were not done, the crops next year would perish from drought.[2] So amongst the Saxons of Transylvania, the person who wears the wreath made of the last corn cut (sometimes the reaper who cut the last corn also wears the wreath) is drenched with water to the skin ; for the wetter he is the better will be next year's harvest, and the more grain there will be threshed out.[3] At the spring ploughing in Prussia, when the ploughmen and sowers returned in the evening from their work in the fields, the farmer's wife and the servants used to splash water over them. The ploughmen and sowers retorted by seizing every one, throwing them into the pond, and ducking them under the water. The

---

[1] See above, p. 16.

[2] W. Mannhardt, *Baumkultus*, p. 214 ; W. Schmidt, *Das Jahr und seine Tage in Meinung und Brauch der Romänen Siebenbürgens*, p. 18 *sq.*

[3] G. A. Heinrich, *Agrarische Sitten und Gebräuche unter den Sachsen Siebenbürgens* (Hermanstadt, 1880), p. 24 ; Wsissocki, *Sitten und Brauch der Siebenbürger Sachsen* (Hamburg, 1888), p. 32.

farmer's wife might claim exemption on payment of a forfeit; but every one else had to be ducked. By observing this custom they hoped to ensure a due supply of rain for the seed.[1] Also after harvest in Prussia, the person who wore a wreath made of the last corn cut was drenched with water, while a prayer was uttered that "as the corn had sprung up and multiplied through the water, so it might spring up and multiply in the barn and granary."[2] In a Babylonian legend, the goddess Istar (Astarte, Aphrodite) descends to Hades to fetch the water of life with which to restore to life the dead Thammuz, and it appears that the water was thrown over him at a great mourning ceremony, at which men and women stood round the funeral pyre of Thammuz lamenting.[3] This legend, as Mannhardt points out, is probably a mythical explanation of a Babylonian festival resembling the Syrian festival of Adonis. At this festival, which doubtless took place in the month Thammuz (June-July)[4] and therefore about midsummer, the dead Thammuz was probably represented in effigy, water was poured over him, and he came to life again. This Babylonian legend is, therefore, of importance, since it confirms the view that the purpose for which the images and gardens of Adonis were thrown into the water was to effect the resurrection of the god, that

---

[1] Matthäus Praetorius, *Deliciae Prussicae*, 55; W. Mannhardt, *Baumkultus*, p. 214 *sq. note.*

[2] Praetorius, *op. cit.*, 60; W. Mannhardt, *Baumkultus*, p. 215, *note.*

[3] A. H. Sayce, *Religion of the ancient Babylonians* (Hibbert Lectures, 1887),p.221 *sqq.*; W. Mannhardt, *Antike Wald-und Feldkulte*, p. 275.

[4] According to Jerome (on Ezechiel, viii. 14), Thammuz was June; but according to modern scholars the month corresponded rather to July, or to part of June and part of July. Movers, *Die Phoenizier*, i. 210; Mannhardt, *A. W.F.* p. 275. My friend, Prof. W. Robertson Smith, informs me that owing to the variations of the local Syrian calendars the month Thammuz fell in different places at different times, from midsummer to autumn, or from June to September.

is, to secure the revival of vegetation.   The connection
of Thammuz with vegetation is proved by a fragment
of a Babylonian hymn, in which Thammuz is described
as dwelling in the midst of a great tree at the centre of
the earth.[1]

The opinion that the gardens of Adonis are
essentially charms to promote the growth of vegetation, especially of the crops, and that they belong
to the same class of customs as those spring and
midsummer folk-customs of modern Europe which
have been described, does not rest for its evidence
merely on the intrinsic probability of the case.
Fortunately, we are able to show that gardens of
Adonis (if we may use the expression in a general
sense) are still planted, first, by a primitive race at
their sowing season, and, second, by European
peasants at midsummer.   Amongst the Oraons and
Mundas of Bengal, when the time comes for planting
out the rice which has been grown in seed-beds, a
party of young people of both sexes go to the forest
and cut a young Karma tree, or the branch of one.
Bearing it in triumph they return dancing, singing,
and beating drums, and plant it in the middle of the
village dancing-ground.   A sacrifice is offered to the
tree ; and next morning the youth of both sexes,
linked arm-in-arm, dance in a great circle round the
Karma tree, which is decked with strips of coloured
cloth and sham bracelets and necklets of plaited straw.
As a preparation for the festival, the daughters of the
head-man of the village cultivate blades of barley in a
peculiar way.   The seed is sown in moist, sandy soil,
mixed with turmeric, and the blades sprout and unfold
of a pale yellow or primrose colour.   On the day of

---

[1] A. H. Sayce, *op. cit.* p. 238.

the festival the girls take up these blades and carry them in baskets to the dancing-ground, where, prostrating themselves reverentially, they place some of the plants before the Karma tree.   Finally, the Karma tree is taken away and thrown into a stream or tank.[1]   The meaning of planting these barley blades and then presenting them to the Karma tree is hardly open to question.   We have seen that trees are supposed to exercise a quickening influence upon the growth of crops, and that amongst the very people in question—the Mundas or Mundaris—"the grove deities are held responsible for the crops."[2]   Therefore, when at the season for planting out the rice the Mundas bring in a tree and treat it with so much respect, their object can only be to foster thereby the growth of the rice which is about to be planted out ; and the custom of causing barley blades to sprout rapidly and then presenting them to the tree must be intended to subserve the same purpose, perhaps by reminding the tree-spirit of his duty towards the crops, and stimulating his activity by this visible example of rapid vegetable growth.   The throwing of the Karma tree into the water is to be interpreted as a rain-charm.   Whether the barley blades are also thrown into the water is not said ; but, if my interpretation of the custom is right, probably they are so.   A distinction between this Bengal custom and the Greek rites of Adonis is that in the former the tree-spirit appears in his original form as a tree ; whereas in the Adonis worship he appears in anthropomorphic form, represented as a dead man, though his vegetable nature is indicated by the gardens of

---

[1] Dalton, *Ethnology of Bengal*, p. 259.   [2] Above, p. 67.

Adonis, which are, so to say, a secondary manifestation of his original power as a tree-spirit.

In Sardinia the gardens of Adonis are still planted in connection with the great midsummer festival which bears the name of St. John. At the end of March or on the 1st of April a young man of the village presents himself to a girl and asks her to be his *comare* (gossip or sweetheart), offering to be her *compare*. The invitation is considered as an honour by the girl's family, and is gladly accepted. At the end of May the girl makes a pot of the bark of the cork-tree, fills it with earth, and sows a handful of wheat and barley in it. The pot being placed in the sun and often watered, the corn sprouts rapidly and has a good head by Midsummer Eve (St. John's Eve, 23d June). The pot is then called *Erme* or *Nenneri*. On St. John's Day the young man and the girl, dressed in their best, accompanied by a long retinue and preceded by children gambolling and frolicking, move in procession to a church outside the village. Here they break the pot by throwing it against the door of the church. Then they sit down in a ring on the grass and eat eggs and herbs to the music of flutes. Wine is mixed in a cup and passed round, each one drinking as it passes. Then they join hands and sing "Sweethearts of St. John" (*Compare e comare di San Giovanni*) over and over again, the flutes playing the while. When they tire of singing, they stand up and dance gaily in a ring till evening. This is the general Sardinian custom. As practised at Ozieri it has some special features. In May the pots are made of cork-bark and planted with corn, as already described. Then on the Eve of St. John the window-sills are draped with rich cloths, on which the pots are placed, adorned with crimson and blue silk and ribbons of various colours. On each of the pots they used formerly to place a statuette or cloth doll dressed as a woman, or a Priapus-like figure made of paste ; but this custom, rigorously forbidden by the Church, has fallen into disuse. The village swains go about in a troop to look at the pots and their decorations and to wait for the girls, who assemble on the public square to celebrate the festival. Here a great bonfire is kindled, round which they dance and make merry. Those who wish to be " Sweethearts of St. John " act as follows. The young man stands on one side of the bonfire and the girl on the other, and they, in a manner, join hands by each grasping one end of a long stick, which they pass three times backwards and forwards across the fire, thus thrusting their hands thrice rapidly into the flames. This seals their relationship to each other. Dancing and music go on till late at night.[1] The correspondence of these Sardinian pots of grain to the gardens of Adonis seems complete, and the images formerly placed in them answer to the images of Adonis which accompanied his gardens.

This Sardinian custom is one of those midsummer customs, once celebrated in many parts of Europe, a chief feature of which is the great bonfire round which people dance and over which they leap. Examples of these customs have already been cited from Sweden and Bohemia.[2] These examples suffici-

---

[1] Antonio Bresciani, *Dei costumi dell' isola di Sardegna comparati cogli antichissimi popoli orientali* (Rome and Turin, 1866), p. 427 *sq.* ; R. Tennant, *Sardinia and its Resources* (Rome and London, 1885), p. 187 ; S. Gabriele, "Usi dei contadini della Sardegna," *Archivio per lo studio delle tradizioni popolari*, vii. (1888) p. 469 *sq.* Tennant says that the pots are kept in a dark warm place, and that the children leap across the fire. [2] See ch. i. p. 78 *sq.*

ently prove the connection of the midsummer bonfire with vegetation; for both in Sweden and Bohemia an essential part of the festival is the raising of a May-pole or Midsummer-tree, which in Bohemia is burned in the bonfire. Again, in the Russian midsummer ceremony cited above,[1] the straw figure of Kupalo, the representative of vegetation, is placed beside a May-pole or Midsummer-tree and then carried to and fro across a bonfire. Kupalo is here represented in duplicate, in tree-form by the Midsummer-tree, and in anthropomorphic form by the straw effigy, just as Adonis was represented both by an image and a garden of Adonis; and the duplicate representatives of Kupalo, like those of Adonis, are finally cast into water. In the Sardinian custom the Gossips or Sweethearts of St. John probably correspond to the Lord and Lady or King and Queen of May. In the province of Blekinge (Sweden), part of the midsummer festival is the election of a Midsummer Bride, who chooses her bridegroom; a collection is made for the pair, who for the time being are looked upon as man and wife.[2] Such Midsummer pairs are probably, like the May pairs, representatives of the spirit of vegetation in its reproductive capacity; they represent in flesh and blood what the images of Siva and Pârvatî in the Indian ceremony, and the images of Adonis and Aphrodite in the Alexandrian ceremony, represented in effigy. The reason why ceremonies whose aim is to foster the growth of vegetation should thus be associated with bonfires; why in particular the representative of vegetation should be burned in tree-form or passed across the fire in effigy or in the form of a living couple, will be explained later on. Here

---

[1] P. 272.　　　[2] L. Lloyd, *Peasant Life in Sweden*, p. 257.

it is enough to have proved the fact of such association and therefore to have obviated the objection which might have been raised to my interpretation of the Sardinian custom, on the ground that the bonfires have nothing to do with vegetation. One more piece of evidence may here be given to prove the contrary. In some parts of Germany young men and girls leap over midsummer bonfires for the express purpose of making the hemp or flax grow tall.[1] We may, there- fore, assume that in the Sardinian custom the blades of wheat and barley which are forced on in pots for the midsummer festival, and which correspond so closely to the gardens of Adonis, form one of those widely- spread midsummer ceremonies, the original object of which was to promote the growth of vegetation, and especially of the crops. But as, by an easy extension of ideas, the spirit of vegetation was believed to exercise a beneficent influence over human as well as animal life, the gardens of Adonis would be supposed, like the May-trees or May-boughs, to bring good luck to the family or to the individual who planted them ; and even after the idea had been abandoned that they operated actively to bring good luck, omens might still be drawn from them as to the good or bad fortune of families or individuals. It is thus that magic dwindles into divination. Accordingly we find modes of divination practised at midsummer which resemble more or less closely the gardens of Adonis. Thus an anonymous Italian writer of the sixteenth century has recorded that it was customary to sow barley and wheat a few days before the festival of St. John (Midsummer Day) and also before that of St. Vitus ; and it was believed that the person for whom they were

---

[1] W. Mannhardt, *Baumkultus*, p. 464 ; Leoprechting, *Aus dem Lechrain*, p. 183.

sown would be fortunate and get a good husband or a good wife, if the grain sprouted well ; but if they sprouted ill, he or she would be unlucky.[1] In various parts of Italy and all over Sicily it is still customary to put plants in water or in earth on the Eve of St. John, and from the manner in which they are found to be blooming or fading on St. John's Day omens are drawn, especially as to fortune in love. Amongst the plants used for this purpose are *Ciuri di S. Giuvanni* (St. John's wort ?) and nettles.[2] In Prussia two hundred years ago the farmers used to send out their servants, especially their maids, to gather St. John's wort on Midsummer Eve or Midsummer Day (St. John's Day). When they had fetched it, the farmer took as many plants as there were persons and stuck them in the wall or between the beams ; and it was thought that the person whose plant did not bloom would soon fall sick or die. The rest of the plants were tied in a bundle, fastened to the end of a pole, and set up at the gate or wherever the corn would be brought in at the next harvest. This bundle was called *Kupole ;* the ceremony was known as Kupole's festival ; and at it the farmer prayed for a good crop of hay, etc.[3] This Prussian custom is particularly notable, inasmuch as it strongly confirms the opinion expressed above that Kupalo (doubtless identical with Kupole) was originally a deity of vegetation.[4] For here Kupalo is represented by a bundle

---

[1] G. Pitrè, *Spettacoli e feste popolari siciliane*, p. 296 *sq.*

[2] G. Pitrè, *op. cit.* p. 302 *sq.*; Antonio de Nino, *Usi Abruzzesi*, i. 55 *sq.*; Gubernatis, *Usi Nuziali*, p. 39 *sq.* Cp. *Archivio per lo studio delle tradizioni popolari*, i. 135. At Smyrna a blossom of the *agnus castus* is used on St. John's Day

for a similar purpose, but the mode in which the omens are drawn is somewhat different, *Archivio per lo studio delle tradizioni popolari*, vii. (1888) p. 128 *sq.*

[3] Matthäus Praetorius, *Deliciae Prussicae*, herausgegeben von Dr. W. Pierson (Berlin, 1871), p. 56.

[4] See p. 274 *sq.*

of plants specially associated with midsummer in folk-custom ; and her influence over vegetation is plainly signified by placing her plant-formed representative over the place where the harvest is brought in, as well as by the prayers for a good crop which are uttered on the occasion. A fresh argument is thus supplied in support of the conclusion that the Death, whose analogy to Kupalo, Yarilo, etc., has been shown, was originally a personification of vegetation, more especially of vegetation as dying or dead in winter. Further, my interpretation of the gardens of Adonis is confirmed by finding that in this Prussian custom the very same kind of plants are used to form the gardens of Adonis (as we may call them) and the image of the deity. Nothing could set in a stronger light the truth of the view that the gardens of Adonis are merely another manifestation of the god himself.

The last example of the gardens of Adonis which I shall cite is the following. At the approach of Easter, Sicilian women sow wheat, lentils, and canary-seed in plates, which are kept in the dark and watered every two days. The plants soon shoot up ; the stalks are tied together with red ribbons, and the plates containing them are placed on the sepulchres which, with effigies of the dead Christ, are made up in Roman Catholic and Greek churches on Good Friday,[1] just as the gardens of Adonis were placed on the grave of the dead Adonis.[2] The whole custom— sepulchres as well as plates of sprouting grain — is

---

[1] G. Pitrè, *Spettacoli e feste popolari siciliane*, p. 211. A similar custom is observed at Cosenza in Calabria. Vincenzo Dorsa, *La tradizione greco-latina*, etc., p. 50. For the Easter ceremonies in the Greek Church, see R. A. Arnold, *From the Levant* (London, 1868), i. 251 *sqq.*

[2] κήπους ὡσίουν ἐπιταφίους Ἀδώνιδι, Eustathius on Homer, *Od.* xi. 590.

probably nothing but a continuation, under a different name, of the Adonis worship.

§ 5.—*Attis*

The next of those gods, whose supposed death and resurrection struck such deep roots into the religious faith and ritual of Western Asia, is Attis. He was to Phrygia what Adonis was to Syria. Like Adonis, he appears to have been a god of vegetation, and his death and resurrection were annually mourned and rejoiced over at a festival in spring. The legends and rites of the two gods were so much alike that the ancients themselves sometimes identified them.[1] Attis was said to have been a fair youth who was beloved by the great Phrygian goddess Cybele. Two different accounts of his death were current. According to the one, he was killed by a boar, like Adonis. According to the other, he mutilated himself under a pine-tree, and died from the effusion of blood. The latter is said to have been the local story told by the people of Pessinus, a great centre of Cybele worship, and the whole legend of which it forms a part is stamped with a character of rudeness and savagery that speaks strongly for its antiquity.[2] But the genuineness of the other story seems also vouched for by the fact that his worshippers, especially the people of Pes-

[1] Hippolytus, *Refut. omn. haeres.* v. 9, p. 168, ed. Duncker and Schneidewin ; Socrates, *Hist. Eccles.* iii. 23, §§ 51 *sqq.* p. 204.

[2] That Attis was killed by a boar was stated by Hermesianax, an elegiac poet of the fourth century B.C. (Pausanias, vii. 17) ; cp. Schol. on Nicander, *Alex.*

8. The other story is told by Arnobius (*Adversus nationes*, v. 5 *sqq.*) on the authority of Timotheus, an otherwise unknown writer, who professed to derive it *ex reconditis antiquitatum libris et ex intimis mysteriis*. It is obviously identical with the account which Pausanias. mentions (*l.c.*) as the story current in Pessinus.

sinus, abstained from eating swine.[1] After his death Attis is said to have been changed into a pine-tree.[2] The ceremonies observed at his festival are not very fully known, but their general order appears to have been as follows.[3] At the spring equinox (22d March) a pine-tree was cut in the woods and brought into the sanctuary of Cybele, where it was treated as a divinity. It was adorned with woollen bands and wreaths of violets, for violets were said to have sprung from the blood of Attis, as anemones from the blood of Adonis; and the effigy of a young man was attached to the middle of the tree.[4] On the second day (23d March) the chief ceremony seems to have been a blowing of trumpets.[5] The third day (24th March) was known as the Day of Blood: the high priest drew blood from his arms and presented it as an offering.[6] It was perhaps on this day or night that the mourning for Attis took place over an effigy, which was afterwards solemnly buried.[7] The fourth day (25th March) was the Festival of Joy (*Hilaria*), at which the resurrection of Attis was probably celebrated—at least the celebration of his resurrection seems to have followed closely upon

---

[1] Pausanias, vii. 17 ; Julian, *Orat.* v. 177 B.

[2] Ovid, *Metam.* x. 103 *sqq.*

[3] On the festival see especially Marquardt, *Römische Staatsverwaltung*, iii.[2] 370 *sqq.* ; Daremberg et Saglio, *Dictionnaire des Antiquités grecques et romaines*, i. p. 1685 *sq.* (article " Cybèle ") ; W. Mannhardt, *Antike Wald-und Feldkulte*, p. 291 *sqq.*; *id.*, *Baumkultus*, p. 572 *sqq.*

[4] Julian, *Orat.* v. 168 C ; Joannes Lydus, *De mensibus*, iv. 41 ; Arnobius, *Advers. nationes*, v. cc. 7, 16 *sq.*; Firmicus Maternus, *De errore profan. relig.* 27.   [5] Julian, *l.c.* and 169 C.

[6] Trebellius Pollio, *Claudius*, 4 ; Tertullian, *Apologet.* 25. For other references, see Marquardt, *l.c.*

[7] Diodorus, iii. 59 ; Firmicus Maternus, *De err. profan. relig.* 3 ; Arnobius, *Advers. nat.* v. 16 ; Schol. on Nicander, *Alex.* 8 ; Servius on Virgil, *Aen.* ix. 116 ; Arrian, *Tactica*, 33. The ceremony described in Firmicus Maternus, c. 22 (*nocte quadam simulacrum in lectica supinum ponitur et per numeros digestis fletibus plangitur. . . . Idolum sepelis. Idolum plangis*, etc.), may very well be the mourning and funeral rites of Attis, to which he had more briefly referred in c. 3.

that of his death.[1] The Roman festival closed on
27th March with a procession to the brook Almo, in
which the bullock-cart of the goddess, her image, and
other sacred objects were bathed. But this bath of the
goddess is known to have also formed part of her
festival in her Asiatic home. On returning from the
water the cart and oxen were strewn with fresh spring
flowers.[2]

The original character of Attis as a tree-spirit is
brought out plainly by the part which the pine-tree
plays in his legend and ritual. The story that he was
a human being transformed into a pine-tree is only one
of those transparent attempts at rationalising the old
beliefs which meet us so frequently in mythology.
His tree origin is further attested by the story that he
was born of a virgin, who conceived by putting in her
bosom a ripe almond or pomegranate.[3] The bringing in
of the pine-tree from the wood, decked with violets
and woollen bands, corresponds to bringing in the
May-tree or Summer-tree in modern folk-custom;
and the effigy which was attached to the pine-tree was
only a duplicate representative of the tree-spirit or

---

[1] On the *Hilaria* see Macrobius,
Saturn. i. 21, 10 ; Julian, *Orat.* v.
168 D, 169 D ; Damascius, *Vita
Isidori*, in Photius, p. 345 A 5 *sqq.* ed.
Bekker. On the resurrection, see
Firmicus Maternus, 3, *reginae suae
amorem [Phryges] cum luctibus annuis
consecrarunt, et ut satis iratae mulieri
facerent aut ut paenitenti solacium
quaererent, quem paulo ante sepelierant
revixisse jactarunt. . . . Mortem ipsius
[i.e.* of Attis] *dicunt, quod semina
collecta conduntur, vitam rursus quod
jacta semina annuis vicibus † recon-
duntur [renascuntur,* C. Halm]. Again
cp. id. 22, *Idolum sepelis]. Idolum
plangis, idolum de sepultura proferis, et
miser cum haec feceris gaudes ;* and

Damascius, *l.c.* τὴν τῶν ἱλαρίων καλου-
μένην ἑορτήν · ὅπερ ἐδήλου τὴν ἐξ ᾅδου
γεγονυῖαν ἡμῶν σωτηρίαν. This last
passage, compared with the formula in
Firmicus Maternus, c. 22

θαρρεῖτε μύσται τοῦ θεοῦ σεσωμένου·
ἔσται γὰρ ἡμῖν ἐκ πόνων σωτηρία,

makes it probable that the ceremony
described by Firmicus, c. 22, is the
resurrection of Attis.
[2] Ovid, *Fast.* iv. 337 *sqq.* ; Ammianus Marcellinus, xxiii. 3. For other
references see Marquardt and Mannhardt, *ll.cc.*
[3] Pausanias, vii. 17 ; Arnobius, *Adv.
nationes*, v. 6. ; cp. Hippolytus, *Refut.
omn. haeres.* v. 9, pp. 166, 168.

Attis. At what point of the ceremonies the violets
and the effigy were attached to the tree is not said,
but we should assume this to be done after the
mimic death and burial of Attis. The fastening of his
effigy to the tree would then be a representation of
his coming to life again in tree-form, just as the
placing of the shirt of the effigy of Death upon a
tree represents the revival of the spirit of vegetation in
a new form.[1] After being attached to the tree, the
effigy was kept for a year and then burned.[2] We have
seen that this was apparently sometimes done with the
May-pole ;[3] and we shall see presently that the effigy
of the corn-spirit, made at harvest, is often preserved
till it is replaced by a new effigy at next year's harvest.
The original intention of thus preserving the effigy for
a year and then replacing it by a new one was
doubtless to maintain the spirit of vegetation in fresh
and vigorous life. The bathing of the image of
Cybele was probably a rain-charm, like the throwing
of the effigies of Death and of Adonis into the
water. Like tree-spirits in general, Attis appears to
have been conceived as exercising power over the
growth of corn, or even to have been identified with the
corn. One of his epithets was "very fruitful ;" he was
addressed as the "reaped green (or yellow) ear of corn,"
and the story of his sufferings, death, and resurrection
was interpreted as the ripe grain wounded by the
reaper, buried in the granary, and coming to life again
when sown in the ground.[4] His worshippers abstained
from eating seeds and the roots of vegetables,[5] just
as at the Adonis ceremonies women abstained from

---

[1] See above, p. 264 *sq.*

[2] Firmicus Maternus, 27.

[3] Above, p. 81.

[4] Hippolytus, *Ref. omn. haeres.* v.
cc. 8, 9, pp. 162, 168 ; Firmicus
Maternus, *De errore prof. relig.* 3.

[5] Julian, *Orat.* v. 174 A B.

eating corn ground in a mill. Such acts would probably have been esteemed a sacrilegious partaking of the life or of the bruised and broken body of the god.

From inscriptions it appears that both at Pessinus and Rome the high priest of Cybele was regularly called Attis.[1] It is therefore a reasonable conjecture that the high priest played the part of the legendary Attis at the annual festival.[2] We have seen that on the Day of Blood he drew blood from his arms, and this may have been an imitation of the self-inflicted death of Attis under the pine-tree. It is not inconsistent with this supposition that Attis was also represented at these ceremonies by an effigy; for we have already had cases in which the divine being is first represented by a living person and afterwards by an effigy, which is then burned or otherwise destroyed.[3] Perhaps we may go a step farther and conjecture that this mimic killing of the priest (if it was such), accompanied by a real effusion of his blood, was in Phrygia, as it has been elsewhere, a substitute for a human sacrifice which in earlier times was actually offered. Professor W. M. Ramsay, whose authority on all questions relating to Phrygia no one will dispute, is of opinion that at these Phrygian ceremonies "the representative of the god was probably slain each year by a cruel death, just as the god himself died."[4] We know from Strabo[5] that the priests of Pessinus were at one time potentates as well as priests; they may, there-

---

[1] Duncker, *Geschichte des Alterthums*,[5] i. 456, note 4; Roscher, *Ausführliches Lexikon d. griech. u. röm. Mythologie*, i. c. 724. Cp. Polybius, xxii. 20 (18).

[2] The conjecture is that of Henzen in *Annal. d. Inst.* 1856, p. 110, referred to in Roscher, *l.c.*

[3] See pp. 84, 231.

[4] Article "Phrygia," in *Encyclopaedia Britannica*, ninth ed. xviii. 853.

[5] xii. 5, 3.

fore, have belonged to that class of divine kings or popes whose duty it was to die each year for their people and the world. As a god of vegetation, annually slain, the representative of Attis would be parallel to the Wild Man, the King, etc., of north European folk-custom, and to the Italian priest of Nemi.

§ 6.—*Osiris*

There seem to be some grounds for believing that Osiris, the great god of ancient Egypt, was one of those personifications of vegetation, whose annual death and resurrection have been celebrated in so many lands. But as the chief of the gods he appears to have absorbed the attributes of other deities, so that his character and rites present a complex of heterogeneous elements which, with the scanty evidence at our disposal, it is hardly possible to sort out. It may be worth while, however, to put together some of the facts which lend support to the view that Osiris or at least one of the deities out of whom he was compounded was a god of vegetation, analogous to Adonis and Attis.

The outline of his myth is as follows.[1] Osiris was the son of the earth-god Qeb (or Seb, as the name is sometimes transliterated).[2] Reigning as a king on earth, he reclaimed the Egyptians from savagery, gave them

---

[1] The myth, in a connected form, is only known from Plutarch, *Isis et Osiris*, cc. 13-19. Some additional details, recovered from Egyptian sources, will be found in the work of Adolf Erman, *Aegypten und aegyptisches Leben im Altertum*, p. 365 *sqq.*

[2] Le Page Renouf, *Hibbert Lectures*, 1879, p. 110; Brugsch, *Religion und Mythologie der alten Aegypter*, p. 614; Ad. Erman, *l.c.*; Ed. Meyer, *Geschichte des Altertums*, i. § 56 *sq.*

laws, and taught them to worship the gods. Before his
time the Egyptians had been cannibals. But Isis, the
sister and wife of Osiris, discovered wheat and barley
growing wild, and Osiris introduced the cultivation of
these grains amongst his people, who forthwith abandoned cannibalism and took kindly to a corn diet.[1]
Afterwards Osiris travelled over the world diffusing
the blessings of civilisation wherever he went. But on
his return his brother Set (whom the Greeks called
Typhon), with seventy-two others, plotted against him,
and having inveigled him into a beautifully decorated
coffer, they nailed it down on him, soldered it fast
with molten lead, and flung it into the Nile. It floated
down to the sea. This happened on the 17th day of
the month Athyr. Isis put on mourning, and wandered
disconsolately up and down seeking the body, till at last
she found it at Byblus, on the Syrian coast, whither it
had drifted with the waves. An *erica* tree had shot up
and enfolded the coffer within its stem, and the King
of Byblus, admiring the fine growth of the tree, had
caused it to be cut down and converted into a pillar of
his palace. From him Isis obtained leave to open the
trunk of the tree, and having taken out the coffer, she
carried it away with her. But she left it to visit her
son Horus at Butus in the Delta, and Typhon found
the coffer as he was hunting a boar by the light of a
full moon.[2] He recognised the body of Osiris, rent it
into fourteen pieces, and scattered them abroad. Isis
sailed up and down the marshes in a papyrus boat
seeking the fragments, and as she found each she
buried it. Hence many graves of Osiris were shown
in Egypt. Others said that Isis left an effigy of Osiris

---

[1] Plutarch, *Isis et Osiris*, 13 ; Diodorus, i. 14 ; Tibullus, i. 7, 29 *sqq.*
[2] Plutarch, *Isis et Osiris*, 8.

in every city, pretending it was his body, in order that Osiris might be worshipped in many places, and to prevent Typhon from discovering the real corpse. Afterwards her son Horus fought against Typhon, conquered him, and bound him fast. But Isis, to whom he had been delivered, loosed his bonds and let him go. This angered Horus, and he pulled the crown from his mother's head ; but Hermes replaced it with a helmet made in the shape of a cow's head. Typhon was subsequently defeated in two other battles. The rest of the myth included the dismemberment of Horus and the beheading of Isis.

So much for the myth of Osiris. Of the annual rites with which his death and burial were celebrated we unfortunately know very little. The mourning lasted five days,[1] from the 8th to the 12th of the month Athyr.[2] The ceremonies began with the "earth-ploughing," that is, with the opening of the field labours, when the waters of the Nile are sinking. The other rites included the search for the mangled body of Osiris, the rejoicings at its discovery, and its solemn burial. The burial took place on the 11th of November, and was accompanied by the recitation of lamentations from the liturgical books. These lamentations, of which several copies have been discovered in modern times, were put in the

---

[1] So Brugsch, *op. cit.* p. 617. Plutarch, *op. cit.* 39, says four days, beginning with the 17th of the month Athyr.

[2] In the Alexandrian year the month Athyr corresponded to November. But as the old Egyptian year was vague, that is, made no use of intercalation, the astronomical date of each festival varied from year to year, till it had passed through the whole cycle of the astronomical year. From the fact,

therefore, that, when the calendar became fixed, Athyr fell in November, no inference can be drawn as to the date at which the death of Osiris was originally celebrated. It is thus perfectly possible that it may have been originally a harvest festival, though the Egyptian harvest falls, not in November, but in April; cp. Selden, *De diis Syris*, p. 335 *sq.*; Parthey on Plutarch, *Isis et Osiris*, c. 39.

mouth of Isis and Nephthys, sisters of Osiris. "In
form and substance," says Brugsch, "they vividly
recall the dirges chanted at the Adonis' rites over the
dead god."[1] Next day was the joyous festival of
Sokari, that being the name under which the hawk-
headed Osiris of Memphis was invoked. The solemn
processions of priests which on this day wound round
the temples with all the pomp of banners, images, and
sacred emblems, were amongst the most stately
pageants that ancient Egypt could show. The whole
festival ended on the 16th of November with a special
rite called the erection of the *Tatu, Tat,* or *Ded* pillar.[2]
This pillar appears from the monuments to have been
a column with cross bars at the top, like the yards of a
mast, or more exactly like the superposed capitals of a
pillar.[3] On a Theban tomb the king himself, assisted
by his relations and a priest, is represented hauling at
the ropes by which the pillar is being raised. The
pillar was interpreted, at least in later Egyptian
theology, as the backbone of Osiris. It might very
well be a conventional representation of a tree stripped
of its leaves; and if Osiris was a tree-spirit, the bare
trunk and branches of a tree might naturally be
described as his backbone. The erection of the
column would then be, as Erman interprets it, a representation of the resurrection of Osiris, which, as we
learn from Plutarch, appears to have been celebrated
at his mysteries.[4] Perhaps the ceremony which

[1] Brugsch, *l.c.* For a specimen of these lamentations see Brugsch, *op. cit.* p. 631 *sq.*; *Records of the Past,* ii. 119 *sqq.* For the annual ceremonies of finding and burying Osiris, see also Firmicus Maternus, *De errore profanarum religionum,* 2 § 3; Servius on Virgil, *Aen.* iv. 609.

[2] Brugsch, *op. cit.* p. 617 *sq.*; Erman, *Aegypten und aegyptisches Leben im Altertum,* p. 377 *sq.*
[3] Erman, *l.c.*; Wilkinson, *Manners and Customs of the Ancient Egyptians* (London, 1878), iii. 68, 82; Tiele, *History of the Egyptian Religion,* p. 46.
[4] Plutarch, *Isis et Osiris,* 35. ὁμο-

Plutarch describes as taking place on the third day of the festival (the 19th day of the month Athyr) may also have referred to the resurrection. He says that on that day the priests carried the sacred ark down to the sea. Within the ark was a golden casket, into which drinking-water was poured. A shout then went up that Osiris was found. Then some mould was mixed with water, and out of the paste thus formed a crescent-shaped image was fashioned, which was then dressed in robes and adorned.[1]

The general similarity of the myth and ritual of Osiris to those of Adonis and Attis is obvious. In all three cases we see a god whose untimely and violent death is mourned by a loving goddess and annually celebrated by their worshippers. The character of Osiris as a deity of vegetation is brought out by the legend that he was the first to teach men the use of corn, and by the fact that his annual festival began with ploughing the earth. He is said also to have introduced the cultivation of the vine.[2] In one of the chambers dedicated to Osiris in the great temple of Isis at Philae the dead body of Osiris is represented with stalks of corn springing from it, and a priest is watering the stalks from a pitcher which he holds in his hand. The accompanying inscription sets forth that " This is the form of him whom one may not name, Osiris of the mysteries, who springs from the returning waters."[3] It would seem impossible to devise a more graphic way of representing Osiris as a personification of the corn ; while the inscription proves that this personification was the kernel of the

λογεῖ δὲ καὶ τὰ τιτανικὰ καὶ νὺξ τελεία τοῖς λεγομένοις Ὀσίριδος διασπασμοῖς καὶ ταῖς ἀναβιώσεσι καὶ παλιγγενεσίαις, ὁμοίως δὲ καὶ τὰ περὶ τὰς ταφάς.

[1] Plutarch, *Isis et Osiris*, 39.

[2] Tibullus, i. 7, 33 *sqq.*

[3] Brugsch, *op. cit.* p. 621.

mysteries of the god, the innermost secret that was only revealed to the initiated. In estimating the mythical character of Osiris very great weight must be given to this monument. The legend that his mangled remains were scattered up and down the land may be a mythical way of expressing either the sowing or the winnowing of the grain. The latter interpretation is supported by the story that Isis placed the severed limbs of Osiris on a corn-sieve.[1] Or the legend may be a reminiscence of the custom of slaying a human victim (probably considered as a representative of the corn-spirit) and distributing his flesh or scattering his ashes over the fields to fertilise them. We have already seen that in modern Europe the figure of " Death " is sometimes torn in pieces, and that the fragments are then buried in the fields to make the crops grow well.[2] Later on we shall meet with examples of human victims being treated in the same way. With regard to the ancient Egyptians, we have it on the authority of Manetho that they used to burn red-haired men and scatter their ashes with winnowing-fans.[3] That this custom was not, as might perhaps have been supposed, a mere way of wreaking their spite on foreigners, amongst whom rather than amongst the native Egyptians red-haired people would generally be found, appears from the fact that the oxen which were sacrificed had also to be red ; a single black or white hair found on a beast would have disqualified it for the sacrifice.[4] The red hair of the human victims was thus probably essential ; the fact that they were generally foreigners was only accidental.

[1] Servius on Virgil, *Georg.* i. 166.

[2] Above, p. 267.

[3] Plutarch, *Isis et Osiris*, 73, cp. 33; Diodorus, i. 88.

[4] Plutarch, *op. cit.* 31 ; Herodotus, ii. 38.

If, as I conjecture, these human sacrifices were intended to promote the growth of the crops—and the *winnowing* of their ashes seems to support this view—red-haired victims were perhaps selected as best fitted to represent the spirit of the golden grain. For when a god is represented by a living person, it is natural that the human representative should be chosen on the ground of his supposed resemblance to the god. Hence the ancient Mexicans, conceiving the maize as a personal being who went through the whole course of life between seed-time and harvest, sacrificed new-born babes when the maize was sown, older children when it had sprouted, and so on till it was fully ripe, when they sacrificed old men.[1] A name for Osiris was the "crop" or "harvest";[2] and the ancients sometimes explained him as a personification of the corn.[3]

But Osiris was not only a corn-spirit; he was also a tree-spirit, and this was probably his original character; for, as we have already observed, the corn-spirit seems to be only an extension of the older tree-spirit. His character as a tree-spirit was represented very graphically in a ceremony described by Firmicus Maternus.[4] A pine-tree was cut down, the centre was hollowed out, and with the wood thus excavated an image of Osiris was made, which was then "buried"

---

[1] Herrera, quoted by Bastian, *Culturländer des alten Amerika*, ii. 639.

[2] Lefébure, *Le mythe Osirien* (Paris, 1874-75), p. 188.

[3] Firmicus Maternus, *De errore profanarum religionum*, 2, § 6, *defensores eorum volunt addere physicam rationem, frugum semina Osirim dicentes esse ; Isim terram, Tyfonem calorem : et quia maturatae fruges calore ad vitam hominum colliguntur et divisae a terrae consortio separantur et rursus adpro-pinquante hieme seminantur, hanc volunt esse mortem Osiridis, cum fruges recondunt, inventionem vero, cum fruges genitali terrae fomento conceptae annua rursus coeperint procreatione generari* ; Eusebius, *Praepar. Evang.* iii. 11, 31, ὁ δὲ Ὄσιρις παρ' Αἰγυπτίοις τὴν κάρπιμον παρίστησι δύναμιν, ἣν θρήνοις ἀπομειλίσσονται εἰς γῆν ἀφανιζομένην ἐν τῷ σπόρῳ, καὶ ὑφ' ἡμῶν καταναλισκομένην εἰς τὰς τροφάς.

[4] *Op. cit.* 27, § 1.

in the hollow of the tree. Here, again, it is hard to imagine how the conception of a tree as tenanted by a personal being could be more plainly expressed. The image of Osiris thus made was kept for a year and then burned, exactly as was done with the image of Attis which was attached to the pine-tree. The ceremony of cutting the tree, as described by Firmicus Maternus, appears to be alluded to by Plutarch.[1] It was probably the ritual counterpart of the mythical discovery of the body of Osiris enclosed in the *erica* tree. We may conjecture that the erection of the *Tatu* pillar at the close of the annual festival of Osiris[2] was identical with the ceremony described by Firmicus; it is to be noted that in the myth the *erica* tree formed a pillar in the King's house. Like the similar custom of cutting a pine-tree and fastening an image to it in the rites of Attis, the ceremony perhaps belonged to that class of customs of which the bringing in the May-pole is among the most familiar. As to the pine-tree in particular, at Denderah the tree of Osiris is a conifer, and the coffer containing the body of Osiris is here represented as enclosed within the tree.[3] A pine-cone is often represented on the monuments as offered to Osiris, and a MS. of the Louvre speaks of the cedar as sprung from Osiris.[4] The sycamore and the tamarisk are also his trees. In inscriptions he is spoken of as residing in them ;[5] and his mother Nut is frequently represented in a sycamore.[6] In a sepulchre

---

[1] *Isis et Osiris*, 21, αἰνῶ δὲ τομὴν ξύλου καὶ σχίσιν λίνου καὶ χοὰς χεομένας, διὰ τὸ πολλὰ τῶν μυστικῶν ἀναμεμῖχθαι τούτοις. Again, c. 42, τὸ δὲ ξύλον ἐν ταῖς λεγομέναις Ὀσίριδος ταφαῖς τέμνοντες κατασκευάζουσι λάρνακα μηνοειδῆ.

[2] See above, p. 304.

[3] Lefébure, *Le mythe Osirien*, pp.

194, 198, referring to Mariette, *Denderah*, iv. 66 and 72.

[4] Lefébure, *op. cit.* pp. 195, 197.

[5] Birch, in Wilkinson's *Manners and Customs of the Ancient Egyptians* (London, 1878), iii. 84.

[6] Wilkinson, *op. cit.* iii. 63 *sq.* ; Ed. Meyer, *Geschichte des Alterthums*, i. §§ 56, 60.

at How (Diospolis Parva) a tamarisk is represented overshadowing the coffer of Osiris; and in the series of sculptures which represent the mystic history of Osiris in the great temple of Isis at Philae, a tamarisk is depicted with two men pouring water on it. The inscription on this last monument leaves no doubt, says Brugsch, that the verdure of the earth is believed to be connected with the verdure of the tree, and that the sculpture refers to the grave of Osiris at Philae, of which Plutarch says that it was overshadowed by a *methide* plant, taller than any olive-tree. This sculpture, it may be observed, occurs in the same chamber in which Osiris is represented as a corpse with ears of corn sprouting from him.[1]   In inscriptions Osiris is referred to as "the one in the tree," "the solitary one in the acacia," etc.[2]   On the monuments he sometimes appears as a mummy covered with a tree or with plants.[3]   It accords with the character of Osiris as a tree-spirit that his worshippers were forbidden to injure fruit-trees, and with his character as a god of vegetation in general that they were not allowed to stop up wells of water, which are so important for purposes of irrigation in hot southern lands.[4]

The original meaning of the goddess Isis is still more difficult to determine than that of her brother and husband Osiris.   Her attributes and epithets were so numerous that in the hieroglyphics she is called

---

[1] Wilkinson, *op. cit.* iii. 349 *sq.*; Brugsch, *Religion und Mythologie der alten Aegypter*, p. 621 ; Plutarch, *Isis et Osiris*, 20.   In Plutarch *l.c.* Parthey proposes to read μυρίκης for μηθίδης, and this conjecture appears to be accepted by Wilkinson, *l.c.*

[2] Lefébure, *Le mythe Osirien*, p. 191.

[3] Lefébure, *op. cit.* p. 188.

[4] Plutarch, *Isis et Osiris*, 35.   One of the points in which the myths of Isis and Demeter agree, is that both goddesses in their search for the loved and lost one are said to have sat down, sad at heart and weary, on the edge of a well.   Hence those who had been initiated at Eleusis were forbidden to sit on a well.   Plutarch, *Isis et Osiris*, 15 ; Homer, *Hymn to Demeter*, 98 *sq.*; Pausanias, i. 39, 1 ; Apollodorus, i. 5, 1 ; Nicander, *Theriaca*, 486 ; Clemens Alex., *Protrept.* ii. 20.

"the many-named," "the thousand-named," and in
Greek inscriptions "the myriad-named."[1] Tiele con-
fesses candidly that "it is now impossible to tell
precisely to what natural phenomena the character
of Isis at first referred."[2] Mr. Renouf states that Isis
was the Dawn,[3] but without assigning any reason
whatever for the identification. There are at least
some grounds for seeing in her a goddess of corn.
According to Diodorus, whose authority appears to
have been the Egyptian historian Manetho, the discovery of wheat and barley was attributed to Isis, and
at her festivals stalks of these grains were carried in
procession to commemorate the boon she had conferred
on men. Further, at harvest-time, when the Egyptian
reapers had cut the first stalks, they laid them down
and beat their breasts, lamenting and calling upon
Isis.[4] Amongst the epithets by which she is designated
on the inscriptions are "creatress of the green crop,"
"the green one, whose greenness is like the greenness
of the earth," and "mistress of bread."[5] According to
Brugsch she is "not only the creatress of the fresh verdure of vegetation which covers the earth, but is actually
the green corn-field itself, which is personified as a
goddess."[6] This is confirmed by her epithet *Sochit* or
Sochet, meaning "a corn-field," a sense which the word
still retains in Coptic.[7] It is in this character of a
corn-goddess that the Greeks conceived Isis, for they

---

[1] Brugsch, *Religion und Mythologie
der alten Aegypter*, p. 645.

[2] C. P. Tiele, *History of Egyptian
Religion*, p. 57.

[3] *Hibbert Lectures*, 1879, p. 111.

[4] Diodorus, i. 14. Eusebius (*Prae-
parat. Evang.* iii. 3) quotes from
Diodorus (i. 11-13) a long passage on
the early religion of Egypt, prefacing

the quotation (c. 2) with the remark
γράφει δὲ καὶ τὰ περὶ τούτων πλατύτερον
μὲν ὁ Μανέθως, ἐπετετμημένως δὲ ὁ
Διόδωρος, which seems to imply that
Diodorus epitomised Manetho.

[5] Brugsch, *op. cit.* p. 647.

[6] Brugsch, *op. cit.* p. 649.

[7] Brugsch, *l.c.*

identified her with Demeter.[1] In a Greek epigram
she is described as "she who has given birth to the
fruits of the earth," and "the mother of the ears of
corn,"[2] and in a hymn composed in her honour she
speaks of herself as "queen of the wheat-field," and is
described as "charged with the care of the fruitful
furrow's wheat-rich path."[3]

Osiris has been sometimes interpreted as the sun-
god; and this view has been held by so many
distinguished writers in modern times that a few
words of reply seem called for. If we inquire on
what evidence Osiris has been identified with the sun
or the sun-god, it will be found on examination that
the evidence is minute in quantity and dubious, where
it is not absolutely worthless, in quality. The diligent
Jablonski, the first modern scholar to collect and examine the testimony of classical writers on Egyptian
religion, says that it can be shown in many ways that
Osiris is the sun, and that he could produce a cloud of
witnesses to prove it, but that it is needless to do so,
since no learned man is ignorant of the fact.[4] Of the
writers whom he condescends to quote, the only two
who expressly identify Osiris with the sun are Diodorus
and Macrobius. The passage in Diodorus runs thus:[5]
"It is said that the aboriginal inhabitants of Egypt,
looking up to the sky, and smitten with awe and wonder
at the nature of the universe, supposed that there were
two gods, eternal and primeval, the sun and the moon,
of whom they named the sun Osiris and the moon
Isis." Even if Diodorus's authority for this statement
is Manetho, as there is some ground for believing,[6]

[1] Herodotus, ii. 59, 156; Diodorus, i. 13, 25, 96; Apollodorus, ii.
1, 3; Tzetzes, *Schol. in Lycophron.* 212.
[2] *Antholog. Planud.* 264, 1.

[3] *Orphica*, ed. Abel, p. 295 *sqq.*
[4] Jablonski, *Pantheon Ageyptiorum*
(Frankfurt, 1750), i. 125 *sq.*
[5] i. 11.   [6] See p. 310, *note.*

little or no weight can be attached to it. For it is plainly a philosophical, and therefore a late, explanation of the first beginnings of Egyptian religion, reminding us of Kant's familiar saying about the starry heavens and the moral law rather than of the rude traditions of a primitive people. Jablonski's second authority, Macrobius, is no better but rather worse. For Macrobius was the father of that large family of mythologists who resolve all or most gods into the sun. According to him Mercury was the sun, Mars was the sun, Janus was the sun, Saturn was the sun, so was Jupiter, also Nemesis, likewise Pan, etc.[1] It was, therefore, nearly a matter of course that he should identify Osiris with the sun.[2] But apart from the general principle, so frankly enunciated by Professor Maspero, that all the gods are the sun ("*Comme tous les dieux, Osiris est le soleil*"),[3] Macrobius has not much cause to show for identifying Osiris in particular with the sun. He argues that Osiris must be the sun because an eye was one of his symbols. The premise is correct,[4] but what exactly it has to do with the conclusion is not clear. The opinion that Osiris was the sun is also mentioned, but not accepted, by Plutarch,[5] and it is referred to by Firmicus Maternus.[6]

Amongst modern Egyptologists, Lepsius, in identifying Osiris with the sun, appears to rely mainly on the passage of Diodorus already quoted. But the monuments, he adds, also show "that down to a late time Osiris was sometimes conceived as *Ra*. In this quality he is named *Osiris-Ra* even in the ' Book of the Dead,'

---

[1] See the *Saturnalia*, bk. i.

[2] *Saturn*. i. 21, 11.

[3] Maspero, *Histoire ancienne des peuples de l'Orient*[4] (Paris, 1886), p. 35.

[4] Wilkinson, *Manners and Customs of the Ancient Egyptians* (London, 1878), iii. 353.

[5] *Isis et Osiris*, 52.

[6] *De errore profan. religionum*, 8.

and Isis is often called 'the royal consort of Ra.'"[1]
That Ra was both the physical sun and the sun-god is
of course undisputed; but with every deference for the
authority of so great a scholar as Lepsius, it may be
doubted whether such identification can be taken as
evidence of the original character of Osiris. For the
religion of ancient Egypt[2] may be described as a con-
federacy of local cults which, while maintaining against
each other a certain measure of jealous and even hostile
independence, were yet constantly subjected to the
fusing and amalgamating action of political centralisa-
tion and philosophical reflection. The history of the
religion appears to have largely consisted of a struggle
between these opposite forces or tendencies. On the
one side there was the conservative tendency to preserve the local cults with all their distinctive features,
fresh, sharp, and crisp, as they had been handed down
from an immemorial past. On the other side there
was the progressive tendency, favoured by the gradual
fusion of the people under a powerful central government, first to dull the edge of these provincial distinc-
tions, and finally to break them down completely and
merge them in a single national religion. The conservative party probably mustered in its ranks the
great bulk of the people, their prejudices and affections
being warmly enlisted in favour of the local deity,
with whose temple and rites they had been familiar
from childhood; and the popular aversion to change,
based on the endearing effect of old association, must

---

[1] Lepsius, "Ueber den ersten
aegyptischen Götterkreis und seine
geschichtlich - mythologische Entsteh-
ung," in *Abhandlungen der könig-
lichen Akademie der Wissenschaften zu
Berlin*, 1851, p. 194 *sq.*

[2] The view here taken of the history
of Egyptian religion is based on the
sketch in Erman's *Aegypten und aegyptisches Leben im Altertum*, p. 351
sqq.

have been strongly reinforced by the less disinterested opposition of the local clergy, whose material interests would necessarily suffer with any decay of their shrines. On the other hand the kings, whose power and glory rose with the political and ecclesiastical consolidation of the nation, were the natural champions of religious unity ; and their efforts would be seconded by the cultured and reflecting minority, who could hardly fail to be shocked by the many barbarous and revolting elements in the local rites. As usual in such cases, the process of religious unification appears to have been largely effected by discovering points of similarity, real or imaginary, between various local gods, which were thereupon declared to be only different names or manifestations of the same god.

Of the deities who thus acted as centres of attraction, absorbing in themselves a multitude of minor divinities, by far the most important was the sun-god Ra. There appear to have been few gods in Egypt who were not at one time or other identified with him. Ammon of Thebes, Horus of the East, Horus of Edfu, Chnum of Elephantine, Atum of Heliopolis, all were regarded as one god, the sun. Even the water-god Sobk, in spite of his crocodile shape, did not escape the same fate. Indeed one king, Amenhôtep IV, undertook to sweep away all the old gods at a stroke and replace them by a single god, the "great living disc of the sun."[1] In the hymns composed in his honour, this deity is referred to as "the living disc of the sun, besides whom there is none other." He is said to have made "the far heaven" and "men, beasts, and birds; he strengtheneth

---

[1] On this attempted revolution in religion see Lepsius in *Verhandl. d. königl. Akad. d. Wissensch. zu Berlin,* 1851, pp. 196-201 ; Erman, *op. cit.* p. 355 *sqq.*

the eyes with his beams, and when he showeth himself, all flowers live and grow, the meadows flourish at his upgoing and are drunken at his sight, all cattle skip on their feet, and the birds that are in the marsh flutter for joy." It is he "who bringeth the years, createth the months, maketh the days, calculateth the hours, the lord of time, by whom men reckon." In his zeal for the unity of god, the king commanded to erase the names of all other gods from the monuments, and to destroy their images. His rage was particularly directed against the god Ammon, whose name and likeness were effaced wherever they were found; even the sanctity of the tomb was violated in order to destroy the memorials of the hated god. In some of the halls of the great temples at Carnac, Luxor, and other places, all the names of the gods, with a few chance exceptions, were scratched out. In no inscription cut in this king's reign was any god mentioned save the sun. He even changed his own name, Amenhôtep, because it was compounded of Ammon, and took instead the name of Chuen-'eten, "gleam of the sun's disc." His death was followed by a violent reaction. The old gods were reinstated in their rank and privileges; their names and images were restored; and new temples were built. But all the shrines and palaces reared by the late king were thrown down; even the sculptures that referred to him and to his god in rock-tombs and on the sides of hills were erased or filled up with stucco; his name appears on no later monument, and was carefully omitted from all official lists.

This attempt of King Amenhôtep IV is only an extreme example of a tendency which appears to have been at work on the religion of Egypt as far back as we can trace it. Therefore, to come back to our point, in attempting to discover the original character of any Egyptian god, no weight can be given to the identification of him with other gods, least of all with the sun-god Ra. Far from helping to follow up the trail, these identifications only cross and confuse it. The best evidence for the original character of the Egyptian gods is to be found in their ritual and myths, so far as these are known (which unfortunately is little enough), and in the figured representations of them on the monuments. It is on evidence drawn from these sources that I rely mainly for the interpretation of Osiris as a deity of vegetation.

Amongst a younger generation of scholars, Tiele is of opinion that Osiris is the sun, because " in the hymns, his accession to the throne of his father is com- pared to the rising of the sun, and it is even said of him in so many words : ' He glitters on the horizon, he sends out rays of light from his double feather and inun- dates the world with it, as the sun from out the highest heaven.' "[1] By the same token Marie Antoinette must have been a goddess of the morning star, because Burke saw her at Versailles "just above the horizon, decorat- ing and cheering the elevated sphere she just began to move in,—glittering like the morning star, full of life, and splendour, and joy." If such comparisons prove any- thing, they prove that Osiris was *not* the sun. There are always two terms to a comparison ; a thing cannot be compared to itself. But Tiele also appeals to the monuments. What is his evidence ? Osiris is some- times represented by a figure surmounted by " the so- called Tat pillar, entirely made up of a kind of superim- posed capitals, one of which has a rude face scratched

---

[1] Tiele, *History of the Egyptian Religion*, p. 44.

upon it." Tiele is of opinion that this rude face is "intended, no doubt, to represent the shining sun."[1] If
every "rude face scratched" is to be taken as a symbol
of the shining sun, sun-worship will be discovered
in some unexpected places. But, on the whole,
Tiele, like Jablonski, prudently keeps to the high
ground of vague generalities, and the result of his
occasional descents to the level of facts is not such as
to encourage him to prolong his stay. "Were we to
come down to details," he says, "and to attend to
slight variations, we should be lost in an ocean of sym-
bolism and mysticism."[2] This is like De Quincey's
attitude towards murder. "General principles I will
suggest. But as to any particular case, once for all I
will have nothing to do with it." There is no having
a man who takes such lofty ground.

Mr. Le Page Renouf also considers that Osiris is
the sun,[3] and his position is still stronger than Tiele's.
For whereas Tiele produces bad arguments for his
view, Mr. Renouf produces none at all, and therefore
cannot possibly be confuted.

The ground upon which some recent writers seem
chiefly to rely for the identification of Osiris with the
sun is that the story of his death fits better with the
solar phenomena than with any other in nature. It
may readily be admitted that the daily appearance and
disappearance of the sun might very naturally be expressed by a myth of his death and resurrection ; and
writers who regard Osiris as the sun are careful to
emphasise the fact that it is the diurnal, and not the
annual, course of the sun to which they understand the
myth to apply. Mr. Renouf expressly admits that the

---

[1] Tiele, *op. cit.* p. 46.
[2] *Ib.* p. 45.
[3] Le Page Renouf, *Hibbert Lectures*, 1879, p. 111 *sqq.*

Egyptian sun cannot with any show of reason be described as dead in winter.[1] But if his *daily* death was the theme of the legend, why was it celebrated by an *annual* ceremony ? This fact alone seems fatal to the interpretation of the myth as descriptive of sunset and sunrise. Again, though the sun may be said to die daily, in what sense can he be said to be torn in pieces ?[2]

In the course of our inquiry, it has, I trust, been made clear that there is another natural phenomenon

---

[1] *Hibbert Lectures*, 1879, p. 113. Cp. Maspero, *Histoire ancienne*,[4] p. 35 ; Ed. Meyer, *Geschichte des Alterthums*, i. §§ 55, 57.

[2] There are far more plausible grounds for identifying Osiris with the moon than with the sun—1. He was said to have lived or reigned twenty-eight years ; Plutarch, *Isis et Osiris*, cc. 13, 42. This might be taken as a mythical expression for a lunar month. 2. His body was rent into fourteen pieces (*ib.* cc. 18, 42). This might be interpreted of the moon on the wane, losing a piece of itself on each of the fourteen days which make up the second half of a lunation. It is expressly mentioned that Typhon found the body of Osiris at the full moon (*ib.* 8) ; thus the dismemberment of the god would begin with the waning of the moon. 3. In a hymn supposed to be addressed by Isis to Osiris, it is said that Thoth

" Placeth thy soul in the bark Ma-at,
In that name which is thine, of GOD
 MOON."

And again,

" Thou *who comest to us as a child each month*,
We do not cease to contemplate thee,
Thine emanation heightens the brilliancy
Of the stars of Orion in the firmament,"
etc.

Records of the Past, i. 121 *sq.*; Brugsch, *Religion und Mythologie der alten Aegypter*, p. 629 *sq.* Here then Osiris is identified with the moon in set terms. If in the same hymn he is said to "illuminate us like Ra" (the sun), this, as we have already seen, is no reason for identifying him with the sun, but quite the contrary. 4. At the new moon of the month Phanemoth, being the beginning of spring, the Egyptians celebrated what they called " the entry of Osiris into the moon." Plutarch, *Is. et Os.* 43. 5. The bull Apis, which was regarded as an image of the soul of Osiris (*Is. et Os.* cc. 20, 29), was born of a cow which was believed to have been impregnated by the moon (*ib.* 43). 6. Once a year, at the full moon, pigs were sacrificed simultaneously to the moon and Osiris. Herodotus, ii. 47 ; Plutarch, *Is. et Os.* 8. The relation of the pig to Osiris will be examined later on.

Without attempting to explain in detail why a god of vegetation, as I take Osiris to have been, should have been brought into such close connection with the moon, I may refer to the intimate relation which is vulgarly believed to subsist between the growth of vegetation and the phases of the moon. See *e.g.* Pliny, *Nat. Hist.* ii. 221, xvi. 190, xvii. 108, 215, xviii. 200, 228, 308, 314 ; Plutarch, *Quaest. Conviv.* iii. 10, 3 ; Aulus Gellius, xx. 8, 7 ; Macrobius, *Saturn.* vii. 16, 29 *sq.* Many examples are furnished by the ancient writers on agriculture, *e.g.* Cato, 37, 4 ; Varro, i. 37 ; *Geoponica*, i. 6.

to which the conception of death and resurrection is as applicable as to sunset and sunrise, and which, as a matter of fact has been so conceived and represented in folk-custom. This phenomenon is the annual growth and decay of vegetation. A strong reason for interpreting the death of Osiris as the decay of vegetation rather than as the sunset is to be found in the general (though not unanimous) voice of antiquity, which classed together the worship and myths of Osiris, Adonis, Attis, Dionysus, and Demeter, as religions of essentially the same type.[1] The consensus of ancient opinion on this subject seems too great to be rejected as a mere fancy. So closely did the rites of Osiris resemble those of Adonis at Byblus that some of the people of Byblus themselves maintained that it was Osiris and not Adonis whose death was mourned by them.[2] Such a view could certainly not have been held if the rituals of the two gods had not been so alike as to be almost indistinguishable. Again, Herodotus found the similarity between the rites of Osiris and Dionysus so great, that he thought it impossible the latter could have arisen independently; they must, he thought, have been recently borrowed, with slight alterations, by the Greeks from the Egyptians.[3] Again, Plutarch, a very intelligent student of comparative religion, insists upon the detailed resemblance of the rites of Osiris to those of Dionysus.[4] We cannot

---

[1] Herodotus, ii. 42, 49, 59, 144, 156 ; Plutarch, *Isis et Osiris*, 13, 35 ; *id.*, *Quaest. Conviv.* iv. 5, 3 ; Diodorus, i. 13, 25, 96, iv. 1 ; *Orphica*, Hymn 42 ; Eusebius, *Praepar. Evang.* iii. 11, 31 ; Servius on Virgil, *Aen.* xi. 287 ; *id.*, on *Georg.* i. 166 ; Hippolytus, *Refut. omn. haeres.* v. 9, p. 168 ; Socrates, *Eccles. Hist.* iii. 23, p. 204 ; Tzetzes, *Schol. in Lycophron*, 212 ;

Διηγήματα, xxii. 2, in *Mythographi Graeci*, ed. Westermann, p.. 368 ; Nonnus, *Dionys.* iv. 269 *sq.*; Cornutus, *De natura deorum*, c. 28 ; Clemens Alexandr. *Protrept.* ii. 19 ; Firmicus Maternus, *De errore profan. relig.* 7.

[2] Lucian, *De dea Syria*, 7.

[3] Herodotus, ii. 49.

[4] Plutarch, *Isis et Osiris*, 35.

reject the evidence of such intelligent and trustworthy witnesses on plain matters of fact which fell under their own cognisance. Their explanations of the worships it is indeed possible to reject, for the meaning of religious cults is often open to question ; but resemblances of ritual are matters of observation. Therefore, those who explain Osiris as the sun are driven to the alternative of either dismissing as mistaken the testimony of antiquity to the similarity of the rites of Osiris, Adonis, Attis, Dionysus, and Demeter, or of interpreting all these rites as sun-worship. No modern scholar has fairly faced and accepted either side of this alternative. To accept the former would be to affirm that we know the rites of these deities better than the men who practised, or at least who witnessed them. To accept the latter would involve a wrenching, clipping, mangling, and distorting of myth and ritual from which even Macrobius shrank.[1] On the other hand, the view that the essence of all these rites was the mimic death and revival of vegetation, explains them separately and collectively in an easy and natural way, and harmonises with the general testimony borne by antiquity to their substantial similarity. The evidence for thus explaining Adonis, Attis, and Osiris has now been presented to the reader ; it remains to do the same for Dionysus and Demeter.

§ 7.—*Dionysus*

The Greek god Dionysus or Bacchus[2] is best known as the god of the vine, but he was also a god

---

[1] Osiris, Attis, Adonis, and Dionysus were all explained by him as the sun ; but he stopped short at Demeter (Ceres), whom, however, he interpreted as the moon. See the *Saturnalia*, bk. i.

[2] On Dionysus in general see Preller,

of trees in general. Thus we are told that almost all the Greeks sacrificed to " Dionysus of the tree."[1] In Boeotia one of his titles was " Dionysus in the tree."[2] His image was often merely an upright post, without arms, but draped in a mantle, with a bearded mask to represent the head, and with leafy boughs projecting from the head or body to show the nature of the deity.[3] On a vase his rude effigy is depicted appearing out of a low tree or bush.[4] He was the patron of cultivated trees;[5] prayers were offered to him that he would make the trees grow;[6] and he was especially honoured by husbandmen, chiefly fruit-growers, who set up an image of him, in the shape of a natural tree-stump, in their orchards.[7] He was said to have discovered all tree-fruits, amongst which apples and figs are particularly mentioned;[8] and he was himself spoken of as doing a husbandman's work.[9] He was referred to as " well-fruited," " he of the green fruit," and "making the fruit to grow."[10] One of his titles was " teeming" or " bursting" (as of sap or blossoms);[11] and there was a Flowery Dionysus in Attica and at Patrae in Achaea.[12] Amongst the trees particularly sacred to him, in addition to the vine, was the pine-tree.[13]

Griechische Mythologie,[3] i. 544 *sqq.*; Fr. Lenormant, article " Bacchus " in Daremberg et Saglio, *Dictionnaire des Antiquités grecques et romaines*, i. 591 *sqq.*; Voigt and Thraemer's article " Dionysus," in Roscher's *Ausführliches Lexikon der griech. und röm. Mythologie*, i. c. 1029 *sqq.*

[1] Plutarch, *Quaest. Conviv.* v. 3, Διονύσῳ δὲ δενδρίτῃ πάντες, ὡς ἔπος εἰπεῖν, Ἕλληνες θύουσιν.

[2] Hesychius, *s.v.* Ἔνδενδρος.

[3] See the pictures of his images, taken from ancient vases, in Bötticher, *Baumkultus der Hellenen*, plates 42, 43, 43 A, 43 B, 44 ; Daremberg et Saglio, *op. cit.* i. 361, 626.

[4] Daremberg et Saglio, *op. cit.* i. 626.

[5] Cornutus, *De natura deorum*, 30.

[6] Pindar, quoted by Plutarch, *Isis et Osiris*, 35.

[7] Maximus Tyrius, *Dissertat.* viii. I.

[8] Athenaeus, iii. pp. 78 C, 82 D.

[9] Himerius, *Orat.* i. 10, Διόνυσος γεωργεῖ.

[10] *Orphica*, Hymn l. 4, liii. 8.

[11] Aelian, *Var. Hist.* iii. 41 ; Hesychius, *s.v.* Φλέω[s]. Cp. Plutarch, *Quaest. Conviv.* v. 8, 3.

[12] Pausanias, i. 31, 4 ; *id.* vii. 21, 6 (2).

[13] Plutarch, *Quaest. Conviv.* v. 3.

The Delphic oracle commanded the Corinthians to worship a particular pine-tree " equally with the god," so they made two images of Dionysus out of it, with red faces and gilt bodies.[1]   In art a wand, tipped with a pine-cone, is commonly carried by the god or his worshippers.[2]   Again, the ivy and the fig-tree were especially associated with him.   In the Attic township of Acharnae there was a Dionysus Ivy;[3] at Lacedaemon there was a Fig Dionysus; and in Naxos, where figs were called *meilicha*, there was a Dionysus Meilichios, the face of whose image was made of fig-wood.[4]

Like the other gods of vegetation whom we have been considering, Dionysus was believed to have died a violent death, but to have been brought to life again; and his sufferings, death, and resurrection were enacted in his sacred rites.   The Cretan myth, as related by Firmicus, ran thus.   He was said to have been the bastard son of Jupiter (Zeus), a Cretan king.   Going abroad, Jupiter transferred the throne and sceptre to the child Dionysus, but, knowing that his wife Juno (Hera) cherished a jealous dislike of the child, he entrusted Dionysus to the care of guards upon whose fidelity he believed he could rely.   Juno, however, bribed the guards, and amusing the child with toys and a cunningly-wrought looking-glass lured him into an ambush, where her satellites, the Titans, rushed upon him, cut him limb from limb, boiled his body

---

[1] Pausanias, ii. 2, 6 (5) *sq.* Pausanias does not mention the kind of tree ; but from Euripides, *Bacchae*, 1064 *sqq.*, and Philostratus, *Imag.* i. 17 (18), we may infer that it was a pine ; though Theocritus (xxvi. 11) speaks of it as a mastich-tree.

[2] Müller-Wieseler, *Denkmäler der*

alten *Kunst*, ii. pl. xxxii. *sqq.*; Baumeister, *Denkmäler des klassischen Altertums*, i. figures 489, 491, 492, 495. Cp. Lenormant in Daremberg et Saglio, i. 623 ; Lobeck, *Aglaophamus*, p. 700.

[3] Pausanias, i. 31, 6 (3).

[4] Athenaeus, iii. p. 78 c.

with various herbs and ate it.   But his sister Minerva, who had shared in the deed, kept his heart and gave it to Jupiter on his return, revealing to him the whole history of the crime.   In his rage, Jupiter put the Titans to death by torture, and, to soothe his grief for the loss of his son, made an image in which he enclosed the child's heart, and then built a temple in his honour.[1] In this version a Euhemeristic turn has been given to the myth by representing Jupiter and Juno (Zeus and Hera) as a king and queen of Crete.   The guards referred to are the mythical Curetes who danced a war-dance round the infant Dionysus as they are said to have done round the infant Zeus.[2]   Pomegranates were supposed to have sprung from the blood of Dionysus,[3] as anemones from the blood of Adonis and violets from the blood of Attis.   According to some, the severed limbs of Dionysus were pieced together, at the command of Zeus, by Apollo, who buried them on Parnassus.[4]   The grave of Dionysus was shown in the Delphic temple beside a golden statue of Apollo.[5]   Thus far the resurrection of the slain god is not mentioned, but in other versions of the myth it is variously related.   One version, which represented Dionysus as a son of Demeter, averred that his mother pieced together his mangled limbs and made him young again.[6]   In others it is simply said that shortly after his burial he rose from

---

[1] Firmicus Maternus, *De errore profanarum religionum*, 6.

[2] Clemens Alexandr., *Protrept.* ii. 17. Cp. Lobeck, *Aglaophamus*, p. 1111 *sqq.*

[3] Clemens Alexandr., *Protrept.* ii. 19.

[4] Clemens Alexandr., *Protrept.* ii. 18; Proclus on Plato's Timaeus, iii. 200 D, quoted by Lobeck, *Aglaophamus*, p. 562, and by Abel, *Orphica*, p. 234.   Others said that the mangled body was pieced together, not by Apollo but by Rhea. Cornutus, *De natura deorum*, 30.

[5] Lobeck, *Aglaophamus*, p. 572 *sqq.* For a conjectural restoration of the temple, based on ancient authorities and an examination of the scanty remains, see an article by Professor J. H. Middleton, in *Journal of Hellenic Studies*, vol. ix. p. 282 *sqq.*

[6] Diodorus, iii. 62.

the dead and ascended up to heaven ;[1] or that Zeus raised him up as he lay mortally wounded ;[2] or that Zeus swallowed the heart of Dionysus and then begat him afresh by Semele,[3] who in the common legend figures as mother of Dionysus. Or, again, the heart was pounded up and given in a potion to Semele, who thereby conceived him.[4]

Turning from the myth to the ritual, we find that the Cretans celebrated a biennial[5] festival at which the sufferings and death of Dionysus were represented in every detail.[6] Where the resurrection formed part of the myth, it also was enacted at the rites,[7] and it even appears that a general doctrine of resurrection, or at least of immortality, was inculcated on the worshippers; for Plutarch, writing to console his wife on the death of their infant daughter, comforts her with the thought of the immortality of the soul as taught by tradition and revealed in the mysteries of Dionysus.[8] A different form of the myth of the death and re- surrection of Dionysus is that he descended into Hades to bring up his mother Semele from the dead.[9] The local Argive tradition was that he descended

---

[1] Macrobius, *Comment. in Somn. Scip.* i. 12, 12 ; *Scriptores rerum mythicarum Latini tres Romae nuper reperti* (commonly referred to as *Mythographi Vaticani*), ed. G. H. Bode (Cellis, 1834), iii. 12, 5, p. 246; Origen, *c. Cels.* iv. 171, quoted by Lobeck, *Aglaophamus*, p. 713.

[2] Himerius, *Orat.* ix. 4.

[3] Proclus, *Hymn to Minerva*, in Lobeck, *Aglaophamus*, p. 561 ; *Orphica*, ed. Abel, p. 235.

[4] Hyginus, *Fab.* 167.

[5] The festivals of Dionysus were biennial in many places. See Schö- mann, *Griechische Alterthümer*,[3] ii. 500 *sqq.* (The terms for the festival were τριετηρίς, τριετηρικός, both terms of

the series being included in the numera- tion, in accordance with the ancient mode of reckoning.) Probably the festivals were formerly annual and the period was afterwards lengthened, as has happened with other festivals. See W. Mannhardt, *Baumkultus*, pp. 172, 175, 491, 533 *sq.*, 598. Some of the festivals of Dionysus, however, were annual.

[6] Firmicus Maternus, *De err. prof. relig.* 6.

[7] *Mythogr. Vatic.* ed. Bode, *l.c.*

[8] Plutarch, *Consol. ad uxor.* 10. Cp. *id.*, *Isis et Osiris*, 35 ; *id.*, *De ei Delphico*, 9 ; *id.*, *De esu carnium*, i. 7.

[9] Pausanias, ii. 31, 2, and 37, 5 ; Apollodorus, iii. 5, 3.

through the Alcyonian lake ; and his return from the lower world, in other words his resurrection, was annually celebrated on the spot by the Argives, who summoned him from the water by trumpet blasts, while they threw a lamb into the lake as an offering to the warder of the dead.[1] Whether this was a spring festival does not appear, but the Lydians certainly celebrated the advent of Dionysus in spring ; the god was supposed to bring the season with him.[2] Deities of vegetation, who are supposed to pass a certain portion of each year underground, naturally come to be regarded as gods of the lower world or of the dead. Both Dionysus and Osiris were so conceived.[3]

A feature in the mythical character of Dionysus, which at first sight appears inconsistent with his nature as a deity of vegetation, is that he was often conceived and represented in animal shape, especially in the form, or at least with the horns, of a bull. Thus he is spoken of as " cow-born," " bull," " bull-shaped," " bull-faced," " bull-browed," " bull-horned," " horn-bearing," "two-horned," "horned."[4] He was believed to appear, at least occasionally, as a bull.[5] His images were often, as at Cyzicus, made in bull shape,[6] or with bull horns;[7] and he was painted with horns.[8] Types of the horned Dionysus are found amongst the sur-

---

[1] Pausanias, ii. 37, 5 *sq.* ; Plutarch, *Isis et Osiris*, 35 ; *id.*, *Quaest Conviv.* iv. 6, 2.

[2] Himerius, *Orat.* iii. 6, xiv. 7.

[3] For Dionysus, see Lenormant in Daremberg et Saglio, i. 632. For Osiris, see Wilkinson, *Manners and Customs of the Ancient Egyptians* (London, 1878), iii. 65.

[4] Plutarch, *Isis et Osiris*, 35 ; *id.*, *Quaest. Graec.* 36 ; Athenaeus, xi. 476 A ; Clemens Alexandr., *Protrept.* ii. 16 ; *Orphica*, Hymn xxx. *vv.* 3, 4,

xlv. 1, lii. 2, liii. 8 ; Euripides, *Bacchae*, 99 ; Schol. on Aristophanes, *Frogs*, 357 ; Nicander, *Alexipharmaca*, 31 ; Lucian, *Bacchus*, 2.

[5] Euripides, *Bacchae*, 920 *sqq.*, 1017.

[6] Plutarch, *Isis et Osiris*, 35 ; Athenaeus, *l.c.*

[7] Diodorus, iii. 64, 2, iv. 4, 2 ; Cornutus, *De natura deorum*, 30.

[8] Diodorus, *l.c.* ; Tzetzes, *Schol. in Lycophr.* 209 ; Philostratus, *Imagines*, i. 14 (15).

viving monuments of antiquity.[1] On one statuette he
appears clad in a bull's hide, the head, horns, and
hoofs hanging down behind.[2] At his festivals Dionysus
was believed to appear in bull form. The women
of Elis hailed him as a bull, and prayed him to come
with his bull's-foot. They sang, "Come here, Dionysus,
to thy holy temple by the sea ; come with the Graces
to thy temple, rushing with thy bull's-foot, O goodly
bull, O goodly bull!"[3] According to the myth, it was
in the shape of a bull that he was torn to pieces by the
Titans;[4] and the Cretans, in representing the sufferings
and death of Dionysus, tore a live bull to pieces with
their teeth.[5] Indeed, the rending and devouring of
live bulls and calves appear to have been a regular
feature of the Dionysiac rites.[6] The practice of representing the god in bull form or with some of the
features of a bull, the belief that he appeared in bull
form to his worshippers at the sacred rites, and the
legend that it was in bull form that he had been torn
in pieces—all these facts taken together leave no room
to doubt that in rending and devouring a live bull at
his festival his worshippers believed that they were
killing the god, eating his flesh, and drinking his blood.

Another animal whose form Dionysus assumed was
the goat. One of his names was " Kid."[7] To save
him from the wrath of Hera, his father Zeus changed

---

[1] Müller-Wieseler, *Denkmäler der
alten Kunst*, ii. pl. xxxiii. ; Daremberg
et Saglio, i. 619 *sq.*, 631 ; Roscher,
Ausführl. Lexikon, i. c. 1149 *sqq.*

[2] Welcker, *Alte Denkmäler*, v. taf.
2.

[3] Plutarch, *Quaest. Graec.* 36 ; *id.*,
Isis et Osiris, 35.

[4] Nonnus, *Dionys.* vi. 205.

[5] Firmicus Maternus, *De errore profan. religionum*, 6.

[6] Euripides, *Bacchae*, 735 *sqq.* ;
Schol. on Aristophanes, *Frogs*, 357.

[7] Hesychius, *s.v.* Ἔριφος ὁ Διόνυσος,
on which there is a marginal gloss
ὁ μικρὸς αἴξ, ὁ ἐν τῷ ἔαρι φαινόμενος,
ἤγουν ὁ πρώϊμος ; Stephanus Byzant.
s.v. 'Ακρώρεια. The title Εἰραφιώτης is
probably to be explained in the same
way. [Homer], *Hymn* xxxiv. 2 ; Porphyry, *De abstin.* iii. 17 : Dionysius,
Perieg. 576 ; *Etymolog. Magnum*, p.
371, 57.

him into a kid;[1] and when the gods fled to Egypt to escape the fury of Typhon, Dionysus was turned into a goat.[2] Hence when his worshippers rent in pieces a live goat and devoured it raw,[3] they must have believed that they were eating the body and blood of the god.

This custom of killing a god in animal form, which we shall examine more fully presently, belongs to a very early stage in human culture, and is apt in later times to be misunderstood. The advance of thought tends to strip the old animal and plant gods of their bestial and vegetable husk, and to leave their human attributes (which are always the kernel of the conception) as the final and sole residuum. In other words, animal and plant gods tend to become purely anthropomorphic. When they have become wholly or nearly so, the animals and plants which were at first the deities themselves, still retain a vague and ill-understood connection with the anthropomorphic gods which have been developed out of them. The origin of the relationship between the deity and the animal or plant having been forgotten, various stories are invented to explain it. These explanations may follow one of two lines according as they are based on the habitual or on the exceptional treatment of the sacred animal or plant. The sacred animal was habitually spared, and only exceptionally slain; and accordingly the myth might be devised to explain either why it was spared or why

---

[1] Apollodorus, iii. 4, 3.

[2] Ovid, *Metam.* v. 329; Antoninus Liberalis, 28; *Mythogr. Vatic.* ed. Bode, i. 86, p. 29.

[3] Arnobius, *Adv. nationes,* v. 19. Cp. Suidas, *s. v.* αἰγίζειν. As fawns appear to have been also torn in pieces at the rites of Dionysus (Photius, *s.v.*

νεβρίζειν; Harpocration, *s.v.* νεβρίζων), it is probable that the fawn was another of the god's embodiments. But of this there seems no direct evidence. Fawn-skins were worn both by the god and his worshippers (Cornutus, *De natura deorum,* c. 30). Similarly the female Bacchanals wore goat-skins (Hesychius, *s.v.* τραγηφόροι).

it was killed. Devised for the former purpose, the myth would tell of some service rendered to the deity by the animal; devised for the latter purpose, the myth would tell of some injury inflicted by the animal on the god. The reason given for sacrificing goats to Dionysus is an example of a myth of the latter sort. They were sacrificed to him, it was said, because they injured the vine.[1] Now the goat, as we have seen, was originally an embodiment of the god himself. But when the god had divested himself of his animal character and had become essentially anthropomorphic, the killing of the goat in his worship came to be regarded no longer as a slaying of the god himself, but as a sacrifice to him; and since some reason had to be assigned why the goat in particular should be sacrificed, it was alleged that this was a punishment inflicted on the goat for injuring the vine, the object of the god's especial care. Thus we have the strange spectacle of a god sacrificed to himself on the ground that he is his own enemy. And as the god is supposed to partake of the victim offered to him, it follows that, when the victim is the god's old self, the god eats of his own flesh. Hence the goat-god Dionysus is represented as eating raw goat's blood;[2] and the bull-god Dionysus is called "eater of bulls."[3] On the analogy of these instances we may conjecture that wherever a god is described as the eater of a particular animal, the animal in question was originally nothing but the god himself.[4]

---

[1] Varro, *De re rustica* i. 2, 19; Virgil, *Georg.* ii. 380, and Servius, *ad l.*, and on *Aen.* iii. 118; Ovid, *Fasti*, i. 353 *sqq.*; *id.*, *Metam.* xv. 114 *sq.*; Cornutus, *De natura deorum*, 30.

[2] Euripides, *Bacchae*, 138 *sq.* ἀγρεύ-ων αἷμα τραγοκτόνον, ὠμοφάγον χάριν.

[3] Schol. on Aristophanes, *Frogs*, 357.

[4] Hera αἰγοφάγος at Sparta, Pausanias, iii. 15, 9 (cp. the representation of Hera clad in a goat's skin, with the animal's head and horns over her head, Müller-Wieseler, *Denkmäler der alten*

All this, however, does not explain why a deity of vegetation should appear in animal form. But the consideration of this point had better be deferred till we have discussed the character and attributes of Demeter. Meantime it remains to point out that in some places, instead of an animal, a human being was torn in pieces at the rites of Dionysus. This was the custom in Chios and Tenedos;[1] and at Potniae in Boeotia the tradition ran that it had been formerly the custom to sacrifice to the goat-smiting Dionysus a child, for whom a goat was afterwards substituted.[2] At Orchomenus the human victim was taken from the women of a certain family, called the Oleiae. At the annual festival the priest of Dionysus pursued these women with a drawn sword, and if he overtook one of them he had a right to slay her. This right was exercised as late as Plutarch's time.[3] As the slain bull or goat represented the slain god, so, we may suppose, the human victim also represented him. It is possible, however, that a tradition of human sacrifice may sometimes have been a mere misinterpretation of a sacrificial ritual in which an animal victim was treated as a human being. For example, at Tenedos the new-born calf sacrificed to Dionysus was shod in buskins, and the mother cow was tended like a woman in child-bed.[4]

Kunst, i. No. 299 B); Apollo ὀψοφάγος at Elis, Athenaeus, 346 B ; Artemis καπροφάγος in Samos, Hesychius, *s.v.* καπροφάγος ; cp. *id.*, *s.v.* κριοφάγος. Divine titles derived from *killing* animals are probably to be similarly explained, as Dionysus αἰγόβολος, Pausanias ix. 8, 2 ; Rhea or Hecate κυνοσφαγής, Tzetzes, *Schol. in Lycophr.*

77 ; Apollo λυκοκτόνος, Sophocles, *Electra*, 6 ; Apollo σαυροκτόνος, Pliny, *Nat. Hist.* xxxiv. 70.
[1] Porphyry, *De abstin.* ii. 55.
[2] Pausanias, ix. 8, 2.
[3] Plutarch, *Quaest. Graec.* 38.
[4] Aelian, *Nat. An.* xii. 34. Cp. W. Robertson Smith, *Religion of the Semites*, i. 286 *sqq.*

§ 8.—*Demeter and Proserpine*

The Greek myth of Demeter and Proserpine is substantially identical with the Syrian myth of Aphrodite (Astarte) and Adonis, the Phrygian myth of Cybele and Attis, and the Egyptian myth of Isis and Osiris. In the Greek myth, as in its Asiatic and Egyptian counterparts, a goddess—Demeter—mourns the loss of a loved one—Proserpine—who personifies the vegetation, more especially the corn, which dies in summer[1] to revive in spring. But in the Greek myth the loved and lost one is the daughter instead of the husband or lover of the goddess; and the mother as well as the daughter is a goddess of the corn.[2] Thus, as modern scholars have recognised,[3] Demeter and Proserpine are merely a mythical reduplication of the same natural phenomenon. Proserpine, so ran the Greek myth,[4] was gathering flowers when the earth gaped, and Pluto, lord of the Dead, issuing from the abyss, carried her off on his golden car to be his bride in the gloomy subterranean world. Her sorrowing mother Demeter sought her over land and sea, and learning from the

---

[1] It is to be remembered that on the Mediterranean coasts the harvest never falls so late as autumn.

[2] On Demeter as a corn-goddess see Mannhardt, *Mythologische Forschungen*, p. 224 *sqq.*; on Proserpine in the same character see Cornutus, *De nat. deor.* c. 28; Varro in Augustine, *Civ. Dei*, vii. 20; Hesychius, *s.v.* Φερσεφόνεια; Firmicus Maternus, *De errore prof. relig.* 17. In his careful account of Demeter as a corn-goddess Mannhardt appears to have overlooked the very important statement of Hippolytus (*Refut. omn. haeres.* v. 8, p. 162, ed. Duncker and Schneidewin) that at the initiation into the Eleusinian mysteries (the most famous of all the rites of Demeter) the central mystery revealed to the initiated was a reaped ear of corn.

[3] Welcker, *Griechische Götterlehre*, ii. 532; Preller, in Pauly's *Real-Encyclopädie für class. Alterthumswiss.* vi. 107; Lenormant, in Daremberg et Saglio, *Dictionnaire des Antiquités grecques et romaines*, i. pt. ii. 1047 *sqq.*

[4] Homer, *Hymn to Demeter*; Apollodorus, i. 5; Ovid, *Fasti*, iv. 425 *sqq.*; *id.*, *Metam.* v. 385 *sqq.*

Sun her daughter's fate, she suffered not the seed to grow, but kept it hidden in the ground, so that the whole race of men would have died of hunger if Zeus had not sent and fetched Proserpine from the nether world. Finally it was agreed that Proserpine should spend a third, or according to others a half,[1] of each year with Pluto underground, but should come forth in spring to dwell with her mother and the gods in the upper world. Her annual death and resurrection, that is, her annual descent into the under world and her ascension from it, appear to have been represented in her rites.[2]

With regard to the name Demeter, it has been plausibly argued by Mannhardt[3] that the first part of the word is derived from *dēai*, a Cretan word for "barley";[4] and that thus Demeter means the Barley-mother or the Corn-mother; for the root of the word appears to have been applied to different kinds of grain by different branches of the Aryans, and even of the Greeks themselves.[5] As Crete appears to have been one of the most ancient seats of the worship of Demeter,[6] it is not surprising that her name should be of Cretan origin. This explanation of the name Demeter is supported by a host of analogies which the diligence of Mannhardt has collected

---

[1] A third, according to Homer, *H. to Demeter*, 399, and Apollodorus, i. 5, 3; a half, according to Ovid, *Fasti*, iv. 614; *id.*, *Metam.* v. 567; Hyginus, *Fab.* 146.

[2] Schömann, *Griech. Alterthümer*,[3] ii. 393; Preller, *Griech. Mythologie*,[3] i. 628 *sq.*, 644 *sq.*, 650 *sq.* The evidence of the ancients on this head, though not full and definite, seems sufficient. See Diodorus, v. 4; Firmicus Maternus, cc. 7, 27; Plutarch, *Isis et Osiris*, 69; Apuleius, *Met.* vi. 2; Clemens Alex., *Protrept.* ii. §§ 12, 17.

[3] *Mythol. Forschungen*, p. 292 *sqq.*

[4] *Etymol. Magnum.* p. 264, 12 *sq.*

[5] O. Schrader, *Sprachvergleichung und Urgeschichte*[2] (Jena, 1890), pp. 409, 422; V. Hehn, *Kulturpflanzen und Hausthiere in ihrem Uebergang aus Asien*,[4] p. 54. Δηαί is doubtless equivalent etymologically to ζειαί, which is often taken to be spelt, but this seems uncertain.

[6] Hesiod, *Theog.* 971; Lenormant, in Daremberg et Saglio, i. pt. ii. p. 1029.

from modern European folk-lore, and of which the following are specimens. In Germany the corn is very commonly personified under the name of the Corn-mother. Thus in spring, when the wind sets the corn in wave-like motion, the peasants say, "There comes the Corn-mother," or "The Corn-mother is running over the field," or "The Corn-mother is going through the corn."[1] When children wish to go into the fields to pull the blue corn-flowers or the red poppies, they are told not to do so, because the Corn-mother is sitting in the corn and will catch them.[2] Or again she is called, according to the crop, the Rye-mother or the Pea-mother, and children are warned against straying in the rye or among the peas by threats of the Rye-mother or the Pea-mother. In Norway also the Pea-mother is said to sit among the peas.[3] Similar expressions are current among the Slavs. The Poles and Czechs warn children against the Corn-mother who sits in the corn. Or they call her the Old Corn-woman, and say that she sits in the corn and strangles the children who tread it down.[4] The Lithuanians say, "The Old Rye-woman sits in the corn."[5] Again the Corn-mother is believed to make the crop grow. Thus in the neighbourhood of Magdeburg it is sometimes said, "It will be a good year for flax; the Flax-mother has been seen." At Dinkelsbühl (Bavaria) down to fifteen or twenty years ago, people believed that when the crops on a particular farm compared unfavourably with those of the neighbourhood, the reason was that the Corn-mother had punished the farmer for his sins.[6] In a village of Styria it is said that the Corn-mother, in the shape of a female

---

[1] W. Mannhardt, *Mythol. Forsch.* p. 296.   [2] *Ib.* p. 297.
[3] *Ib.* p. 297 *sq.*   [4] *Ib.* p. 299.   [5] *Ib.* p. 300.   [6] *Ib.* p. 310.

puppet made out of the last sheaf of corn and dressed in white, may be seen at midnight in the corn-fields, which she fertilises by passing through them ; but if she is angry with a farmer, she withers up all his corn.[1]

Further, the Corn-mother plays an important part in harvest customs. She is believed to be present in the handful of corn which is left standing last on the field ; and with the cutting of this last handful she is caught, or driven away, or killed. In the first of these cases, the last sheaf is carried joyfully home and honoured as a divine being. It is placed in the barn, and at threshing the corn-spirit appears again.[2] In the district of Hadeln (Hanover) the reapers stand round the last sheaf and beat it with sticks in order to drive the Corn-mother out of it. They call to each other, " There she is ! hit her ! Take care she doesn't catch you ! " The beating goes on till the grain is completely threshed out ; then the Corn-mother is believed to be driven away.[3] In the neighbourhood of Danzig the person who cuts the last ears of corn makes them into a doll, which is called the Corn-mother or the Old Woman, and is brought home on the last waggon.[4] In some parts of Holstein the last sheaf is dressed in woman's clothes and called the Corn-mother. It is carried home on the last waggon, and then thoroughly drenched with water. The drenching with water is doubtless a rain-charm.[5] In the district of Bruck in Styria the last sheaf, called the Corn-mother, is made up into the shape of a woman by the oldest married woman in the village, of an age from fifty to fifty-five years. The finest ears are plucked out of it

---

[1] W. Mannhardt, *Mythol. Forsch.* p. 310 *sq.*   [2] *Ib.* p. 316.
[3] *Ib.* p. 316.   [4] *Ib.* p. 316 *sq.*   [5] See above, pp. 16 *sq.*, 286 *sq.*

and made into a wreath, which, twined with flowers, is
carried on her head by the prettiest girl of the village
to the farmer or squire, while the Corn-mother is laid
down in the barn to keep off the mice.[1] In other
villages of the same district the Corn-mother, at the
close of harvest, is carried by two lads at the top of a
pole. They march behind the girl who wears the
wreath to the squire's house, and while he receives
the wreath and hangs it up in the hall, the Corn-
mother is placed on the top of a pile of wood, where
she is the centre of the harvest supper and dance.
Afterwards she is hung up in the barn and remains
there till the threshing is over. The man who gives
the last stroke at threshing is called the son of the
Corn-mother; he is tied up in the Corn-mother, beaten,
and carried through the village. The wreath is
dedicated in church on the following Sunday ; and on
Easter Eve the grain is rubbed out of it by a seven
years' old girl and scattered amongst the young corn.
At Christmas the straw of the wreath is placed in the
manger to make the cattle thrive.[2] Here the fertilising power of the Corn-mother is plainly brought out
by scattering the seed taken from her body (for the
wreath is made out of the Corn-mother) among the
new corn ; and her influence over animal life is
indicated by placing the straw in the manger. At
Westerhüsen in Saxony the last corn cut is made in
the shape of a woman decked with ribbons and cloth.
It is fastened on a pole and brought home on the last
waggon. One of the people on the waggon keeps
waving the pole, so that the figure moves as if alive.
It is placed on the threshing-floor, and stays there till
the threshing is done.[3] Amongst the Slavs also the

---

[1] W. Mannhardt, *op. cit.* p. 317.   [2] *Ib.* p. 317 *sq.*   [3] *Ib.* p. 318.

last sheaf is known as the Rye-mother, the Wheat-
mother, the Oats-mother, the Barley-mother, etc.,
according to the crop.   In the district of Tarnow,
Galicia, the wreath made out of the last stalks is
called the Wheat-mother, Rye-mother, or Pea-mother.
It is placed on a girl's head and kept till spring, when
some of the grain is mixed with the seed-corn.[1]   Here
again the fertilising power of the Corn-mother is
indicated.   In France, also, in the neighbourhood of
Auxerre, the last sheaf goes by the name of the
Mother of the Wheat, Mother of the Barley, Mother of
the Rye, or Mother of the Oats.   It is left standing
in the field till the last waggon is about to wend
homewards.   Then a puppet is made out of it, dressed
with clothes belonging to the farmer, and adorned
with a crown and a blue or white scarf.   A branch
of a tree is stuck in the breast of the puppet, which
is now called the Ceres.   At the dance in the evening
the Ceres is placed in the middle of the floor, and the
reaper who reaped fastest dances round it with the
prettiest girl for his partner.   After the dance a pyre is
made.   All the girls, each wearing a wreath, strip the
puppet, pull it to pieces, and place it on the pyre, along
with the flowers with which it was adorned.   Then
the girl who was the first to finish reaping sets fire
to the pile, and all pray that Ceres may give a fruitful
year.   Here, as Mannhardt observes, the old custom
has remained intact, though the name Ceres is a bit of
schoolmaster's learning.[2]   In Upper Britanny the last
sheaf is always made into human shape ; but if the
farmer is a married man, it is made double and consists
of a little corn-puppet placed inside of a large one.
This is called the Mother-sheaf.   It is delivered to the

---

[1] W. Mannhardt, *Mythol. Forsch.* p. 318.   [2] *Ib.* p. 318 *sq.*

farmer's wife, who unties it and gives drink-money in return.[1]

Sometimes the last sheaf is called, not the Corn-mother, but the Harvest-mother or the Great Mother. In the province of Osnabrück (Hanover) it is called the Harvest-mother; it is made up in female form, and then the reapers dance about with it. In some parts of Westphalia the last sheaf at the rye harvest is made especially heavy by fastening stones in it. It is brought home on the last waggon and is called the Great Mother, though no special shape is given it. In the district of Erfurt a very heavy sheaf (not necessarily the last) is called the Great Mother, and is carried on the last waggon to the barn, where it is lifted down by all hands amid a fire of jokes.[2]

Sometimes again the last sheaf is called the Grandmother, and is adorned with flowers, ribbons, and a woman's apron. In East Prussia, at the rye or wheat harvest, the reapers call out to the woman who binds the last sheaf, " You are getting the Old Grandmother." In the neighbourhood of Magdeburg the men and women servants strive who shall get the last sheaf, called the Grandmother. Whoever gets it will be married in the next year, but his or her spouse will be old; if a girl gets it, she will marry a widower; if a man gets it, he will marry an old crone. In Silesia the Grandmother—a huge bundle made up of three or four sheaves by the person who tied the last sheaf—was formerly fashioned into a rude likeness of the human form.[3] In the neighbourhood of Belfast the last sheaf is sometimes called Granny. It is not cut in the usual way, but all the reapers throw

[1] Sébillot, Coutumes populaires de la Haute-Bretagne, p. 306.

[2] W. Mannhardt, M. F. p. 319.
[3] Ib. p. 320.

their sickles at it and try to bring it down. It is
plaited and kept till the (next?) autumn. Whoever
gets it will marry in the course of the year.[1]

Oftener the last sheaf is called the Old Woman
or the Old Man. In Germany it is often shaped and
dressed as a woman, and the person who cuts it or binds
it is said to "get the Old Woman.[2] At Altisheim in
Swabia when all the corn of a farm has been cut
except a single strip, all the reapers stand in a row
before the strip; each cuts his share rapidly, and he
who gives the last cut " has the Old Woman."[3] When
the sheaves are being set up in heaps, the person who
gets hold of the Old Woman, which is the largest and
thickest of all the sheaves, is jeered at by the rest, who
sing out to him, " He has the Old Woman and must
keep her."[4] The woman who binds the last sheaf
is sometimes herself called the Old Woman, and it
is said that she will be married in the next year.[5] In
Neusaass, West Prussia, both the last sheaf—which is
dressed up in jacket, hat and ribbons—and the woman
who binds it are called the Old Woman. Together
they are brought home on the last waggon and are
drenched with water.[6] At Hornkampe, near Tiegen-
hof (West Prussia), when a man or woman lags behind
the rest in binding the corn, the other reapers dress
up the last sheaf in the form of a man or woman,
and this figure goes by the laggard's name, as "the
old Michael," " the idle Trine." It is brought home
on the last waggon, and, as it nears the house, the
bystanders call out to the laggard, " You have got the
Old Woman and must keep her."[7]

---

[1] Mannhardt, *Mythol. Forsch.* p. 321.   *deutschen Mythologie*, ii. p. 219, No. 403.
[2] *Ib.* pp. 321, 323, 325 *sq.*   [4] W. Mannhardt, *op. cit.* p. 325.
[3] *Ib.* p. 323; Panzer, *Beitrag zur*   [5] *Ib.* p. 323.   [6] *Ib.*   [7] *Ib.* p. 323 *sq.*

In these customs, as Mannhardt has remarked, the person who is called by the same name as the last sheaf and sits beside it on the last waggon is obviously identified with it ; he or she represents the corn-spirit which has been caught in the last sheaf; in other words, the corn-spirit is represented in duplicate, by a human being and by a sheaf.[1] The identification of the person with the sheaf is made still clearer by the custom of wrapping up in the· last sheaf the person who cuts or binds it. Thus at Hermsdorf in Silesia it used to be the regular custom to tie up in the last sheaf the woman who had bound it.[2] At Weiden in Bavaria it is the cutter, not the binder, of the last sheaf who is tied up in it.[3] Here the person wrapt up in the corn represents the corn-spirit, exactly as a person wrapt in branches or leaves represents the tree-spirit.[4]

The last sheaf, designated as the Old Woman, is often distinguished from the other sheaves by its size and weight. Thus in some villages of West Prussia the Old Woman is made twice as long and thick as a common sheaf, and a stone is fastened in the middle of it. Sometimes it is made so heavy that a man can barely lift it.[5] Sometimes eight or nine sheaves are tied together to make the Old Woman, and the man who sets it up complains of its weight.[6] At Itzgrund, in Saxe-Coburg, the last sheaf, called the Old Woman, is made large with the express intention of thereby securing a good crop next year.[7] Thus the custom of making the last sheaf unusually large or heavy is a charm, working by sympathetic magic, to secure a large and heavy crop in the following year.

---

[1] W. Mannhardt, op. cit. p. 324.
[2] Ib. p. 320.
[3] Ib. p. 325.
[4] See above, p. 83 sqq.
[5] W. Mannhardt, op. cit. p. 321
[6] Ib. p. 324 sq.   [7] Ib. p. 325.

In Denmark also the last sheaf is made larger than the others, and is called the Old Rye-woman or the Old Barley-woman. No one likes to bind it, because whoever does so will, it is believed, marry an old man or an old woman. Sometimes the last wheat-sheaf, called the Old Wheat-woman, is made up in human shape, with head, arms, and legs, is dressed in clothes and carried home on the last waggon, the harvesters sitting beside it, drinking and huzzaing.[1] Of the person who binds the last sheaf it is said, "She (or he) is the Old Rye-woman."[2]

In Scotland, when the last corn was cut after Hallowmas, the female figure made out of it was sometimes called the Carlin or Carline, *i.e.* the Old Woman. But if cut before Hallowmas, it was called the Maiden; if cut after sunset, it was called the Witch, being supposed to bring bad luck.[3] We shall return to the Maiden presently. In County Antrim, down to a few years ago, when the sickle was finally expelled by the reaping machine, the few stalks of corn left standing last on the field were plaited together; then the reapers, blindfolded, threw their sickles at the plaited corn, and whoever happened to cut it through took it home with him and put it over his door. This bunch of corn was called the Carley[4]—probably the same word as Carlin.

Similar customs are observed by Slavonic peoples. Thus in Poland the last sheaf is commonly called the Baba, that is, the Old Woman. "In the last sheaf," it is said, "sits the Baba." The sheaf itself is also called the Baba, and is sometimes composed of twelve

[1] W. Mannhardt, *op. cit.* p. 327.
[2] *Ib.* p. 328.
[3] Jamieson, *Dictionary of the Scottish Language*, *s.v.* "Maiden"; W. Mannhardt, *Mythol. Forschungen*, p. 326.
[4] Communicated by my friend Prof. W. Ridgeway, of Queen's College, Cork.

smaller sheaves lashed together.[1] In some parts of
Bohemia the Baba, made out of the last sheaf, has the
figure of a woman with a great straw hat. It is carried
home on the last harvest-waggon and delivered, along
with a garland, to the farmer by two girls. In binding
the sheaves the women strive not to be last, for
she who binds the last sheaf will have a child next
year.[2] The last sheaf is tied up with others into a
large bundle, and a green branch is stuck on the top
of it.[3] Sometimes the harvesters call out to the woman
who binds the last sheaf, "She has the Baba," or "She
is the Baba." She has then to make a puppet, sometimes in female, sometimes in male form, out of the
corn ; the puppet is occasionally dressed with clothes,
often with flowers and ribbons only. The cutter of
the last stalks, as well as the binder of the last sheaf,
was also called Baba ; and a doll, called the Harvest-
woman, was made out of the last sheaf and adorned
with ribbons. The oldest reaper had to dance, first
with this doll, and then with the farmer's wife.[4] In
the district of Cracow, when a man binds the last
sheaf, they say, "The Grandfather is sitting in it ;"
when a woman binds it, they say, "The Baba is sitting
in it," and the woman herself is wrapt up in the sheaf,
so that only her head projects out of it. Thus encased
in the sheaf, she is carried on the last harvest-waggon
to the house, where she is drenched with water by the
whole family. She remains in the sheaf till the dance
is over, and for a year she retains the name of Baba.[5]

In Lithuania the name for the last sheaf is Boba
(Old Woman), answering to the Polish name Baba.
The Boba is said to sit in the corn which is left

---

[1] W. Mannhardt, *op. cit.* p. 328.   [2] *Ib.*   [3] *Ib.* p. 328 *sq.*
[4] *Ib.* p. 329.   [5] *Ib.* p. 330.

standing last.[1] The person who binds the last sheaf
or digs the last potato is the subject of much banter,
and receives and long retains the name of the Old
Rye-woman or the Old Potato woman.[2] The last
sheaf—the Boba—is made into the form of a woman,
carried solemnly through the village on the last harvest-
waggon, and drenched with water at the farmer's house;
then every one dances with it.[3]

In Russia also the last sheaf is often shaped and
dressed as a woman, and carried with dance and song
to the farmhouse. Out of the last sheaf the Bulgarians
make a doll which they call the Corn-queen or Corn-
mother; it is dressed in a woman's shirt, carried round
the village, and then thrown into the river in order to
secure plenty of rain and dew for the next year's crop.
Or it is burned and the ashes strewn on the fields,
doubtless to fertilise them.[4] The name Queen, as
applied to the last sheaf, has its analogies in Northern
Europe. Thus Brand quotes from Hutchinson's *History
of Northumberland* the following : " I have seen, in
some places, an image apparelled in great finery,
crowned with flowers, a sheaf of corn placed under
her arm, and a scycle in her hand, carried out of the
village in the morning of the conclusive reaping day,
with music and much clamour of the reapers, into the
field, where it stands fixed on a pole all day, and when
the reaping is done, is brought home in like manner.
This they call the Harvest Queen, and it represents
the Roman Ceres."[5] From Cambridge also Dr. E.
D. Clarke reported that " at the Hawkie [harvest-
home], as it is called, I have seen a clown dressed in

---

[1] W. Mannhardt, *op. cit.* p. 330.

[2] *Ib* p. 331.   [3] *Ib.* p. 331.

[4] *Ib.* p. 332.

[5] Hutchinson, *History of Northum-
berland*, ii. *ad finem*, 17, quoted by
Brand, *Popular Antiquities*, ii. 20,
Bohn's ed.

woman's clothes, having his face painted, his head decorated with ears of corn, and bearing about him other symbols of Ceres, carried in a waggon, with great pomp and loud shouts, through the streets, the horses being covered with white sheets ; and when I inquired the meaning of the ceremony, was answered by the people, that they were drawing the Harvest Queen."[1]

Often the customs we have been examining are practised, not on the harvest field, but on the threshing-floor. The spirit of the corn, fleeing before the reapers as they cut down the corn, quits the cut corn and takes refuge in the barn, where it appears in the last sheaf threshed, either to perish under the blows of the flail or to flee thence to the still unthreshed corn of a neighbouring farm.[2] Thus the last corn to be threshed is called the Mother-corn or the Old Woman. Sometimes the person who gives the last stroke with the flail is called the Old Woman, and is wrapt in the straw of the last sheaf, or has a bundle of straw fastened on his back. Whether wrapt in the straw or carrying it on his back, he is carted through the village amid general laughter. In some districts of Bavaria, Thüringen, etc., the man who threshes the last sheaf is said to have the Old Woman or the Old Corn-woman ; he is tied up in straw, carried or carted about the village, and set down at last on the dunghill, or taken to the threshing-floor of a neighbouring farmer who has not finished his threshing.[3] In Poland the man who gives the last stroke at threshing is called Baba (Old Woman) ; he is wrapt in corn and wheeled through the village.[4] Sometimes in Lithuania the last sheaf is not threshed, but is fashioned into female

---

[1] Quoted by Brand, *op. cit.* ii. 22.
[2] W. Mannhardt, *Mythol. Forsch.* p. 333 *sq.*   [3] *Ib.* p. 334.   [4] *Ib.* p. 334.

shape and carried to the barn of a neighbour who has
not finished his threshing.[1]   In some parts of Sweden,
when a stranger woman appears on the threshing-
floor, a flail is put round her body, stalks of corn are
wound round her neck, a crown of ears is placed on
her head, and the threshers call out, "Behold the
Corn-woman."   Here the stranger woman, thus
suddenly appearing, is taken to be the corn-spirit who
has just been expelled by the flails from the corn-
stalks.[2]   In other cases the farmer's wife represents
the corn-spirit.   Thus in the Commune of Saligné,
Canton de Poiret (Vendée), the farmer's wife, along
with the last sheaf, is tied up in a sheet, placed on a
litter, and carried to the threshing machine, under
which she is shoved.   Then the woman is drawn out
and the sheaf is threshed by itself, but the woman is
tossed in the sheet (in imitation of winnowing).[3]   It
would be impossible to express more clearly the identification of the woman with the corn than by this
graphic imitation of threshing and winnowing her.

In these customs the spirit of the ripe corn is
regarded as old, or at least as of mature age.   Hence
the names of Mother, Grandmother, Old Woman, etc.
But in other cases the corn-spirit is conceived as young,
sometimes as a child who is separated from its mother
by the stroke of the sickle.   This last view appears in
the Polish custom of calling out to the man who cuts
the last handful of corn, "You have cut the navel-
string."[4]   In some districts of West Prussia the figure
made out of the last sheaf is called the Bastard, and a boy
is wrapt up in it.   The woman who binds the last sheaf

---

[1] W. Mannhardt, *op. cit.* p. 336.
[2] *Ib.* p. 336.
[3] *Ib.* p. 336 ; *Baumkultus*, p. 612.

[4] W. Mannhardt, *Die Korndämonen*, p. 28.

and represents the Corn-mother, is told that she is about
to be brought to bed ; she cries like a woman in travail,
and an old woman in the character of grandmother
acts as midwife. At last a cry is raised that the child
is born ; whereupon the boy who is tied up in the
sheaf whimpers and squalls like an infant. The grandmother wraps a sack, in imitation of swaddling bands,
round the pretended baby, and it is carried joyfully to
the barn, lest it catch cold in the open air.[1] In other
parts of North Germany, the last sheaf, or the puppet
made out of it, is called the Child, the Harvest Child,
etc. In the North of England the last handful of
corn was cut by the prettiest girl and dressed up as
the Corn Baby or Kern Baby ; it was brought home
to music, set up in a conspicuous place at the harvest
supper, and generally kept in the parlour for the rest of
the year. The girl who cut it was the Harvest Queen.[2]
In Kent the Ivy Girl is (or was) " a figure composed of
some of the best corn the field produces, and made as
well as they can into a human shape ; this is afterwards
curiously dressed by the women, and adorned with
paper trimmings, cut to resemble a cap, ruffles, handkerchief, etc., of the finest lace. It is brought home
with the last load of corn from the field upon the waggon, and they suppose entitles them to a supper at the
expense of the employer."[3] In the neighbourhood of
Balquhidder, Perthshire, the last handful of corn is cut
by the youngest girl on the field, and is made into the
rude form of a female doll, clad in a paper dress, and
decked with ribbons. It is called the Maiden, and is
kept in the farmhouse, generally above the chimney,

---

[1] W. Mannhardt, *l.c.*

[2] *Ib.* ; Henderson, *Folk-lore of the Northern Counties*, p. 87 ; Brand, *Popular Antiquities*, ii. 20, Bohn's ed. ; Chambers's *Book of Days*, ii. 377 *sq.* Cp. *Folk-lore Journal*, vii. 50.

[3] Brand, *op. cit.* ii. 21 *sq.*

for a good while, sometimes till the Maiden of the next
year is brought in.   The writer of this book witnessed
the ceremony of cutting the Maiden at Balquhidder in
September 1888.[1]   On some farms on the Gareloch,
Dumbartonshire, about sixty years ago the last handful of standing corn was called the Maiden.   It was
divided in two, plaited, and then cut with the sickle by
a girl, who, it was thought, would be lucky and would
soon be married.   When it was cut the reapers
gathered together and threw their sickles in the air.
The Maiden was dressed with ribbons and hung in the
kitchen near the roof, where it was kept for several
years with the date attached.   Sometimes five or six
Maidens might be seen hanging at once on hooks.
The harvest supper was called the Kirn.[2]   In other
farms on the Gareloch the last handful of corn was
called the Maidenhead or the Head ; it was neatly
plaited, sometimes decked with ribbons, and hung in
the kitchen for a year, when the grain was given to
the poultry.[3]   In the North of Scotland, the Maiden
is kept till Christmas morning, and then divided
among the cattle " to make them thrive all the year
round."[4]   In Aberdeenshire also the last sheaf (called
the clyack sheaf) was formerly cut, as it is still cut at
Balquhidder, by the youngest girl on the field ; then
it was dressed in woman's clothes, carried home in
triumph, and kept till Christmas or New Year's morning, when it was given to a mare in foal, or, failing
such, to the oldest cow.[5]   Lastly, a somewhat maturer,
but still youthful age is assigned to the corn-spirit by

---

[1] *Folk-lore Journal*, vi. 268 *sq.*

[2] From information supplied by
Archie Leitch, gardener, Rowmore,
Garelochhead.

[3] Communicated by Mr. Macfarlane
of Faslane, Gareloch.

[4] Jamieson, *Dictionary of the Scottish
Language, s.v.* " Maiden."

[5] W. Gregor, in *Revue des Traditions
populaires*, iii. 533 (485 B) ; *id., Folk-
lore of the North - East of Scotland*, p.
182.   An old Scottish name for the

the appellations of Bride, Oats-bride, and Wheat-bride, which in Germany and Scotland are sometimes bestowed both on the last sheaf and on the woman who binds it.[1] Sometimes the idea implied in these names is worked out more fully by representing the productive powers of vegetation as bride and bridegroom, Thus in some parts of Germany a man and woman dressed in straw and called the Oats-wife and the Oats-man, or the Oats-bride and the Oats-bridegroom dance at the harvest festival; then the corn-stalks are plucked from their bodies till they stand as bare as a stubble field. In Silesia, the woman who binds the last sheaf is called the Wheat-bride or the Oats-bride. With the harvest crown on her head, a bridegroom by her side, and attended by bridesmaids, she is brought to the farmhouse with all the solemnity of a wedding procession.[2]

The harvest customs just described are strikingly analogous to the spring customs which we reviewed in the first chapter. (1.) As in the spring customs the tree-spirit is represented both by a tree and by a person,[3] so in the harvest customs the corn-spirit is represented both by the last sheaf and by the person who cuts or binds or threshes it. The equivalence of the person to the sheaf is shown by giving him or her the same name as the sheaf, or *vice versâ*; by wrapping him or her in the sheaf; and by the rule observed in some places, that when the sheaf is called the Mother, it must be cut by the oldest married woman; but when it is called

---

Maiden (*autumnalis nymphula*) was *Rapegyrne*. See Fordun, *Scotichron.* ii. 418, quoted in Jamieson's *Dict. of the Scottish Language, s.v.* "Rapegyrne."

[1] W. Mannhardt, *Die Korndämonen,* p. 30; *Folk-lore Journal,* vii. 50.
[2] W. Mannhardt, *l.c.*; Sommer, *Sagen, Märchen und Gebräuche aus Sachsen und Thüringen,* p. 160 *sq.*
[3] See above, p. 83 *sqq.*

the Maiden, it must be cut by the youngest girl.[1]
Here the age of the personal representative of the
corn-spirit corresponds with that of the supposed age
of the corn-spirit, just as the human victims offered by
the Mexicans to promote the growth of the maize
varied with the age of the maize.[2] For in the Mexican,
as in the European, custom the human beings were
probably representatives of the corn-spirit rather than
victims offered to him. (2.) Again, the same fertilising
influence which the tree-spirit is supposed to exert over
vegetation, cattle, and even women [3] is ascribed to the
corn-spirit. Thus, its supposed influence on vegetation is shown by the practice of taking some of the
grain of the last sheaf (in which the corn-spirit is regularly supposed to be present), and scattering it among
the young corn in spring.[4] Its influence on cattle is
shown by giving the straw of the last sheaf to the
cattle at Christmas with the express intention of making them thrive.[5] Lastly, its influence on women is
indicated by the custom of delivering the Mother-sheaf,
made into the likeness of a pregnant woman, to the
farmer's wife ;[6] by the belief that the woman who binds
the last sheaf will have a child next year ;[7] perhaps,
too, by the idea that the person who gets it will marry
next year.[8]

Plainly, therefore, these spring and harvest customs
are based on the same ancient modes of thought, and
form parts of the same primitive heathendom, which
was doubtless practised by our forefathers long before
the dawn of history, as it is practised to this day by

---

[1] Above, pp. 333, 344.
[2] Above, p. 307.
[3] Above, p. 67 *sqq.*
[4] Above, pp. 334, 335.
[5] Above, pp. 334, 345.

[6] See above, p. 335 *sq.*
[7] Above, p. 340 ; cp. Kuhn, *West-fälische Sagen, Gebräuche und Märchen,* ii. No. 516.
[8] Above, pp. 336, 337, 345.

many of their descendants. Amongst the marks of a primitive religion, we may note the following :—

(1.) No special class of persons is set apart for the performance of the rites ; in other words, there are no priests. The rites may be performed by any one, as occasion demands.

(2.) No special places are set apart for the performance of the rites ; in other words, there are no temples. The rites may be performed anywhere, as occasion demands.

(3.) Spirits, not gods, are recognised. (*a*.) As distinguished from gods, spirits are restricted in their operations to definite departments of nature. Their names are general, not proper. Their attributes are generic, rather than individual ; in other words, there is an indefinite number of spirits of each class, and the individuals of a class are all much alike ; they have no definitely marked individuality ; no accepted traditions are current as to their origin, life, adventures, and character. (*b*.) On the other hand gods, as distinguished from spirits, are not exclusively restricted in their operations to definite departments of nature. It is true that there is generally some one department over which they preside as their special province ; but they are not rigorously confined to it ; they can exert their power for good or evil in many other spheres of nature and life. Again, they bear individual or proper names, such as Ceres, Proserpine, Bacchus ; and their individual characters and histories are fixed by current myths and the representations of art.

(4.) The rites are magical rather than propitiatory. In other words, the desired objects are attained, not by propitiating the favour of divine beings through sacrifice, prayer, and praise, but by ceremonies which, as has been explained,[1] are believed to influence the course of nature directly through a physical sympathy or resemblance between the rite and the effect which it is the intention of the rite to produce.

Judged by these tests, the spring and harvest customs of our European peasantry deserve to rank as primitive. For no special class of persons and no special places are set exclusively apart for their performance ; they may be performed by any one, master or man, mistress or maid, boy or girl ; they are practised, not in temples or churches, but in the woods and meadows, beside brooks, in barns, on harvest fields and cottage floors. The supernatural beings whose existence is taken for granted in them are spirits rather than deities ; their functions are limited to certain well-defined departments of nature; their names are general, like the Barley-mother, the Old Woman, the Maiden, not proper names like Ceres, Proserpine, Bacchus. Their generic attributes are known, but their individual histories and characters are not the subject of myths. For they exist in classes rather than as individuals, and the members of each class are indistinguishable. For example, every farm has its Corn-mother, or its Old Woman, or its Maiden ; but every Corn-mother is much like every other Corn-mother, and so with the Old Women and Maidens. Lastly, in these harvest, as in the spring, customs, the ritual is magical rather than propitiatory. This is shown by throwing the Corn-mother into the river in order to secure rain and dew for the crops ;[2] by making the Old Woman heavy in order to get a heavy crop next year ;[3] by strewing grain from the last sheaf amongst the young crops in

[1] See above, p. 9 *sqq.*   [2] Above, p. 341.   [3] Above, p. 338.

spring;[1] and giving the last sheaf to the cattle to make them thrive.[2]

Further, the custom of keeping the puppet—the representative of the corn-spirit—till next harvest, is a charm to maintain the corn-spirit in life and activity throughout the year.[3] This is proved by a similar custom observed by the ancient Peruvians, and thus described by the historian Acosta. " They take a certain portion of the most fruitefull of the Mays [*i.e.* maize] that growes in their farmes, the which they put in a certaine granary which they doe call *Pirua*, with certaine ceremonies, watching three nightes ; they put this Mays in the richest garments they have, and beeing thus wrapped and dressed, they worship this *Pirua*, and hold it in great veneration, saying it is the mother of the mays of their inheritances, and that by this means the mays augments and is preserved. In this moneth [the sixth month, answering to May] they make a particular sacrifice, and the witches demaund of this *Pirua*, if it hath strength sufficient to continue untill the next yeare; and if it answers no, then they carry this Mays to the farme to burne, whence they brought it, according to every man's power ; then they make another *Pirua*, with the same ceremonies, saying that they renue it, to the end the seede of Mays may not perish, and if it answers that it hath force sufficient to last longer, they leave it untill the next yeare. This foolish vanity continueth to this day, and it is very common amongest the Indians to have these *Piruas.*"[4] There seems to

---

[1] Above, p. 334, cp. 335.

[2] Above, pp. 334, 345.

[3] Above, p. 344 *sq.* ; W. Mannhardt, *Korndämonen*, pp. 7, 26. Amongst the Wends the last sheaf, made into a puppet and called the Old Man, is hung in the hall till next year's Old Man is brought in. Schulenburg,

Wendisches Volksthum, p. 147. In Inverness and Sutherland the Maiden is kept till the next harvest. *Folk-lore Journal*, vii. 50, 53 *sq.* Cp. Kuhn, *Westfälische Sagen, Gebräuche und Märchen*, ii. Nos. 501, 517.

[4] Acosta, *Hist. of the Indies*, v. c. 28, vol. ii. p. 374 (Hakluyt Society, 1880).

be some error in this description of the custom.   Probably it was the dressed-up bunch of maize, not the
granary (*Pirua*), which was worshipped by the Peruvians and regarded as the Mother of the Maize.   This
is confirmed by what we know of the Peruvian custom
from another source.   The Peruvians, we are told,
believed all useful plants to be animated by a divine
being who causes their growth.   According to the
particular plant, these divine beings were called the
Maize - mother (*Zara-mama*), the Quinoa - mother
(*Quinoa-mama*), the Cocoa-mother (*Coca-mama*), and
the Potato-mother (*Axo-mama*).   Figures of these
divine mothers were made respectively of ears of
maize and leaves of the quinoa and cocoa plants ; they
were dressed in women's clothes and worshipped.
Thus the Maize-mother was represented by a puppet
made of stalks of maize, dressed in full female attire ;
and the Indians believed that "as mother, it had the
power of producing and giving birth to much maize."[1]
Probably, therefore, Acosta misunderstood his inform-
ant, and the Mother of the Maize which he describes
was not the granary (*Pirua*) but the bunch of maize
dressed in rich vestments.   The Peruvian Mother of
the Maize, like the harvest Maiden at Balquhidder,
was kept for a year in order that by her means the
corn might grow and multiply.   But lest her strength
might not suffice to last out the year, she was asked in
the course of the year how she felt, and if she answered
that she felt weak, she was burned and a fresh Mother
of the Maize made, "to the end the seede of Mays

---

[1] W. Mannhardt, *Mythol. Forsch.*
p. 342 *sq.*   Mannhardt's authority is a
Spanish tract (*Carta pastoral de exorta-
cion e instruccion contra las idolatrias de
los Indios del arçobispado de Lima*) by
Pedro de Villagomez, Archbishop of
Lima, published at Lima in 1649, and
communicated to Mannhardt by J. J.
v. Tschudi.

may not perish." Here, it may be observed, we have
a strong confirmation of the explanation already given
of the custom of killing the god, both periodically and
occasionally. The Mother of the Maize was allowed,
as a rule, to live through a year, that being the period
during which her strength might reasonably be supposed to last unimpaired ; but on any symptom of her
strength failing she was put to death and a fresh and
vigorous Mother of the Maize took her place, lest
the maize which depended on her for its existence
should languish and decay.

Hardly less clearly does the same train of thought
come out in the harvest customs formerly observed
by the Zapotecs of Mexico. At harvest the priests,
attended by the nobles and people, went in procession
to the maize fields, where they picked out the largest
and finest sheaf. This they took with great ceremony
to the town or village, and placed it in the temple upon
an altar adorned with wild flowers. After sacrificing
to the harvest god, the priests carefully wrapt up the
sheaf in fine linen and kept it till seed-time. Then the
priests and nobles met again at the temple, one of them
bringing the skin of a wild beast, elaborately ornamented, in which the linen cloth containing the sheaf
was enveloped. The sheaf was then carried once
more in procession to the field from which it had been
taken. Here a small cavity or subterranean chamber
had been prepared, in which the precious sheaf was
deposited, wrapt in its various envelopes. After
sacrifice had been offered to the gods of the fields for
an abundant crop, the chamber was closed and covered
over with earth. Immediately thereafter the sowing
began. Finally, when the time of harvest drew near,
the buried sheaf was solemnly disinterred by the

priests, who distributed the grain to all who asked for it. The packets of grain so distributed were carefully preserved as talismans till the harvest.[1] In these ceremonies, which continued to be annually celebrated long after the Spanish conquest, the intention of keeping the finest sheaf buried in the maize field from seed-time to harvest was undoubtedly to quicken the growth of the maize.

In the Punjaub, to the east of the Jumna, when the cotton boles begin to burst, it is usual "to select the largest plant in the field, and having sprinkled it with butter-milk and rice-water, it is bound all over with pieces of cotton, taken from the other plants of the field. This selected plant is called Sirdar, or Bhogaldaı, i.e. mother-cotton, from bhogla, a name sometimes given to a large cotton-pod, and daí (for daiya) a mother, and after salutations are made to it, prayers are offered that the other plants may resemble it in the richness of their produce."[2]

If the reader still feels any doubts as to the original meaning of the harvest customs practised by our peasantry, these doubts may be dispelled by comparing the harvest customs of the Dyaks of Borneo. At harvest the Dyaks of Northern Borneo have a special feast, the object of which is "to secure the soul of the rice, which if not so detained, the produce of their farms would speedily rot and decay." The mode of securing the soul of the rice varies in different tribes. Sometimes the priest catches it, in the form of a few grains of rice, in a white cloth. Sometimes a large shed is erected outside the village, and near it

---

[1] Brasseur de Bourbourg, *Histoire des Nations civilisées du Mexique*, iii. 40 *sqq.*

[2] H. M. Elliot, *Supplemental Glos-* *sary of Terms used in the North West-* *ern Provinces*, edited by J. Beames, i. 254.

is reared a high and spacious altar. The corner-posts of the altar are lofty bamboos with leafy tops, from one of which there hangs a long narrow streamer of white cloth. Here gaily-dressed men and women dance with slow and solemn steps. Suddenly the elders and priests rush at the white streamer, seize the end of it, and begin dancing and swaying to and fro, amid a burst of wild music and the yells of the spectators. An elder leaps on the altar and shakes the bamboos violently, whereupon small stones, bunches of hair and grains of rice fall at the feet of the dancers and are carefully picked up by attendants. These grains of rice are the soul of the rice. At sowing-time some of this soul of the rice is planted with the other seeds, "and is thus propagated and communicated."[1] The same need of securing the soul of the rice, if the crop is to thrive, is keenly felt by the Karens of Burma. When a rice-field does not flourish, they suppose that the soul (*kelah*) of the rice is in some way detained from the rice. If the soul cannot be called back, the crop will fail. The following formula is used in recalling the *kelah* (soul) of the rice: "O come, rice-*kelah*, come! Come to the field. Come to the rice. With seed of each gender, come. Come from the river Kho, come from the river Kaw ; from the place where they meet, come. Come from the West, come from the East. From the throat of the bird, from the maw of the ape, from the throat of the elephant. Come from the sources of rivers and their mouths. Come from the country of the Shan and Burman. From the distant kingdoms come. From all granaries come. O rice-*kelah*, come to the

---

[1] Spenser St. John, *Life in the Forests of the Far East*,[2] i. 187, 192 *sqq.*

rice."[1] Again, the European custom of representing the
corn-spirit in the double form of bride and bridegroom[2]
is paralleled by a custom observed at the rice-harvest
in Java.   Before the reapers begin to cut the rice, the
priest or sorcerer picks out a number of ears of rice,
which are tied together, smeared with ointment, and
adorned with flowers.   Thus decked out, the ears are
called the *padi-pĕngantèn*, that is, the Rice-bride and
the Rice-bridegroom; their wedding feast is celebrated,
and the cutting of the rice begins immediately afterwards.   Later on, when the rice is being got in, a
bridal chamber is partitioned off in the barn, and
furnished with a new mat, a lamp, and all kinds of
toilet articles.   Sheaves of rice, to represent the
wedding guests, are placed beside the Rice-bride
and the Rice-bridegroom.   Not till this has been
done may the whole harvest be housed in the barn.
And for the first forty days after the rice has been
housed, no one may enter the barn, for fear of disturbing the newly-wedded pair.[3]

Compared with the Corn-mother of Germany and
the harvest Maiden of Balquhidder, the Demeter and
Proserpine of Greece are late products of religious
growth.   But, as Aryans, the Greeks must at one time
or another have observed harvest customs like those
which are still practised by Celts, Teutons, and Slavs,
and which, far beyond the limits of the Aryan world,
have been practised by the Incas of Peru, the Dyaks
of Borneo, and the Malays of Java—a sufficient proof
that the ideas on which these customs rest are not confined to any one race, but naturally suggest themselves

---

[1] E. B. Cross, "On the Karens,"
in *Journal of the American Oriental
Society*, iv. 309.

[2] See above, p. 346.
[3] Veth, *Java*, i. 524-526.

to all untutored peoples engaged in agriculture. It is probable, therefore, that Demeter and Proserpine, those stately and beautiful figures of Greek mythology, grew out of the same simple beliefs and practices which still prevail among our modern peasantry, and that they were represented by rude dolls made out of the yellow sheaves on many a harvest-field long before their breathing images were wrought in bronze and marble by the master hands of Phidias and Praxiteles. A reminiscence of that olden time—a scent, so to say, of the harvest-field—lingered to the last in the title of the Maiden (*Kore*) by which Proserpine was commonly known. Thus if the prototype of Demeter is the Corn-mother of Germany, the prototype of Proserpine is the harvest Maiden, which, autumn after autumn, is still made from the last sheaf on the Braes of Balquhidder. Indeed if we knew more about the peasant-farmers of ancient Greece we should probably find that even in classical times they continued annually to fashion their Corn-mothers (Demeters) and Maidens (Proserpines) out of the ripe corn on the harvest fields. But unfortunately the Demeter and Proserpine whom we know are the denizens of towns, the majestic inhabitants of lordly temples; it was for such divinities alone that the refined writers of antiquity had eyes; the rude rites performed by rustics amongst the corn were beneath their notice. Even if they noticed them, they probably never dreamed of any connection between the puppet of corn-stalks on the sunny stubble-field and the marble divinity in the shady coolness of the temple. Still the writings even of these town-bred and cultured persons afford us an occasional glimpse of a Demeter as rude as the rudest that a remote German village can show. Thus the story that Iasion begat a child Plutus ("wealth," "abundance") by Demeter on a thrice-ploughed field,[1] may be compared with the West Prussian custom of the mock birth of a child on the harvest field.[2] In this Prussian custom the pretended mother represents the Corn-mother (*Žytniamatka*) ; the pretended child represents the Corn-baby, and the whole ceremony is a charm to ensure a crop next year.[3] There are other folk-customs, observed both in spring and at harvest, with which the legend of the begetting of the child Plutus is probably still more intimately connected. Their general purport is to impart fertility to the fields by performing, or at least mimicking, upon them the process of procreation.[4] Another glimpse of the savage under the civilised Demeter will be afforded farther on, when we come to deal with another aspect of these agricultural divinities.

The reader may have observed that in modern folk-customs the corn-spirit is generally represented either by a Corn-mother (Old Woman, etc.) or by a Maiden (Corn-baby, etc.), not both by a Corn-mother

---

[1] Homer, *Od.* v. 125 *sqq.* ; Hesiod, *Theog.* 969 *sqq.*

[2] See above, p. 343 *sq.*

[3] It is possible that a ceremony performed in a Cyprian worship of Ariadne may have been of this nature. Plutarch, *Theseus*, 20, ἐν δὴ τῇ θυσίᾳ τοῦ Γορπιαίου μηνὸς ἱσταμένου δευτέρᾳ κατακλινόμενόν τινα τῶν νεανίσκων φθέγγεσθαι καὶ ποιεῖν ἅπερ ὠδινούσαι γυναῖκες. We have already seen grounds for regarding Ariadne as a goddess or spirit of vegetation (above, p. 104). If, however, the reference is to the Syro-Macedonian calendar, in which Gorpiaeus corresponds to September (Daremberg et Saglio, i. 831), the ceremony could

not have been a harvest celebration, but may have been a vintage one. Amongst the Minnitarees in North America, the Prince of Neuwied saw a tall strong woman pretend to bring up a stalk of maize out of her stomach ; the object of the ceremony was to secure a good crop of maize in the following year. Maximilian, Prinz zu Wied, *Reise in das innere Nord-Amerika*, ii. 269.

[4] W. Mannhardt, *Baumkultus*, pp. 468 *sq.*, 480 *sqq.* ; *id.*, *Antike Wald- und Feldkulte*, p. 288 *sq.* ; *id.*, *Mythologische Forschungen*, pp. 146 *sqq.*, 340 *sqq.* ; Van Hoëvell, *Ambon en de Oeliasers*, p. 62 *sq.* ; Wilken, in *Indische Gids*, June 1884, pp. 958, 963 *sq.* Cp. Marco Polo, trans. Yule,[2] i. 212 *sq.*

and by a Maiden. Why then did the Greeks represent the corn both as a mother and a daughter? In
the Breton custom the mother-sheaf—a large figure
made out of the last sheaf with a small corn-doll inside
of it—clearly represents both the Corn-mother and the
Corn-daughter, the latter still unborn.[1] Again, in the
Prussian custom just described, the woman who plays
the part of Corn-mother represents the ripe corn ; the
child appears to represent next year's corn, which may
be regarded, naturally enough, as the child of this
year's corn, since it is from the seed of this year's
harvest that next year's corn will spring. Demeter
would thus be the ripe corn of this year ; Proserpine
the seed-corn taken from it and sown in autumn, to
reappear in spring. The descent of Proserpine into
the lower world[2] would thus be a mythical expression for the sowing of the seed ; her reappearance
in spring[3] would express the sprouting of the young
corn. Thus the Proserpine of this year becomes
the Demeter of the next, and this may very well
have been the original form of the myth. But
when with the advance of religious thought the
corn came to be personified, no longer as a being
that went through the whole cycle of birth, growth,
reproduction, and death within a year, but as an
immortal goddess, consistency requires that one of
the two personifications, the mother or the daughter,
should be sacrificed. But the double conception of
the corn as mother and daughter was too old and too

[1] See above, p. 335 *sq.*
[2] Cp. Preller, *Griech. Mythol.*[3] i.
628, *note* 3. In Greece the annual descent of Proserpine appears to have
taken place at the Great Eleusinian
Mysteries and at the Thesmophoria,
that is, about the time of the autumn

sowing. But in Sicily her descent
seems to have been celebrated when
the corn was fully ripe (Diodorus, v. 4),
that is, in summer.
[3] Homer, *Hymn to Demeter*, 401
sqq.; Preller, *l.c.*

deeply rooted in the popular mind to be eradicated by logic, and so room had to be found in the reformed myth both for mother and daughter. This was done by assigning to Proserpine the rôle of the corn sown in autumn and sprouting in spring, while Demeter was left to play the somewhat vague and ill-defined part of mother of the corn, who laments its annual disappearance underground, and rejoices over its reappearance in spring. Thus instead of a regular succession of divine beings, each living a year and then giving birth to her successor, the reformed myth exhibits the conception of two divine and immortal beings, one of whom annually disappears into and reappears from the ground, while the other has little to do but to weep and rejoice at the appropriate times.

This explanation of the double personification of the corn in Greek myth assumes that both personifications (Demeter and Proserpine) are original. But if we assume that the Greek myth started with a single personification, the after-growth of a second personification may perhaps be explained as follows. On looking over the peasant harvest customs which have been passed under review, it may be noticed that they involve two distinct conceptions of the corn-spirit. For whereas in some of the customs the corn-spirit is treated as immanent in the corn, in others it is regarded as external to it. Thus when a particular sheaf is called by the name of the corn-spirit, and is dressed in clothes and treated with reverence,[1] the corn-spirit is clearly regarded as immanent in the corn. But when the corn-spirit is said to make

---

[1] In some places it was customary to kneel down before the last sheaf, in others to kiss it. W. Mannhardt, *Korn-dämonen*, 26 ; *id.*, *Mytholog. Forschungen*, p. 339; *Folk-lore Journal*, vi. 270.

the corn grow by passing through it, or to blight the corn of those against whom she has a grudge,[1] she is clearly conceived as quite separate from, though exercising power over, the corn. Conceived in the latter way the corn-spirit is in a fair way to become a deity of the corn, if she has not become so already. Of these two conceptions, that of the corn-spirit as immanent in the corn is doubtless the older, since the view of nature as animated by indwelling spirits appears to have generally preceded the view of it as controlled by deities external to it ; to put it shortly, animism precedes deism. In the harvest customs of our European peasantry the conception of the corn-spirit as immanent appears to be the prevalent one ; the conception of it as external occurs rather as an exception. In Greek mythology, on the other hand, Demeter is distinctly conceived in the latter way ; she is the deity of the corn rather than the spirit immanent in it.[2] The process of thought which seems to be chiefly instrumental in producing the transition from the one mode of conception to the other is anthropomorphism, or the gradual investment of the immanent spirits with more and more of the attributes of humanity. As men emerge from savagery the tendency to anthropomorphise or humanise their divinities gains strength ; and the more anthropomorphic these become, the wider is the breach which severs them from those natural objects of which they were at first merely the animating spirits or souls. But in the progress upwards from savagery, men of the same generation do not march abreast ; and though the anthropomorphic gods may satisfy the religious wants

---

[1] Above, p. 332 *sq.*

[2] In the Homeric Hymn to Demeter, she is represented as controlling the growth of the corn. See above, p. 331.

of more advanced individuals, the more backward members of the community will cling by preference to the older animistic notions. Now when the spirit of any natural object (as the corn) has been invested with human qualities, detached from the object, and converted into a deity controlling it, the object itself is, by the withdrawal of its spirit, left inanimate, it becomes, so to say, a spiritual vacuum. But the popular fancy, intolerant of such a vacuum, in other words, unable to conceive anything as inanimate, immediately creates a fresh mythical being, with which it peoples the vacant object. Thus the same natural object is now represented in mythology by two separate beings; first, by the old spirit now separated from it and raised to the rank of a deity; second, by the new spirit, freshly created by the popular fancy to supply the place vacated by the old spirit on its elevation to a higher sphere. The problem for mythology now is, having got two separate personifications of the same object, what to do with them? How are their relations to each other to be adjusted, and room found for both in the mythological system? When the old spirit or new deity is conceived as creating or producing the object in question, the problem is easily solved. Since the object is believed to be produced by the old spirit, and animated by the new one, the latter, as the soul of the object, must also owe its existence to the former; thus the old spirit will stand to the new one as producer to produced, that is (in mythology), as parent to child, and if both spirits are conceived as female, their relation will be that of mother and daughter. In this way, starting from a single personification of the corn as female, mythology might in time reach a double personification of it as mother and daughter. It would be very rash to affirm that this was the way in which the myth of Demeter and Proserpine actually took shape ; but it seems a legitimate conjecture that the reduplication of deities, of which Demeter and Proserpine furnish an example, may sometimes have arisen in the way indicated. For example, among the pairs of deities whom we have been considering, it has been shown that there are grounds for regarding both Isis and her companion god Osiris as personifications of the corn.[1] On the hypothesis just suggested, Isis would be the old corn-spirit, and Osiris would be the newer one, whose relationship to the old spirit was variously explained as that of brother, husband, and son ;[2] for of course mythology would always be free to account for the coexistence of the two divinities in more ways than one. Further, this hypothesis offers at least a possible explanation of the relation of Virbius to the Arician Diana. The latter, as we have seen,[3] was a tree-goddess ; and if, as I have conjectured, the Flamen Virbialis was no other than the priest of Nemi himself, that is, the King of the Wood, Virbius must also have been a tree-spirit. On the present hypothesis he was the newer tree-spirit, whose relation to the old tree-spirit (Diana) was explained by representing him as her favourite or lover. It must not, however, be forgotten that this proposed explanation of such pairs of deities as Demeter and Proserpine, Isis and Osiris, Diana and Virbius, is purely conjectural, and is only given for what it is worth.

---

[1] See above, pp. 305 *sqq.*, 309 *sqq.*
[2] Pauly, *Real-Encyclopädie der class. Alterthumswiss.* v. 1011.
[3] Above, p. 105 *sq.*

§ 9.—*Lityerses*

In the preceding pages an attempt has been made to show that in the Corn-mother and harvest Maiden of Northern Europe we have the prototypes of Demeter and Proserpine. But an essential feature is still wanting to complete the resemblance. A leading incident in the Greek myth is the death and resurrection of Proserpine ; it is this incident which, coupled with the nature of the goddess as a deity of vegetation, links the myth with the cults of Adonis, Attis, Osiris, and Dionysus ; and it is in virtue of this incident that the myth is considered in this chapter. It remains, therefore, to see whether the conception of the annual death and resurrection of a god, which figures so prominently in these great Greek and Oriental worships, has not also its origin in the rustic rites observed by reapers and vine-dressers amongst the corn-shocks and the vines.

Our general ignorance of the popular superstitions and customs of the ancients has already been confessed. But the obscurity which thus hangs over the first beginnings of ancient religion is fortunately dissipated to some extent in the present case. The worships of Osiris, Adonis, and Attis had their respective seats, as we have seen, in Egypt, Syria, and Phrygia ; and in each of these countries certain harvest and vintage customs are known to have been observed, the resemblance of which to each other and to the national rites struck the ancients themselves, and, compared with the harvest customs of modern peasants and barbarians, seem to throw some light on the origin of the rites in question.

It has been already mentioned, on the authority of Diodorus, that in ancient Egypt the reapers were wont to lament over the first sheaf cut, invoking Isis as the goddess to whom they owed the discovery of corn.[1] To the plaintive song or cry sung or uttered by Egyptian reapers the Greeks gave the name of Maneros, and explained the name by a story that Maneros, the only son of the first Egyptian king, invented agriculture, and, dying an untimely death, was thus lamented by the people.[2] It appears, however, that the name Maneros is due to a misunderstanding of the formula *mââ-ne-hra*, " come thou back," which has been discovered in various Egyptian writings, for example in the dirge of Isis in the Book of the Dead.[3] Hence we may suppose that the cry *mââ-ne-hra* was chanted by the reapers over the cut corn as a dirge for the death of the corn-spirit (Isis or Osiris) and a prayer for its return. As the cry was raised over the first ears reaped, it would seem that the corn-spirit was believed by the Egyptians to be present in the first corn cut and to die under the sickle. We have seen that in Java the first ears of rice are taken to represent the Corn-bride and the Corn-bridegroom.[4] In parts of Russia the first sheaf is treated much in the same way that the last sheaf is treated elsewhere. It is reaped by the mistress herself, taken home and set in the place of honour near the holy pictures ; afterwards it is threshed separately, and some of its grain is mixed with the next year's seed-corn.[5]

---

[1] Diodorus, i. 14, ἔτι γὰρ καὶ νῦν κατὰ τὸν θερισμὸν τοὺς πρώτους ἀμηθέντας στάχυς θέντας τοὺς ἀνθρώπους κόπτεσθαι πλησίον τοῦ δράγματος κ.τ.λ. For θέντας we should perhaps read σύνθεντας, which is supported by the following δράγματος.

[2] Herodotus, ii. 79 ; Pollux, iv. 54 ; Pausanias, ix. 29 ; Athenaeus, 620 A.

[3] Brugsch, *Adonisklage und Linoslied*, p. 24.

[4] Above, p. 355.

[5] Ralston, *Songs of the Russian People*, p. 249 *sq*.

In Phoenicia and Western Asia a plaintive song, like that chanted by the Egyptian corn-reapers, was sung at the vintage and probably (to judge by analogy) also at harvest. This Phoenician song was called by the Greeks Linus or Ailinus and explained, like Maneros, as a lament for the death of a youth named Linus.[1] According to one story Linus was brought up by a shepherd, but torn to pieces by his dogs.[2] But, like Maneros, the name Linus or Ailinus appears to have originated in a verbal misunderstanding, and to be nothing more than the cry *ai lanu*, that is "woe to us," which the Phoenicians probably uttered in mourning for Adonis;[3] at least Sappho seems to have regarded Adonis and Linus as equivalent.[4]

In Bithynia a like mournful ditty, called Bormus or Borimus, was chanted by Mariandynian reapers. Bormus was said to have been a handsome youth, the son of King Upias or of a wealthy and distinguished man. One summer day, watching the reapers at work in his fields, he went to fetch them a drink of water and was never heard of more. So the reapers sought for him, calling him in plaintive strains, which they continued to use ever afterwards.[5]

In Phrygia the corresponding song, sung by harvesters both at reaping and at threshing, was called Lityerses. According to one story, Lityerses was a bastard son of Midas, King of Phrygia. He used to reap the corn, and had an enormous appetite. When a stranger happened to enter the corn-field or to pass

---

[1] Homer, *Il.* xviii. 570; Herodotus, ii. 79; Pausanias, ix. 29; Conon, *Narrat.* 19. For the form Ailinus see Suidas, *s.v.*; Euripides, *Orestes*, 1395; Sophocles, *Ajax*, 627. Cp. Moschus, *Idyl.* iii. 1; Callimachus, *Hymn to Apollo*, 20.

[2] Conon, *l.c.*

[3] W. Mannhardt, *A. W. F.* p. 281.

[4] Pausanias, *l.c.*

[5] Pollux, iv. 54; Athenaeus, 619 F, 620 A; Hesychius, *svv.* Βῶρμον and Μαριανδυνὸς θρῆνος.

by it, Lityerses gave him plenty to eat and drink, then took him to the corn-fields on the banks of the Maeander and compelled him to reap along with him. Lastly, he used to wrap the stranger in a sheaf, cut off his head with a sickle, and carry away his body, wrapt in the corn stalks. But at last he was himself slain by Hercules, who threw his body into the river.[1] As Hercules was probably reported to have slain Lityerses in the same way that Lityerses slew others (as Theseus treated Sinis and Sciron), we may infer that Lityerses used to throw the bodies of his victims into the river. According to another version of the story, Lityerses, a son of Midas, used to challenge people to a reaping match with him, and if he vanquished them he used to thrash them ; but one day he met with a stronger reaper, who slew him.[2]

There are some grounds for supposing that in these stories of Lityerses we have the description of a Phrygian harvest custom in accordance with which certain persons, especially strangers passing the harvest field, were regularly regarded as embodiments of the corn-spirit and as such were seized by the reapers, wrapt in sheaves, and beheaded, their bodies, bound up in the corn-stalks, being afterwards thrown into water as a rain-charm. The grounds for this supposition are, first, the resemblance of the Lityerses story to the harvest customs of European peasantry, and, second, the fact that human beings have been commonly killed by savage races to promote the fertility of the fields. We

---

[1] The story was told by Sositheus in his play of *Daphnis*. His verses have been preserved in the tract of an anonymous writer. See *Scriptores rerum mirabilium*, ed. Westermann, p. 220 ; also Athenaeus, 415 B ; Schol. on Theocritus, x. 41 ; Photius, Suidas, and Hesychius, *s.v. Lityerses* ; Apostolius, x. 74. Photius mentions the sickle. Lityerses is the subject of a special study by Mannhardt (*Mythologische Forschungen*, p. 1 *sqq.*), whom I follow.

[2] Pollux, iv. 54.

will examine these grounds successively, beginning with the former.

In comparing the story with the harvest customs of Europe,[1] three points deserve special attention, namely : I. the reaping match and the binding of persons in the sheaves; II. the killing of the corn-spirit or his representatives ; III. the treatment of visitors to the harvest-field or of strangers passing it.

I. In regard to the first head, we have seen that in modern Europe the person who cuts or binds or threshes the last sheaf is often exposed to rough treatment at the hands of his fellow-labourers. For example, he is bound up in the last sheaf, and, thus encased, is carried or carted about, beaten, drenched with water, thrown on a dunghill, etc. Or, if he is spared this horseplay, he is at least the subject of ridicule or is believed destined to suffer some misfortune in the course of the year. Hence the harvesters are naturally reluctant to give the last cut at reaping or the last stroke at threshing or to bind the last sheaf, and towards the close of the work this reluctance produces an emulation among the labourers, each striving to finish his task as fast as possible, in order that he may escape the invidious distinction of being last.[2] For example, in the neighbourhood of Danzig, when the winter corn is cut and mostly bound up in sheaves, the portion which still remains to be bound is divided amongst the women binders, each of whom

---

[1] In this comparison I closely follow Mannhardt, *Myth. Forsch.* p. 18 *sqq.*

[2] Cp. above, p. 340. On the other hand, the last sheaf is sometimes an object of desire and emulation. See p. 336. It is so at Balquhidder also, *Folk-lore Journal*, vi. 269 ; and it was formerly so on the Gareloch, Dumbartonshire, where there was a competition for the honour of cutting it, several handfuls of standing corn being concealed under sheaves.—(From the information of Archie Leitch. See note on p. 345).

receives a swath of equal length to bind. A crowd of reapers, children, and idlers gathers round to witness the contest, and at the word, " Seize the Old Man," the women fall to work, all binding their allotted swaths as hard as they can. The spectators watch them narrowly, and the woman who cannot keep pace with the rest and consequently binds the last sheaf has to carry the Old Man (that is, the last sheaf made up in the form of a man) to the farmhouse and deliver it to the farmer with the words, "Here I bring you the Old Man." At the supper which follows, the Old Man is placed at the table and receives an abundant portion of food which, as he cannot eat it, falls to the share of the woman who carried him. Afterwards the Old Man is placed in the yard and all the people dance round him. Or the woman who bound the last sheaf dances for a good while with the Old Man, while the rest form a ring round them ; afterwards they all, one after the other, dance a single round with him. Further, the woman who bound the last sheaf goes herself by the name of the Old Man till the next harvest, and is often mocked with the cry, " Here comes the Old Man."[1] At Aschbach, Bavaria, when the reaping is nearly finished, the reapers say, " Now we will drive out the Old Man." Each of them sets himself to reap a patch of corn and reaps as fast as he can ; he who cuts the last handful or the last stalk is greeted by the rest with an exulting cry, " You have the Old Man." Sometimes a black mask is fastened on the reaper's face and he is dressed in woman's clothes ; or if the reaper is a woman, she is dressed in man's clothes ; a dance follows. At the supper the Old Man gets twice as large a portion of food as the others. At threshing, the proceedings are the same ;

---

[1] W. Mannhardt, *Myth. Forsch.* p. 19 *sq.*

the person who gives the last stroke is said to have the Old Man.[1]

These examples illustrate the contests in reaping, threshing, and binding which take place amongst the harvesters, on account of their unwillingness to suffer the ridicule and personal inconvenience attaching to the individual who happens to finish his work last. It will be remembered that the person who is last at reaping, binding, or threshing, is regarded as the representative of the corn-spirit,[2] and this idea is more fully expressed by binding him or her in corn-stalks. The latter custom has been already illustrated, but a few more instances may be added. At Kloxin, near Stettin, the harvesters call out to the woman who binds the last sheaf, "You have the Old Man, and must keep him." The Old Man is a great bundle of corn decked with flowers and ribbons, and fashioned into a rude semblance of the human form. It is fastened on a rake or strapped on a horse, and brought with music to the village. In delivering the Old Man to the farmer, the woman says—

> " Here, dear Sir, is the Old Man.
> He can stay no longer on the field,
> He can hide himself no longer,
> He must come into the village.
> Ladies and gentlemen, pray be so kind
> As to give the Old Man a present."

Forty or fifty years ago the custom was to tie up the woman herself in pease-straw, and bring her with music to the farmhouse, where the harvesters danced with her till the pease-straw fell off.[3] In other villages round Stettin, when the last harvest-waggon is being loaded, there is a regular race amongst the women,

---

[1] W. Mannhardt, *Myth. Forsch.* p. 20 ; Panzer, *Beitrag zur deutschen Mythologie*, ii. 217.

[2] Above, p. 346 *sq.*

[3] W. Mannhardt, *Myth. Forsch.* p. 22.

each striving not to be last. For she who places
the last sheaf on the waggon is called the Old Man,
and is completely swathed in corn-stalks ; she is also
decked with flowers, and flowers and a helmet of straw
are placed on her head. In solemn procession she
carries the harvest-crown to the squire, over whose
head she holds it while she utters a string of good
wishes. At the dance which follows, the Old Man
has the right to choose his (or rather her) partner ;
it is an honour to dance with him.[1] At Blankenfelde,
in the district of Potsdam, the woman who binds the
last sheaf at the rye-harvest is saluted with the cry,
"You have the Old Man." A woman is then tied
up in the last sheaf in such a way that only her
head is left free ; her hair also is covered with a
cap made of rye-stalks, adorned with ribbons and
flowers. She is called the Harvest-man, and must keep
dancing in front of the last harvest-waggon till it reaches
the squire's house, where she receives a present, and is
released from her envelope of corn.[2] At Gommern,
near Magdeburg, the reaper who cuts the last ears
of corn is often wrapt up in corn-stalks so completely
that it is hard to see whether there is a man in the
bundle or not. Thus wrapt up he is taken by another
stalwart reaper on his back, and carried round the
field amid the joyous cries of the harvesters.[3] At
Neuhausen, near Merseburg, the person who binds the
last sheaf is wrapt in ears of oats and saluted as
the Oats-man, whereupon the others dance round
him.[4] At Brie, Isle de France, the farmer himself
is tied up in the *first* sheaf.[5] At the harvest-home
at Udvarhely, Transylvania, a person is encased in

corn - stalks, and wears on his head a crown made out of the last ears cut. On reaching the village he is soused with water over and over.[1] At Dingelstedt, in the district of Erfurt, about fifty years ago it was the custom to tie up a man in the last sheaf. He was called the Old Man, and was brought home on the last waggon, amid huzzas and music. On reaching the farmyard he was rolled round the barn and drenched with water.[2] At Nördlingen, Bavaria, the man who gives the last stroke at threshing is wrapt in straw and rolled on the threshing - floor.[3] In some parts of Oberpfalz, Bavaria, he is said to "get the Old Man," is wrapt in straw, and carried to a neighbour who has not yet finished his threshing.[4] In Thüringen a sausage is stuck in the last sheaf at threshing, and thrown, with the sheaf, on the threshing-floor. It is called the *Barrenwurst* or *Banzenwurst*, and is eaten by all the threshers. After they have eaten it a man is encased in pease-straw, and thus attired is led through the village.[5]

" In all these cases the idea is that the spirit of the corn—the Old Man of vegetation—is driven out of the corn last cut or last threshed, and lives in the barn during the winter. At sowing-time he goes out again to the fields to resume his activity as animating force among the sprouting corn." [6]

Much the same ideas are attached to the last corn in India ; for we are told that in the Central Provinces, " when the reaping is nearly done, about a *bisvá*, say a rood of land, of corn is left standing in the culti-

---

[1] W. Mannhardt, *Myth. Forsch.* p. 24.
[2] *Ib.* p. 24.   [3] *Ib.* p. 24 *sq.*
[4] *Ib.* p. 25.

[5] Witzschel, *Sagen, Sitten und Gebräuche aus Thüringen*, p. 223.
[6] W. Mannhardt, *op. cit.* p. 25 *sq.*

vator's last field, and the reapers rest a little. Then they rush at this *bisvá*, tear it up, and cast it into the air, shouting victory to Omkár Maháráj or Jhámájí, or Rámjí Dás, etc., according to their respective possessions. A sheaf is made up of this corn, tied to a bamboo, and stuck up in the last harvest cart, and carried home in triumph. It is fastened up in the threshing-floor to a tree, or to the cattle-shed, where its services are essential in averting the evil-eye." [1]

II. Passing to the second point of comparison between the Lityerses story and European harvest customs, we have now to see that in the latter the corn-spirit is often believed to be killed at reaping or threshing. In the Romsdal and other parts of Norway, when the haymaking is over, the people say that "the Old Hay-man has been killed." In some parts of Bavaria the man who gives the last stroke at threshing is said to have killed the Corn-man, the Oats-man, or the Wheat-man, according to the crop.[2] In the Canton of Tillot, in Lothringen, at threshing the last corn the men keep time with their flails, calling out as they thresh, "We are killing the Old Woman! We are killing the Old Woman!" If there is an old woman in the house she is warned to save herself, or she will be struck dead.[3] In Lithuania, near Ragnit, the last handful of corn is left standing by itself, with the words, "The Old Woman (*Boba*) is sitting in there." Then a young reaper whets his scythe, and, with a strong sweep, cuts down the handful. It is now said of him that "He has cut off the Boba's head;" and he receives a gratuity from the farmer and a jugful of

---

[1] C. A. Elliot, *Hoshangábád Settlement Report*, p. 178, quoted in *Panjab Notes and Queries*, iii. Nos. 8, 168.

[2] W. Mannhardt, *Myth. Forsch.* p. 31.

[3] *Ib.* p. 334.

water over his head from the farmer's wife.[1] According
to another account, every Lithuanian reaper makes haste
to finish his task ; for the Old Rye-woman lives in the
last stalks, and whoever cuts the last stalks kills the Old
Rye-woman, and by killing her he brings trouble on
himself.[2] In Wilkischken (district of Tilsit) the man
who cuts the last corn goes by the name of " The killer
of the Rye-woman."[3] In Lithuania, again, the corn-
spirit is believed to be killed at threshing as well as at
reaping. When only a single pile of corn remains to be
threshed, all the threshers suddenly step back a few
paces, as if at the word of command. Then they fall
to work plying their flails with the utmost rapidity
and vehemence, till they come to the last bundle.
Upon this they fling themselves with almost frantic
fury, straining every nerve, and raining blows on it till
the word " Halt ! " rings out sharply from the leader.
The man whose flail is the last to fall after the
command to stop has been given is immediately
surrounded by all the rest, crying out that " He has
struck the Old Rye-woman dead." He has to expiate
the deed by treating them to brandy ; and, like the
man who cuts the last corn, he is known as " The
killer of the Old Rye - woman." [4] Sometimes in
Lithuania the slain corn-spirit was represented by a
puppet. Thus a female figure was made out of
corn-stalks, dressed in clothes, and placed on the
threshing-floor, under the heap of corn which was to
be threshed last. Whoever thereafter gave the
last stroke at threshing " struck the Old Woman
dead."[5] We have already had examples of burning
the figure which represents the corn-spirit.[6] Some-

---

[1] W. Mannhardt, *Myth. Forsch.*   [4] *Ib.* p. 335.   [5] *Ib.* p. 335.
p. 330.   [2] *Ib.*   [3] *Ib.* p. 331.   [6] Above, pp. 335, 341, 350.

times, again, the corn-spirit is represented by a man, who lies down under the last corn ; it is threshed upon his body, and the people say that " the Old Man is being beaten to death."[1] We have already seen that sometimes the farmer's wife is thrust, together with the last sheaf, under the threshing-machine, as if to thresh her, and that afterwards a pretence is made of winnowing her.[2] At Volders, in the Tyrol, husks of corn are stuck behind the neck of the man who gives the last stroke at threshing, and he is throttled with a straw garland. If he is tall, it is believed that the corn will be tall next year. Then he is tied on a bundle and flung into the river.[3] In Carinthia, the thresher who gave the last stroke, and the person who untied the last sheaf on the threshing-floor, are bound hand and foot with straw bands, and crowns of straw are placed on their heads. Then they are tied, face to face, on a sledge, dragged through the village, and flung into a brook.[4] The custom of throwing the representative of the corn-spirit into a stream, like that of drenching him with water, is, as usual, a rain-charm.[5]

III. Thus far the representatives of the corn-spirit have generally been the man or woman who cuts, binds, or threshes the last corn. We now come to the cases in which the corn-spirit is represented either by a stranger passing the harvest-field (as in the Lityerses tale), or by a visitor entering it for the first time. All over Germany it is customary for the reapers or threshers to lay hold of passing strangers and bind them with a rope made of corn-stalks, till

---

[1] W. Mannhardt, *Korndäm.*, p. 26.
[2] Above, p. 343.
[3] W. Mannhardt, *M. F.* p. 50.
[4] *Ib.* p. 50 *sq.*
[5] See above, pp. 286 *sq.*, 333, 337, 340, 341.

they pay a forfeit; and when the farmer himself or one of his guests enters the field or the threshing-floor for the first time, he is treated in the same way. Sometimes the rope is only tied round his arm or his feet or his neck.[1] But sometimes he is regularly swathed in corn. Thus at Solör in Norway, whoever enters the field, be he the master or a stranger, is tied up in a sheaf and must pay a ransom. In the neighbourhood of Soest, when the farmer visits the flax-pullers for the first time, he is completely enveloped in flax. Passers-by are also surrounded by the women, tied up in flax, and compelled to stand brandy.[2] At Nördlingen strangers are caught with straw ropes and tied up in a sheaf till they pay a forfeit. At Brie, Isle de France, when any one who does not belong to the farm passes by the harvest-field, the reapers give chase. If they catch him, they bind him in a sheaf and bite him, one after the other, in the forehead, crying "You shall carry the key of the field."[3] "To have the key" is an expression used by harvesters elsewhere in the sense of to cut or bind or thresh the last sheaf;[4] hence, it is equivalent to the phrases "You have the Old Man," "You are the

---

[1] W. Mannhardt, *op. cit.* p. 32 *sqq.* Cp. *Revue des Traditions populaires*, iii. 598.

[2] W. Mannhardt, *Mythol. Forsch.* p. 35 *sq.*

[3] *Ib.* p. 36.

[4] For the evidence, see *ib.* p. 36, *note* 2. The idea which lies at the bottom of the phrase seems to be explained by the following Cingalese custom. "There is a curious custom of the threshing-floor called 'Goigote' —the tying of the cultivator's knot. When a sheaf of corn has been threshed out, before it is removed the grain is heaped up and the threshers, generally six in number, sit round it, and taking a few stalks, with the ears of corn attached, jointly tie a knot and bury it in the heap. It is left there until all the sheaves have been threshed and the corn winnowed and measured. The object of this ceremony is to prevent the devils from diminishing the quantity of corn in the heap." C. J. R. Le Mesurier, "Customs and Superstitions connected with the Cultivation of Rice in the Southern Province of Ceylon," in *Journal of the Royal Asiatic Society*, N.S., xvii. (1885) 371. The "key" in the European custom is probably intended to serve the same purpose as the "knot" in the Cingalese custom.

Old Man," which are addressed to the cutter, binder, or thresher of the last sheaf. Therefore, when a stranger, as at Brie, is tied up in a sheaf and told that he will "carry the key of the field," it is as much as to say that he is the Old Man, that is, an embodiment of the corn-spirit.

Thus, like Lityerses, modern reapers lay hold of a passing stranger and tie him up in a sheaf. It is not to be expected that they should complete the parallel by cutting off his head ; but if they do not take such a strong step, their language and gestures are at least indicative of a desire to do so. For instance, in Mecklenburg on the first day of reaping, if the master or mistress or a stranger enters the field, or merely passes by it, all the mowers face towards him and sharpen their scythes, clashing their whet-stones against them in unison, as if they were making ready to mow. Then the woman who leads the mowers steps up to him and ties a band round his left arm. He must ransom himself by payment of a forfeit.[1] Near Ratzeburg when the master or other person of mark enters the field or passes by it, all the harvesters stop work and march towards him in a body, the men with their scythes in front. On meeting him they form up in line, men and women. The men stick the poles of their scythes in the ground, as they do in whetting them ; then they take off their caps and hang them on the scythes, while their leader stands forward and makes a speech. When he has done, they all whet their scythes in measured time very loudly, after which they put on their caps. Two of the women binders then come forward ; one of them ties the master or stranger (as the case may be) with corn-ears

---

[1] W. Mannhardt, *op. cit.* p. 39.

or with a silken band ; the other delivers a rhyming
address.   The following are specimens of the speeches
made by the reaper on these occasions.   In some parts
of Pomerania every passer-by is stopped, his way
being barred with a corn-rope.   The reapers form a
circle round him and sharpen their scythes, while their
leader says—

> " The men are ready,
> The scythes are bent,
> The corn is great and small,
> The gentleman must be mowed."

Then the process of whetting the scythes is repeated.[1]
At Ramin, in the district of Stettin, the stranger, standing encircled by the reapers, is thus addressed—

> " We'll stroke the gentleman
> With our naked sword,
> Wherewith we shear meadows and fields.
> We shear princes and lords.
> Labourers are often athirst ;
> If the gentleman will stand beer and brandy
> The joke will soon be over.
> But, if our prayer he does not like,
> The sword has a right to strike." [2]

That in these customs the whetting of the scythes
is really meant as a preliminary to mowing appears
from the following variation of the preceding customs.
In the district of Lüneburg when any one enters the
harvest-field, he is asked whether he will engage a
good fellow.   If he says yes, the harvesters mow some
swaths, yelling and screaming, and then ask him for
drink-money.[3]

On the threshing-floor strangers are also regarded
as embodiments of the corn-spirit, and are treated

---

[1] W. Mannhardt, *Myth. Forsch.*
p. 39 *sq.*
[2] *Ib.* p. 40.   For the speeches made
by the woman who binds the stranger
or the master, see *ib.* p. 41 ; Lemke,
Volksthümliches in Ostpreussen, i. 23 *sq.*
[3] W. Mannhardt, *Myth. Forsch.* p.
41 *sq.*

accordingly. At Wiedingharde in Schleswig when a
stranger comes to the threshing-floor he is asked
"Shall I teach you the flail-dance?" If he says yes,
they put the arms of the threshing-flail round his neck
(as if he were a sheaf of corn), and press them together
so tightly that he is nearly choked.[1] In some parishes
of Wermland (Sweden) when a stranger enters the
threshing-floor where the threshers are at work, they
say that "they will teach him the threshing-song."
Then they put a flail round his neck and a straw rope
about his body. Also, as we have seen, if a stranger
woman enters the threshing-floor, the threshers put
a flail round her body and a wreath of corn-stalks
round her neck, and call out, " See the Corn-woman!
See! that is how the Corn-maiden looks!"[2]

In these customs, observed both on the harvest-
field and on the threshing-floor, a passing stranger is
regarded as a personification of the corn, in other
words, as the corn-spirit; and a show is made of
treating him like the corn by mowing, binding, and
threshing him. If the reader still doubts whether
European peasants can really regard a passing stranger
in this light, the following custom should set their
doubts at rest. During the madder-harvest in the
Dutch province of Zealand a stranger passing by a
field where the people are digging the madder-roots
will sometimes call out to them *Koortspillers* (a term
of reproach). Upon this, two of the fleetest runners

---

[1] W. Mannhardt, *op. cit.* p. 42.

[2] *Ib.* p. 42. See above, p. 343. In
Thüringen a being called the Rush-
cutter used to be much dreaded. On
the morning of St. John's Day he was
wont to walk through the fields with
sickles tied to his ankles cutting avenues
in the corn as he walked. To detect
him, seven bundles of brushwood were
silently threshed with the flail on the
threshing-floor, and the stranger who
appeared at the door of the barn during
the threshing was the Rush-cutter.
Witzschel, *Sagen, Sitten und Gebräuche aus Thüringen,* p. 221. With
the *Binsenschneider* compare the *Bil-
schneider.* Panzer, *Beitrag zur deutschen
Mythologie,* ii. 210 *sq.*

make after him, and, if they catch him, they bring
him back to the madder-field and bury him in the
earth up to his middle at least, jeering at him the
while ; then they ease nature before his face.[1] This
last act is to be explained as follows. The spirit
of the corn and of other cultivated plants is sometimes conceived, not as immanent in the plant, but
as its owner ; hence the cutting of the corn at harvest,
the digging of the roots, and the gathering of fruit
from the fruit-trees are each and all of them acts
of spoliation, which strip him of his property and
reduce him to poverty. Hence he is often known as
" the Poor Man " or " the Poor Woman." Thus in the
neighbourhood of Eisenach a small sheaf is sometimes
left standing on the field for " the Poor Old Woman."[2]
At Marksuhl, near Eisenach, the puppet formed out of
the last sheaf is itself called " the Poor Woman." At

---

[1] W. Mannhardt, *op. cit.* p. 47 *sq.*

[2] *Ib.* p. 48. To prevent a rationalistic explanation of this custom, which,
like most rationalistic explanations of
folk-custom, would be wrong, it may be
pointed out that a little of the crop is
sometimes left on the field for the spirit
under other names than " the Poor Old
Woman." Thus in a village of the
Tilsit district, the last sheaf was left
standing on the field " for the Old
Rye-woman." *M. F.* p. 337. In Neften-
bach (Canton of Zürich) the first three
ears of corn reaped are thrown away
on the field " to satisfy the Corn-
mother and to make the next year's
crop abundant." *Ib.* In Thüringen
when the after-grass (*Grummet*) is
being got in, a little heap is left lying
on the field ; it belongs to " the Little
Wood-woman " in return for the blessing she has bestowed. Witzschel,
*Sagen, Sitten una Gebräuche aus
Thüringen,* p. 224. At Kupferberg,
Bavaria, some corn is left standing on
the field when the rest has been cut.
Of this corn left standing, they say

that " it belongs to the Old Woman,"
to whom it is dedicated in the following words—

  " We give it to the Old Woman ;
    She shall keep it.
    Next year may she be to us
    As kind as this time she has been."

M. F. p. 337 *sq.* These last expressions
are quite conclusive. See also Mannhardt, *Korndämonen,* p. 7 *sq.* In
Russia a patch of unreaped corn is
left in the field and the ears are knotted
together ; this is called " the plaiting
of the beard of Volos." " The unreaped patch is looked upon as tabooed ; and it is believed that if any
one meddles with it he will shrivel up,
and become twisted like the inter-
woven ears." Ralston, *Songs of the
Russian People,* p. 251. In the North-
east of Scotland a few stalks were
sometimes left unreaped for the benefit of " the aul' man." W. Gregor,
Folk-lore of the North-East of Scotland,
p. 182. Here " the aul' man " is
probably the equivalent of the Old Man
(*der Alte*) of Germany.

Alt Lest in Silesia the man who binds the last sheaf is called the Beggar-man.[1] In a village near Roeskilde, in Zealand (Denmark), old-fashioned peasants sometimes make up the last sheaf into a rude puppet, which is called the Rye-beggar.[2] In Southern Schonen the sheaf which is bound last is called the Beggar; it is made bigger than the rest and is sometimes dressed in clothes. In the district of Olmütz the last sheaf is called the Beggar; it is given to an old woman, who must carry it home, limping on one foot.[3] Thus when the corn-spirit is conceived as a being who is robbed of his store and impoverished by the harvesters, it is natural that his representative—the passing stranger—should upbraid them; and it is equally natural that they should seek to disable him from pursuing them and recapturing the stolen property. Now, it is an old superstition that by easing nature on the spot where a robbery is committed, the robbers secure themselves, for a certain time, against interruption.[4] The fact, therefore, that the madder-diggers resort to this proceeding in presence of the stranger proves that they consider themselves robbers and him as the person robbed. Regarded as such, he must be the natural owner of the madder-roots; that is, their spirit or demon; and this conception is carried out by burying him, like the madder-roots, in the ground.[5] The Greeks, it may be observed, were quite familiar with the idea that a passing stranger may be a god. Homer says that the gods in the likeness of foreigners roam up and down cities.[6]

---

[1] *M. F.* p. 48.

[2] *Ib.* p. 48 *sq.*   [3] *Ib.* p. 49.

[4] *Ib.* p. 49 *sq.*; Wuttke, *Der deutsche Volksaberglaube,*[2] § 400; Töppen, *Aberglaube aus Masuren,*[2] p. 57.

[5] The explanation of the custom is Mannhardt's. *M. F.* p. 49.

[6] *Odyssey,* xvii. 485 *sqq.* Cp. Plato, *Sophist,* 216 A.

Thus in these harvest-customs of modern Europe the person who cuts, binds, or threshes the last corn is treated as an embodiment of the corn-spirit by being wrapt up in sheaves, killed in mimicry by agricultural implements, and thrown into the water.[1] These coincidences with the Lityerses story seem to prove that the latter is a genuine description of an old Phrygian harvest-custom. But since in the modern parallels the killing of the personal representative of the corn-spirit is necessarily omitted or at most enacted only in mimicry, it is necessary to show that in rude society human beings have been commonly killed as an agricultural ceremony to promote the fertility of the fields. The following examples will make this plain.

The Indians of Guayaquil (Ecuador) used to sacrifice human blood and the hearts of men when they sowed their fields.[2] At a Mexican harvest-festival, when the first-fruits of the season were offered to the sun, a criminal was placed between two immense stones, balanced opposite each other, and was crushed by them as they fell together. His remains were buried, and a feast and dance followed. This sacrifice was known as "the meeting of the stones."[3] Another series of human sacrifices offered in Mexico to make the maize thrive has been already referred to.[4] The Pawnees annually sacrificed a human victim in spring when they sowed their fields. The sacrifice was believed to have been enjoined on them by the Morning Star, or by a certain bird which the Morning

---

[1] For throwing him into the water, see p. 374.

[2] Cieza de Leon, *Travels*, translated by Markham, p. 203 (Hakluyt Society, 1864).

[3] Brasseur de Bourbourg, *Histoire des Nations civilisées du Mexique*, i. 274; Bancroft, *Native Races of the Pacific States*, ii. 340.

[4] Bastian, *Die Culturländer des alten Amerika*, ii. 639 (quoting Herrara). See above, p. 307.

Star had sent to them as its messenger. The bird
was stuffed and preserved as a powerful " medicine."
They thought that an omission of this sacrifice would
be followed by the total failure of the crops of maize,
beans, and pumpkins. The victim was a captive of
either sex. He was clad in the gayest and most costly
attire, was fattened on the choicest food, and carefully
kept in ignorance of his doom. When he was fat
enough, they bound him to a cross in the presence of
the multitude, danced a solemn dance, then cleft his
head with a tomahawk and shot him with arrows.
According to one trader, the squaws then cut pieces of
flesh from the victim's body, with which they greased
their hoes ; but this was denied by another trader who
had been present at the ceremony. Immediately after
the sacrifice the people proceeded to plant their fields.
A particular account has been preserved of the sacrifice of a Sioux girl by the Pawnees in April 1837 or
1838. The girl had been kept for six months and
well treated. Two days before the sacrifice she was
led from wigwam to wigwam, accompanied by the
whole council of chiefs and warriors. At each lodge
she received a small billet of wood and a little paint,
which she handed to the warrior next to her. In this
way she called at every wigwam, receiving at each the
same present of wood and paint. On the 22d of
April she was taken out to be sacrificed, attended by
the warriors, each of whom carried two pieces of wood
which he had received from her hands. She was
burned for some time over a slow fire, and then shot
to death with arrows. The chief sacrificer next tore
out her heart and devoured it. While her flesh was
still warm it was cut in small pieces from the bones,
put in little baskets, and taken to a neighbouring corn-

field. Here the head chief took a piece of the flesh
from a basket and squeezed a drop of blood upon
the newly-deposited grains of corn. His example
was followed by the rest, till all the seed had been
sprinkled with the blood ; it was then covered up
with earth.[1]

A West African queen used to sacrifice a man and
woman in the month of March. They were killed with
spades and hoes, and their bodies buried in the middle
of a field which had just been tilled.[2] At Lagos in
Guinea it was the custom annually to impale a young
girl alive soon after the spring equinox in order to
secure good crops. Along with her were sacrificed
sheep and goats, which, with yams, heads of maize,
and plantains, were hung on stakes on each side of
her. The victims were bred up for the purpose in the
king's seraglio, and their minds had been so powerfully
wrought upon by the fetish men that they went cheer-
fully to their fate.[3] A similar sacrifice is still annually
offered at Benin, Guinea.[4] The Marimos, a Bechuana
tribe, sacrifice a human being for the crops. The
victim chosen is generally a short, stout man. He is
seized by violence or intoxicated and taken to the
fields, where he is killed amongst the wheat to serve
as "seed " (so they phrase it). After his blood has
coagulated in the sun it is burned along with the
frontal bone, the flesh attached to it, and the brain ;

[1] E. James, *Account of an Expedition from Pittsburgh to the Rocky Mountains,* ii. 80 *sq.*; Schoolcraft, *Indian Tribes,* v. 77 *sqq.*; De Smet, *Voyages aux Montagnes Rocheuses,* nouvelle ed. 1873, p. 121 *sqq.* The accounts by Schoolcraft and De Smet of the sacrifice of the Sioux girl are independent and supplement each other.

[2] Labat, *Relation historique de l'Ethiopie occidentale,* i. 380.

[3] John Adams, *Sketches taken during Ten Voyages in Africa between the years* 1786 *and* 1800, p. 25.

[4] P. Bouche, *La Côte des Esclaves,* p. 132.

the ashes are then scattered over the ground to fertilise it. The rest of the body is eaten.[1]

The Gonds of India, a Dravidian race, kidnapped Brahman boys, and kept them as victims to be sacrificed on various occasions. At sowing and reaping, after a triumphal procession, one of the lads was slain by being punctured with a poisoned arrow. His blood was then sprinkled over the ploughed field or the ripe crop, and his flesh was devoured.[2]

But the best known case of human sacrifices, systematically offered to ensure good crops, is supplied by the Khonds or Kandhs, another Dravidian race in Bengal. Our knowledge of them is derived from the accounts written by British officers who, forty or fifty years ago, were engaged in putting them down.[3] The sacrifices were offered to the Earth Goddess, Tari Pennu or Bera Pennu, and were believed to ensure good crops and immunity from all disease and accidents. In particular, they were considered necessary in the cultivation of turmeric, the Khonds arguing that the turmeric could not have a deep red colour without the shedding of blood.[4] The victim or Meriah was acceptable to the goddess only if he had been purchased, or had been born a victim—that is, the son of a victim father—or had been devoted as a child by his father or guardian. Khonds in distress often sold their children for victims, " considering the beatification of their souls certain, and their death, for the benefit of mankind, the most honourable possible."

[1] Arbousset et Daumas, *Voyage d'exploration au Nord-est de la Colonie du Cap de Bonne-Esperance*, p. 117 *sq.*
[2] *Panjab Notes and Queries*, ii. No. 721.

[3] Major S. C. Macpherson, *Memorials of Service in India*, p. 113 *sq.*; Major-General John Campbell, *Wild Tribes of Khondistan*, pp. 52-58, etc.
[4] J. Campbell, *op. cit.* p. 56.

A man of the Panua tribe was once seen to load a Khond with curses, and finally to spit in his face, because the Khond had sold for a victim his own child, whom the Panua had wished to marry. A party of Khonds, who saw this, immediately pressed forward to comfort the seller of his child, saying, "Your child has died that all the world may live, and the Earth Goddess herself will wipe that spittle from your face." [1] The victims were often kept for years before they were sacrificed. Being regarded as con-secrated beings, they were treated with extreme affection, mingled with deference, and were welcomed wherever they went. A Meriah youth, on attaining maturity, was generally given a wife, who was herself usually a Meriah or victim ; and with her he received a portion of land and farm-stock. Their offspring were also victims. Human sacrifices were offered to the Earth Goddess by tribes, branches of tribes, or villages, both at periodical festivals and on extra-ordinary occasions. The periodical sacrifices were generally so arranged by tribes and divisions of tribes that each head of a family was enabled, at least once a year, to procure a shred of flesh for his fields, generally about the time when his chief crop was laid down. [2]

The mode of performing these tribal sacrifices was as follows. Ten or twelve days before the sacrifice, the victim was devoted by cutting off his hair, which, until then, was kept unshorn. Crowds of men and women assembled to witness the sacri-fice ; none might be excluded, since the sacrifice was declared to be "for all mankind." It was preceded by several days of wild revelry and gross

---

[1] S. C. Macpherson, *op. cit.* p. 115 *sq.*   [2] *Ib.* p. 113.

debauchery.[1]   On the day before the sacrifice the
victim, dressed in a new garment, was led forth from
the village in solemn procession, with music and dancing, to the Meriah grove, which was a clump of high
forest trees standing a little way from the village and
untouched by the axe.   In this grove the victim was
tied to a post, which was sometimes placed between
two plants of the sankissar shrub.   He was then
anointed with oil, ghee, and turmeric, and adorned
with flowers ; and " a species of reverence, which it
is not easy to distinguish from adoration," was paid
to him throughout the day.[2]   A great struggle now
arose to obtain the smallest relic from his person ;
a particle of the turmeric paste with which he was
smeared, or a drop of his spittle, was esteemed
of sovereign virtue, especially by the women.   The
crowd danced round the post to music, and, addressing
the earth, said, " O God, we offer this sacrifice to you ;
give us good crops, seasons, and health." [3]

On the last morning the orgies, which had been
scarcely interrupted during the night, were resumed,
and continued till noon, when they ceased, and the
assembly proceeded to consummate the sacrifice.
The victim was again anointed with oil, and each
person touched the anointed part, and wiped the oil
on his own head.   In some places the victim was
then taken in procession round the village, from door
to door, where some plucked hair from his head, and
others begged for a drop of his spittle, with which
they anointed their heads.[4]   As the victim might
not be bound nor make any show of resistance, the

---

[1] S. C. Macpherson, *op. cit.* p. 117
sq. ; J. Campbell, p. 112.

[2] S. C. Macpherson, p. 118.
[3] J. Campbell, p. 54.
[4] *Ib.* pp. 55, 112.

bones of his arms and, if necessary, his legs were broken ; but often this precaution was rendered unnecessary by stupefying him with opium.[1] The mode of putting him to death varied in different places. One of the commonest modes seems to have been strangulation, or squeezing to death. The branch of a green tree was cleft several feet down the middle ; the victim's neck (in other places, his chest) was inserted in the cleft, which the priest, aided by his assistants, strove with all his force to close.[2] Then he wounded the victim slightly with his axe, whereupon the crowd rushed at the victim and cut the flesh from the bones, leaving the head and bowels untouched. Sometimes he was cut up alive.[3] In Chinna Kimedy he was dragged along the fields, surrounded by the crowd, who, avoiding his head and intestines, hacked the flesh from his body with their knives till he died.[4] Another very common mode of sacrifice in the same district was to fasten the victim to the proboscis of a wooden elephant, which revolved on a stout post, and, as it whirled round, the crowd cut the flesh from the victim while life remained. In some villages Major Campbell found as many as fourteen of these wooden elephants, which had been used at sacrifices.[5] In one district the victim was put to death slowly by fire. A low stage was formed, sloping on either side like a roof ; upon it

---

[1] S. C. Macpherson, p. 119 ; J. Campbell, p. 113.

[2] S. C. Macpherson, p. 127. Instead of the branch of a green tree, Campbell mentions two strong planks or bamboos (p. 57) or a slit bamboo (p. 182).

[3] J. Campbell, pp. 56, 58, 120.

[4] Dalton, *Ethnology of Bengal*, p. 288, quoting Colonel Campbell's Report.

[5] J. Campbell, p. 126. The elephant represented the Earth Goddess herself, who was here conceived in elephant-form ; Campbell, pp. 51, 126. In the hill tracts of Goomsur she was represented in peacock-form, and the post to which the victim was bound bore the effigy of a peacock, Campbell, p. 54.

the victim was placed, his limbs wound round with cords to confine his struggles. Fires were then lighted and hot brands applied, to make him roll up and down the slopes of the stage as long as possible ; for the more tears he shed the more abundant would be the supply of rain. Next day the body was cut to pieces.[1]

The flesh cut from the victim was instantly taken home by the persons who had been deputed by each village to bring it. To secure its rapid arrival, it was sometimes forwarded by relays of men, and conveyed with postal fleetness fifty or sixty miles.[2] In each village all who stayed at home fasted rigidly until the flesh arrived. The bearer deposited it in the place of public assembly, where it was received by the priest and the heads of families. The priest divided it into two portions, one of which he offered to the Earth Goddess by burying it in a hole in the ground with his back turned, and without looking. Then each man added a little earth to bury it, and the priest poured water on the spot from a hill gourd. The other portion of flesh he divided into as many shares as there were heads of houses present. Each head of a house rolled his shred of flesh in leaves, and buried it in his favourite field, placing it in the earth behind his back without looking.[3] In some places each man carried his portion of flesh to the stream which watered his fields, and there hung it on a pole.[4] For three days thereafter no house was swept ; and, in one district, strict silence was observed, no fire might be given out, no wood cut, and no strangers received.

---

[1] S. C. Macpherson, p. 130.

[2] Dalton, *Ethnology of Bengal*, p. 288, referring to Colonel Campbell's Report.

[3] S. C. Macpherson, p. 129. Cp. J. Campbell, pp. 55, 58, 113, 121, 187.

[4] J. Campbell, p. 182.

The remains of the human victim (namely, the head, bowels, and bones) were watched by strong parties the night after the sacrifice; and next morning they were burned, along with a whole sheep, on a funeral pile. The ashes were scattered over the fields, laid as paste over the houses and granaries, or mixed with the new corn to preserve it from insects.[1] Sometimes, however, the head and bones were buried, not burnt.[2] After the suppression of the human sacrifices, inferior victims were substituted in some places; for instance, in the capital of Chinna Kimedy a goat took the place of a human victim.[3]

In these Khond sacrifices the Meriahs are represented by our authorities as victims offered to propitiate the Earth Goddess. But from the treatment of the victims both before and after death it appears that the custom cannot be explained as merely a propitiatory sacrifice. A part of the flesh certainly was offered to the Earth Goddess, but the rest of the flesh was buried by each householder in his fields, and the ashes of the other parts of the body were scattered over the fields, laid as paste on the granaries, or mixed with the new corn. These latter customs imply that to the body of the Meriah there was ascribed a direct or intrinsic power of making the crops to grow, quite independent of the indirect efficacy which it might have as an offering to secure the good-will of the deity. In other words, the flesh and ashes of the victim were believed to be endowed with a magical or physical power of fertilising the land. The same intrinsic power was ascribed to the blood and tears of the Meriah, his blood causing the redness of the turmeric and his tears

---

[1] S. C. Macpherson, p. 128; Dalton, *l.c.*
[2] J. Campbell, pp. 55, 182.   [3] J. Campbell, p. 187.

producing rain ; for it can hardly be doubted that, originally at least, the tears were supposed to produce rain, not merely to prognosticate it. Similarly the custom of pouring water on the buried flesh of the Meriah was no doubt a rain-charm. Again, intrinsic supernatural power as an attribute of the Meriah appears in the sovereign virtue believed to reside in anything that came from his person, as his hair or spittle. The ascription of such power to the Meriah indicates that he was much more than a mere man sacrificed to propitiate a deity. Once more, the extreme reverence paid him points to the same conclusion. Major Campbell speaks of the Meriah as " being regarded as something more than mortal,"[1] and Major Macpherson says, " A species of reverence, which it is not easy to distinguish from adoration, is paid to him." [2] In short, the Meriah appears to have been regarded as divine. As such, he may originally have represented the Earth deity or perhaps a deity of vegetation ; though in later times he came to be regarded rather as a victim offered to a deity than as himself an incarnate deity. This later view of the Meriah as a victim rather than a god may perhaps have received undue emphasis from the European writers who have described the Khond religion. Habituated to the later idea of sacrifice as an offering made to a god for the purpose of conciliating his favour, European observers are apt to interpret all religious slaughter in this sense, and to suppose that wherever such slaughter takes place, there must necessarily be a deity to whom the slaughter is believed by the slayers to be acceptable. Thus their preconceived ideas unconsciously colour and warp their descriptions of savage rites.

[1] J. Campbell, p. 112.   [2] S. C. Macpherson, p. 118.

The same custom of killing the representative of a god, of which strong traces appear in the Khond sacrifices, may perhaps be detected in some of the other human sacrifices described above. Thus the ashes of the slaughtered Marimo were scattered over the fields; the blood of the Brahman lad was put on the crop and field; and the blood of the Sioux girl was allowed to trickle on the seed.[1] Again, the identification of the victim with the corn, in other words, the view that he is an embodiment or spirit of the corn, is brought out in the pains which seem to be taken to secure a physical correspondence between him and the natural object which he embodies or represents. Thus the Mexicans killed young victims for the young corn and old ones for the ripe corn; the Marimos sacrifice, as "seed," a short, fat man, the shortness of his stature corresponding to that of the young corn, his fatness to the condition which it is desired that the crops may attain; and the Pawnees fattened their victims probably with the same view. Again, the identification of the victim with the corn comes out in the African custom of killing him with spades and hoes, and the Mexican custom of grinding him, like corn, between two stones.

One more point in these savage customs deserves to be noted. The Pawnee chief devoured the heart of the Sioux girl, and the Marimos and Gonds ate the victim's flesh. If, as we suppose, the victim was regarded as divine, it follows that in eating his flesh his worshippers were partaking of the body of their god. To this point we shall return later on.

The savage rites just described offer analogies to the harvest customs of Europe. Thus the fer-

---

[1] Above, pp. 383, 384.

tilising virtue ascribed to the corn - spirit is shown
equally in the savage custom of mixing the victim's
blood or ashes with the seed-corn and the European
custom of mixing the grain from the last sheaf with
the young corn in spring.[1]   Again, the identification
of the person with the corn appears alike in the
savage custom of adapting the age and stature of
the victim to the age and stature (actual or expected)
of the crop ; in the Scotch and Styrian rules that when
the corn-spirit is conceived as the Maiden the last corn
shall be cut by a young maiden, but when it is conceived
as the Corn-mother it shall be cut by an old woman ; [2]
in the Lothringian warning given to old women to save
themselves when the Old Woman is being killed, that
is, when the last corn is being threshed ; [3] and in the
Tyrolese expectation that if the man who gives the last
stroke at threshing is tall, the next year's corn will be
tall also.[4]   Further, the same identification is implied
in the savage custom of killing the representative of
the corn-spirit with hoes or spades or by grinding him
between stones, and in the European custom of pretending to kill him with the scythe or the flail.   Once
more the Khond custom of pouring water on the buried
flesh of the victim is parallel to the European customs
of pouring water on the personal representative of the
corn-spirit or plunging him into a stream.[5]   Both the
Khond and the European customs are rain-charms.

To return now to the Lityerses story.   It has been
shown that in rude society human beings have been
commonly killed to promote the growth of the crops.
There is therefore no improbability in the supposition
that they may once have been killed for a like purpose

---

[1] Above, pp. 334, 335.   [2] Above, pp. 333, 344, 345.   [3] Above, p. 372.
[4] Above, p. 374.   [5] Above, pp. 286 *sq.*, 337, 340, 374.

in Phrygia and Europe ; and when Phrygian legend and
European folk-custom, closely agreeing with each other,
point to the conclusion that men were so slain, we are
bound, provisionally at least, to accept the conclusion.
Further, both the Lityerses story and European
harvest customs agree in indicating that the person
slain was slain as a representative of the corn-spirit,
and this indication is in harmony with the view which
savages appear to take of the victim slain to make the
crops flourish. On the whole, then, we may fairly
suppose that both in Phrygia and in Europe the representative of the corn-spirit was annually killed upon the
harvest-field. Grounds have been already shown for
believing that similarly in Europe the representative of
the tree-spirit was annually slain. The proofs of these
two remarkable and closely analogous customs are
entirely independent of each other. Their coincidence
seems to furnish fresh presumption in favour of both.

To the question, how was the representative of
the corn-spirit chosen? one answer has been already
given. Both the Lityerses story and European folk-
custom show that passing strangers were regarded
as manifestations of the corn-spirit escaping from
the cut or threshed corn, and as such were seized
and slain. But this is not the only answer which
the evidence suggests. According to one version
of the Phrygian legend the victims of Lityerses were
not passing strangers but persons whom he had
vanquished in a reaping contest ; and though it is not
said that he killed, but only that he thrashed them, we
can hardly avoid supposing that in one version of the
story the vanquished reapers, like the strangers in the
other version, were said to have been wrapt up by
Lityerses in corn-sheaves and so beheaded. The

supposition is countenanced by European harvest-customs. We have seen that in Europe there is sometimes a contest amongst the reapers to avoid being last, and that the person who is vanquished in this competition, that is, who cuts the last corn, is often roughly handled. It is true we have not found that a pretence is made of killing him ; but on the other hand we have found that a pretence is made of killing the man who gives the last stroke at threshing, that is, who is vanquished in the threshing contest.[1] Now, since it is in the character of representative of the corn-spirit that the thresher of the last corn is slain in mimicry, and since the same representative character attaches (as we have seen) to the cutter and binder as well as to the thresher of the last corn, and since the same repugnance is evinced by harvesters to be last in any one of these labours, we may conjecture that a pretence has been commonly made of killing the reaper and binder as well as the thresher of the last corn, and that in ancient times this killing was actually carried out. This conjecture is corroborated by the common superstition that whoever cuts the last corn must die soon.[2] Sometimes it is thought that the person who binds the last sheaf on the field will die in the course of next year.[3] The reason for fixing on the reaper, binder, or thresher of the last corn as the representative of the corn-spirit may be this. The corn-spirit is supposed to lurk as long as he can in the corn, retreating before the reapers, the binders, and the threshers at their work. But when he is forcibly expelled from his ultimate refuge in the last corn cut or the last sheaf bound or the last grain threshed, he necessarily assumes some other form than

---

[1] Above, p. 374.   [2] W. Mannhardt, *Korndämonen*, p. 5.
[3] Pfannenschmid, *Germanische Erntefeste*, p. 98.

that of the corn-stalks which had hitherto been his
garments or body. And what form can the expelled
corn-spirit assume more naturally than that of the person
who stands nearest to the corn from which he (the
corn-spirit) has just been expelled? But the person in
question is necessarily the reaper, binder, or thresher
of the last corn. He or she, therefore, is seized and
treated as the corn-spirit himself.

Thus the person who was killed on the harvest-
field as the representative of the corn-spirit may have
been either a passing stranger or the harvester who
was last at reaping, binding, or threshing. But there
is a third possibility, to which ancient legend and
modern folk-custom alike point. Lityerses not only
put strangers to death; he was himself slain, and
probably in the same way as he had slain others,
namely, by being wrapt in a corn-sheaf, beheaded, and
cast into the river; and it is implied that this happened
to Lityerses on his own land. Similarly in modern
harvest-customs the pretence of killing appears to be
carried out quite as often on the person of the master
(farmer or squire) as on that of strangers.[1] Now when
we remember that Lityerses was said to have been the
son of the King of Phrygia, and combine with this the
tradition that he was put to death, apparently as a
representative of the corn-spirit, we are led to conjecture that we have here another trace of the custom of
annually slaying one of those divine or priestly kings
who are known to have held ghostly sway in many
parts of Western Asia and particularly in Phrygia.
The custom appears, as we have seen,[2] to have been
so far modified in places that the king's son was
slain in the king's stead. Of the custom thus

---

[1] Above, p. 376 *sq.*   [2] Above, p. 235.

modified the story of Lityerses would therefore be a reminiscence.

Turning now to the relation of the Phrygian Lityerses to the Phrygian Attis, it may be remembered that at Pessinus—the seat of a priestly kingship —the high-priest appears to have been annually slain in the character of Attis, a god of vegetation, and that Attis was described by an ancient authority as " a reaped ear of corn."[1]   Thus Attis, as an embodiment of the corn-spirit, annually slain in the person of his representative, might be thought to be ultimately identical with Lityerses, the latter being simply the rustic prototype out of which the state religion of Attis was developed.   It may have been so ; but, on the other hand, the analogy of European folk-custom warns us that amongst the same people two distinct deities of vegetation may have their separate personal representatives, both of whom are slain in the character of gods at different times of the year.   For in Europe, as we have seen, it appears that one man was commonly slain in the character of the tree-spirit in spring, and another in the character of the corn-spirit in autumn.   It may have been so in Phrygia also.   Attis was especially a tree-god, and his connection with corn may have been only such an extension of the power of a tree-spirit as is indicated in customs like the Harvest-May.[2]   Again, the representative of Attis appears to have been slain in spring ; whereas Lityerses must have been slain in summer or autumn, according to the time of the harvest in Phyrgia.[3]   On the whole, then, while we are not justified in regard-

---

[1] Above, p. 299.   [2] Above, p. 68.

[3] I do not know when the corn is reaped in Phrygia ; but considering the high upland character of the country, harvest is probably later there than on the coasts of the Mediterranean.

ing Lityerses as the prototype of Attis, the two may
be regarded as parallel products of the same religious
idea, and may have stood to each other as in Europe
the Old Man of harvest stands to the Wild Man, the
Leaf Man, etc., of spring. Both were spirits or deities
of vegetation, and the personal representatives of both
were annually slain. But whereas the Attis worship
became elevated into the dignity of a state religion
and spread to Italy, the rites of Lityerses seem
never to have passed the limits of their native
Phrygia, and always retained their character of rustic
ceremonies performed by peasants on the harvest-field.
At most a few villages may have clubbed together, as
amongst the Khonds, to procure a human victim to
be slain as representative of the corn-spirit for their
common benefit. Such victims may have been drawn
from the families of priestly kings or kinglets, which
would account for the legendary character of Lityerses
as the son of a Phrygian king. When villages did
not so club together, each village or farm may have
procured its own representative of the corn-spirit
by dooming to death either a passing stranger or the
harvester who cut, bound, or threshed the last sheaf.
It is hardly necessary to add that in Phrygia, as in
Europe, the old barbarous custom of killing a man on
the harvest-field or the threshing-floor had doubtless
passed into a mere pretence long before the classical
era, and was probably regarded by the reapers and
threshers themselves as no more than a rough jest
which the license of a harvest-home permitted them
to play off on a passing stranger, a comrade, or even
on their master himself.

I have dwelt on the Lityerses song at length
because it affords so many points of comparison with

European and savage folk-custom. The other harvest
songs of Western Asia and Egypt, to which attention
has been called above,[1] may now be dismissed much
more briefly. The similarity of the Bithynian Bormus[2]
to the Phrygian Lityerses helps to bear out the interpretation which has been given of the latter. Bormus,
whose death or rather disappearance was annually
mourned by the reapers in a plaintive song, was, like
Lityerses, a king's son or at least the son of a wealthy
and distinguished man. The reapers whom he watched
were at work on his own fields, and he disappeared in
going to fetch water for them; according to one version of the story he was carried off by the (water)
nymphs.[3] Viewed in the light of the Lityerses story
and of European folk-custom, this disappearance of
Bormus is probably a reminiscence of the custom of
binding the farmer himself in a corn-sheaf and throwing him into the water. The mournful strain which
the reapers sang was probably a lamentation over the
death of the corn-spirit, slain either in the cut corn or
in the person of a human representative; and the call
which they addressed to him may have been a prayer
that the corn-spirit might return in fresh vigour next
year.

The Phoenician Linus song was sung at the vintage,
at least in the west of Asia Minor, as we learn from
Homer; and this, combined with the legend of Syleus,
suggests that in ancient times passing strangers were
handled by vintagers and vine-diggers in much the
same way as they are said to have been handled by
the reaper Lityerses. The Lydian Syleus, so ran the
legend, compelled passers-by to dig for him in his
vineyard, till Hercules came and killed him and dug

---

[1] Above, p. 364 *sq.* [2] Above, p. 365. [3] Hesychius, *s.v.* Βῶρμον.

up his vines by the roots.[1]   This seems to be the outline of a legend like that of Lityerses; but neither
ancient writers nor modern folk-custom enable us to
fill in the details.[2]   But, further, the Linus song was
probably sung also by Phoenician reapers, for Herodotus compares it to the Maneros song, which, as we
have seen, was a lament raised by Egyptian reapers
over the cut corn.   Further, Linus was identified with
Adonis, and Adonis has some claims to be regarded
as especially a corn-deity.[3]   Thus the Linus lament,
as sung at harvest, would be identical with the Adonis
lament; each would be the lamentation raised by
reapers over the dead corn-spirit.   But whereas
Adonis, like Attis, grew into a stately figure of mythology, adored and mourned in splendid cities far beyond
the limits of his Phoenician home, Linus appears to
have remained a simple ditty sung by reapers and
vintagers among the corn-sheaves and the vines.   The
analogy of Lityerses and of folk-custom, both European
and savage, suggests that in Phoenicia the slain corn-
spirit—the dead Adonis—may formerly have been
represented by a human victim; and this suggestion
is possibly supported by the Harrân legend that
Thammuz (Adonis) was slain by his cruel lord, who
ground his bones in a mill and scattered them to the
wind.[4]   For in Mexico, as we have seen, the human
victim at harvest was crushed between two stones;
and both in India and Africa the ashes of the victim
were scattered over the fields.[5]   But the Harrân
legend may be only a mythical way of expressing the

---

[1] Apollodorus, ii. 6, 3.

[2] The scurrilities exchanged in both ancient and modern times between vine-dressers, vintagers, and passers-by seem to belong to a different category.

See W. Mannhardt, *Myth. Forsch.* p. 53 *sq.*

[3] Above, p. 282 *sqq.*

[4] Above, p. 283 *sq.*

[5] Above, pp. 381, 384, 389.

grinding of corn in the mill and the scattering of the seed. It seems worth suggesting that the mock king who was annually killed at the Babylonian festival of the Sacaea on the 16th of the month Lous may have represented Thammuz himself. For the historian Berosus, who records the festival and its date, probably used the Macedonian calendar, since he dedicated his history to Antiochus Soter; and in his day the Macedonian month Lous appears to have corresponded to the Babylonian month Thammuz.[1] If this conjecture is right, the view that the mock king at the Sacaea was slain in the character of a god would be established.

There is a good deal more evidence that in Egypt the slain corn-spirit—the dead Osiris—was represented by a human victim, whom the reapers slew on the harvest-field, mourning his death in a dirge, to which the Greeks, through a verbal misunderstanding, gave the name of Maneros.[2] For the legend of Busiris seems to preserve a reminiscence of human sacrifices once offered by the Egyptians in connection with the worship of Osiris. Busiris was said to have been an Egyptian king who sacrificed all strangers on the altar of Zeus. The origin of the custom was traced to a barrenness which afflicted the land of Egypt for nine years. A Cyprian seer informed Busiris that the barrenness would cease if a man were annually sacri-

---

[1] For this fact of the probable correspondence of the months, which supplies so welcome a confirmation of the conjecture in the text, I am indebted to my friend Professor W. Robertson Smith, who furnishes me with the following note: "In the Syro-Macedonian calendar Lous represents Ab, not Tammuz. Was it different in Babylon? I think it was, and one month different, at least in the early times of the Greek monarchy in Asia. For we know from a Babylonian observation in the Almagest (*Ideler*, i. 396) that in 229 B.C. Xanthicus began on February 26. It was therefore the month before the equinoctial moon, not Nisan but Adar, and consequently Lous answered to the lunar month Tammuz."   [2] Above, p. 364.

ficed to Zeus. So Busiris instituted the sacrifice. But
when Hercules came to Egypt, and was being dragged
to the altar to be sacrificed, he burst his bonds and
slew Busiris and his son.[1] Here then is a legend
that in Egypt a human victim was annually sacrificed
to prevent the failure of the crops, and a belief is
implied that an omission of the sacrifice would have
entailed a recurrence of that infertility which it was the
object of the sacrifice to prevent. So the Pawnees, as
we have seen, believed that an omission of the human
sacrifice at planting would have been followed by a
total failure of their crops. The name Busiris was
in reality the name of a city, *pe-Asar*, "the house
of Osiris"[2] the city being so called because it con-
tained the grave of Osiris. The human sacrifices
were said to have been offered at his grave, and the
victims were red-haired men, whose ashes were scattered abroad by means of winnowing-fans.[3] In the
light of the foregoing discussion, this Egyptian tradition admits of a consistent and fairly probable explanation. Osiris, the corn-spirit, was annually represented
at harvest by a stranger, whose red hair made him a
suitable representative of the ripe corn. This man,
in his representative character, was slain on the harvest-
field, and mourned by the reapers, who prayed at the
same time that the corn-spirit might revive and return
(*mââ-ne-rha*, Maneros) with renewed vigour in the
following year. Finally, the victim, or some part of
him, was burned, and the ashes scattered by winnow-

---

[1] Apollodorus, ii. 5, 11; Schol. on
Apollonius Rhodius, iv. 1396; Plutarch, *Parall.* 38. Herodotus (ii. 45)
discredits the idea that the Egyptians
ever offered human sacrifices. But his
authority is not to be weighed against

that of Manetho (Plutarch, *Is. et Os.*
73), who affirms that they did.

[2] E. Meyer, *Geschichte des Alterthums*, i. § 57.

[3] Diodorus, i. 88; Plutarch, *Is. et
Os.* 73; cp. *id.*, 30, 33.

ing-fans over the fields to fertilise them. Here the
choice of the representative on the ground of his
resemblance to the corn which he was to represent
agrees with the Mexican and African customs already
described.[1] Similarly the Romans sacrificed red-haired
puppies in spring, in the belief that the crops would
thus grow ripe and ruddy;[2] and to this day in sowing
wheat a Bavarian sower will sometimes wear a golden
ring, that the corn may grow yellow.[3] Again, the
scattering of the Egyptian victim's ashes is identical
with the Marimo and Khond custom.[4] His identification with the corn comes out again in the fact that
his ashes were winnowed ; just as in Vendée a pretence is made of threshing and winnowing the farmer's
wife, regarded as an embodiment of the corn-spirit ; or
as in Mexico the victim was ground between stones ;
or as in Africa he was slain with spades and hoes.[5]
The story that the fragments of Osiris's body were
scattered up and down the land, and buried by Isis
on the spots where they lay,[6] may very well be a
reminiscence of a custom, like that observed by the
Khonds, of dividing the human victim in pieces and
burying the pieces, often at intervals of many miles
from each other, in the fields. However, it is possible
that the story of the dismemberment of Osiris, like
the similar story told of Thammuz, may have been
simply a mythical expression for the scattering of the
seed. Once more, the story that the body of Osiris
enclosed in a coffer was thrown by Typhon into the

[1] Above, pp. 307, 383, 391.
[2] Festus, *s.v. Catularia.* Cp. *id.,*
s.v. rutilae canes ; Columella, x. 343 ;
Ovid, *Fasti,* iv. 905 *sqq.*; Pliny, *N. H.*
xviii. § 14.
[3] Panzer, *Beitrag zur deutschen*
Mythologie, ii. 207, No. 362 ; *Bavaria,*
Landes-und Volkskunde des Königreichs
Bayern, iii. 343.
[4] Above, pp. 384, 389.
[5] Above, pp. 381, 383.
[6] Plutarch, *Is. et Os.* 18.

Nile perhaps points to a custom of throwing the body
of the victim, or at least a portion of it, into the Nile
as a rain-charm, or rather to make the Nile rise. For
a similar purpose Phrygian reapers seem to have
thrown the headless bodies of their victims, wrapt in
corn-sheaves, into a river, and the Khonds poured
water on the buried flesh of the human victim. Probably when Osiris ceased to be represented by a human
victim, an effigy of him was annually thrown into the
Nile, just as the effigy of his Syrian counterpart,
Adonis, used to be thrown into the sea at Alexandria.
Or water may have been simply poured over it, as on
the monument already mentioned a priest is seen
pouring water over the body of Osiris, from which corn
stalks are sprouting. The accompanying inscription,
" This is Osiris of the mysteries, who springs from
the returning waters," bears out the view that at the
mysteries of Osiris a water-charm or irrigation-charm
was regularly performed by pouring water on his
effigy, or by throwing it into the Nile.

It may be objected that the red-haired victims were
slain as representatives not of Osiris, but of his enemy
Typhon ; for the victims were called Typhonian, and
red was the colour of Typhon, black the colour of
Osiris.[1] The answer to this objection must be reserved
for the present. Meantime it may be pointed out that
if Osiris is often represented on the monuments as
black, he is still more commonly depicted as green,[2]
appropriately enough for a corn-god, who may be conceived as black while the seed is under ground, but as
green after it has sprouted. So the Greeks recognised

---

[1] Plutarch, *Is. et Os.* 22, 30, 31, 33, 73.

[2] Wilkinson, *Manners and Customs of the Ancient Egyptians* (ed. 1878), iii. 81.

both a green and a black Demeter,[1] and sacrificed to
the green Demeter in spring with mirth and gladness.[2]

Thus, if I am right, the key to the mysteries of
Osiris is furnished by the melancholy cry of the
Egyptian reapers, which down to Roman times could
be heard year after year sounding across the fields,
announcing the death of the corn-spirit, the rustic
prototype of Osiris. Similar cries, as we have seen,
were also heard on all the harvest-fields of Western Asia. By the ancients they are spoken of as
songs; but to judge from the analysis of the names
Linus and Maneros, they probably consisted only of a
few words uttered in a prolonged musical note which
could be heard for a great distance. Such sonorous
and long-drawn cries, raised by a number of strong
voices in concert, must have had a striking effect,
and could hardly fail to arrest the attention of any
traveller who happened to be within hearing. The
sounds, repeated again and again, could probably be
distinguished with tolerable ease even at a distance;
but to a Greek traveller in Asia or Egypt the foreign
words would commonly convey no meaning, and he
might take them, not unnaturally, for the name of some
one (Maneros, Linos, Lityerses, Bormus), upon whom
the reapers were calling. And if his journey led him
through more countries than one, as Bithynia and
Phrygia, or Phoenicia and Egypt, while the corn was
being reaped, he would have an opportunity of comparing the various harvest cries of the different peoples.
Thus we can readily account for the fact that these
harvest cries were so often noted and compared with
each other by the Greeks. Whereas, if they had been

[1] Pausanias, i. 22, 3, viii. 5, 8, viii. 42, 1.
[2] Cornutus, *De nat. deor.* c. 28.

regular songs, they could not have been heard at such
distances, and therefore could not have attracted the
attention of so many travellers ; and, moreover, even
if the traveller were within hearing of them, he could
not so easily have picked out the words.   To this day
Devonshire reapers utter cries of the same sort, and
perform on the field a ceremony exactly analogous
to that in which, if I am not mistaken, the rites of
Osiris originated.   The cry and the ceremony are thus
described by an observer who wrote in the first half
of this century.   " After the wheat is all cut, on most
farms in the north of Devon, the harvest people have
a custom of 'crying the neck.'   I believe that this practice is seldom omitted on any large farm in that part
of the country.   It is done in this way.   An old man,
or some one else well acquainted with the ceremonies
used on the occasion (when the labourers are reaping
the last field of wheat), goes round to the shocks and
sheaves, and picks out a little bundle of all the best
ears he can find ; this bundle he ties up very neat and
trim, and plats and arranges the straws very tastefully.
This is called ' the neck ' of wheat, or wheaten-ears.
After the field is cut out, and the pitcher once more
circulated, the reapers, binders, and the women, stand
round in a circle.   The person with ' the neck ' stands
in the centre, grasping it with both his hands.   He
first stoops and holds it near the ground, and all the
men forming the ring take off their hats, stooping and
holding them with both hands towards the ground.
They then all begin at once in a very prolonged and
harmonious tone to cry ' the neck ! ' at the same time
slowly raising themselves upright, and elevating their
arms and hats above their heads ; the person with ' the
neck ' also raising it on high.   This is done three times.

They then change their cry to ' wee yen !'—' way yen !'
—which they sound in the same prolonged and slow
manner as before, with singular harmony and effect,
three times.   This last cry is accompanied by the same
movements of the body and arms as in crying ' the
neck.' . . . After having thus repeated 'the neck'
three times, and 'wee yen,' or 'way yen,' as often,
they all burst out into a kind of loud and joyous laugh,
flinging up their hats and caps into the air, capering
about and perhaps kissing the girls.   One of them
then gets ' the neck' and runs as hard as he can down
to the farmhouse, where the dairymaid or one of the
young female domestics stands at the door prepared
with a pail of water.   If he who holds 'the neck' can
manage to get into the house, in any way unseen, or
openly, by any other way than the door at which the
girl stands with the pail of water, then he may lawfully
kiss her ; but, if otherwise, he is regularly soused with
the contents of the bucket.   On a fine still autumn
evening, the 'crying of the neck' has a wonderful
effect at a distance, far finer than that of the Turkish
muezzin, which Lord Byron eulogises so much, and
which he says is preferable to all the bells in Christen-
dom.   I have once or twice heard upwards of twenty
men cry it, and sometimes joined by an equal number
of female voices.   About three years back, on some
high grounds, where our people were harvesting, I
heard six or seven ' necks ' cried in one night, although
I know that some of them were four miles off.   They
are heard through the quiet evening air, at a considerable distance sometimes."[1]   Again, Mrs. Bray tells
how, travelling in Devonshire, "she saw a party of
reapers standing in a circle on a rising ground, holding

---

[1] Hone, *Every-day Book*, ii. c. 1170 *sq.*

their sickles aloft.   One in the middle held up some
ears of corn tied together with flowers, and the party
shouted three times (what she writes as) 'Arnack,
arnack, arnack, we *haven*, we *haven*, we *haven*.'   They
went home, accompanied by women and children
carrying boughs of flowers, shouting and singing.   The
man-servant who attended Mrs. Bray, said, 'it was only
the people making their games, as they always did, *to
the spirit of harvest*.'"[1]   Here, as Miss. Burne remarks,
"'arnack, we haven!' is obviously in the Devon dialect,
'a neck (or nack)! we have un!'"   "The neck" is
generally hung up in the farmhouse, where it sometimes remains for two or three years.[2]   A similar
custom is still observed in some parts of Cornwall, as I
am informed by my friend Professor J. H. Middleton.
"The last sheaf is decked with ribbons.   Two strong-
voiced men are chosen and placed (one with the sheaf)
on opposite sides of a valley.   One shouts, 'I've
gotten it.'   The other shouts, 'What hast gotten?'
The first answers, 'I'se gotten the neck.'"

In these Devonshire and Cornish customs a particular bunch of ears, generally the last left standing,[3]
is conceived as the neck of the corn-spirit, who is consequently beheaded when the bunch is cut down.
Similarly in Shropshire the name "neck," or "the
gander's neck," used to be commonly given to the last
handful of ears left standing in the middle of the field,
when all the rest of the corn was cut.   It was plaited
together, and the reapers, standing ten or twenty
paces off, threw their sickles at it.   Whoever cut it
through was said to have cut off the gander's neck.

---

[1] Miss C. S. Burne and Miss G. F.
Jackson, *Shropshire Folk-lore*, p. 372
sq., referring to Mrs. Bray's *Traditions
of Devon*, i. 330.

[2] Hone, *op. cit.* ii. 1172.
[3] Brand, *Popular Antiquities*, ii. 20
(Bohn's ed.); Burne and Jackson, *op.
cit.* p. 371.

The "neck" was taken to the farmer's wife, who was supposed to keep it in the house "for good luck" till the next harvest came round.[1] Near Trèves, the man who reaps the last standing corn "cuts the goat's neck off."[2] At Faslane, on the Gareloch (Dumbartonshire), the last handful of standing corn was sometimes called the "head."[3] At Aurich, in East Friesland, the man who reaps the last corn "cuts the hare's tail off."[4] In mowing down the last corner of a field French reapers sometimes call out, "We have the cat by the tail."[5] In Bresse (Bourgogne) the last sheaf represented the fox. Beside it a score of ears were left standing to form the tail, and each reaper, going back some paces, threw his sickle at it. He who succeeded in severing it "cut off the fox's tail," and a cry of "*You cou cou !*" was raised in his honour.[6] These examples leave no room to doubt the meaning of the Devonshire and Cornish expression "the neck," as applied to the last sheaf. The corn-spirit is conceived in human or animal form, and the last standing corn is part of its body—its neck, its head, or its tail. Sometimes, as we have seen, it is regarded as the navel-string.[7] Lastly, the Devonshire custom of drenching with water the person who brings in "the neck" is a rain-charm, such as we have had many examples of. Its parallel in the mysteries of Osiris was the custom of pouring water on the image of Osiris or on the person who represented him.

In Germany cries of *Waul!* or *Wol!* or *Wôld!* are sometimes raised by the reapers at cutting the last corn. Thus in some places the last patch of standing

---

[1] Burne and Jackson, *l.c.*
[2] W. Mannhardt, *Myth. Forsch.* p. 185.
[3] See above, p. 345.
[4] W. Mannhardt, *Myth. Forsch.* p. 185. [5] *Ib.*
[6] *Revue des Traditions populaires*, ii. 500. [7] Above, p. 343.

corn was called the *Waul*-rye ; a stick decked with flowers was inserted in it, and the ears were fastened to the stick.   Then all the reapers took off their hats and cried thrice, *Waul! Waul! Waul!*   Sometimes they accompany the cry by clashing with their whetstones on their scythes.[1]

---

[1] U. Jahn, *Die deutschen Opfergebräuche bei Ackerbau und Viehzucht*, pp. 166-169 ; Pfannenschmid, *Germanische Erntefeste*, p. 104 *sq.* ; Kuhn, *Westfälische Sagen, Gebräuche und Märchen*, ii. Nos. 491, 492; Kuhn und Schwartz, *Norddeutsche Sagen, Märchen und Gebräuche*, p. 395, No. 97 ; Lynker, *Deutsche Sagen und Sitten in hessischen Gauen*, p. 256, No. 340.

END OF VOL. I

Printed by R. & R. CLARK, *Edinburgh.*

CPSIA information can be obtained at www.ICGtesting.com
Printed in the USA
BVOW032008250712

296213BV00001B/44/P